THE PASSAGE OF LITERATURE

THE PASSAGE OF LITERATURE

Genealogies of Modernism in Conrad, Rhys, and Pramoedya

Christopher GoGwilt

UNIVERSITY PRESS

UNIVERSITY PRESS

Oxford University Press is a department of the University of Oxford.
It furthers the University's objective of excellence in research, scholarship,
and education by publishing worldwide.

Oxford   New York
Auckland   Cape Town   Dar es Salaam   Hong Kong   Karachi
Kuala Lumpur   Madrid   Melbourne   Mexico City   Nairobi
New Delhi   Shanghai   Taipei   Toronto

With offices in
Argentina   Austria   Brazil   Chile   Czech Republic   France   Greece
Guatemala   Hungary   Italy   Japan   Poland   Portugal   Singapore
South Korea   Switzerland   Thailand   Turkey   Ukraine   Vietnam

Oxford is a registered trade mark of Oxford University Press
in the UK and certain other countries.

Published in the United States of America by
Oxford University Press
198 Madison Avenue, New York, NY 10016

© Oxford University Press 2011

First issued as an Oxford University Press paperback, 2013.

All rights reserved. No part of this publication may be reproduced, stored in a retrieval system, or transmitted, in any form or by any means, without the prior permission in writing of Oxford University Press, or as expressly permitted by law, by license, or under terms agreed with the appropriate reproduction rights organization. Inquiries concerning reproduction outside the scope of the above should be sent to the Rights Department, Oxford University Press, at the address above.

You must not circulate this work in any other form
and you must impose this same condition on any acquirer.

Library of Congress Cataloging-in-Publication Data
GoGwilt, Christopher Lloyd.
The passage of literature : genealogies of modernism in Conrad, Rhys,
and Pramoedya / Christopher GoGwilt.
p. cm.
Includes bibliographical references and index.
ISBN 978-0-19-975162-4 (hardcover); 978-0-19-933013-3 (paperback)
1. Modernism (Literature)—Great Britain.   2. Modernism (Literature)—
Caribbean Area.   3. Modernism (Literature)—Indonesia.   4. Postcolonialism in
literature.   5. Comparative literature—English and Caribbean (English)   6. Comparative
literature—Caribbean (English) and English.   7. Comparative literature—English
and Indonesian.   8. Comparative literature—Indonesian and English.   9. Conrad,
Joseph, 1857–1924—Criticism and interpretation.   10. Rhys, Jean, 1890–1979—
Criticism and interpretation.   11. Toer, Pramoedya Ananta,
1925–2006—Criticism and interpretation.   I. Title.
PR888.M63G64 2010
823'.91209—dc22   2010009507

untuk Go Tie Siem

ACKNOWLEDGMENTS

This book has emerged from a number of different conversations, exchanges, and crossings of paths. Growing from so many different occasions, the book has been enriched by many more people than I can possibly thank individually here.

I owe an enormous debt to all those who have supported my informal apprenticeship in Indonesian studies: Ben Anderson, for his generous comments and advice in 1995 and 1996; Go Gien Tjwan, for many conversations about Indonesian history and politics; and all those who helped organize and who participated in the events of April 1999, during Pramoedya's visit to New York, especially Joesoef Isak, Maemoenah Thamrin, and Pramoedya Ananta Toer; and also the co-organizers, Will Schwalbe and John McGlynn. For ongoing conversations, I thank Alex Bardsley, Nancy Florida, Peter Hitchcock, Sanjay Krishnan, Max Lane, Henk Maier, John Pemberton, and André Vltchek. Above all, I thank my father-in-law, Go Tie Siem, for the wealth of his experience, for material help in translating Indonesian texts, and for the generosity of his time arranging meetings with Go Gien Tjwan, Wim Wertheim, and Oei Tjoe Tat, not to mention Pram himself.

The book has been enriched by conversations at many different academic conferences and seminars, including several MLA panels, conferences on Conrad in Philadelphia (1997), Gdańsk (1997), Vancouver, BC (2002), and Orange, California (2010); and events organized for the Symposium on the Diaspora of Cultural Studies and the Literary Studies Program at Fordham. I have drawn numerous insights from conversations at these and other events, and thank (among many others) Andrzej Busza, Robert Caserio, Yvette Christiansë, Arnaldo Cruz-Malavé, Laurence Davies, Kim Hall, Nico Israel, James Kim, Jakob Lothe, Peter Mallios, Roz Morris, Zdzisław Najder, Francesca Parmeggiani, John Peters,

Nicola Pitchford, Ann Stoler, and Andrea White. I acknowledge my debt to three very different readers of Conrad I was privileged to be able to meet while they were alive: Eloise Knapp Hay, Hans van Marle, and G. J. Resink. I continue to learn from all my students, colleagues, and friends, and I thank those who have read portions of the manuscript, or who have provided crucial advice at critical moments: John M. Archer, Madeleine Brainerd, Fraser Easton, T. Kaori Kitao, and Fawzia Mustafa.

Formally, I acknowledge the support of two Fordham faculty fellowships—one in the academic year 2000–1 that enabled me to conceive the overall shape of the project; and one in fall 2005 that helped me complete a substantial portion of the manuscript. I thank Liz Foley O'Connor and Fordham's Graduate School of Arts & Sciences for providing her the research assistantship to help with the final stages of this book manuscript. I owe special thanks to both of Oxford's anonymous reviewers for their invaluable suggestions. I would also like to thank Brendan O'Neill and the entire editorial team at Oxford for their invaluable assistance in realizing the final shape of the book.

Parts of the following study have appeared in earlier versions elsewhere. A version of chapter 2 was published in *Conrad in the Twenty-First Century: Contemporary Critical Approaches and Perspectives*, edited by Carola Kaplan, Peter Mallios, and Andrea White (New York: Routledge, 2005). I thank Routledge for permission to republish an expanded and revised version of this essay. I thank the editors, too, for their valuable comments. The photographs from Rob Nieuwenhuys's *Tempo Doeloe* referred to in chapter 2 were reproduced in that essay (with permission from Querido), but I have not reprinted these photographs here, wishing to emphasize the medium of the printed word rather than the photographic record, while at the same time underscoring the fact that the printed word is itself inscribed in relation to a photographic— and phonographic—archive. A version of chapter 4 was published in *Geographies of Modernism*, edited by Peter Brooker and Andrew Thacker (New York: Routledge, 2005). I thank Routledge for permission to republish an expanded and revised version of this article. I thank the editors, too, for the opportunity to publish this essay and for their comments on the essay itself. A version of chapter 6 was published in *Comparative Literature Studies* 44, no. 4 (Winter 2007), 409–33. I thank the Penn State Press for permission to republish an expanded and revised version of this article.

Last, but by no means least, I want to thank my family. I have an impressionistic childhood memory, before I could read myself, almost a baby, of seeing the title cover of Jean Rhys's *Wide Sargasso Sea* on a bookshelf at home. The distortion of memory is all my own, but whatever I may have learned right about reading and writing words I owe both to my mother and to my father. I trust

Richard and Philip can patiently correct my childhood memory and I thank them for a brotherly apprenticeship in listening to the inevitably distorting Scottish effects of English words. I thank Cai and Keir for allowing me to bring dictionaries to the dinner table so often. No words can express my thanks to Siu Li. I owe her everything. For their wisdom, experience, and practical help, I thank May Li and Soesilowati. I have already acknowledged the debt this work owes to my father-in-law, Go Tie Siem. For the countless ways he has supported my study of Pramoedya, I dedicate the book to him. I hope that dedication might also be understood as acknowledgment of my debt to the family he raised in Rome, the family he now lives with in Toronto, and the extended family of Tan sisters, whose *Stamboek (Tan Tjwan Liong. Soerabaia. 1915)* now includes Cai and Keir, along with many other family relatives (*kerna kita bisa taoe kita ampoenja toeroennan*). Their genealogies cross paths with the genealogies of modernism traced in this book.

CONTENTS

A Note on Abbreviations and Quotations   xiii

Introduction   1

1   The Linguistic-Literary Coordinates of English, Creole, and Indonesian Modernisms   3
  Joseph Conrad's Polish English   12
  Jean Rhys's Creole English   18
  Pramoedya Ananta Toer's "Pre-Indonesian" Indonesian   23

Part I   English Modernism   37

2   Opera, Modernism, and Modernity: Reading Counterpoint in Joseph Conrad's Malay Trilogy and Pramoedya's Buru Tetralogy   39
  The Cultural Dialectic of Abysmal Taste in Opera   43
  Conrad's Malay Trilogy   48
  Pramoedya's Buru Tetralogy   53
  Philology and Counterpoint   57

3   The Repetitive Formation of English Modernism: Jean Rhys, Ford Madox Ford, and the Memory of Joseph Conrad   61
  Ford Madox Ford and the Repetitive Formation of English Modernism   65
  Re-Citing Conrad in Modernist Memory   69
  Jean Rhys and the Transatlantic Modernism of Ford's *the transatlantic review*   82
  Reading Modernist Memory   89

Part II   Creole Modernism   95

4   Jean Rhys's Francophone English and the Creole "Impasse" of Modernity   97
Anterior Interiors: The First-Person Narrators of *Good Morning, Midnight* and *The Shadow-Line*   98
The "Impasse" of *Good Morning, Midnight*   101
The "Impasse" of Jean Rhys's Creole Consciousness   104
The Shock of Racial Pofiles and the Trace of Creole Culture   119

5   Creole Legacies in Rhys's *Wide Sargasso Sea* and Pramoedya's *This Earth of Mankind*   127
The Creole Heiress   129
Creole Family Romances   137
Creole Literary Passages   148

Part III   Indonesian Modernism   151

6   The Vanishing Genre of the *Nyai* Narrative: Reading Genealogies of English and Indonesian Modernism   153
Defining the *Nyai*   155
The *Nyai* as Disappearing Subaltern Figure   160
The Appearance of the *Nyai* in English Modernism   166
The Transnational Matrix of Indonesian Modernism   171

7   Decolonizing Tradition: Pramoedya's Indonesian Modernism   177
Lingkaran Setan: The "Vicious Circle" of History and the Rescue Work of Buru   179
"*Mata Rantai*": The Genealogical Link as Break   187
Pramoedya's Revolutionary Family Romance   197
Pesangon and *Warisan:* The "All-Round" Decolonizing of Tradition   212

Conclusion   215

8   Postcolonial Philology and the Passage of Literature   217
Between Orientalism and Literary Criticism   220
The Postcolonial Philological Turn   227
The Trope of Theory and the Passage of Postcolonial Philology   235
Decolonizing English and the *O.E.D.*   243

Notes   253
Bibliography   285
Index   301

A NOTE ON ABBREVIATIONS AND QUOTATIONS

Unless otherwise indicated, all references to Conrad's works are to Joseph Conrad, *The Collected Works* (26 vols., Garden City, New York Doubleday, Page, 1926) and are abbreviated as follows:

AF	*Almayer's Folly*
LJ	*Lord Jim*
OI	*An Outcast of the Islands*
PR	*A Personal Record*
R	*The Rescue*
SL	*The Shadow-Line*
TU	*Tales of Unrest*
VI	*Victory*
Y	*Youth and Two Other Stories*

References to the following editions of Rhys's works are abbreviated accordingly:

AL	*After Leaving Mr. Mackenzie* (New York: Norton, 1997)
CS	*The Collected Short Stories* (New York: Norton, 1992)
GM	*Good Morning, Midnight* (New York: Norton, 1986)
Q	*Quartet* (New York: Norton, 1997)
S	*Smile Please: An Unfinished Autobiography* (New York: Harper & Row, 1979)
V	*Voyage in the Dark* (New York: Norton, 1982)
WSS	*Wide Sargasso Sea* (New York: Norton Critical Edition, 1999)

References to the following translations and editions of Pramoedya's work are abbreviated accordingly:

ASB	*Anak Semua Bangsa* (Jakarta: Hasta Mitra, 1981)
BM	*Bumi Manusia* (Jakarta: Hasta Mitra, 1981)

C	*Child of All Nations* (Trans. Max Lane [New York: Penguin, 1996])
CI	*The Chinese in Indonesia* (Trans. Max Lane [Singapore: Select Books, 2007])
F	*Footsteps* (Trans. Max Lane [New York: Penguin, 1990])
H	*House of Glass* (Trans. Max Lane [New York: Penguin, 1992])
HI	*Hoakiau di Indonesia* (Jakarta: Hasta Mitra, 1995)
J	*Jejak Langkah* (Jakarta: Hasta Mitra, 1985)
MS	*The Mute's Soliloquy* (Trans. Willem Samuels [New York: Hyperion, 1999])
NS I	*Nyanyi Sunyi Seorang Bisu: Catatan-catatan dari Buru*. I. (Jakarta: Lentera, 1995)
NS II	*Nyanyi Sunyi Seorang Bisu: Catatan-catatan dari Buru*. II. (Jakarta: Lentera, 1997)
RK	*Rumah Kaca* (Jakarta: Hasta Mitra, 1988)
TE	*This Earth of Mankind* (Trans. Max Lane [New York: Penguin, 1996])

Introduction

1

THE LINGUISTIC-LITERARY COORDINATES OF ENGLISH, CREOLE, AND INDONESIAN MODERNISM

I

This book examines the interrelations between English, Creole, and Indonesian formations of modernism through a comparative study of Joseph Conrad (1857–1924), Jean Rhys (1890–1979), and Pramoedya Ananta Toer (1925–2006). Taking "modernism" in its literary-historical sense to refer to a particular formation of literary experimentation and innovation, this study considers three distinct, linguistic, literary, and historical modernisms.[1] The decision to focus on Conrad, Rhys, and Pramoedya is dictated in large part by the canonical status each has come to occupy in relation to these three modernist formations—Conrad as a representative early figure in the formation of English modernism;[2] Rhys as a writer whose relation to Creole modernism remains contested;[3] and Pramoedya as the most celebrated Indonesian writer whose work sought to recapture a lost history of Indonesian modernism.[4] In the first part of this introductory chapter, I briefly discuss the sense of modernism used in this study, outlining the linguistic and literary coordinates of these three modernisms. In the second part, I introduce the genealogies of modernism implicit in the work of Conrad, Rhys, and Pramoedya, as these emerge in autobiographical fragments from the work of each writer.

If each author provides an opportunity to trace distinct genealogies of modernist formations, their work also underscores an overlapping and contested relation between these three forms of modernism. The relation between English, Creole, and Indonesian modernist formations reveals an ongoing contest over transnational genealogies of modernism. The argument of the present study is that this ongoing contest is registered in each and every passage of literature. As both a practical and a theoretical matter of citation, translation, and cultural authority, the individual passage of literature constitutes a contestation over linguistic and literary capital. As I discuss more fully in the final chapter, the nineteenth-century philological principles that make the passage of literature a touchstone for European forms of cultural capital have continued to shape literary criticism, cultural studies, and the teaching of language and literature into the twenty-first century. Defined by the colonial coordinates of European comparative philology, the theory and practice of textual study have made the individual passage of literature a privileged point of reference for linguistic and literary capital. If the cultural capital of any individual passage of literature singled out for authoritative citation is shaped by residual colonial forms of philology, those same forms of philology reveal, too, emergent decolonizing forms of postcolonial philology. This study follows the emergence of postcolonial philology from the interrelations between English, Creole, and Indonesian modernisms.

Over the past twenty years or so, a wide range of studies have challenged received accounts of canonical modernism, deepening and extending understandings of the transnational contexts within which European "high modernism" emerged in the first half of the twentieth century.[5] Although "modernism" continues to be used as a descriptive label defining a specific historical period of literary innovation between the 1890s and 1930s, and largely centered in the metropolitan cities of Western Europe and North America, there has been a notable shift in attention to its transnational coordinates. Postcolonial studies, in particular, have drawn renewed attention to the significance of colonialism for European and American modernist writers,[6] to the links between writers from metropolitan centers and writers from colonial peripheries,[7] and to the significance of non-European artistic and literary innovation in shaping transnational modernism. There is no one overarching argument that unifies these approaches; indeed, there has been a proliferation of approaches, pluralizing and multiplying the number of modernisms and modernities that can and should be studied with historical, cultural, and linguistic specificity. Nonetheless, the cumulative effect of these studies has been to create an overall paradigm shift in the historical, theoretical, and linguistic grasp of modernism. It is now increasingly more plausible to view modernism, once considered a product of Europe and America, as the effect of a wider, transnational phenomenon. In this view, literary and artistic modernism properly belongs within a history of decolonization. The current study seeks to contribute to this paradigm shift by paying close attention to the work of Pramoedya Ananta Toer and its implications for transnational modernist studies. Encompassing both the formation and the dismantling of Third World revolutionary nationalism, Pramoedya's work registers as personal, literary, and historical experience the seismic shocks of twentieth-century decolonization. If English modernism has increasingly been reconceived from the transnational perspective of Creole modernism, both Creole and English modernism can, in turn, be reconceived in light of Indonesian modernism.

In particular, the underlying aim of the study is to reconceive the largely Anglophone coordinates of modernist studies (past and present) by reframing canonical English modernism within the linguistic, literary, and historical coordinates of Indonesian modernism. Following the lead of Pramoedya's own work, but also following recent developments within modernist studies, this comparative study of the work of Conrad, Rhys, and Pramoedya seeks to reconceive the transnational coordinates of literary modernism. As Susan Stanford Friedman points out, even the recent innovations in modernist studies (represented by the journal of the Modernist Studies Association, *Modernism/modernity*) have tended to consolidate a conventional model of periodizing modernism as "a loose affiliation of aesthetic movements in the first half of the twentieth century," a periodizing that "privileges Anglo-American modernism."[8] This conventional understanding repeatedly frames many of the most innovative and up-to-date approaches in modernist studies in a sort of compulsively Anglophone repetition entirely in keeping with what I examine (in part I) as the genealogy of "English modernism."

The literary historical focus on Pramoedya's work promises to resituate the colonial coordinates of Conrad's work—and the continuing efforts to evaluate the relation between English modernism and colonialism—within the wider global and historical context of decolonization. In this sense, the study responds to Friedman's imperative to "respatialize" and "reperiodize" modernism in light of the "creative agencies in the colonies and newly emergent nations":

> We must not close the curtain on modernism before the creative agencies in the colonies and newly emergent nations have their chance to perform. Their nationalist movements and liberations from the political dimensions of colonial rule are central to the story of their modernities. Therefore, the creative forces within those modernities—the writers, the artists, the musicians, the dancers, the philosophers, the critics, and so forth—are engaged in producing modernisms that accompany their own modernities. To call their postliberation arts "postmodern"—as they often are—is to miss the point entirely. Multiple modernities create multiple modernisms. Multiple modernisms require respatializing and reperiodizing modernism.[9]

Following this imperative, however, involves a further step already implied in Friedman's return to the singular, nominal "modernism" she seeks to pluralize, respatialize, and reperiodize.

Although the nationalist movements of decolonization produce "their own modernities," those modernities do not merely coexist side by side with other modernities. Multiple modernisms and modernities involve a contest over genealogies of modernism and modernity.

This contest over a singular history of modernism and a universalizing form of modernity is a characteristic feature of what Françoise Lionnet calls "transcultural Creole modes of being and forms of linguistic and social agency."[10] Drawing on theoretical concepts (opacity, anonymity, and creolization itself) associated with prominent Caribbean writers and theorists (Glissant, Brathwaite, Benítez-Rojo), Lionnet articulates the combined political and philosophical contest over a universalizing definition of modernism that, while most clear within the Francophone context Lionnet examines, also constitutes the weak universalism that Friedman exposes in Anglo-American assumptions about the periodizing of modernism. Lionnet distills a set of theoretical arguments drawn from Creole modernism that have for some time now reshaped modernist studies. (Friedman, for example, explicitly draws from Glissant's "poetics of relation" and "créolité" in calling for the displacement of "nominal" with "relational modes" of defining modernism.) Simplifying though the category "Creole modernism" certainly is, it signals a shift in definition from presumed cultural, geographical, or national coordinates (as in a definition like "Anglo-American modernism") toward linguistic coordinates that complicate in turn those cultural, geographical, or national coordinates. Juxtaposing Creole modernism with English modernism not only unsettles the presumed periodizing of Anglo-American modernism but also unsettles the linguistic premises of canonical modernism and European modernity.

The designations "English," "Creole," and "Indonesian" refer primarily to the languages that distinguish these three formations of literary modernism. The "English" language of English modernism, in the main period of its formation from the 1880s and 1890s to the 1930s, extends beyond England—encompassing an English spoken and written not only in the British Isles but also throughout Britain's existing and former colonial territories. "Creole," by contrast to the monolingual basis of English modernism, encompasses a range of Caribbean languages—above all, Creole forms of English, French, and Spanish—from which writers drew in the formative period of Creole modernism from the 1950s through the 1980s. The "Indonesian" language of "Indonesian modernism" refers to the language developed from a form of Malay during the turn of the century, adopted in 1928 as the language of anti-colonial nationalism and officially constituted as a national language with the founding of the Republic of Indonesia (proclaimed in 1945, recognized by the outside world in 1949).

To foreground the linguistic coordinates for these three formations of literary modernism is to underscore the different historical and political coordinates of each writer's work. "English modernism" coincides with the period of late colonialism (or "high imperialism") during which Conrad's work appeared (between 1895 and 1924). "Creole modernism," although more difficult to date, refers primarily to the period of explosion in Anglophone, Francophone, and Hispanophone Caribbean literature from the 1950s (Derek Walcott, Edward Brathwaite, Wilson Harris, V. S. Naipaul; Aimé Césaire, Édouard Glissant; Alejo Carpentier); but it should also be traced back to the 1930s (with such seminal works as C. L. R. James's *The Black Jacobins* and Fernando Ortiz's *Cuban Counterpoint*). This backdating of Creole modernism is particularly relevant for Rhys's work, itself split between the prewar stories and novels and the later, now canonical *Wide Sargasso Sea*.

Pramoedya's work calls attention to three different moments in the formation of "Indonesian modernism": first, the period from 1945 to the early 1960s when Pramoedya himself, as part of the so-called Generation of 1945, produced a self-consciously modern Indonesian literature as part of the experience of revolutionary anti-colonial nationalism; second, the period of Pramoedya's Buru imprisonment (from the late 1960s until 1979), when Pramoedya composed the most celebrated work of Indonesian literature, the "Buru" quartet of novels about the awakening of Indonesian anti-colonial nationalism; and third, the formative period of what Pramoedya called "pre-Indonesian literature" during the turn from the nineteenth to the twentieth century.

Plotting the historical coordinates of English, Creole, and Indonesian modernism does not, then, yield a straightforward literary history of successive formations of modernism. It demands, rather, the kind of reperiodizing and respatializing of literary history called for by Friedman. It also demands renewed attention to the forms of linguistic "creolization" operating within and between different modernist formations. Caribbean forms of contest over the hegemony of European languages have provided something like the linguistic paradigm for postcolonial studies (informing the early model of "writing back" to Empire and Homi Bhabha's ideas of mimicry and hybridity). There are already a number of well-established examples of how Creole modernism has displaced the coordinates of canonical European modernism, reconceiving "modernity," more broadly, in light of the historical experience of decolonization embodied in very particular forms of "Creole" linguistic contest.[11] Less attention has been paid (at least in Anglophone modernist studies) to the influence of a related process of "creolization" in the Indonesian or Malay Archipelago.[12] Here, the interaction among Malay, Arab, Chinese, Dutch, and other European languages embodies another side of the same historical experience of decolonization. Their convergence in the shared space of a newly romanized print form of Malay—the precursor to *bahasa Indonesia*—makes the literary-linguistic roots of Indonesian modernism potentially as significant, alongside the forms of Caribbean "creolization" that underwrite Creole modernism.

Benedict Anderson's *Imagined Communities* is the one striking example of how this moment of early Indonesian modernism has already effected a paradigm shift in studies of modernism and modernity, provoking ways to reconceive the relation between language and anti-colonial nationalism. What is less visible is how much Anderson's influential idea of "imagining community" is underwritten (and also complicated, in turn) by the particular historical phenomenon of the emergent print form of Malay that shaped the coordinates of Indonesian modernism. Pramoedya's own attention to the linguistic-literary roots of Indonesian modernism provides, I argue (in part III), an important model for theorizing the passage of literary text (in its romanized print form) as an especially important locus of authority and contest in the history of decolonization. Each passage of literature, as I explore throughout the study in both a practical and a theoretical sense, is the scene of a crossing and contestation between different genealogies of literary modernism and modernity.

Two parallel linguistic developments within English and Indonesian, respectively, illustrate this overlapping of modernist formations and provide a useful guiding point of historical reference for the book's overall trajectory. Although the Indonesian language is a new language—dating from 1928, and officially used as a national language only since the middle of the twentieth century—the moment of its formation during the turn of the nineteenth to the twentieth centuries coincides with a parallel, contrasting development in the English language: the work of the *Oxford English Dictionary* (*O.E.D.*), which began publication in the 1880s and whose last volume (before the *Supplement* of 1933) appeared in 1928, coincidentally the same year Indonesian was adopted by the "oath of youth" as the language of a projected new national identity. These parallel developments are related to apparently opposed political dynamics—the reactive formation of colonialism, on the one hand, and the revolutionary process of decolonization, on the other. This parallel provides a useful comparative historical frame of reference for the study as a whole. It draws attention, first, to the contemporaneity of two processes—colonization and decolonization—usually plotted in succession. In highlighting the importance of language in forging the colonial hegemony of the one and the anti-colonial nationalist imagining of the other, this parallel also calls attention to the comparative linguistic frame of reference within which transnational modernism needs to be reexamined.

In both a theoretical and a practical sense, the linguistic is also the literary frame of reference for this comparative study of English, Creole, and Indonesian modernism. The individual passage of literature singled out for critical analysis foregrounds this linguistic-literary frame of reference. Practically speaking, the study seeks to reevaluate the linguistic and literary coordinates of English-based studies of literary modernism by reading passages of English-language texts side by side with Indonesian texts. This is not a claim to philological expertise in Indonesian and Malay studies but, rather, a deliberate effort to confront the limits of predominantly Anglophone approaches to literary modernism. These limits will likely be clearest where I cite a passage from Pramoedya's work first in its English translation and then in its Indonesian original. But the linguistic work of translation is inextricable from the literary work of reading any passage of text. The philological assumptions that underpin each are simultaneously linguistic and literary in ways that constitute the authority and cultural capital of any passage of literature. The *O.E.D.* grounds its authoritative claim to English on the basis of a huge archive of passages of literature. There is no corresponding archive of passages for the Indonesian language, although Pramoedya's own work, as I argue in the conclusion, stands in revealing counterpoint to that archive of English modernism. The very lack of a comparably rich archive has produced a theory and practice of what I call postcolonial philology. The disparity between different archives of literary modernism draws attention to a complex dialectic of linguistic and literary authority that shadows the study of transnational modernism. It is this dialectic that the following study seeks to engage by tracking the interrelations between English, Creole, and Indonesian modernisms.

II

> What concern have we with the shades of dialect in Homer or Theocritus, provided they speak the spiritual *lingua franca* that abolishes all alienage of race?
>
> —James Russell Lowell, *Among My Books,* Series I, 170
> (as cited in the *O.E.D.* entry on *lingua franca*)

Turning now to consider the work of Conrad, Rhys, and Pramoedya, I want to dwell on autobiographical fragments in which each writer attempts to articulate his or her own authorial relation to the coordinates of English, Creole, and Indonesian modernism, respectively. Each of these reflections concerns a childhood scene of learning to read and a family romance of reading. Since it constitutes the basic condition of possibility for a writer, the experience of learning how to read is both an autobiographical commonplace and a kind of authorial primal scene. Simultaneously recording the birth of an anonymous reading subject and the emergence of a writer's authorial identity, the attempt to recall the moment of learning to read constitutes a paradoxically primordial relation to the written word. This almost prototypically modernist predicament of an authorship confronting itself as an effect of textuality involves each author in the attempt to recapture in writing an experience of writing before writing.[13]

What links each writer's autobiographical recollection is the complex role of the spoken language generally, and in particular the formation of what might be described as an idealized *lingua franca*. Conrad's memory of reading his father's translation from English into Polish (from *A Personal Record*), Jean Rhys's memory of her nurse's hostility to reading (in her unfinished autobiography, *Smile Please*), and Pramoedya's memory of his mother's reading stories from a range of different traditions (from the prison memoir-notes, *The Mute's Soliloquy* [*Nyanyi Sunyi Seorang Bisu*]), all form miniature studies in the linguistic-cultural imperatives—what we might now call variously the modernizing, globalizing, or worlding imperatives—of literacy. In each of these accounts, the linguistic appeal of a *lingua franca*, as the common language shared by speakers from different linguistic backgrounds, underwrites an idealized conception of world literature, as the coordination of different cultural traditions and different racial, ethnic, or national identities into a shared genealogy of literary heritage. This is the lure of the *lingua franca* that underwrites, for all three writers, albeit in different ways, the mirage of "world" literature as the universal heritage of all humankind.[14]

A *lingua franca* generally refers to any mixed language used by speakers of different languages, following the *O.E.D.*'s definition: "any mixed jargon formed as a medium of intercourse between people speaking different languages." The Malay "market" or "bazaar" language—what Pramoedya calls the Malay *lingua franca* (*Melayu lingua franca*)[15]—that was the basis for the Indonesian language in which Pramoedya writes is a paradigmatic example, providing a shared medium of communication among the multiplicity of linguistic groups throughout the Malay Archipelago. There are a number of exemplary cases in which English, too, has served as a *lingua franca*. It was a form of English *lingua franca* on board the ships of the British merchant marine that provided Joseph Conrad with his first sustained exposure to spoken English.[16] The spoken English of Jean Rhys's childhood experience growing up on the small island of Dominica, in the Windward Islands, would have been an English shared—and contested—among different kinds of both Creole and standard English speakers. The term "contact language" might alternatively suggest that space of interaction between speakers of different languages that characterizes the linguistic idea—and ideal—of the *lingua franca*. Mary Louise Pratt, extending the term to an analysis of the "contact zones" of colonial encounters and the process of "transculturation," explains: "[T]he term contact language refers to improvised languages that develop among speakers of different native languages who need to communicate with each other consistently, usually in context of trade. Such languages begin as pidgins, and are called creoles when they come to have native speakers of their own."[17] The less precise term *lingua franca*, however, is helpful because it suggests the simultaneity of both fragmentation (the emergence of "pidgins") and the consolidation of distinct languages (with the formation of creoles); a double process that implies a historical interrelation between the *lingua franca* and a variety of national languages. Recalling what Bakhtin calls "heteroglossia"—the interactions between different languages, across dialects and jargons, forming the social and linguistic diversity from which the European novel springs—also suggests the dream of a shared space of world literary discourse—the ideal of Goethe's *Weltliteratur*—on which Bakhtin's own theories might be seen to depend.

The *O.E.D.* makes just such a connection in its illustrative citation—from James Russell Lowell—for the figurative use of the term *lingua franca:* "What concern have we with the shades of dialect in Homer or Theocritus, provided they speak the spiritual *lingua franca* that abolishes all alienage of race?" The idea of a shared *language* unifying people otherwise separated by language or dialect provides the model for a shared *literary* heritage for peoples otherwise separated by culture, history, or "race." As one might expect from the nineteenth-century poet, Harvard professor of modern languages and literatures, and second president of the Modern Language Association of America, Lowell's metaphor is full of nineteenth-century philological assumptions—about the relations between "dialect," language, and "race"; and about the relation of language to literature. If this matrix of assumptions is precisely what Bakhtin's notion of "heteroglossia," and Pratt's adoption of the term "contact languages," seek to displace, it nonetheless remains the academic foundation for the contemporary study of modern languages and literatures. As an illustrative citation for the figurative English meaning of *lingua franca*, as established by the authority of the monumental *Oxford English Dictionary*, Lowell's figurative metaphor condenses a set of philological debates from Goethe to the present day. As I want to show, these are the assumptions that Conrad, Rhys, and Pramoedya, in their rather different ways, confront and unravel.

Conrad's childhood memory of learning to read is found embedded in a set of autobiographical reminiscences serialized in *The English Review* between December 1908 and May 1909. Written at a key moment in Conrad's career—just as he was turning to the "Russian" novel, *Under Western Eyes,* and on the heels of completing *The Secret Agent—A Personal Record,* as "Some Reminiscences" were later retitled, stands as a revealing document in a number of ways. Its appearance in the pages of Ford Madox Ford's recently established *English Review* situates Conrad more or less self-consciously on the threshold between two generations of English modernists—between the older generation of Henry James, Ford Madox Ford, and Conrad himself, on the one hand, and a newer generation represented by D. H. Lawrence, Ezra Pound, and Wyndham Lewis. The reminiscences are complicated, however, by the fact that Conrad sought to write about his Polish background at a time when he was increasingly reacting against the "Slavic" label used by critics—even hugely sympathetic critics like Edward Garnett—to explain the relevance of his Polish background. The whole autobiography, then, represents a complex combination of self-promotion and evasive camouflage.[18]

Both of these elements are evident in the way he stages his reflection on his origins as a writer. Creating a mock-biographical subject in the form of the manuscript of his first novel, *Almayer's Folly,* the first four reminiscences recount the adventures of the manuscript as it travels with him from France to Central Africa to Austria and Germany and to Poland. In the fourth reminiscence, as he returns to reflect on the very first moment when he came to write (that beginning moment his reminiscences have constantly circled around and constantly deferred), he characteristically swerves away from the question of writing to reading, recalling that "I don't even know now what were the books then lying about the room. Whatever they were they were not the works of great masters, where the secret of clear thought and exact expression can be found" (*PR,* 70). The form of this digression allows him to displace discussion of when and how he first came to write to the question of when and how he first came to read—"Since the age of five I have been a great reader, as is not perhaps wonderful in a child who was never aware of learning to read" (*PR,* 70).

In what follows, Conrad gives an account of the wide range of books he had grown up reading, incidentally developing a fairly explicit hierarchy, following the comment on the "clear thought and exact expression" to be found in "the works of great masters," in which he distinguishes between "English novelists whose works I read for the first time in English" (he mentions Trollope) and those "men of European reputation" (Dickens, Scott, and

Thackeray are specified) whose work Conrad first read in translation. If this discussion of reading displaces some more obvious questions about the origins of his writing—When did he learn to read and write in English? Why did he choose to write in English?—it nonetheless indirectly condenses those questions into the idealized space of an English literature of "European" reputation. Conrad's reminiscence here works to affiliate his writing with a cosmopolitan European ideal of English literature; and in this respect, indeed, his remarks are entirely in keeping with the ideals of Ford Madox Ford's *English Review*, whose deliberate aim was to establish a *European* reputation for English literature. The English modernism with which Ford associated himself, Henry James, and Joseph Conrad was a modernism that translated the techniques of the great French "masters" (Flaubert above all, who presides over the opening to Conrad's reminiscences) into English.

Embedded in this idealized projection of an English literature in translation Conrad improvises what comes closest to being a recollection of the scene of learning to read and hence, as noted above, a sort of authorial primal scene. Conrad recalls when he was eight years old, discovering a manuscript on his father's desk: "What emboldened me to clamber into his chair I am sure I don't know, but a couple of hours afterwards [my father] discovered me kneeling in it with my elbows on the table and my head held in both hands over the MS. of loose pages." Expecting "to get into trouble," Conrad is surprised when "the only thing he said after a moment of silence was: 'Read the page aloud.'" The passage continues:

> Luckily the page lying before me was not over-blotted with erasures and corrections, and my father's handwriting was otherwise extremely legible. When I got to the end he nodded and I flew out of doors thinking myself lucky to have escaped reproof for that piece of impulsive audacity. I have tried to discover since the reason of this mildness, and I imagine that all unknown to myself I had earned, in my father's mind, the right to some latitude in my relations with his writing-table. It was only a month before, or perhaps it was only a week before that I had read him aloud from beginning to end, and to his perfect satisfaction, as he lay on his bed, not being very well at the time, the proofs of his translation of Victor Hugo's "Toilers of the Sea." Such was my title to consideration, I believe, and also my first introduction to the sea in literature. If I do not remember where, how and when I learned to read, I am not likely to forget the process of being trained in the art of reading aloud. My poor father, an admirable reader himself, was the most exacting of masters. I reflect proudly that I must have read that page of "Two Gentlemen of Verona" tolerably well at the age of eight. (*PR*, 72)

Embedded within a reminiscence of what he was reading the day he began writing—itself embedded within the long-deferred account of the beginnings of his first novel—this recollection of his father condenses a number of other learning moments. Besides the forgotten moment of learning how to read, there is also the prior experience of basic language acquisition, and—particularly significant for Conrad's autobiographical record—the later experience of learning English.

Citing Victor Hugo's *Toilers of the Sea* as "my first introduction to the sea in literature" is an especially interesting condensation and displacement of the sort of English-learning experience Conrad received at sea. Hugo's novel itself dwells at length on the "patois"[19] of the Normandy coast, weaving throughout the novel comments on the creolized French and English language of fishing peoples, at points idealizing that "patois" as the "classic dialect of the sea" (*"l'idiome marin classique"*)[20] and the very foundations of the French language. There is, then, a complex and idealized order of the relation between languages and literature condensed in the memory Conrad rehearses of reading aloud the Polish text of his father's translation of Shakespeare.

Conrad's idealized childhood memory of reading invokes many of the same assumptions that inform the model of Lowell's "spiritual *lingua franca*"—above all, the ability to translate the opacity of spoken dialect into the transparent clarity of written text. Conrad's memory of being tested in "the art of reading aloud" acts out the metaphorical effect of Lowell's figuring the written text as speech; there is, as it were, a double testing going on: the young eight-year-old Conrad is being tested to see if he can read his father's Polish text out loud; and then in turn the Polish text's translation is being tested to see if it can "speak the spiritual *lingua franca* that abolishes all alienage of race." For Conrad, this is the privileged space of English literature, a space of reading in translation that resolves in advance questions he has been evading, or holding at bay.

If Conrad follows some of Lowell's assumptions, however, he does so with important differences—foregrounding, for example, the "shades of dialect" that need to be transcended in the process of turning literature into what Conrad describes as the "clear thought and exact expression" of the "great masters." Implied already in the image of the eight-year-old learning "the art of reading aloud" is the need to overcome whatever difficulties a translation inevitably faces. These difficulties, incidentally, are revealingly condensed, in Conrad's reminiscence, in the metaphor of script ("luckily the page...was not over blotted with erasures and corrections"): the materiality of writing, here, has quietly substituted for the questions of linguistic and literary translation with which the episode is invested. Immediately following this, moreover, Conrad goes on to exaggerate these linguistic and literary translation effects: "My first introduction to English imaginative literature was 'Nicholas Nickleby.' It is extraordinary how well Mrs. Nickleby could chatter disconnectedly in Polish and the sinister Ralph rage in that language. As to the Crummles family and the family of the learned Squeers, it seemed as natural to them as their native speech" (*PR*, 71). This order of reading, translation, and reported "native speech" foregrounds those "shades of dialect" Lowell would have us disregard in the "spiritual" region of classic literature—disrupting, for humorous effect, the expected hierarchy of written to spoken language. In one sense this complication emphasizes what is after all implicit in Lowell's ideal: though rooted in its own vernacular, and the linguistic circumstances of a particular environment ("shades of dialect"), the literary value of a work—the sign that it belongs to what Lowell elsewhere calls "pure literature"—is what survives in translation. Both Lowell and Conrad use a familiar rhetorical inversion of speaking and writing to convey this point: for Lowell, Homer and Theocritus "speak" in the metaphorical *lingua franca* of literature; for Conrad, the "native speech" of Dickens's characters comes to seem "natural" for the reader of a Polish translation.

Yet whereas Lowell's metaphor completes the inversion by fixing the hierarchical opposition between speech and writing in an implied opposition between the "spiritual" *lingua franca* of literature and the actual spoken, as it were material *lingua franca*, Conrad emphasizes a persistent dependence of the one on the other: the materiality of spoken English gets inscribed into the "spiritual *lingua franca*" of an ideal literary translation. Incidentally, this testing of the living language against an idealized order of literature might be compared to the principle by which the *O.E.D.* selects passages of literature—such as the Lowell citation—to illustrate the meaning of English words and phrases. Reading must always negotiate the passage from the one to the other, from the literal to the figurative, or the material to the spiritual *lingua franca*. There is a shared philological assumption governing the Lowell citation and Conrad's scene of childhood reading: the passage of literature (and also the passage *into* literacy and literature) is the site of a testing of linguistic and literary authority and authorship. There are also, of course, important differences. The English dialects of Dickens come to shape for Conrad an idealized *literary* order of English in European translation—a literary order of spoken English, moreover, whose claim to the status of "spiritual *lingua franca*" is all the more spiritualized for having negotiated the *linguistic* materiality of English. Thus, whereas for Lowell the "spiritual *lingua franca*" of world literature assumes the translation of classical and modern languages into English, Conrad's example presents a spiritual *lingua franca* of English in European literary translation.

Conrad stages his relation to English as both native and foreign: native as a literature, foreign as a language. Adjusting his claim that Dickens was his first introduction to English literature, Conrad introduces the memory of reading aloud to his father through a humorous stumbling over English grammar that modulates the translation effects of Dickens: "But I really believe that I am wrong. That book was not my first introduction to English literature. My first acquaintance was (or were) the 'Two Gentlemen of Verona,' and that in the very MS. of my father's translation" (*PR*, 71). English emerges as the dream of a spoken *lingua franca* embedded in a literary order of translation effects.

This linguistic-literary register of English—fully in accord, as noted earlier, with the cosmopolitan claims of *The English Review*—stages a humorous resolution of national differences that recalls a number of Goethe's celebrated comments on "world literature"; as, for example, when Eckermann recalls his statement that "The phenomenon which I call world literature will come about mainly when the disputes within one nation are settled by the opinions and judgments of others" ("*dasjenige was ich Weltliteratur nenne dadurch vorzüglich entstehen wird, wenn die Differenzen, die innerhalb der einen Nation obwalten, durch Ansicht und Urtheil der übrigen ausgeglichen würden*").[21] English, for Conrad, is certainly a privileged language for embodying this essentially cosmopolitan ideal. Within the scope of *A Personal Record*—within the scope, indeed, of Conrad's overall career—it is an "English" at least potentially open to translating any and all languages. Toward the beginning of the *Record*, and as an initial attempt to recount the moment he first started writing, he conjures the image of himself in his Pimlico apartments in London, "unknown to my respectable land-lady...[holding] animated receptions of Malays, Arabs, and half-castes" (*PR*, 9). This reference to the Malay characters and material of his first novel—and by extension, too, the projected Malay trilogy with which he began his literary career, finishing it only at the very end of that career—is especially interesting from our perspective since it links Conrad's early Malay-English colonial family romance to a form of Malay *lingua franca* quite closely related to the Malay *lingua franca* that would become Indonesian. For Conrad, however, the "words and gestures" of these characters may naturally be admitted (albeit "unknown to my respectable landlady") to the space of that "English" where differences (or disputes—*Differenzen*) can be staged as grammatical error and correction. The idealized "spiritual *lingua franca*" of Conrad's English remains a specifically European ideal—as, indeed, it was for Goethe. But the linguistic materiality with which it embodies the differences, disputes, or *Differenzen* of "native speech" is open to the world.

The unevenness of development implied in this distinction between the linguistic and literary registers of Conrad's English modernism deserves one further point of clarification in terms of the specific scene of reading in question. Although Conrad appears to echo Goethe's European ideal of world literature in the literary register of English writers translated into Polish—what Conrad conveys in the phrase "men of European reputation"—this ideal is not only quite fragile, a mirage on the horizon not unlike some of the famously hesitant and prospective formulations of Goethe himself. Associated as it is with his father's career, this European ideal is also perhaps already recognized as a mirage that has evaporated. What Conrad resolves humorously at the level of his English grammatical error and correction remains deeply unresolved within the context of the overall memory of his father's literary endeavors. The idealized fantasy of an English literary *lingua franca* emerges, after all, in the reconstruction of a painful childhood memory, the consequences of his father's failed political involvement in the 1863 Polish rebellion against Russia:

> It was during our exile in Russia, and it must have been less than a year after my mother's death, because I remember myself in the black blouse with a white border of my heavy mourning. We were living together, quite alone, in a small house on the outskirts of the town of T___. That afternoon, instead of going out to play in the large yard which we shared with our landlord, I had lingered in the room in which my father wrote. (*PR*, 71)

Conrad's evocation of an idealized European order of English reading and writing emerges in response to a far from humorous memory—that of his mother's death and his father's exile from Poland to Russia, both of which figure a specifically resonant disorder of European political and cultural identification.

If, with Conrad, the lure of English as a *lingua franca* is measured against, but always discontinuous with, the mirage of a European order of world literature, the scene of writing becomes a space of recognized misunderstandings—the scene of writing where, characteristically, Conrad can stumble over the correct grammatical form in which to explain how "My first acquaintance was (or were) the 'Two Gentlemen of Verona'" (*PR*, 71). This suggests the point Homi Bhabha argues for in revising Goethe's concept of world literature as "an emergent, prefigurative category that is concerned with a form of cultural dissensus and alterity."[22] Conrad (as one of those case studies in Bhabha's revision of world literature as "the study of the way in which cultures recognize themselves through their projections of 'otherness'"[23]) stands as an important figure both in looking ahead to the "worlding" of English in the twentieth century from Naipaul to Rushdie and in looking back to the kind of "worlding" of English at work in such "men of European reputation" as Scott and Dickens. As I explore at greater length in chapter 2, it is this discontinuity between the idealized *lingua franca* of English and the imagined order of a European literary reputation that situates the coordinates of "English modernism." Underlying the logic of this "English modernism" is the discontinuous relation between "English" (as an idealized *lingua franca*) and "world" literature.

Jean Rhys's Creole English

With the work of Jean Rhys, at least from the retrospect of *Wide Sargasso Sea* (1966), this "worlding" of English (as language and literature) is fully imbricated in the process of "creolization" as theorized by, among others, Édouard Glissant and Edward Kamau Brathwaite.[24] In general, the attraction of a creolized *lingua franca* is that it affords the opportunity to realize that polyglot linguistic and plural cultural space in the transparency of the written page. One thinks of Glissant's imperative: "A language does not require initiation but apprenticeship: it must be accessible to all" (*"Une langue ne suppose pas initiation mais apprentissage; elle doit être accessible à tout"*).[25] As an essential part of this attraction, however, the "movement" of creolization contains a sort of hidden clause: again, quoting Glissant, "One could imagine—this is, moreover, a movement that is emerging almost everywhere—a kind of revenge by oral languages over written ones, in the context of a global civilization of the nonwritten" (*"On pourrait concevoir—c'est d'ailleurs un mouvement qui se dessine à peu près partout—une sorte de revanche des langues orales sur les langues écrites, dans le context d'une civilization planétaire du non-écrit"*).[26] This hostility to literature is something that Rhys's *Wide Sargasso Sea* captures in a literary form that has come, paradoxically and problematically, to canonize the postcolonial possibilities of a Creole rereading of English literature.

In the second section of her "unfinished autobiography" *Smile Please* (1979), the problematic relation—even hostility—between oral and written language surfaces in her recollection of the process of learning to read. Troubling the apparently normative rite of passage into literacy, this section, entitled "Books," might also invite a rereading of Conrad's own insistence on the impossibility of accounting for that passage into literacy. Embedded already in Conrad's account of "learning to read aloud" is a problematic relation between the oral and written that appears, in light of Rhys's autobiographical fragment, more self-referentially trapped in the impasse of any original passage into literacy: "If I do not remember where, how and when I learned to read, I am not likely to forget the process of being trained in the art of reading aloud" (*PR*, 72). Is it possible to ignore entirely a hidden pun in the sound of the word *aloud* ("allowed")? What are the conditions that allow for a continuing relation and hierarky between the oral and the written? It is a question embedded not only in Conrad's primal scene of learning to read but also in many of the classic moments of "Conradian" prose—as, for example, when the narrator Marlow is introduced: "Marlow (at least I think that is how he spelt his name)" (*Y*, 3).

Rhys's recollection is organized around an impossibility: the attempt to describe, in writing, what it is like not to know how to read. This impossibility assumes narrative form in the antagonism between her younger self and her nurse, Meta: "My nurse, who was called Meta, didn't like me much anyway, and complete with a book it was too much" (*S*, 20). Meta embodies a hostility to writing that enables Rhys to formulate that impossibility of experience:

> She said, 'If all you read so much, you know what will happen to you? Your eyes will drop out and they will look at you from the page.'
> 'If my eyes dropped out I wouldn't see,' I argued.
> She said, 'They drop out except the little black points you see with.' (*S*, 21)

This description of reading as loss of eyesight and bodily mutation (or mutilation) stands, then, as an alternative account of the passage into literacy. One thing that remains haunting about the image of the reading process is its refusal of any obvious contrast between the oral and the written, the literate and the illiterate. Meta seems to embody the kind of defiant illiteracy Rhys ascribes to Christophine in her final confrontation with Rochester toward the end of *Wide Sargasso Sea* ("'Read and write I don't know. Other things I know'" [*WSS*, 97]). Yet Meta's description of the reading process, itself governed by the linguistic power of its Creole linguistic articulation, asserts an authority of knowledge about the power of the printed page that cannot be ascribed to some nonliterate ignorance (whether pre-literate or illiterate). In this way, the hostility Rhys personifies in the figure of Meta dramatizes Glissant's "revenge by oral languages over written ones"—perhaps still more clearly than Glissant's own expression, which seems to retain the consolation of a difference between oral and written forms, whereas the "revenge" lies precisely in the abolition of that distance. In terms of the autobiography of the vignette (and, like Conrad's reminiscence, it occupies a privileged place in the autobiographical fiction of authorship), the account of a normative transition from pre-literate ignorance to literate knowledge is confounded. Meta's terrifying image of the reading process confirms the cluster of perceptions about books with which the vignette begins, in its apparent attempt to recapture the lost childhood experience of the mysteries of reading. The seemingly illogical, aliterate grasp of "books," the vignette suggests, constitutes the logic of the reading process—that process that will continue despite, or because of, the in-built hostility: "But I went on reading."

In effect, Rhys reformulates the process of learning to read as an incomplete process. Although the narrative develops an account of the "leap" whereby she learned to "manage quite long words," could "make sense of the fairy stories," and then "read everything I could get hold of," this successful movement into literacy is reversed in the vignette's denouement. Ultimately, the reading process itself is grasped as a perpetual negotiation of the passage back and forth between the literate and the nonliterate.

The lure of a *lingua franca* (by analogy to our discussion of Conrad) surfaces in the attempt to reason with Meta about the reading process—a realm of recognition, dialogue, and disagreement, strongly registered in a Creole English by contrast with and hostile to that order of books with which Rhys recalls the standard reading matter of her childhood. It might be too simple to see in this a contrast between a colonial English canon of world literature and an oral compendium of Creole stories and folk wisdom, such as does get developed in stages throughout the unfinished autobiography. Certainly, the unfinished autobiography is itself organized around the lure of a Creole past constituted by oral traditions. Those memories of stories, songs, and sayings, however, are always reconstructed through an order of reading, although not necessarily a reading ordered by the space of the printed page: television organizes Rhys's retrospective memory of West Indian carnival; and the very first memory is mediated by the reading of a "chosen photograph" that gives title to the autobiography—*Smile Please*—as an unfinished whole. Rhys's memories are also premised on a disturbing process of split racial, cultural, and linguistic identifications—as with the splitting of identity and identification in the estranged bodily image of the "little black points you see with." There is a profound ambivalence about the relation between the assumptions of literacy and the hostility to literacy, and this ambivalence constitutes the idealized linguistic space of creolized *lingua franca*—indeed, the title word *books* ambiguously names not only that set of canonical works of literature Rhys recalls reading but also that, as it were, nonliterary knowledge of print literacy. The dialectic between these two—dramatized in the deadlocked dialectic of postcolonial/postemancipation violence enacted over the Creole madwoman of Brontë's *Jane Eyre*—is already implied in the split sense of "books" with which the vignette opens: between the singular "large" book imagined as God and the "smaller" book, with its implied plurality and heterogeneity of "sharp flashing things," retrospectively surmised as "my mother's needle book" (S, 20).

The lure of the *lingua franca*, within this logic of creolization, or Creole modernism, is then both the undoing of the literary and the reconstitution of the space of the literary; of the role of "books" in the world; of world literature. Within Rhys's work this contested order of the oral, the written, and "books" is measured, in a number of important instances, against the model of the newspaper—incidentally, one of Benedict Anderson's privileged models for the national consciousness of "imagined communities" (the other being the novel).[27] The "creole pioneers"[28] Anderson credits with originating this modular form of "print capitalism" are "creole" in a rather different sense from the linguistic and literary register of the Creole modernism associated with Caribbean writers of the twentieth century; and this is a difference to which we will need to return (in chapter 5) in considering the overall trajectory of Rhys's career in relation to the changing meaning of the word *creole* itself.[29]

What differentiates Anderson's historical emphasis on the "creole pioneers" of "print capitalism" in the Americas of the eighteenth century, from Rhys's interest in a Creole contest over the space of print literacy, however, is the discontinuity between the space of the newspaper and the space of the literary. This discontinuity is made clear in an early short story, "Again the Antilles"—one of three stories about Rhys's "Antillean" childhood that inaugurates her literary career with a sort of farewell to that West Indian social, political, and literary world. In the anecdote this story develops about the feud between Mr. Musgrave and Papa Dom—between the white sugar and lime owner and the "coloured" editor of the *Dominica Herald and Leeward Islands Gazette*—Rhys articulates something of the basic social antagonism between landowning whites and a nonwhite middle class. What is interesting about the story is the narrative perspective it creates to formulate the stereotyped colonial standoff (or, perhaps rather, the standoff of colonial stereotypes: "'Coloured' we West Indians call the intermediate shades…" [*CS*, 39])—constituted around a collectively imagined community (although this imagined community is, characteristically, split between "we West Indians" and "the whole island" [*CS*, 40]). On the one hand, this image reveals the limits of a shared educated, literate consciousness able to transcend what Lowell's phrase calls the "alienage of race"—the limit signaled, perhaps, by that sense of the word *creole* Jean Rhys discarded as the title for *Wide Sargasso Sea:* a "Creole" community of readers—the readers of the *Dominica Herald and Leeward Island Gazette*. On the other hand, the crystallization of that image as a nostalgic construction, the image of a shared language and shared space of print, constitutes precisely what might be described as one of the lures of a *lingua franca*—a shared space of contestation. This is that precarious passage to "an openly accessible language" ("*en langue ouverte*")[30] Glissant discusses, but which he claims passes Martinican Creole by: "The dilemma of Martinican Creole is that the stage of secret code has been passed, but language (as a new opening) has not been attained" ("*Le drame Martiniquais du créole est qu'en lui le pacte s'éteint, mais que la langue [en tant qu'ouverture] n'apparait pas*").[31]

What Rhys does is to crystallize this impasse around a disputed literary passage from English literature, Papa Dom's quotation of the line "He was a very gentle, perfect knight." Our reading of that passage, and the various gradations of irony involved in the disputed authorship and context of the passage—Papa Dom's ascription of the quote to "the Marquis of Montrose" via Shakespeare prompts Mr. Musgrave's letter asserting that the line is from Chaucer—compels us to consider that third position between Mr. Musgrave's arrogant and racist claims to literary authority and Papa Dom's literary pretensions and racial conscience. This emerges in the interpretive knot forced on the reader by the narrator's comment that "Mr. Musgrave had really written 'damn niggers'" where Papa Dom's edited version of the letter reads "the ignorant of another race and colour" (*CS*, 41). One might well ask on what authority the narrator knows this; but the point is not so much that the story invites the reader to contemplate the possibility that she has a privileged relation to Mr. Musgrave or that this was common knowledge for "the whole island." The point, rather, is that the phrase "damn niggers" acts as an expletive whose edited deletion from the printed page constitutes the sense of community on which the narrative reflects. It is a study in the question of civility Homi Bhabha takes up in "Sly Civility," although it apparently inverts the effect of mimicry, showing how much labor of editorial work goes into keeping the page of civil discourse and open debate free from the reciprocities of racial hatred. The *Dominica Herald and Leeward Islands Gazette* provides a study in organized modern civility (which is, in many respects, Rhys's abiding topic); and in Papa Dom two seemingly irreconcilable current senses of "Creole" come together: Benedict Anderson's use of the old term in defining the "creole pioneers" of nationalism and the literary-linguistic sense of the term as developed by Glissant. The two are brought together in Papa Dom, paradoxically, to show how Creole literary consciousness becomes the guardian of English against creolization.

To put this another way—in order to emphasize the question of what Rhys has to tell us about the social, historical, and linguistic coordinates of Creole modernism—the narrative perspective produced by the story "Again the Antilles" is one constituted through the possibility of reading the language of "print capitalism" (in Anderson's phrase) as a space of contestation and of community. The passage of literature—what Papa Dom sententiously (mis)-quotes as a line from Shakespeare—and what Musgrave corrects (again, slightly misquoting from the original Chaucerian English) as a passage from Chaucer—might at first seem to signal a writer's

(Rhys's) abandoning as hopelessly undignified the literary and social context of her home. Yet it also signals (as an impasse of literary consciousness) the question of reading that gets reformulated years later in "Books." It is a question of reading that turns Lowell's rhetorical question into a more than rhetorical question: "what concern have we with the shades of dialect in Homer or Theocritus, provided they speak the spiritual *lingua franca* that abolishes all alienage of race?" A suspicious, anagrammatical, and Creole modernist rereading of this passage itself might have some cause to see in Lowell's "alienage of race" an unconscious effort to "abolish a *lineage* of race" from the printed page of world literature. The question of race is simultaneously written into and effaced from the space of print in a way that marks Rhys's career-long engagement with the writing and rewriting of English as a contested effect of Creole language, print literature, and culture.[32]

Pramoedya Ananta Toer's "Pre-Indonesian" Indonesian

In a section entitled "Flowers for Mother" ("Karangan Bunga pada Kakinya") from the prison notes rescued from Pramoedya's Buru exile, Pramoedya recalls an early scene of childhood reading that provides a revealing companion piece to these early childhood reading scenes of Conrad and Rhys. In a number of ways it might be read as an idealized evocation of a worldly, proto-nationalist sense of world literature, an Indonesian version of Lowell's "spiritual *lingua franca*." Recalling his mother as a "brilliant storyteller," Pramoedya writes:

> My mother liked to read and could understand Javanese in Roman script, as well as Malay and Dutch. She kept up with the Surabaya and Semarang daily papers and all the books and magazines that we received. (My father, as the principal of a school, was given numerous publications free of charge.) At night, when encircled by her children, or sometimes when lying down and nursing the youngest child, she'd weave for us stories based on the materials she had read. She was a brilliant storyteller, able to entwine us in her spell. Over a series of nights she might relate the story of *Angling Darmo* and her favorite hero, Amir Hamzah. Or one of the many stories published by Balai Pustaka. [Or European stories: *Klein Duimpje, Robinson Crusoe, Gulliver's Travels, Putri Genoveva* (all of which I would later read myself), and many more besides, although for sure it would be boring to mention them all.] (*MS*, 128)[33]
>
> *Ibuku seorang yang suka membaca majalah dan buku: Jawa, selama tidak berhuruf Jawa, Melayu dan Belanda. Ia setiap hari mengikuti koran, baik dari Surabaya maupun Semarang, yang dikirimkan cuma-cuma pada alamat kami. Buku dan majalah juga dikirimkan*

pada ayahku dengan cuma-cuma. Dari bacaan itu ia suka bercerita. Ia seorang pencerita yang baik dan selalu memikat. Kadang ia bercerita di malam hari sambil duduk dalam kerumunan anak-anaknya. Tidak jarang anak-anak titipan mendengarkan juga dari sesuatu jarak. Kadang ia bercerita sambil tiduran menyusui bayinya.

Ia dapat bercerita bersambung-sambung sampai beberapa malam tentang cerita berangkai Amir Hamzah, yang dalam terjemahan Jawa jadi Bagindo Ambyah, Angling Darmo, *atau cerita lain dari* Almanak Balai Pustaka, *atau cerita-cerita Eropa:* Klein Duimpje, Robinson Crusoe, Guiliver, Putri Genoveva *(yang semua ini kemudian aku baca sendiri), dan banyak yang lain, dan tentu akan membosankan bila disebut semua.* (NS II, 50)

What emerges from the memory of his mother's reading is a wide-ranging, multicultural, and syncretic approach to the world—an Indonesian modernism entirely at home in a world of diverse literatures.

Within this idealized, world literary space—the space of what Lowell calls a "spiritual *lingua franca*"—there is, however, no explicit account of the role of that material *lingua franca*, the form of Malay adopted in 1928 as a nationalist language that would become *bahasa Indonesia,* the language of independent, post-45 Indonesia. Even as it stands in for an account of Pramoedya's initiation into just such a language, the recollection of his mother's "brilliant storytelling" seems to elide the question of *bahasa Indonesia*. Other than stating that his mother knew how to read Malay as well as Javanese and Dutch, there is no explicit mention of *bahasa Indonesia*. The world of *bahasa Indonesia* is evoked only indirectly. Pramoedya calls attention to what his mother did *not* read: "Though my father included among his prized possessions copies of the Javanese classics, Pustaka Raja Jarwa and Pustaka Raja Purwa, she never drew stories from them to tell to us" (*MS*, 129) ("*walaupun ayah mempunyai buku kesayangan* Pustaka Raja Jarwa *dan* Pustaka Raja Purwa, *ia pun tidak pernah mengutipnya dalam cerita-ceritanya*" [*NS* II, 50]). In addition, we learn (though in a passage not translated in the English edition): "From amongst all this there was not a mention of the *wayang* stories. My mother was not as familiar with the world of *wayang* as my father was, and liked even less to be enthralled by [*mengagumi*] gamelan, the absolute opposite of my father" ("*Di antara sekian banyak tak ada terselip cerita wayang. Ibuku tidak mengenal alam wayang sebagai ayahku, juga tidak suka apalagi mengagumi gamelan, sebaliknya dari ayahku*" [*NS* II, 50]). And: "I later learned of a whole set of books that were in the library by Indo writers, in beautiful yellow-coloured binding, in Dutch, but she never once read to us from any of these" ("*Kelak aku ketahui dalam perpustakaan rumah terdapat seri tulisan pengarang-pengarang Indo, dalam jilidan indah berwarna kuning, dalam Belanda, tetapi ia tidak pernah menceritakan satu pun di antaranya"* [*NS* II, 50–51]).

Such exclusions—against Javanese literature, on the one hand, and Dutch literature, on the other—delineate the idealized order of an Indonesian reading. The political dimensions of this ideal are suggested by the recollection that "from when I was in the fifth grade, she began to tell me stories about contemporary nationalist figures" and of "Gandhi and the Indian nationalists" (*MS*, 128) ("*Setelah aku mulai duduk di kelas 5 sekolah dasar, ia mulai bercerita tentang tokoh-tokoh nasionalis semasa...tentang Gandhi dan gerakannya di India*" [*NS* II, 50]). "Her stories with their beautiful fantasies," he continues, underscoring the idealized shape of his own recollection, "stimulated the imagination and nurtured in our young souls the dream of building a better, more perfect world" (*MS*, 129) ("*Ceritanya selalu membangkitkan fantasi yang indah-indah... Maka fantasi ini memimpin jiwa kanak-kanak itu memasuki dunia gambarannya sendiri yang lebih baik, lebih sempuirna, lebih berpengharapan, juga lebih berkemanusiaan*" [*NS* II, 51]). Their political orientation is reinforced by the repertoire of the mother's songs. Writing of the songs she liked to sing—"In the middle of a story my mother might interrupt her tale with a song" (*MS*, 129) ("*Di tengah-tengah cerita kadang-kadang ia menyelinginya dengan nyanyian*" [*NS* II, 51])—Pramoedya comments "Strangely, she didn't even once sing what was at the time a popular song, *Als de Orchidieen Bloeien*" (omitted from *MS*) ("*Anehnya waktu sedang populernya lagu* Als de Orchidieen Bloeien, *ia sama sekali tak pernah menyanyikannya*" [*NS* II, 51]). Although there is no explicit comment on the role of the *lingua franca* of Malay, its presence is implicit in an idealized model of an oral storytelling, translation, and singing that distances itself both from Dutch and from Javanese. Not unlike Conrad's scene of learning the "art of reading aloud," Pramoedya's scene of reading projects a *literary* order of language (a "spiritual *lingua franca*") *prior* to the acquisition of spoken language.

The literary order of writing and reading conjured in this passage is introduced by an account of a Javanese family book of advice for children that his father put together. He recalls finding, among the handwritten and typewritten manuscripts of his father, a written copy of a piece of advice his mother had given him, the advice that he is not "made out to be a farmer"—"You're too lazy for that. You're a person who's meant to be free, an *all-round* person. Later she explained what that strange word meant" (*MS*, 128; English translation modified[34]) ("*Kau takkan cocok jadi petani. Untuk itu kau terlalu malas. Yang paling tepat kau sebaiknya jadi orang bebas, dan* all-round. *Kemudian ia menerangkan apa artinya kata asing itu*" [*NS* II, 49]). This piece of advice—whose written form Pramoedya says he took a copy of to keep for himself—is presented as one of a set of such pieces of advice: "These little words and sayings, spoken and written, part of the soul of my childhood, have become the concepts that today I keep in the foreground" (*"Kata-kata yang sedikit itu, lisan dan tulisan, dalam jiwa kanak-kanakku telah menjadi konsep tentang hari depanku"* [*NS* II, 50]). The word *all-round*, spoken, and then written down among the various forms of presumably Javanese manuscript and roman typescript, provides a revealing point of reference for the multilingual formation of a language that has not yet fully crystallized as the language, literature, or political idea of Indonesian. Although this key word of advice appears to be English, it might alternatively be read as an Indonesian formation.[35]

In this Indonesian childhood scene of learning to read we find elements of both the European and the Creole scene of learning English in Conrad's and Rhys's respective autobiographical accounts. There is something similar to Conrad's European order of world literature in the detail with which Pramoedya remembers the titles of particular European tales, as well as in his retrospective comment that he later read all of them himself. The oral storytelling form of his mother's reading, however, recalls both the complicating feature of Conrad's memory of learning the art of "reading aloud" and the suspicion and hostility toward literature encountered in Rhys's childhood reading scene. Although there is no such Meta figure of hostility in Pramoedya's account, the emphasis on the mother's exclusions nurtures suspicion about the excluded texts—and notably about the collection of Indo writers (that "whole set of books... in beautiful yellow-coloured binding in Dutch"), on the one hand, and on the other, the Javanese classics (the father's "prized possessions"). The suspicion itself—born of the retrospective narrative reflection back on the remembered scene of reading—is ambiguously directed both against the literary tradition of the Dutch colonizers and against the literary tradition of his native Javanese culture. Although these excluded books prompt questions that remain unanswered in the narrative present, the suspicion they engender anticipates the emerging form of Indonesian linguistic and literary modernism outlined against a European literary tradition, on the one hand, and against a Javanese tradition, on the other.

This absent presence in "Flowers for Mother" of what Pramoedya elsewhere calls the "Malay *lingua franca*" might also be read, historically and materially, as a sign of the gaps of historical memory on which Pramoedya's reconstruction of Indonesian history, and all of the work of Buru, is premised. As we shall explore in greater detail in later chapters, the Buru quartet of novels must account for at least two moments of lost documentation: the destruction of almost all of Pramoedya's own historical and fictional works during the events of 1965; and the prior destruction, at the beginning of the twentieth century, of the works of proto-nationalist writers and journalists, notably Tirto Adi Suryo, the historical model for Minke, the first-person narrator of the first three volumes of the Buru quartet. Among the works destroyed in 1965 was a preliminary history of the development of *bahasa Indonesia* as a language, various studies and anthologies of "pre-Indonesian" literature, and the remainder of a trilogy about his parents, only the first part of which (concerning his grandmother) has survived (*Gadis Pantai; The Girl from the Coast*).[36] The loss of the trilogy about his parents leaves an obvious mark on the fragmentary memories of his parents collected, above all, in the two sections "One Link in a Chain" and "Flowers for Mother" from the prison notes (discussed at greater length in chapter 7). The loss of all these earlier efforts to document the historical formation of a "pre-Indonesian" language and literature shapes all of the work of Buru. This is especially important for the Buru quartet, where the conflicting claims of different languages—Dutch, Javanese, Malay, even English—shape Minke's decision to write in the *lingua franca* Melayu to crystallize an alliance of anti-colonial political forces among the heterogeneity of ethnic groups throughout the Dutch East Indies.

The year 1928 is repeatedly cited as "the real beginning of *Bahasa Indonesia*, as both the medium and symbol of national freedom";[37] and specifically October 28, 1928, the "oath of youth" (*soempah pemoeda*), when the all-Indonesia association, *Indonesia Muda* (Young Indonesia), proclaimed the "three-fold ideal of one country, one nation, and one language" (*satu nusa, satu bangsa, satu bahasa*).[38] As Benedict Anderson notes, though, this event had already been "shaped by two generations of urban writers and readers."[39] One important earlier historical point of reference is the case of a famous newspaper article published by Suwardi Surjaningrat in *De Expres* on July 13, 1913, and quickly translated into Malay. Entitled "Als ik eens Nederlander was"—in Malay, "Jika saja Nederlander" [If I Were Ever a Dutchman]. Its satirical comment on the celebrations of Dutch independence from Napoleon's rule was, as Benedict Anderson explains, to turn "Dutch history against the Dutch" by questioning the political rationale behind the celebrations: "If I were a Dutchman, I would not organize an independence celebration in a country where the independence of the people has been stolen."[40] Anderson goes on to claim that the article "is exemplary of a world-wide twentieth-century phenomenon. For the paradox of imperial official nationalism was that it inevitably brought what were increasingly thought of and written about as European 'national histories' into the consciousness of the colonized."[41] This key moment in the process of "imagining community" might be described as a Creole modernist consciousness that appears in print to challenge the complacencies of a European colonial "I." Taken as a watershed moment in the awakening of Indonesian national consciousness, it is a moment toward which Pramoedya's Buru tetralogy looks, and one prefigured by the narrative "I" of Minke, based on the historical figure of Tirto Adi Suryo, who narrates the first three volumes.[42]

James Siegel examines the nuances of this "consciousness" from a slightly different angle:

> The question is how this can take place and also how it can involve masses of people. It is not naturally given in Melayu lingua franca. The one who embarrasses [the colonized appropriating the colonizer's language] is someone who sees what he should not see. He is present inappropriately. In the case [of Suwardi's pamphlet], his presense [sic] is not noticed. He is invisible; he is present without being seen. That is, the "I" of the sentence, translated into Melayu, is one that suddenly appears to the Dutch, having been there all the time; a fact that one knows only in retrospect, only after the title of Soewardi's piece is produced and then translated.[43]

Siegel's interest in the disruptive effects of Suwardi's intervention focuses on the moment before *bahasa Indonesia* takes shape as vehicle for imagining nationalism in Anderson's sense. As he puts it, "The thrust of Indonesian nationalism in 1913 was not for independence; it was for a certain recognition."[44] This casts the watershed moment in Indonesian nationalism as a paradigmatic realization of Goethe's ideal "world literature"—a moment of longing for transnational, translingual recognition.

To read this historical moment as the simultaneous realization of Goethe's ideal and the formation of a specifically Indonesian modernism might, in turn, shed light on the inherent problem of world literature that haunts the formation of "English" and "Creole" modernism, respectively. It signals the moment when the linguistic hegemony of a colonizing language is assumed by the *lingua franca* of colonial exchange—the moment when the "I" (*ik*) of the one colonizing language (Dutch) can be exchanged with, and recognized in its equivalence for, the "I" (*saja*) of the colonized other. Whether regarded from the point of view of Anderson's speculations on the modern forms of nationalism, or in terms of Siegel's analysis of the failed trajectory of revolutionary anti-colonial nationalism, this is clearly an important moment in the history of decolonization. Its implications may be gauged in relation to Lowell's metaphor for the "spiritual *lingua franca*" of universal literary value: world literature depends on the linguistic materiality (of "dialect" and "alienage of race") that gives it hegemony. What Indonesian modernism may further illuminate about the formation of an "English" and a "Creole" modernism, respectively, is how the specifically "English" ideal of Lowell's "spiritual *lingua franca*" has, all along, been haunted by the material *lingua franca* of colonial exchange.

As Anderson, Siegel, and Henk Maier have all explored, each from different perspectives and each following in the footsteps of Pramoedya, these early twentieth-century coordinates for Indonesian nationalism—1928 and 1913—are shaped by an even earlier moment of what Pramoedya called "pre-Indonesian" literature. The "two generations of urban writers and readers"[45] who shaped the form of Indonesian adopted in 1928 include not only proto-nationalists like Suwardi and, before him, Tirto Adi Suryo but also writers, often anonymous and usually publishing under pseudonyms, who used a nonstandard form of print Malay to produce a wide variety of tales, often translations from Arab, Chinese, European, or Malay literatures. Siegel writes of this important, transitional moment of literary exchange that "works designed for one group—Chinese, 'native,' European, Arab—were read by all."[46] Citing the work of Maier, Siegel describes this as a moment of "staggering polyphony and heterogeneity in printed materials."[47] One of the "pre-Indonesian" texts Pramoedya reprints in his anthology, *Tempo Doeloe*, in order to illustrate "the structure of feeling" ("*semangat semasa*")[48] of this time, is *Nyai Dasima*, by G. Francis, published in 1896, a tale that has an important, if ghostly presence throughout the Buru tetralogy.

Henk Maier's more recent "survey of Malay writing" has added to this already complex picture of multi-ethnic and transnational exchange in the print Malay of "pre-Indonesian" literature by drawing attention to the overlap between older forms of oral composition and manuscript circulation and the newer forms of romanized print Malay. Although modern Indonesian literature can be traced to the shift from those older forms of oral and manuscript "reading" (*baca*) and "composition" (*karang*) to the newer forms of print culture, Maier suggests that, in some respects, the older interplay between oral and manuscript reading, writing, and recomposition may still persist, and notably in the work of Pramoedya.[49] Pramoedya's childhood scene of his mother's reading may, indeed, itself be read as a form of commemoration of this interplay between reading, writing, and oral commemoration, especially since it weaves together both of the key words—*baca* and *karang;* "reading" and "composition"—Maier attributes to this longer history of Malay literature.[50]

Looking back to this complex moment of "pre-Indonesian" literature, Pramoedya's historical vision of Indonesian modernism raises a set of questions about reading that remains at the heart of all three of the major works of these three Indonesian specialists: Benedict Anderson's *Imagined Communities;* James Siegel's *Fetish, Recognition, Revolution;* and Henk Maier's *We Are Playing Relatives*. Whether focusing on the success in crystallizing a new Indonesian "imagined community" (Anderson), on its failure (Siegel), or on the modern repetition of older Malay forms of reading and writing

(Maier), all three return to the questions Pramoedya poses about the emergence of Indonesian literary modernism from this moment of "pre-Indonesian" literature. In the introduction to *Tempo Doeloe,* he formulates these questions around an open historical question about the readership of all the texts of "pre-Indonesian literature" reprinted in his anthology: "What is published here has not yet for certain been read, but what is read here has already for certain been published" (*"Ada penerbitan memang belum tentu ada pembaca, tetapi ada pembaca sudah tentu ada penerbitan"*).[51] This almost aphoristic formulation for a readership of "pre-Indonesian" texts constitutes something of a riddle not only for Indonesian modernism but also, I propose, for transnational modernism over the turn from the nineteenth to the twentieth century.

In some respects, it is a very straightforward historical question about the readership for these texts produced in a multi-ethnic colonial society in which only a tiny fraction of the total population was literate. As Pramoedya notes, however, the very question of what constitutes a "reading" (*pembaca*) suggests a much wider audience than simply those who are literate. This is not only because such texts became the scripts for popular operatic theater. These texts, produced at the crossroads of a range of cultures and traditions—Arab, Chinese, European, Malay—and in a relatively recent, not yet standardized romanized script, signal a moment of enormous revolutionary transformation. As we shall explore in discussing the Buru tetralogy, the disappearance of many of these texts (and notably the genre of the *nyai* narrative) turns the problem of readership into a still more important and haunting question. With the setting up of the official Malay-language colonial publishing house, Balai Pustaka (referred to in Pramoedya's childhood memory of his mother's reading), the "staggering polyphony and heterogeneity" of published materials gets regulated. The problem of reading to which Pramoedya turns, in writing back to the "roots" of Indonesian nationalism and Indonesian literary modernism, is the prior moment of polyphony and heterogeneity, a moment that coincides historically with the moment of the English modernism of Conrad's idealized order of literature in translation; and that looks back from a position of colonial contest that overlaps with the Creole modernism to which Rhys's work constitutes a complex response.

Each of the scenes of learning to read I have discussed in this introductory chapter present embryonic genealogies of English, Creole, and Indonesian modernism. These genealogies—which form the basis for the genealogies of reading transnational modernism we shall be tracing in the pages that follow—are also inscribed, in still more condensed and encoded form, in the names of the authors. As Foucault discusses in "What Is an Author?" the name of the author serves a complex "variable" "function" in organizing the texts ascribed to an individual author.[52] Foucault is interested, in part, in complicating the poststructuralist notion of a space of writing, or *écriture*, freed from the psychological, phenomenological, or theological illusion of an original author. This conception of a writing "where the writing subject endlessly disappears" ("*où le sujet écrivant ne cesse de disparaître*")[53] famously proclaimed by Roland Barthes in "The Death of the Author," but derived from the French modernist ideal of *l'oeuvre pur* (Mallarmé), does not, after all, do away with the function of the author's name in classifying, regulating, delimiting, or authorizing a complex relation between texts. Each of the scenes of reading discussed above is part of an autobiographical work that seeks to redeploy the "variable" "function" of the author's name. Each of these author's names presents questions of reading, writing, and authorial self-reference, moreover, that suggest an intimate link between his or her individual, authorial family romance of reading and the genealogies of English, Creole, and Indonesian modernism registered in their writing.

What Conrad himself once called "the neutral pseudonym of 'Joseph Conrad'"[54] translates essential parts of his full original Polish name—Józef Teodor Konrad Nałęcz Korzeniowski—into a form legible in English, elaborating an authorial identity that seems to embody the "neutral" transparency of an idealized linguistic and literary space of English modernism. To call it a "neutral pseudonym," however, invites attention to the variable forms of allegiance, antagonism, and betrayal concealed behind the name. The resonance of Conrad's original, non-English name has, indeed, regularly drawn critical attention to problems of reading, translation, and legibility that have come to constitute the signature modernist effects of any Conradian passage of literature. As David R. Smith points out, Conrad was "preoccupied with the semiotics" of his name, as revealed in the alternating emphasis on the letters "K" and "C" scribbled into the margins of his manuscripts.[55] This preoccupation, which extends to the naming of his fictional characters, too, calls attention to a semiotics of cross-cultural identity at work in all his fiction. While most apparent in the vexed antagonism between Polish and Russian identities that surfaced explicitly in the writing of *A Personal Record* and *Under Western Eyes*, the authorial function of this signature translation from the "K" of Konrad to its Anglicized "C" points to many other forms of cross-cultural antagonism that inflect Conrad's "English" with potentially creolizing forms of hybridity and difference. At the very beginning of his literary career, he submitted the manuscript of *Almayer's Folly* for publication under the pseudonym Kamudi, the Malay word for "rudder."[56] Had Conrad adopted Kamudi as his pen name, it would have drawn all the more attention to the family romance of reading Malay culture and history in his fiction. His authorial identity would have appeared much closer, too, to the sorts of pseudonyms adopted by the authors of the *lingua franca* Malay that Pramoedya called "pre-Indonesian." Although displaced by the "neutral pseudonym" of "Joseph Conrad," the resonance of that discarded name, Kamudi, nonetheless emphasizes Conrad's career-long investment in attempting to rescue the romance of a shared, if also contested, Malay and English historical identity projected in the Malay trilogy that was not completed until near the very end of his career, with the publication of *The Rescue* in 1920.

"Jean Rhys" is an authorial pseudonym in many respects perfectly suited to the moment of transatlantic English modernism that gave it birth—1924, in the *transatlantic review* edited by Ford Madox Ford (who may perhaps have suggested the pseudonym). There is something oddly marked about the otherwise unremarkable English name. The ambiguity, for example, in the possibly French or English accenting of the first name is linked to an ambiguity in the possibly male or female gender of the pseudonym. (Rhys may have adopted her husband's first name, Jean.) In retrospect, this ambiguously gendered and culturally unmarked English pseudonym may also reveal a career-long contest over the Creole white associations embedded in her birth name, Ella Gwendoline Rees Williams.[57] When, in the opening section of *Smile Please*, Rhys recalls her discomfort with the name by which she was known as a child, she retrospectively disturbs the seemingly neutral cultural provenance of the name: "why was I singled out to be the only fair one, to be called Gwendolen, which means white in Welsh I was told?" (S, 14). Whether or not the pseudonym marked a symbolic economy of displaced racial, cultural, and linguistic identity from the beginning of Rhys's writing career, the change of names has certainly since come to serve as a critical point of reference for what Peter Hulme calls the "creole family romance" of her relation to her family's Caribbean background.[58] Not unlike the neutral pseudonym of Joseph Conrad, then, the pseudonym of Jean Rhys proves far from neutral. It invites attention to the way Rhys creates a narrative voice and consciousness from the displaced effects of reading the printed page—such as when Anna's narrative perspective, in *Voyage in the Dark*, emerges from a reading of the "endless procession of words" (V, 9) in Zola's *Nana;* or, more famously, when Antoinette from *Wide Sargasso Sea* finds herself retracing the steps of Bertha Mason as she walks along "the passages" of the "cardboard house" of Charlotte Brontë's *Jane Eyre* (WSS, 107). As with the effects produced by such moments, the function of Jean Rhys's authorial name marks a complex relation between the literary and linguistic formations of English and Creole modernism. If their relation to Indonesian modernism may not be as obvious, Rhys herself draws attention to a possible family entanglement between the writing of *Wide Sargasso Sea* and the period of political crisis in Indonesia from 1957 to 1965. In 1957, Rhys's daughter, Maryvonne Moerman, who had moved to Indonesia with her husband and baby daughter in 1948, was forced to return to Europe because of the political instability throughout Indonesia that prompted the suspension of parliamentary democracy.[59] In a letter to her daughter in July 1957, as she made her way back to Europe from Indonesia, Rhys wrote: "It is strange that your ship is called Rees Williams or nearly, for it was my name. A good omen—it must be so!"[60] The authorial function of Rhys's name is far more invested, of course, in the Creole family romance of her relation to the Caribbean childhood of her past than in her family's relation to the crisis of postcolonial Indonesia. But the overlap between her daughter's family having to leave Indonesia and her literary attempt to recapture a West Indian past she herself had left behind calls attention to the general historical conjuncture linking the writing of her last major novel with the politics of decolonization in the Caribbean and in Indonesia.

Although Pramoedya's books appeared under his full name, Pramoedya Ananta Toer, and although he consistently used the initials P.A.T. as signature for prefaces or notes, I use the single name Pramoedya throughout this study (as I do Conrad and Rhys) because this, rather than the last name Toer, would more normally be used as the surname, according to the Indonesian custom of using only one name.[61] One of his early stories, "Blora," creates the authority and authorship of its autobiographical first-person narrative voice by hailing the author's name from within the Dutch prison (*Bukitduri*) from which Pramoedya's first published work emerged: "The jailer returned from the camp office and yelled, 'Pram!' I yelled back in response. And he went on, 'You're being released.'"[62] This dialogue gives a particular shape to the authorial identity of the writer, all at once autobiographical and fictional, immediate and distanced, since the guard's proclamation of release turns out to be a fantasy, a "daydream" of release and freedom that governs the story's disturbing account of a murderous homecoming encounter with the narrator's family. The intimate estrangement of addressing himself as "Pram" helps emphasize the dissonance between this disturbing early instance of Pramoedya's revolutionary family romance and the autobiographical experience of imprisonment. In the much later prison notes from Buru, Pramoedya reflects on the possible Javanese significance his father may have attached to his personal name, and on the peculiarities of the last, family name Toer. In a recollection that signals the revolutionary value Pramoedya places in the Indonesian language over against the ossified forms of Javanese tradition, he recalls, first, how non-Javanese the name Toer sounded: "It is an odd name—not at all 'Javanese'—and in the 1950s, when the name first began to become known nationally through my published works, it stirred numerous questions about its origins, especially among those who knew that its bearer was ethnic Javanese" (*MS*, 104) ("*Pada tahun 1950 waktu nama ini muncul di depan umum melalui tulisan-tulisanku, orang merasai kejanggalannya. Apalagi setelah mengetahui itu nama keluarga orang Jawa*" [*NS* II, 3]). Later, he recalls how his father broke from the hierarchies of Javanese tradition by striking off the honorific *Mas*—"An opponent of feudalism, with a firm break he cast off the 'Mas' in front of his personal name, leaving: Toer" ("*Sebagai pembenci feodalisme, dengan putusan yang kukuh ia buang Mas pada nama pribadinya, tinggal: Toer*" [*NS* II, 5]). As I discuss at greater length in chapter 7, this meditation on what was, for Javanese, "odd," discordant, or improper (*kejanggalannya*) about the name reveals a key feature of that revolutionary family romance by which Pramoedya enacts an intimate estrangement of Javanese traditions.

In the "variables" of each author's name, and from the scenes of early childhood reading rehearsed above, we can already see the outlines of what I call, loosely following Freud, a "family romance" of modernist literary affiliation: Conrad's colonial English family romance (especially as this shapes Lingard's piratical family romance in the Malay trilogy); Rhys's Creole family romance (most obvious in *Wide Sargasso Sea*); and Pramoedya's revolutionary Indonesian family romance. These family romances of reading are themselves fundamentally estranging in ways that embed within each writer's work alien genealogies of modernism: Conrad's affiliation with an English linguistic and literary tradition that is open to the Malay subject of his fiction and inscribed in the European ideals of his Polish childhood memories; Rhys's relation to a Creole cultural and linguistic environment hostile to English affiliations; and Pramoedya's genealogy of an Indonesian language and literature suspicious of the traditional hierarchies of both Javanese and Dutch.[63]

Implicit in these childhood scenes of reading are genealogies of modernism that emerge from the practical and theoretical problems posed by the passage of literature. For Conrad, an affiliation with English modernism emerges from a successful negotiation over the passage of literature—idealized as his father's Polish translation of a passage of English literature—where English itself constitutes a space of cosmopolitan recognition over against a narrower national or racial designation. The passage of literature for English modernism in this sense converts material differences ("dialects") into literary dialogue legible to any English reader. If the passage of literature constitutes for English modernism the acquisition of cultural capital, for Creole modernism the passage of literature stages an unresolved contest over cultural capital. Creole modernism threatens the legibility of English print, for Rhys, by reopening the differences—and disputes—embedded in the "shades of dialect" that haunt all language. The passage of literature for

Indonesian modernism constitutes elements of both the transparency in translation of English modernism and the opacity of contest and dispute of Creole modernism. As suggested by the detail of the piece of spoken and written advice to be "a free, *all-round*" person (*orang bebas, dan* all-round), the passage of literature for Indonesian modernism constitutes a space of reading between linguistic systems.

The genealogies of reading modernism implicit in each of these autobiographical fragments, however, also constitute genealogies of reading the passage between English, Creole, and Indonesian modernisms. The word *all-round*, for example, belongs to the coordinates of all three linguistic-literary formations of modernism. If the *O.E.D.*'s definition of "an all-round man" hardly intimates the history of decolonization Pramoedya associates with the word, what Pramoedya registers invites a reconsideration of the *O.E.D.* definition, a rereading that might recall the resonance of the word in the work, for example, of C. L. R. James, whose autobiography, *Beyond a Boundary* (1963), gives the colonial accenting of the *O.E.D.*'s definition its potential anti-colonial resonance in his book's opening anecdote of an old friend of his father's, "an intercolonial cricketer and a great all-round sportsman."[64]

In terms of the parallel formations of the *O.E.D.* and the historical emergence of *bahasa Indonesia,* both Joseph Conrad and Jean Rhys clearly have more to do with the colonial linguistic claims of the former than the anti-colonial linguistic claims of the latter. If the *O.E.D.* represents the consolidation of English as a hegemonic colonial language, it mirrors what Conrad is able to do with English modernism, on the one hand, making "English" accessible to readers from a range of different linguistic backgrounds. At the same time, it opens this "English" to the sort of disruptive "Creole" rereadings that preoccupy Rhys in a literary and linguistic sense. Both kinds of modernism, indeed, might be seen at work in the *O.E.D.*'s characteristic practice of anchoring its definitions of words in select passages of text—not only privileged passages of canonical texts but also the prose of daily newspapers. In ways that find their counterpart in the avant-garde poetics of high modernists such as Eliot, Pound, and Joyce, the *O.E.D.* anchors its authoritative monument to the English language in a form of literary-linguistic modernism that simultaneously detaches texts from their literary, historical, and cultural context and attaches to those fragments of text a newly privileged philological value. Each passage of literature held up as an authority for proper English usage not only consolidates a hegemonic English meaning but invites, too, a contest over the possible priority of its Creole sense. As we have already noted, the philological assumptions of the passage from Lowell cited by the *O.E.D.* in its definition of a *lingua franca* unearth a Creole modernist rereading of what the literary passage does. That unsettling of the difference between spoken and written language produces more than a modernist deconstruction of the text; it unearths, too, a repressed history of contest over lineages of slavery and racial representation, over the "lineage" and "alienage" of multiple alien genealogies of modernism and modernity.

The *O.E.D.*'s use of passages of text as cultural capital might appear to stand in striking contrast to the modernizing function of *bahasa Indonesia* as a vehicle of communication, the model vehicle for "imagining community" in Benedict Anderson's sense. *Bahasa Indonesia*, after all, is a new language whose primary function would appear to be to break from forms of cultural and political capital regulated according to colonial rule. In fact, however, in both cases, there is a double process of valuation and devaluation, conservation and modernization, related to what Bakhtin describes as the centripetal and centrifugal forces always operating in languages. The extreme contrasts suggest an inner, dialectical affinity. For Indonesian modernism, as for English modernism, the modernizing moment of linguistic and literary innovation takes place in the form of print literature. The moment of exchange, when print culture is opened up to readers of various ethnic and cultural backgrounds, forms the basis for the later claims for *bahasa Indonesia* as the vehicle for imagining nationalism. In the process these literary texts (and the trace of those that have been lost) acquire an archival cultural and political value. The passage of literary text, for Indonesian literary modernism, may not be privileged in quite the same way that it is with the *O.E.D.*; but the modernizing, political reconfiguration of colonial hierarchies does privilege a literary exchange in print (the moment of "pre-Indonesian literature"). The linguistic and literary evidence it provides—even in the place of its *absence* as a text that has been erased from the archive—serves a corresponding function, investing literary texts with a particular cultural and political charge. This moment of literary exchange, coinciding historically with the publication of the *O.E.D.* and the emergence of *bahasa Indonesia*, defines the period during which English, Creole, and Indonesian modernisms take shape as a matrix of overlapping, interacting formations of transnational literary modernism. It is this moment of literary exchange, archived in the passage of literature between English, Creole, and Indonesian modernisms, that I examine in the following study.

PART I

English Modernism

2

OPERA, MODERNISM, AND MODERNITY
Reading Counterpoint in Joseph Conrad's Malay Trilogy and Pramoedya's Buru Tetralogy

In the following chapter I offer a comparative reading of the novel sequence with which Joseph Conrad began his literary career and the novel sequence that established Pramoedya Ananta Toer's international reputation as Indonesia's most important twentieth-century novelist. Conrad's Malay or Lingard trilogy—*Almayer's Folly* (1895), *An Outcast of the Islands* (1896), and *The Rescue* (1920)—not only inaugurated but also haunted Conrad's literary career, since he was unable to complete the final novel until 1919.[1] Pramoedya's Buru tetralogy—*Bumi Manusia* (*This Earth of Mankind*) (1980), *Anak Semua Bangsa* (*Child of All Nations*) (1980), *Jejak Langkah* (*Footsteps*) (1985), and *Rumah Kaca* (*House of Glass*) (1988)—was composed in the infamous Buru Island prison camps during the 1970s and published (but quickly banned) following his release in 1979. Each of these novel sequences establishes the significance of Conrad and Pramoedya, respectively, for the linguistic-literary formations of English and Indonesian modernism. In order to explore this, I examine the role of opera, comparing the problem of cultural and aesthetic judgment that operatic form foregrounds in each novel sequence.

Readers have often been struck by the operatic qualities of Conrad's early Malay tales, and Conrad's own comments in letters suggest that he thought of the Malay (or "Lingard") trilogy of his first projected novel sequence in terms of a specifically operatic aesthetic.[2] While the operatic effects in these Malay novels would seem to confirm the exoticist distortion that critics have found in their East Indies settings, I argue here that this operatic aesthetic helps identify the historical and cultural specificity of Conrad's Malay Archipelago and the importance of this for Conrad's formative relation to English modernism. This argument follows, in part, a recent trend in reading Conrad historically, and with careful attention to the way his fiction registers the historical facts of colonial and anti-colonial contest.³ The significance of opera in Conrad's Malay fiction, however, is by no means only a matter of historical representation. The question of aesthetic form remains a fundamental theoretical problem for literary and cultural studies. To situate Conrad's interest in opera historically, and especially as it relates to his imaginative investment in Malay cultural formations, also entails examining the theoretical challenge Conrad's work presents for literary criticism today and to come: in particular, the imperative to find a viable model for studying literature within a global and comparative historical-cultural perspective.⁴

One such model is the "contrapuntal reading" of texts proposed by Edward Said in *Culture and Imperialism:* "As we look back at the cultural archive, we begin to reread it not univocally but *contrapuntally*, with a simultaneous awareness both of the metropolitan history that is narrated and of those other histories against which (and together with which) the dominating discourse acts."⁵ Conrad's Malay novels might usefully be read in "contrapuntal" relation to Pramoedya's "Buru" quartet of novels, composed in prison exile on Buru Island during the 1970s and published—but immediately banned in Indonesia itself—in the 1980s.⁶ This comparison offers a paradigmatic instance of Said's call for "contrapuntal analysis" not only because of the contrast between the two authors' experiences—Conrad's experience of colonialism, Pramoedya's experience of decolonization—but also because these novel sequences each attempt to narrate overlapping histories. The historical settings for both novel sequences coincide with the period of high Dutch colonialism between the 1870s and the 1920s—Conrad's trilogy moving backward historically from the late 1880s to the 1860s, Pramoedya's tetralogy moving forward historically from the 1890s to the 1910s.

Opera provides an important cultural point of comparative reference for this historical period primarily because it presents a problem of aesthetic taste that informs the narrative scope of each of these novel sequences. In what follows I examine two passages from each novel sequence that concern European grand opera, and specifically Verdi. Edward Said's model of "contrapuntal analysis" is fitting both because of the musical metaphor of counterpoint and because Said himself applies it to an analysis of the cultural work of imperialism in Verdi opera. If Said's "contrapuntal analysis" underscores the problem of European cultural capital that is both put on display and contested within the colonial contexts elaborated by Conrad and Pramoedya, there is an important sense in which the very premise of "contrapuntal analysis" is itself a part of the problem of cultural taste these novels elaborate. Fernando Coronil, comparing Said's form of contrapuntal reading with the earlier model of Fernando Ortiz's *Cuban Counterpoint,* points out that "while Said derived his notion of counterpoint from Western classical music, Ortiz was inspired by Cuban musical and liturgical popular traditions." Coronil goes on to suggest: "Perhaps a contrapuntal reading of Said and Ortiz points to a counterpoint between classic and popular music, and beyond that, to one between the cultures of Europe, Africa, and America."[7]

Coronil's call for a contrapuntal reading of Said and Ortiz has a particular relevance for the problem of opera in the Malay context of Conrad's and Pramoedya's novel sequences. An emergent popular form of Malay opera has played an important role in defining the period during the turn of the century that is the overlapping historical moment for both novel sequences. This historical period, coinciding with Conrad's writing career, is often "recalled nostalgically" (as John Pemberton puts it) "through the haunting compound linguistic expression *tempo* (Dutch) *doeloe* (Malay), 'the old days,' 'former times.'"[8] *Tempo doeloe* is associated with a specific kind of operatic performance variously called "Komedi Bangsawan," "Komedi Stamboul," or "East Indies opera."[9] Rob Nieuwenhuys's anthology of photographs, significantly entitled *Tempo Doeloe*, provides photographic documentation of this specific kind of operatic performance. One photo, of an "amateur krontjong band from Semarang, 1910" (*Een amateur-krontjongorkest te Semarang*)[10] illustrates the cultural mix of instruments used to play the popular "krontjong" music that often accompanied this form of opera. The hybrid opera form is evoked in another photo of "a Stamboul women's orchestra," which illustrates the multiracial (and often mixed-gender) cast of traveling opera groups performing plots drawn from Arab, European, and Chinese stories.[11] A third photo (from 1912) shows a group of young Indo men and women *pretending* to be an orchestra group—a spatula, tennis racket, and rattan stick masquerade here as musical instruments. It is difficult to read with what sort of humor of ironic cultural, racial, class, or gender identification the photographic record is framed. One thing that makes for the puzzle is the object around which the photo image is composed—the hand organ—which not only mimics whatever form of musical performance the group is imitating but also mirrors the mechanical means of photographic reproduction that records the composition.[12]

This popular form of operatic theater presents a number of exemplary problems for reading culture during this period. One question we need to consider—in counterpoint to the examples of classical European operatic form—is why the popular form of East Indies opera depicted in these photographs is mostly absent from the historical vision of Conrad's Malay trilogy and Pramoedya's Buru tetralogy. This question, to which we will return at the end of the chapter, depends on a question of reading that is closely related to the form of opera and the riddle of its representation in photographs (and lack of representation in the novels). In the foreword to an anthology of stories from the turn of the century, under the title *Tempo Doeloe,* Pramoedya turns to the form of "Komedi Stamboul" to address the question of who was reading the texts first published during the turn of the century and reprinted by Pramoedya in 1981, after his release from Buru. Pointing to links between the form of this popular traveling opera and the texts he anthologizes as "pre-Indonesian" literature, some of which were used as plots for the operatic performances, Pramoedya also emphasizes that the question of readership remains an open historical question: "What is published here has not yet for certain been read, but what is read here has already for certain been published" ("*Ada penerbitan memang belum tentu ada pembaca, tetapi ada pembaca sudah tentu ada penerbitan*").[13] Linking this emergent popular opera form with an emergent, "pre-Indonesian" form of literature, Pramoedya suggests that both present the riddle of a modern Indonesian consciousness in formation.

To emphasize the fact that part of our concern here is the theoretical and critical model of a "contrapuntal reading" both in Said's sense and in the sense Coronil finds in Fernando Ortiz, we should note that Pramoedya's novel calls attention to a further contrapuntal, comparative perspective to add to the classical model of Said's European counterpoint and the popular model of Ortiz's Cuban counterpoint. The counterpoint of Indonesian, and more specifically Javanese gamelan music in the *wayang* opera tradition, has an important place in Pramoedya's work as a whole. This highly stratified type of counterpoint used in gamelan music belongs to a form of opera with a prestige and cultural distinction within Indonesian traditions much higher than that of either the popular form of East Indies opera or the classical European form of grand opera. Claude Debussy, writing in 1913 about the charm of gamelan music that he first heard at the 1889 Exposition Universelle in Paris, commented: "Javanese music is based on a type of counterpoint by comparison with which that of Palestrina is child's play. And if we listen without European prejudice to the charm of their percussion, we must confess that our percussion is like primitive noises at a country fair."[14]

Measuring each writer's work against the historical specificity of *tempo doeloe,* I follow a "contrapuntal reading" of the way Conrad's Malay trilogy and Pramoedya's Buru tetralogy grasp the historical period designated by that phrase. This "contrapuntal reading," however, must also itself negotiate a problem of reading counterpoint within a global and historical frame of reference. In attempting to do this, I want to suggest a threefold elaboration of Said's "contrapuntal analysis" already premised on the overlapping formations of English, Creole, and Indonesian modernism: counterpoint in the European musical tradition as Said presents it; counterpoint in the model of Ortiz's "Cuban counterpoint"; and counterpoint in the Javanese (and more generally Indonesian) musical sense.

The Cultural Dialectic of Abysmal Taste in Opera

One memorable moment from almost exactly midway through Conrad's first novel, *Almayer's Folly* (1895), depicts the playing of a Verdi opera in the novel's East Indies setting:

> Lakamba listened with closed eyes and a delighted smile; Babalatchi turned, at times dozing off and swaying over, then catching himself up in a great fright with a few quick turns of the handle. Nature slept in an exhausted repose after the fierce turmoil, while under the unsteady hand of the statesman of Sambir the Trovatore fitfully wept, wailed, and bade good-bye to his Leonore again and again in a mournful round of tearful and endless iteration. (*AF*, 88–89)

The hand-organ rendition of Manrico's farewell aria from Verdi's *Il Trovatore* locks into place a set of incongruous contrasts on which the irony of the passage depends—recapitulating, in turn, the ironic narrative perspective of the whole novel's grasp of the deluded European dreams of the Indies-born title character (whose death by poisoning has just been planned by Lakamba and Babalatchi). In some ways, this is merely a humorous digression from the main unfolding of plot—light relief from the climax to come in the next chapter, when the reader, along with Almayer, will momentarily be confronted with the death of Dain Maroola, a Balinese prince to whom Almayer is trading gunpowder, and (as Almayer has yet to learn and will refuse to acknowledge) the lover of his daughter, Nina.

But the humor of the passage is not easy to decode. Deploying the stereotypes of lazy chief and wily schemer—Lakamba and Babalatchi, respectively—the passage replicates what Frantz Fanon called the "perverted logic" of colonialism: "not satisfied merely with…emptying the native's brain of all form and content…, it turns to the past of the oppressed people, and distorts, disfigures, and destroys it" ("*Par une sorte de perversion de la logique, il s'oriente vers le passé du people opprimé, le distord, le défigure, l'anéantit*").[15] Conrad, however, ironically inverts the set of implied oppositions between native barbarism and European civilization with which the whole passage plays. In order to decode the racist "native" stereotypes, a reader must measure the incongruity of Lakamba's and Babalatchi's appreciation of opera against his or her own. And so the troubling racism is troubled in turn by the work of irony, in a sort of vicious circle of racist stereotyping and its critique. The vicious circle provoked by this question of opera appreciation frames a set of assumptions of race, civilization, and modernity whose very unsettling ensures a foundational instability in the inauguration of an implied Conradian readership. This abysmal taste in opera generates the ironies of Conrad's first novel and organizes, too, the entire corpus of his work and the way it continues to be received critically today. I call this "abysmal taste" not only because it concerns questionable aesthetic judgments but also because it involves a narrative mirroring effect of *mise-en-abyme*, a problem of modernist narrative and critical reading.[16]

A contrasting question of opera emerges in *Footsteps* (*Jejak Langkah* [1985]), the third volume of Pramoedya's quartet of novels about the period of Indonesian anti-colonial nationalism during the turn of the century. In the midst of this increasingly historical-narrative account of mass political organizing throughout the Dutch-controlled East Indies, Minke, the narrator of the first three books of the quartet (a figure based on the historical journalist and political activist Tirto Adi Suryo), pauses to account for "something that I will always remember" (*F*, 200) ("*peristiwa yang cukup meninggalkan kesan*" [*J*, 194]). What follows is a description of his listening to a recording of Verdi's *Rigoletto:*

> Sandiman was just putting on a recording of Verdi's opera *Rigoletto*. I'd started the practice of setting aside three hours a week to listen to European music, copying what had been the practice of Mama and her children.
>
> Perhaps because this had been our practice in Surabaya, Verdi always took me back to old memories, to Mama and her business, to Annelies and to all the happiness that had ended with tragedy.
>
> It was true that I didn't yet appreciate European music as fully as I did gamelan. European music stimulated in me many different thoughts. Gamelan music instead enveloped me in beauty, in a harmony of feeling that was without form, in an atmosphere that rocked my emotions to an eternal sleep. (*F*, 200–201)
>
> *Sandiman sedang memutar phonograf, memainkan lagu-lagu dari opera* Rigoletto Verdi. *Sejak tiga bulan yang lalu kusediakan waktu membiasakan diri mendengarkan musik Eropa, meniru kebiasaan Mama dan anaknya.*
>
> *Entah karena kebiasaan di Surabaya dulu, Verdi selalu membawa aku kembali pada kenangan lama, pada Mama, pada anaknya, pada perusahaannya, pada semua kesenangan yang diakhiri dengan tragedi.*
>
> *Memang belum sepenuhnya dapat merasakan musik Eropa sebagaimana halnya dengan gamelan. Namun musik membawa aku pada macam-macam kenangan dan pikiran. Gamelan membawa aku pada keindahan, ketenangan perasaan yang menyangkal wujud, ke suasana yang membawa pikiran terayun dalam tidur abadi.* (J, 194)

As with Conrad's *Almayer's Folly*, Verdi presents a problem of opera appreciation, although here it is internalized in the narrator's judgment of his own non-European appreciation of European opera. Complicating this problem and making it all the more abysmal in the formal narrative sense in which the Conrad passage implicates its readership, is the further comparison between European and Javanese gamelan music.

Both passages serve as miniature narrative cues for the larger unfolding of the plots within which they appear. Minke's split musical sensibility recalls the conflict of racial and cultural identification between his native Javanese and his educated European identity, recapitulating one of the main thematic elements of his sentimental education in the first two novels, *This Earth of Mankind* and *Child of All Nations*. Verdi serves as a metonym for those lost attachments of youth, recalling the tragic loss of his first wife, the "creole beauty" (*TE*, 205) ("*kreol kecantikan*" [*BM*, 200]) Annelies and—as if invoked by the very playing of European opera—bringing back into the narrative that mixed racial cast of characters from the first novel that constitutes what might be called Minke's Creole family romance.[17] Verdi opera thus signals a riddle of European cultural capital embedded in the narrative form of the tetralogy. Where one expects a critique of colonial nostalgia, as the narrative approaches the historic founding of Boedi Oetomo in 1908 (on "what is now celebrated annually in Indonesia as the Day of National Awakening"[18]), the narrative seems to evoke the colonial nostalgia of *tempo doeloe* as the reader's own nostalgic attachment to Minke's narrative voice. This attachment is strengthened all the more with the abrupt dislocation of narrative voice that occurs in the transition from the third to the fourth volume, *House of Glass*, when Minke's narrative voice is replaced by that of the native Menadonese police commissioner charged with containing and ultimately eliminating him as a political threat to the colonial regime. Minke's abysmal taste in opera, a *mise-en-abyme* of narrative form, marks the disjuncture between narrative and history on which the entire tetralogy is premised. Ostensibly tracing the "awakening" of Indonesian nationalism during the turn of the century, the narrative inquest into the erasure of Tirto Adi Suryo from the historical record provides a genealogy of official amnesia about twentieth-century Indonesia, retracing the lineaments of the postcolonial state around the policing apparatus of colonial governance and its systematic subversion of early anti-colonial nationalist organizations.

Verdi opera provides a corresponding *mise-en-abyme* of narrative form for Conrad's Malay or Lingard trilogy. Set in the remote Borneo region of Conrad's fictional Sambir—that "model state" (*AF*, 34) whose independence from European interests Lakamba and Babalatchi seek to maintain through nominal dependence on

Dutch colonial rule—*Almayer's Folly* plots the premise for the trilogy on a retrospective grasp of the contemporary politics of archipelago-wide anti-colonial nationalism.[19] The full significance of this for the historical scope of the trilogy remains contingent on the ironic force of racial stereotyping. Already split between the appreciative repose of Lakamba and the less-than-appreciative position of Babalatchi, the "native" stereotype is itself complicated by what Cedric Watts identifies as the "covert plot" of *Almayer's Folly*—the betrayal of Dain Maroola to the Dutch authorities by Lingard's rival, the Arab trader Abdulla.

Although Watts argues that the novel's "ironic complex of racial, national and sexual revenge" transcends racial stereotypes, Babalatchi's role as archschemer suggests, on the contrary, that racial stereotype is the very motor force of Conrad's "covert plotting."[20] As the most distorted of racialized figures,[21] Babalatchi's voyeuristic manipulation of the Nina-Dain love affair taints romance with the insinuation of perversity in interracial desire. *An Outcast of the Islands* adds to his one-eyed disfigurement the completely blind Omar el-Badavi who, with his daughter Aïssa and Babalatchi, constitute a sinister counter-family to the other mixed-racial families of the first two novels: Willems's respectably creolized family in Macassar (undermined by the Aïssa-Willems affair, again manipulated by Babalatchi), and the somewhat less respectably mixed-racial Almayer family at Sambir. By contrast to Minke's nostalgic association of Verdi with a Creole family romance, any such association here must be viewed—as Verdi is heard—through the distorted perspective of Babalatchi. To the extent that the romance plot of *Il Trovatore* mirrors the romance plot of the Nina–Dain affair, it only serves to reinforce the distortion of racial stereotype at the heart of each story of "racial, national and sexual revenge." Far from providing some final interpretive key, the allusion produces a permanent ellipsis of relation between narration and plot, forever deferring comparison of the story of *Il Trovatore* to the plot of *Almayer's Folly* and the novel sequence it inaugurates.

Both passages confirm the argument Said develops in his own reading of another Verdi opera, *Aida*, in *Culture and Imperialism*. As "an imperial spectacle designed to alienate and impress an almost exclusively European audience,"[22] *Aida* exemplifies the riddle of European cultural capital that Conrad and Pramoedya each take as the point of reference for their non-European characters' appreciation of European opera.[23] In all three cases, dependence on European cultural capital stands in varying degrees of ironic contrast to aspirations of independence from European political power. By contrast to Said's extended reading of *Aida*, however, neither Conrad nor Pramoedya offers a "full contrapuntal appreciation" of the operas—*Il Trovatore* and *Rigoletto*, respectively—to which they allude. In each case, the problem of operatic appreciation is refracted through the medium of mechanical reproduction—the hand-organ rendition in *Almayer's Folly* and the phonograph recording in *Footsteps*.

Recalling Walter Benjamin's famous thesis—"that which withers in the age of mechanical reproduction is the aura of the work of art" (*"was im Zeitalter der technischen Reproduzierbarkeit des Kunstwerks verkümmert, das ist seine Aura"*)[24]—each citation invokes an operatic aesthetic in the very moment of its distortion through the agency of mechanical mass reproduction. Far from realizing their revolutionary potential, however, in each case the instrument of mechanical reproduction becomes a fetishized luxury item, emphasizing the negative moment in Benjamin's cultural dialectic and anticipating Adorno's more pessimistic application of Benjamin's argument to the regressive "fetish character" (*Fetischcharakter*) of music appreciation.[25] It is indeed a fetishized pleasure Lakamba takes in having Babalatchi bring out the "box of music the white captain gave me" (*AF*, 88). This comic fetish of European modernity emblematizes the ironic situation of Lingard's betrayal by Lakamba—the "covert plot" more fully explored in *An Outcast of the Islands*. The fact that it was once Lingard's hand organ makes it an emblem, too, of what in *The Rescue* will be revealed as Lingard's own sentimental attachment to opera. The phonograph plays an analogous function in Pramoedya's tetralogy. An early instance of Minke's fascination for all things modern, the phonograph is singled out, on his first visit to the Mellema house in *This Earth of Mankind*, as a luxury item of furniture whose beauty is associated with the stunning "creole beauty" of Annelies.[26] This combination of erotic, racial, and commodity fetishism will again be attached to the image of the phonograph when, in the final volume, Pangemanann describes the scene of his early seduction into the political work of subversive police activities against Minke: by means of the prostitute Rientje de Roo and to the accompaniment of Verdi's *La Traviata* played on an expensive new phonograph.[27]

Both opera citations illustrate the fetishism Adorno decried in the practice of making musical arrangements that "snatch[] the reified bits and pieces out of their context and set[s] them up as a potpourri...destroy[ing] the multilevel unity of the whole work and bring[ing] forward only isolated popular passages."[28] Conrad's choice of "what used to be the best-known of all *Trovatore* melodies in the days of the barrel organ and the street piano"[29] compounds racial stereotyping with the insinuation of a class distinction between the bad taste pedaled by street musicians and the fuller appreciation of the opera-goer who knows its place within the context of the work as a whole. Although it is Verdi's *Rigoletto* that is cited in Pramoedya's novel, what Minke recalls hearing a few lines later is, through some phonographic distortion of memory, "The Last Rose of Summer," a popular aria from Flotow's *Martha*.

The very diminishment of opera enacted by the work of mechanical reproduction calls attention to a paradoxical and exemplary estrangement of the literary text at the very heart of the operatic aesthetic. The barrel-organ theme from *Il Trovatore* may once have evoked the text of the song, but now the Trovatore's "mournful round of tearful and endless iteration" repeats itself wordlessly. And although Minke remembers the title of an aria, the song itself, based on an Irish folk melody adapted by Thomas Moore, confirms the estrangement that opera typically effects in literary form.[30]

Hegel's *Aesthetics* grasps this estrangement of the literary in the formal question of priority in the relation between music and text. By contrast to either "operetta" (*Operette*) or "vaudeville" (*Vaudeville*), in "real opera" (*in der eigentliche* Oper) the music transcends the words.[31] This operatic moment of musical transcendence and subordination of words leaves its mark both on the Hegelian dialectic and on the grand narrative assumptions of nineteenth-century Europe. In the *Phenomenology of Spirit*, that touchstone for the grand narrative tradition, the figure of the "Minstrel" (*Sänger*) appears in the penultimate chapter before "Absolute Knowing" ("*Das absolute Wissen*") as "the organ that vanishes in its content" ("*das in seinem Inhalte verschwindende Organ*") to sing the "universal song" ("*allgemeiner Gesang*") or epic of the dialectic of individual, national, and universal unfolding of self-consciousness into absolute knowledge.[32] Grasping opera as the epitome of just such European grand narrative claims, Conrad and Pramoedya use their operatic examples to foreground a crisis of literary consciousness, and one that ruptures the very form of developmental narrative with which their projected novel sequences engage.

Conrad's Malay Trilogy

The crisis of European literary consciousness foregrounded in Conrad's Verdi passage is premised, like much in Conrad, on the example of Flaubert.[33] It recalls two scenes from *Madame Bovary*—Emma Bovary's enraptured identification with the soprano (in contrast to her husband's incomprehension) at a performance of Donizetti's *Lucia di Lammermoor;* and an earlier description of Emma's enchantment with the tunes of an organ grinder in the street. In the opening to *A Personal Record*, Conrad associates the first of these scenes with the scene of his own writing of *Almayer's Folly* "in the neighbourhood of the [Rouen] Opera House" in view of "the very" café "where the worthy Bovary and his wife...had some refreshment after the memorable performance of an opera which was the tragic story of Lucia di Lammermoor in a setting of light music" (*PR*, 5). The famous scene of abysmal operatic taste in *Madame Bovary* is itself informed by the earlier description of a vulgar street organ grinder playing "tunes that were heard elsewhere—tunes played in the theatre, sung in drawing-rooms, danced to at night beneath lighted chandeliers—echoes reaching Emma from the great world outside" ("*des airs que l'on jouait ailleurs, sur les théatres, que l'on chantait dans les salons, que l'on dansait le soir sous des lustres éclairs, échos du monde qui arrivaient jusqu'à Emma*").[34] Splicing together these two moments to grasp the double displacement of a European romantic tradition—operatic adaptation of literary works; barrel-organ arrangements of operatic aria—Conrad displaces, in turn, that literary consciousness (Emma Bovary's) Flaubert dissects as the novel's pathological point of literary identification.

With the playing of Verdi on a barrel organ in Borneo, Conrad pushes the "bovarysme" of his own novel to an extreme, widening the gap Flaubert rigorously details between romantic illusion and the banalities of middle-class consumer culture. Conrad's corresponding dissection of European literary sensibilities, however, stakes its claim to recognition by an *English*-reading public on a projected long-term narrative investment in *Malay* culture. The linguistic register may be more fundamental than the cultural, historical, or ethnological resonance of these two designations for assessing Conrad's place in the formation of the field of English literary modernism. As Michael North has discussed, one thing that makes Conrad so paradigmatic for the "dialect of modernism"— for modernist experimentations with linguistic and racial difference—is the fact that his English was rooted in the *lingua franca* of shipboard English.[35] The affinities between Malay and English each as a *lingua franca* are foregrounded in significant moments, such as the very opening of the novel—"Kaspar! Makan!"—and in Conrad's proposed pseudonym, Kamudi (the Malay word for "rudder"). As the spoken language of the characters, and as the linguistic disguise of pseudonymous authorship, Malay provides something of a foil for what Conrad was attempting to achieve using English as his literary medium: to reorient the coordinates of European literary traditions through the translingual, transnational, literary *lingua franca* of English. If *Almayer's Folly* implies a cosmopolitan readership for Conrad's projected first novel sequence, and by extension also for the literary career that trilogy launches—a readership familiar with Verdi opera, barrel-organ renditions, not to mention Flaubert—it also places that cosmopolitan perspective within a wider global context. The center of literary consciousness is located neither in an English literary tradition nor in a Malay literary tradition but, rather, in the gap between the two marked by the problem of an abysmal taste in opera.

This point is foregrounded in the last novel of the sequence, *The Rescue*. Edith Travers, one of the shipwrecked Europeans Lingard will rescue at the cost of the plans—and lives—of his Malay friends, compares her involvement in the political intrigues of Lingard's Wajo romance to the "unreal" and "artificial" feeling of "walking on a splendid stage in a scene from an opera, in a gorgeous show fit to make an audience hold its breath" (*R*, 300). Not only does Lingard share a knowledge of opera. It is the seemingly illiterate sailor who has a passion for opera, finding it "more real than anything in life," while the refined Edith Travers "never knew anything" of that kind of "feeling": "Would real people go singing through their life anywhere except in a fairy tale?" (*R*, 301). Whereas *Almayer's Folly* measures the ironic limits of cross-cultural perspective against the musical taste of the two Malay characters, Lakamba and Babalatchi, in *The Rescue* this perspectival limit is measured against the operatic taste of the two English characters, Edith Travers and Tom Lingard. At both ends of the trilogy, an abysmal taste in opera marks the limitation of an English investment in Malay culture.

In the middle novel, *An Outcast of the Islands*, the vanishing point of comparative English-Malay cultural-historical perspectives is grasped through the distorted perspective of Babalatchi's "frivolous desire to sing"—prompted, significantly, by the sight of the lovers Aïssa and Willems:

> It could hardly be called a song; it was more in the nature of a recitative without any rhythm, delivered rapidly but distinctly in a croaking and unsteady voice; and if Babalatchi considered it a song, then it was a song with a purpose and, perhaps for that reason, artistically defective. It had all the imperfections of unskilful improvisation and its subject was gruesome. (*OI*, 138)

Like the contrast between European music and gamelan in Pramoedya's novel, Babalatchi's song appears to introduce an alternative cultural category of artistic performance to that of European opera—perhaps some form of Malay *pantun*. The narrative, however, immediately denigrates that form, suggesting even more strongly what Fanon calls the colonial work of "devaluing pre-colonial history." Despite the "inartistic" privileging of words over music, the words themselves—along with any sense of a Malay literary context—remain closed to the text. Its "subject" is, however, briefly described: "It told a tale of shipwreck and of thirst, and of one brother killing another for the sake of a gourd of water. A repulsive story which might have had a purpose but possessed no moral whatever" (*OI*, 138). An ornamental coda to the rumors of how Babalatchi arrived in Sambir,[36] Babalatchi's song proves to be a grotesque miniature inversion of the plot of *The Rescue*—another story of shipwreck and brotherly betrayal, whose motif repeatedly punctuates the narrative of the second novel.

Babalatchi's song suggests a further twist to what Cedric Watts describes as the "covert plotting" that resiliently defies successive interpretations. Anticipating the link between Babalatchi and Lingard's failed rescue plot, made explicit half way through *An Outcast of the Islands,* the cryptic doubling of shipwreck plots signals an untold story: indeed, Conrad never will tell of their prior meeting, although Babalatchi's reminder precipitates Lingard's disturbed memories of "the past sweetness and strife of Carimata days" (*OI,* 223). This untold story emphasizes all the more the masculine romance of a piratical past that defines both Babalatchi's and Lingard's sense of the "good old days" (*OI,* 196). As Robert Hampson suggests, these two characters register a contrapuntal Malay-English grasp of piracy as a shared, contested sense of the "good old days" (itself set in counterpoint to the Dutch East Indies notion of *tempo doeloe*): "Lingard's evocation of 'the good old days'…chimes intriguingly with Babalatchi's nostalgia for the good old days of 'throat-cutting, kidnapping, slave-dealing, and fire-raising.'"[37]

This contrapuntal Malay-English grasp of piracy is historically grounded in Conrad's use of James Brooke's journals and their archival record of his celebrated campaign against piracy along the northwest coast of Borneo. Hampson has argued that the trilogy enacts a reversal of that archival perspective, retelling Brooke's destruction of pirate villages from the Malay point of view. Babalatchi's exploits with Omar el-Badavi following the Brooke campaign register both heroic and distinctly unheroic possibilities.[38] According to Hampson, for example, the Virgilian allusion to "that piratical and son-less Aeneas" (*OI,* 54) "vacillates between ironic discrepancy and genuine equivalence."[39] What enables this fundamental ambiguity of perspective, moreover, is a drastic foreshortening of epic scale—precisely the effect produced by the *mise-en-abyme* of Conrad's operatic aesthetic. As with the disfigured form of Babalatchi's song, or the operatic allusion to *Il Trovatore,* the scope of romance or epic is truncated, reducing grand narrative to fragments, turning the literary passage into what Lyotard called the "differend."

The general, generic sense of Lyotard's "differend" helps identify the problem of aesthetic judgment, or abysmal taste in opera, that generates the narrative form of Conrad's Malay trilogy. As Lyotard puts it, explaining his title "The Differend," "The title of this book suggests…that a universal rule of judgment between heterogeneous genres is lacking in general" (*"Le titre du livre suggère…qu'une règle universelle de jugement entre des genres hétérogènes fait défaut en general"*).[40] As already suggested by Babalatchi's barrel-organ rendition of Verdi, the narrative sequence of Conrad's trilogy, and its retrospective historical trajectory, turns on a *mise-en-abyme* of the philosophical ideal (Kantian or Hegelian) of a universal aesthetic judgment. The counterpointing of Lingard's English piratical ethos against Babalatchi's Malay piratical ethos in *An*

Outcast of the Islands confirms this *mise-en-abyme* of narrative not only around "heterogeneous genres" in general but also around what Lyotard, playing off of legal terminology, calls (in his subtitle) "phrases in dispute"—"As distinguished from a litigation, a differend [*différend*] would be a case of conflict, between (at least) two parties, that cannot be equitably resolved for lack of a rule of judgment applicable to both arguments" ("*À la différence d'un litige, un différend serait un cas de conflit entre deux parties [au moins] qui ne pourrait pas être tranché équitablement faute d'une règle du jugement applicable aux deux argumentations*").[41] So, the phrase "that piratical and son-less Aeneas" encodes the "different" of a shared and contested genealogy of English and Malay piracy; a retrospective grasp of disputes and conflicts over territorial and legal control over Malay waters that constitutes Conrad's extended Lingard family romance—and his grasp of Malay history generally—around an anti-epic vanishing point of comparative perspective.[42]

This may be seen in the distorting effects of racial stereotype, most particularly in the case of Babalatchi, who, as we have already seen, initiates the vicious circle of racist stereotyping and its critique that inaugurates an implied Conradian readership. In *Almayer's Folly* his background is specified as Sulu in origin, and in *An Outcast of the Islands* he is associated with the Islamic militancy of Omar. Even as Conrad manipulates these distinctly negative racial stereotypes, however, the narrative insists on a historical specificity that refuses fixation on any one racist stereotype. The description of his role in *Almayer's Folly* as "prime minister, harbour master, financial advisor, and general factotum" (*AF*, 38)—confirmed in *An Outcast* through Almayer's disparaging comments on his status as "shahbandar" (*OI*, 364)—situates Babalatchi's role as a quite specific functionary. Indeed, as G. J. Resink has pointed out, the *shahbandar* is a key figure of international law and diplomacy in Indonesian and Malay history, involved in regulating legal and political disputes over inter-island relations throughout the Malay Archipelago.[43]

This simultaneous indexing and disfigurement of historical fact is encoded in the name itself. Although suggestively Orientalist, evoking Ali Baba of the Arabian Nights, it is also based in historical fact—a bill of lading found in Conrad's possession shows goods shipped by "Babalatchie" on the west coast of Sulawesi.[44] There is also, moreover, a distinctly Chinese resonance to his name—"Baba" (the specific form of address for an elderly Chinese man) and "La-Tchi" suggest an ethnic Chinese, rather than (or perhaps in addition to) his purported Sulu origin.[45] Whether or not Conrad was aware of the possibility, the name marks a highly volatile repertoire of unresolvable racial identifications and antagonisms (Malay and Sulu, possibly also Bugis; Moslem and Chinese). This chain of racial stereotypes ensures a fundamental ambiguity of historical perspective whichever way one attempts to read the trilogy's plot—whether chronologically, toward the Indies-wide rebellion imagined in *Almayer's Folly*, or sequentially as a retrospective account of Lingard's role in the failed restoration of a Wajo Bugis kingdom in southern Celebes. In this sense the perversity of Babalatchi's racial stereotype—as "the statesman of Sambir" (*AF*, 89) condemned to crank out the music of Verdi, and maligned for his "artistically defective" (*OI*, 138) singing—epitomizes the fragmentary narrative logic at work in the trilogy's operatic aesthetic.[46]

Pramoedya's own reading of Conrad emphasizes the significance of this distorting aesthetic.[47] As he puts it, simply: "In Conrad's works there are historical facts which have not been recorded elsewhere."[48] Far from suggesting that the literary text is simply the repository of historical facts, this positions the literary work in counterpoint to the archival record. With his use of the Brooke journals, Conrad's fiction engages in a critical reading of the cultural archive, in Said's terms, "not univocally but *contrapuntally*." With the name of Babalatchi, Conrad's fiction also registers what is "not recorded" elsewhere. The operatic qualities in Conrad's Malay fiction are not merely exoticist distortions of history. In the very distortion of their effects, they constitute questions of political and cultural identity and identification that haunt the historical record.

Pramoedya's Buru Tetralogy

The corresponding function of operatic taste in Pramoedya's tetralogy reveals a shared problem of global and comparative perspective in each of these novel sequences, as well as in the musical metaphor of Said's model of "contrapuntal" comparative analysis. In all three, music foregrounds a crisis of literary form. The phonographic replaying and distortion of European operatic tradition in Pramoedya's tetralogy presents a crisis not only of European but also of Javanese literary consciousness. As a Dutch-educated, Javanese noble (*priyayi*), whose narrative is based on notes written in Dutch according to his European training, rearranged and rewritten according to later experience, Minke constitutes a self-evidently hybrid, split literary consciousness. His very name marks this as an internalized estrangement of European consciousness. As revealed in the first novel, the name comes from the half-articulated Dutch pronunciation of the English word *monkey*, a racist epithet directed at him by his Dutch high school teacher, immediately adopted by his grandfather on the assumption that it signaled a sign of respect, although Minke's own suspicions are confirmed in English classes. Thereafter, the name signals a paradigmatic "double consciousness" (to borrow W. E. B. Du Bois's celebrated formulation for the internalized experience of racial stereotype).[49]

This "double consciousness" is reflected in a doubly abysmal problem of taste. As a man of European taste, Minke's appreciation of opera reenacts the pathologies of opera appreciation and the distortions of literary tradition that constitute the European operatic aesthetic.[50] Perhaps more significantly, though, as a man of Javanese taste, loss of appreciation for Javanese opera threatens the very essence of the Javanese *priyayi* worldview. Gamelan music and the *wayang* shadow puppet performances it traditionally accompanies are defining features of cultural refinement for the Javanese *priyayi*, inseparable from the Javanese notion of taste, or *rasa*, in its full, traditional, and ineffable spiritual sense. Clifford Geertz has explained the significance of gamelan as an essential component of the *priyayi*—aristocratic Javanese—worldview. Shaped by all three of the "major foci" of *priyayi* belief—"etiquette, art, and mystical practice"—gamelan music is inseparable from that "common element in them all which ties them together and makes them but different modes of the same reality": "what the Javanese, borrowing a concept from India, call *rasa*."[51] Although, as Nancy Florida has pointed out, "there is no translating the polysemic *rasa*,"[52] Geertz explains that it "has two primary meanings: 'feeling' and 'meaning,'" covering—with the first—all of the traditional five senses and their figurative application beyond sense-perception; and—with the second—"As 'meaning,' *rasa* is applied to the words in a letter, in a poem, or even in speech, to indicate the...type of allusive suggestion that is so important in Javanese communication."[53]

By the end of *Footsteps*, however, Minke has come to reject that world in his critique of the forms of superstitious thinking he calls "Javanism" (*F, 373*) ("*javanisme*" [*J, 371*]). Although European and Javanese operatic forms seem to present opposing registers of aesthetic taste, Minke's problem of opera appreciation in fact signals a fundamental collusion of both forms. "Javanism" is the term used to articulate this abysmal doubling and splitting of Minke's aesthetic sensibility in *Footsteps*, and it reflects Pramoedya's own use of modern Indonesian against the complex hierarchies of the Javanese language.[54] Recalling Edward Said's celebrated critique of "Orientalism," what Minke calls "Javanism" names the colonial sponsorship of ossified Javanese traditions and "superstitious thinking"—"those beliefs that had become so embedded in people's consciousness over centuries of colonization" (*F, 374*) ("*yang kokoh-kuat dalam jiwa kolonial berabad*" [*J, 372*]). Minke's reflection on his own abysmal sense of musical taste coincides, indeed, with a crisis of political consciousness signaled by the word *priyayi* in the name of the first native political organization, Sarekat Priyayi. In the preceding chapter, Sandiman—the man operating Minke's phonograph in our opera passage—has questioned the use of that exclusive designation *priyayi* for an organization that purports to be Indies-wide, embracing those of all classes and reaching beyond Java, too. Since the critique of "Javanism" and Minke's *priyayi* taste is implied in the very language Pramoedya uses,[55] however, this passage foregrounds a problem of abysmal taste that has informed the tetralogy from the very start—attending each comment on gamelan and *wayang*, reduplicating a simultaneously European and Javanese sensibility in the same passage, whether transmitted through the voice of a European, a native Javanese, an Indo, or some other voice.

So, in the first novel, Minke imagines himself as a leader for his people by comparison with the largest gong in the gamelan orchestra: "Become a gong to be heard booming out everywhere" (*TE*, 195) ("*Jadilah gung! terdengar bergaung-gaung*" [*BM*, 190]). Since the gamelan accompanies *wayang*, the Javanese operatic form of shadow puppetry, theater, and dance, Javanese operatic associations remain important throughout the tetralogy. In one of Minke's last conversations with his mother, she tells him: "Don't become a kedasih [bird] that does not sing, that does not make music. Don't become a dalang that has no stories. A dalang can survive without puppets, Child, but not without stories...." (*F*, 295) ("*Jangan kau jadi kedasih yang tidak bersahut tidak bersambut. Jangan jadi dalang tiada cerita. Tanpa anakwayang pun dalang masih bisa, tapi tanpa cerita....*" [*J*, 289]). Given the specifically Javanese operatic aesthetic sensibility, it is significant that the cultural model of gamelan is first pressed by Miriam de la Croix, the daughter of the high colonial Dutch official, the Assistant Resident Herbert de la Croix: "Papa had ordered us to study your people's music. You have studied gamelan for a long time now, he said to us, and perhaps you can already enjoy it. Listen to how all the tones wait upon the sound of the gong. That is how it is in Javanese music, but that is not how it is in real life, because this pathetic people has still not found their gong, a leader, a thinker who can come forth with words of resolution" (*TE*, 193) ("*Sudah lebih dua tahun ini Papa menyuruh kami memperhatikan musik menurut pengucapan bangsamu itu. Kalian memang sudah lama belajar mendengarkan dan mungkin sudah bisa menikmatinya, katanya lagi. Perhatikan, semua nada bercurahan rancak menuju dan menunggu bunyi gung. Begitu dalam musik Jawa, tetapi tidak begitu dalam kehidupannya yang nyata, karena bangsa yang mengibakan ini dalam kehidupannya tak juga mendapatkan gungnya, seorang pemimpin, pemikir, yang bisa memberikan kataputus*" [*BM*, 187]). It is this that prompts Minke to consider: "Become a gong to be heard booming out everywhere." By the end of *Footsteps*, however, Minke hears a different sense in Herbert de la Croix's arguments: "A pathetic people, Herbert de la Croix had said. For me too it was pathetic. This people waited for the Gong, the Messiah, the Mahdi, the Just King. And he whom they awaited never came.... And Minke is no savior; neither is it his work. At the most, I am a drum that introduces some disharmony into the melody" (*F*, 373) ("*Bangsa yang mengibakan, kata Herbert de la Croix. Bagiku juga mengibakan. Dia, bangsa ini, mengimpikan datangnya gong, si Messias, si Imam Mahdi, si Ratu Adil. Yang ditunggu-tunggu tak kunjung datang.... Ratu Adil yang sekarang bukan Minke, bukan juga pekerjaanya. Paling-paling aku sebuah gendang, yang riuh-rendah memencak-mencak*" [*J*, 370]). This refusal of the metaphor of the "gong" may be seen to complete the process of Minke's rejection of the *priyayi* worldview that culminates, toward the end of *Footsteps*, in Minke's critique of the forms of superstitious thinking he calls "Javanism."

The specifically musical effects of gamelan call attention to a philological problem of literary form at the heart of both European and Javanese operatic forms. In the prison memoirs, in a passage that echoes Minke's reflections in *Footsteps*, Pramoedya reflects on the mesmeric effect of the gamelan accompaniment to *wayang* performance:

> All is accompanied by gamelan music and women's voices, those wayang recitations that connect all at once wisdom, prayer, and worship, drugging and putting the mind to sleep, and absorbing the people in an illusory world of stasis. Alone. Empty. *Non-existing*.
>
> And that gamelan—what polyphony! reaching such heights as have also been reached by Western music. [my translation; italics added to show English in original]
>
> *Semua ditingkah gamelan dan suara pesinden, yang* suluk-suluknya *membubungkan hikmat dan doa dan puja sekaligus, membius dan mematikan akal, membawa orang tertelan oleh dunia ilusi yang menghentikan segala gerak. Sunya. Sunyi. Kosong. Non-existing.*
>
> *Dan gamelan itu—kepolifonikannya! dia telah capai yang juga dicapai oleh musik Barat.* (NS I, 35)

Pramoedya here refers to the special songs called *suluk* in the interconnected accompaniment of gamelan to *wayang*. As Geertz explains, "As the *suluk* are derived from ancient Javanese versions of Hindu poems, and so are in great part incomprehensible both to the *wajang* audience and to the *dalang* himself, the emphasis tends not to be on their intrinsic meaning but, as in the music generally, on the mood they suggest."[56] This "mood" or "feeling" is what Minke describes, by comparison to the mood evoked by Verdi, as "a harmony of feeling that was without form" ("*ketenangan perasaan yang menyangkal wujud*").[57] Revealing his own abysmal taste for gamelan and *wayang*, Pramoedya associates gamelan with the most sublime, as it were most refined annihilation of Javanese literariness.

This exegetical abyss—the rendering meaningless, or "non-existing," the sacred text of song—defines, both for European and for Javanese opera, the aesthetic power of polyphonic counterpoint. In Javanese opera it is not only the *suluk* songs that are accompanied by the polyphonic "stratification" of gamelan; the "recitations" to which Pramoedya refers constitute only one of the many kinds of voices or themes developed to the accompaniment of gamelan, since, as A. L. Becker points out:

> A wayang includes within it, in each performance, the entire history of the literary language, from Old Javanese, pre-Hindu incantation and mythology to the era of the Sanskrit gods and their language, blending with Javanese in the works of ancient poets (the suluks), adding Arabic and Colonial elements, changing with the power of Java to new locations and dialects, up to the present Bahasa Indonesia and even a bit of American English (in which one clown often instructs another).[58]

One of the best examples of a comparable effect in European opera is the familiar barrel-organ tune from *Il Trovatore* around which Conrad organizes the *mise-en-abyme* of modernist narrative irony in *Almayer's Folly*. The troubador's song, set in counterpoint to the lamentations of Leonora's voice, has, as its contrapuntal backdrop, the "Miserere" of the chorus, a homophonic imitation of the polyphonic performance of the sacred text of Psalm 51. Stereotypically, as a repetitively sung fragment of text that acquires familiarity in translation across languages and artistic media, the operatic aria performs a paradoxical and exemplary estrangement of literature: the simultaneous *passing away* of literary form, and its reconstitution in the isolated *passage* of text held up for textual exegesis. Conrad's handorgan and Pramoedya's gramophone renditions of Verdi stage a fundamental philological problem of the passage of literature for modernism: the negation of an original literary text, the estrangement of a prior literary tradition (European or Javanese), and the loss of origin for literary tradition.

Philology and Counterpoint

The contrast in Pramoedya's Buru tetralogy between European and Javanese systems of musical counterpoint foregrounds a central philological, or exegetical, problem at work in the dialectic of abysmal taste in opera. This problem of philology also centrally informs Said's critical model of "contrapuntal reading." Said's use of the specifically "Western classical" musical term "counterpoint" at first suggests a markedly Eurocentric philological model. When Said associates the art of musical counterpoint with the exegetical and interpretive practice of philology—as he repeatedly does—he usually invokes the heroic figure of Erich Auerbach. As Emily Apter has argued, however, Leo Spitzer may be a more revealing precursor for contemporary comparative literary theory.[59] Spitzer's projected *opus magnum, Classical and Christian Ideas of World Harmony,* traces the German philological tradition in which Auerbach and Spitzer were both trained back to those "ideas of world harmony" that bring medieval counterpoint, literature, and biblical hermeneutics together, for Spitzer, into a single historical evolution. Spitzer notes that the Latin terms *contropare, adtropare* from the Greek term (*tropologein*) used "to explain or compare biblical passages by harmonizing them" "led to *contropare,* 'to compare, corroborate legal documents.'"[60] Said's "contrapuntal analysis" may indeed echo the sense of this Spitzerian insight. But for Said—as arguably for Spitzer, too—this philological sense of *contropare* provides a model for a postphilological discordant analysis of textual passages.

Toward the end of *Culture and Imperialism,* a sort of covert plot emerges in Said's argument when he writes: "But this global, contrapuntal analysis should be modeled not (as earlier notions of comparative literature were) on a symphony but rather on an atonal ensemble."[61] The shift from a tonal to atonal music recalls Adorno's argument, developed in his *Philosophy of Modern Music* (and used for the plot of Thomas Mann's *Doctor Faustus*), about the collapse of tonal music at the turn of the twentieth century. Within this argument, the autonomous work of art's aura is threatened, and with it the continuity of a presumed whole organic historical tradition. As Spitzer's argument underscores, a key part of this tradition, if not the harmonic system that holds it together, is the art of "hermeneutics or exegesis," which was

> destined to become most important to the Bible-minded Middle Ages, in which the authority of the Scriptures was as strong as the variety of interpretations was overwhelming. Agreement of the passages of Holy Writ with each other (involving a balancing of Old Testament and New Testament passages, or of the parts of the New Testament against each other) as well as agreement of the Bible with the documents of heathendom (Virgil, etc.)—this was most eagerly sought. And how could this 'concordance' appear otherwise than as musical harmony?[62]

The contrast between European and Javanese systems of musical counterpoint foregrounds this philological problem of textual exegesis informing the model of Said's "contrapuntal analysis." For Conrad, the problem of abysmal operatic taste stages the lost origins of a European literary tradition. For Pramoedya, opera stages the lost origins of a Javanese literary tradition. And for all three, Said included, the model of a "contrapuntal analysis" stages the lost origins of a tradition of philology, or exegetical interpretation.[63]

The question of philology brings us back to the significance of the kind of East Indies opera depicted in the photo images from Nieuwenhuys's *Tempo Doeloe*. These photo images provide something of an answer to the philological question of global comparative analysis at the heart of the cultural dialectic of abysmal operatic taste in both Conrad and Pramoedya. As Pramoedya himself discusses, in his own anthology, *Tempo Doeloe* (an anthology of stories, not photographs), East Indies opera provides a crucial linguistic, and literary record of what he calls "pre-Indonesian literature." Like the tales Pramoedya anthologizes, East Indies opera records, not some nostalgic evocation of a lost colonial world, but the "structure of feeling of the time" (*"semangat semasa"*).[64] Written and performed by European, Indo, or Chinese writers, the stories and theatrical performances record the shared linguistic medium of that matrix of Indies-wide social, political, and cultural exchanges that shaped the climate of anti-colonial nationalism. One of the tales Pramoedya anthologizes, *Nyai Dasima* (a key text for the Buru tetralogy, as will be discussed in chapter 6), was also part of the stock repertoire for East Indies opera. More significant, however, is the fact that most of the repertoire of East Indies opera vanished with the eclipse of this form of popular opera in the 1920s. Whatever the reasons for this, the phenomenon of East Indies opera remains the record of a *lost* moment in the cultural cross-fertilization of different literary traditions. Even more graphically than Conrad's and Pramoedya's examples, then, these photos show how an unfathomable taste in opera constitutes the literary as a fundamental vanishing point of cultural perspective.

This cultural logic emerges politically and historically in the puzzle of each of the figures operating the mechanical object of operatic reproduction (whether hand organ or phonograph). Babalatchi's racial stereotype embeds a central historical and perspectival deformation in Conrad's Malay or Lingard trilogy. He embodies the puzzling problem of cross-cultural perspective that organizes the colonial family romance not only of the Lingard trilogy but of all of Conrad's Malay fiction. Sandiman remains a shadowy figure in Pramoedya's Buru tetralogy: a fictional character among the historical figures (Marco Kartodikromo, Suwardi) who appear in the third volume, his presence in *House of Glass* is invoked by Pangemanann as a *dalang* figure: "Sandiman disappeared from circulation. But, Modern Pitung, I think it is Sandiman who is Marko's *dalang*. He lives in the shadows" (*H*, 175) ("*Sandiman hilang dari peredaran. Tapi aku duga, Pitung Modern, dialah dalang Marko. Dia hidup dalam bayang-bayang*" [*RK*, 176]). Figured as a ghostly fictional puppeteer orchestrating the opera of recorded history, Sandiman presents the puzzle of Pramoedya's fictional reading of the archives, to which we will return. Such figures necessarily complicate the historical picture of what Nieuwenhuys's photographs evoke as *tempo doeloe*.[65] The hand organ, along with its technological cousin the phonograph, binds together each of these examples into a single dialectical image of the relation between opera and the passage of literature at the turn of the century. In all three of our examples, regardless of the different forms and traditions of opera on display (East Indies opera, European grand opera, or Javanese *wayang*), the hand organ and phonograph provide points of ironic and distorting perspective from which to grasp opera in general as a fundamental cultural—and political—problem of taste. Simultaneously signaling the formation and the deformation of culture, opera is the *mise-en-abyme* of modern cultural capital.

In the third photograph from Nieuwenhuys's *Tempo Doeloe* East Indies opera is illustrated without actually being depicted—there are just so many people and objects mimicking the form of an orchestral opera troupe. So, too, in a sense, with Pramoedya's and Conrad's novels. If East Indies opera is not itself represented in their novel sequences, the novels themselves have a great deal in common with this hybrid cultural and artistic form.[66] Both draw on its characteristic multi-ethnic masquerade and melodramatic grasp of exotic stories. Both draw, moreover, on the same linguistic medium: for Pramoedya, the *lingua franca* of Malay is the precursor for modern *bahasa Indonesia;* for Conrad's Malay fiction, it is the common language of the characters, and the mirror image, as it were, of what he himself does with the translingual, transcultural medium of English.[67] Both also grasp opera as the performance of a fundamental estrangement of literary tradition: the loss of origin, and the loss of temporality, for literature.

In applying Said's "contrapuntal analysis" to the novel sequences of Conrad and Pramoedya, we find models for global comparative study that productively complicate Said's metaphorical use of the specifically Western classical musical term "counterpoint."[68] Applied to the historical period of colonialism—roughly 1600 to 1900—during which European counterpoint and the polyphony of Javanese (alongside Balinese and other Indonesian) gamelan music formed discrete and discrepant tonal systems—Said's metaphor opens up a set of overlapping models of counterpoint: the counterpoint of Said's Western classical music; the "Cuban counterpoint" of Fernando Ortiz; and the counterpoint of Indonesian gamelan. Each of these forms of musical counterpoint may be linked to modes of modern consciousness related to the formations of English, Creole, and Indonesian literary modernism whose interrelation I am tracing through this book. The dialectic of abysmal taste in opera at work in the narrative form of Conrad's Malay trilogy and Pramoedya's Buru tetralogy outlines in what sense each of these apparently different systems of musical counterpoint precipitates a modern break from tradition, an awakening to modernity that finds its own modern genealogy inscribed within a genealogy of modernism that strangely precedes its own.

3

THE REPETITIVE FORMATION OF ENGLISH MODERNISM
Jean Rhys, Ford Madox Ford, and the Memory of Joseph Conrad

In this chapter I trace a pattern of repetition in the formation of English modernism around the founding of two literary journals, *The English Review* in 1908 and *the transatlantic review* in 1924. This repetitive formation emerges through a combination of memoir and literary citation (beginning with Conrad's own "reminiscences" in *The English Review* and repeated with Ford's "remembrance" of Conrad in *the transatlantic review*) through which Conrad becomes a canonical point of reference for genealogies of English literary modernism. This focus might be compared, and contrasted, to what Pierre Bourdieu, in *The Rules of Art*, analyzes as the "genesis and structure of the literary field" (*"genèse et structure du champ littéraire"*) of French modernism from Flaubert to Gide and beyond. Attending to the social milieu—or habitus—of the artistic salons of the late nineteenth century and the literary reviews of the early twentieth century, Bourdieu analyzes a dialectic of distinction by which the "literary field" emerges from a hierarchy of different arts organized according to a logic of "symbolic" or "cultural capital." The English modernism examined here forms an adjacent and overlapping field, more narrowly focused on the double formation of Ford Madox Ford's two ventures in literary review editing, the short-lived *transatlantic review* of 1924 and the earlier *English Review* of 1908.

Following Bourdieu's formulation of "an opposition between the avant-garde and the consecrated avant-garde" within the "unified literary field" of French modernism,[1] it is possible to recognize in the field of English modernism an analogous kind of opposition. Here, we should distinguish between the avant-garde writers with whom Jean Rhys first appeared in print in Ford Madox Ford's *transatlantic review*, in 1924, and the old avant-garde ideals consecrated by the same review, both in its repetition of (including reprinting passages from) the older avant-garde *English Review* and in its memorial "Conrad Supplement" dedicated to the work of Joseph Conrad who had died earlier in the same year. The specifically Ford-ian symbolic economy of English modernism, as examined here around Ford's collaborative affairs with Conrad and Rhys, respectively, yields an important difference in attention to the literary field, but one that might supplement Bourdieu's approach by drawing attention to an inter-dependency of rival national literary avant-gardes and the complex cultural affiliations and antagonisms that form and deform them. One thing that makes the analogy between Bourdieu's French and our English literary field so fitting, after all, is the fact that it was from within a French avant-garde milieu that *the transatlantic review*, based in Paris and edited by expatriate British and American writers, sought to lay claim to a transatlantic "English" modernism.[2]

Rhys's first published story appeared in 1924, the year of Conrad's death. By that time, Conrad's work had been granted near-canonical status. Virginia Woolf was able to write with assurance not only about the place of Conrad's books "amongst our classics," but also about "those famous passages which it is becoming the habit to lift from their context and exhibit among other cut flowers of English prose."[3] André Gide (soon to follow Conrad's footsteps into the Congo) had already translated "Typhoon," and was supervising the series of translations of Conrad's work into French for the *Nouvelle Revue Française*. Impressed by Gide's claim that he learned English in order to read Conrad, Thomas Mann would write an influential introduction to the German translation of two Conrad novels in 1926, ensuring Conrad's canonical place as a representative English voice at the heart of "high" European modernism. The process of Conrad's literary canonization, and the European reputation of the English modernism it helped consolidate, is a longer and more complex affair than these three examples—each with their own English, French, and German mythologies of modernism—might suggest. The purpose here is not to examine the dense network of institutional links and affiliations that established the modernist profile of Conrad within the overlapping literary and linguistic formations of various European modernisms. Rather, by isolating two moments in this process, and focusing on Ford's role in simultaneously consecrating Conrad's memory and promoting the work of Rhys, the aim is to examine a constitutive problem of cultural memory attached to the formation of English modernism within the wider literary field of transnational literary modernism.

Situating the established reputation of Conrad within the same field of reference as the then-unrecognized (indeed, only newly named) Rhys enables a study attuned to the inherent misrecognition of the "English" linguistic and cultural coordinates of English modernism. Ford's memory of each provides an important point of reference, and precisely because of, rather than in spite of, the notorious unreliability of its deliberately "impressionist" promotion of the modernist artistic principles he associates with each writer. What is of particular interest here is the question of how Ford situates the Malay and Caribbean cultural coordinates, respectively, of each writer's imaginative investments. We have already discussed the importance of Conrad's career-long investment in the Malay settings with which he began—and ended—his literary career. Malay language, history, and culture play a complex role in mediating his own authorial relation to English and organizing his entire *oeuvre* around the delayed retrospective reconstruction of Lingard's Malay historical romance. As we shall explore at greater length later, Rhys's work is shaped by her career-long investment in memories of the Caribbean environment of her childhood. What role do these respective investments play in each writer's relation to the "English" and "transatlantic" coordinates of the modernism Ford sought to manage in his role as editor of *The English Review* and *the transatlantic review?*

An important difference from Bourdieu's approach is our interest in the modernist citation of literary passages. Perhaps the most celebrated form of this is the use of allusions in T. S. Eliot's *The Waste Land;* and Eliot's citations from Conrad's "Heart of Darkness" in the draft version, famously cut by Ezra Pound, already provide a miniature case study of the role of Conrad in the formation of English modernism. But the creative and critical practice of literary citation might generally be recognized as the strategy by which what Huyssen calls the "historical avant-garde"—a term used to designate a historically bounded, yet European-wide range of experimental and iconoclastic artistic and literary movements—gets assimilated into the "symbolic" or "cultural capital" of literary modernism.[4] Woolf's image of "famous passages" taken out of context like "cut flowers of English prose" conveniently suggests the importance of citation in the Bourdieuian dialectic of cultural capital. It indicates a tension and contrast between the creative work of the avant-garde writer and the canonizing work of criticism and anthologization, a contrast reminiscent of John Guillory's argument (itself drawing on Bourdieu) about the formation of English literary capital from the eighteenth century on, and its dependence on the use of commonplace passages for memorization in schools.[5]

Woolf's image seems intended to construct an opposition between passages of Conradian prose appreciated in context and passages mindlessly repeated as canonical. Her argument belongs, too, though, to the moment of memorialization and canonization during which Conrad's champions and critics sought to evaluate Conrad's reputation after his death, and this is the moment of the Conrad Memorial supplement to *the transatlantic review*. Woolf does not allude to the debates then stirred up by Ford Madox Ford's memorial, but she offers another, characteristically classical image of her own that suggests in what sense the critical work of selecting "famous passages" of Conrad to hold up as "cut flowers of English prose" concerns the work of remembering and consecrating an ideal of literary, linguistic, and aesthetic form:

> One opens his pages and feels as Helen must have felt when she looked in her glass and realized that, do what she would, she could never in any circumstances pass for a plain woman. So Conrad had been gifted, so he had schooled himself, and such was his obligation to a strange language wooed characteristically for its Latin qualities rather than the Saxon that it seemed impossible for him to make an ugly or insignificant movement of the pen.[6]

The complex combination of classical literary allusions (the ancient Greek model of Helen) and linguistic lineages (Conrad's preference for the "Latin" over the "Saxon" features of English) produces an idealized genealogy of "English" as literary and linguistic "cultural capital."

Woolf may be measuring her own distance from this lineage, but in so doing she makes Conrad an exemplary point of reference for literary and linguistic genealogies of English modernism around this time. Woolf's picture stands in contrast with the one Ford Madox Ford elaborated at length in *Joseph Conrad: A Personal Remembrance*. Begun in *the transatlantic review* in 1924, already anticipated by Ford's 1911 essay on Conrad in *The English Review*, Ford's *Joseph Conrad* was modeled on Conrad's own *A Personal Record*, published as "Some Reminiscences" in *The English Review* in 1908–1909. The underlying similarity, though, is the shared recognition of the importance of Conrad's attention to formal style—what Woolf calls "the incessant care for appearances," subtly undercutting the prior image of Helen; and what Ford elevates into Conrad's "conquest of a language" and "conspiracy against a literature."[7]

Rhys offers a rather different reading of the canonized Conradian passage of literature. In *After Leaving Mr. Mackenzie*, a novel that looks back on the Anglo-French milieu of Ford's English modernism (and the symbolic economy of her own affair with Ford for which the novel is sometimes read as a *roman à clef*), Rhys cites a passage from Conrad's first novel, *Almayer's Folly*. The quotation appears to illustrate the state of mind of Norah, the sister of the novel's main character, Julia Martin. Norah is distraught over her sister's reappearance from France: "It was as if meeting Julia had aroused some spirit of rebellion to tear her to bits. She thought over and over again, 'It isn't fair, it isn't fair'" (*AL*, 103). It is this repeated complaint that leads to the Conrad citation:

> She picked up the book lying on her bed-table—*Almayer's Folly*—and had begun to read:

> The slave had no hope, and knew of no change. She knew of no other sky, no other water, no other forest, no other world, no other life. She had no wish, no hope, no love.... The absence of pain and hunger was her happiness, and when she felt unhappy she was tired, more than usual, after the day's labour.
> Then she had got up and looked at herself in the glass.... (*AL*, 103)

An example of the way Rhys cites all sorts of cultural fragments—borrowing, perhaps, from avant-garde surrealist uses of photomontage and collage—the citation might itself be taken as Rhys's memorial to the English modernism of Ford's and Conrad's generation. Like Woolf, Rhys frames the Conradian passage as a problem of gendered reading; like Woolf, too, this scene of a woman reading Conrad's prose as if in a mirror seems troubled by a question of racial identity—the repeated refrain "it's not fair, it's not fair" carries at least the connotation of a "fair" racial complexion,[8] albeit one likely *not* mirrored in the English prose of the Conradian passage. By contrast to the idealized genealogy of the "English" of Conrad's prose, Rhys's citation frames the passage as a problem of reading, race, and identity. Without any reference to the Malay setting of the novel from which the passage is taken, however, the coordinates of culture, race, and identity seem to have been erased entirely from the scene of reading. What is the effect of this forgetting and erasure of the novel's Malay setting? Does it repeat or displace the symbolic economy of Ford's remembrance of Conrad? Where does it situate the linguistic and literary coordinates of the field of English modernism? The accumulating questions of reading and identification that proliferate around this cited passage, and to which I shall return at the end of this chapter, form the starting point of my inquiry into the necessary misrecognition of cultural identity at the heart of the formation of English modernism.

Ford Madox Ford and the Repetitive Formation of English Modernism

From *The English Review* (1908) to *the transatlantic review* (1924)

If Joseph Conrad and Jean Rhys exemplify two different moments in the formation of English modernism, Ford Madox Ford is the central mediating figure. *The English Review* and *the transatlantic review* confirm, twice over (first as Hueffer, then as Ford[9]), Ford's formative influence on English and American literary modernism. In the prewar period, *The English Review* became one of the key "battlegrounds" of English modernism (shoring up the James-Conrad-Hueffer "Rye revolution" of one generation of modernists and anticipating the "revolution of the word" of the next, introducing Ezra Pound, D. H. Lawrence, and Wyndham Lewis).[10] In the postwar period, *the transatlantic review* published a striking constellation of "high" modernist documents—stories from Hemingway's *In Our Time*, the serial appearance of Gertrude Stein's *The Making of Americans*, poems by e. e. cummings, Ezra Pound, and Tristan Tzara, the first published fragment of Joyce's *Finnegans Wake*, the serial publication of Ford's own *Some Do Not*—all this (and more) appearing in the twelve issues between the review's first issue, dated January 1924, and its last, in December of the same year.

Ford's editorial instinct for managing literary modernism is showcased by his role in consecrating the modernist reputation of Conrad and inaugurating the career of Rhys. In the opening issue of *the transatlantic review*, Ford republished *The Nature of a Crime*, a story collaboratively written with Conrad, which had originally appeared under the pseudonym Baron Ignatz von Aschendrof in *The English Review* in 1909. In his inaugural editorial communications, Ford included a letter from Conrad authorizing republication, wishing Ford well in his new editorial venture, and reflecting on the spirit of the earlier *English Review*.[11] In this retrospective reflection on the work of collaboration, Ford began a process of memorialization that would result in *Joseph Conrad: A Personal Remembrance*, which began serialization in *the transatlantic review* following Conrad's death in August. It was still being serialized in the last issue, dated December 1924, in which Jean Rhys appeared in print for the very first time, as author of a short story entitled "Vienne." These two editorial acts—capitalizing on Conrad's established reputation and promoting Rhys as one of a new generation of avant-garde writers—illustrate the double movement of inaugurating the new while consecrating the old avant-garde, that informs *The English Review* as much as its postwar successor, *the transatlantic review*, itself founded to consecrate that earlier modernist venture.

An essential part of this instinct for managing modernism, however, is Ford's spectacular mismanagement of affairs. As he put it himself, writing about *the transatlantic review* in *It Was the Nightingale* (1933), "I am a very good business man when it comes to other people's affairs. I know the ins and outs of printing, publishing, and business-editing a review as few others do. But when it comes to managing my own affairs I am worse than hopeless. I do not manage them at all, and if they have any chance of becoming complicated at all they become incredibly complicated."[12] Just as he had lost control of *The English Review* in 1909, by the end of 1924 he had lost control, too, of *the transatlantic review*.[13] The loss of both is bound up with the scandal of his collaborative affairs, respectively, with Joseph Conrad and Jean Rhys. "Affair" is a loaded term for Ford, as Max Saunders has pointed out,[14] implying all at once a business venture, a sexual affair—of the kind Ford repeatedly and compulsively fell into—and signifying, in a technical literary sense, the subject matter of novel writing. As Ford wrote, introducing his Conrad memorial, "according to our view of the thing, a novel should be the biography of a man or of an affair, and a biography, whether of a man or an affair, should be a novel, both being, if they are efficiently performed, renderings of such affairs as are our human lives."[15]

Ford's affair with Rhys (what Rhys herself called "L'Affaire Ford") has been the subject for numerous mythologized accounts—at least three novels (Jean Lenglet's *Sous les Verrous*, Jean Rhys's *Quartet* [but also *After Leaving Mr. Mackenzie*], Ford's *When the Wicked Man*), various autobiographical reminiscences (Stella Bowen's, and Jean Rhys's sparse comments), and an accumulating set of critical accounts.[16] The affair can be read as part of an economy of financial, imaginative, and literary, as well as sexual affairs, that helped shore up the cultural prestige of Ford's English modernism. Ford's memorial to Conrad attempted just such an accounting of collaborative affairs. Taking the Conrad–Ford collaboration as its subject, it provoked a charge of exploitation and opportunism, beginning with Jessie Conrad's denunciation in December 1924 (but anticipated already by Conrad's own break with Ford over *The English Review* in 1909),[17] that has shaped much of Conrad criticism throughout the twentieth century. As with Rhys, Ford helped secure Conrad's reputation at the expense of his own.

It is difficult not to notice a Freudian pattern of repetitive compulsion in Ford's inability to manage his own affairs. In addition to the psychological and sexual complications involved, the financial, cultural, and literary consequences of Ford's affairs make this repetitive pattern a revealing part of the symbolic economy of the modernist field marked by the two reviews. Ford's insistence on returning to the memory of Conrad is especially revealing for this symbolic economy, pointing in turn to the problematic notion of identification in Freud's hypothesis of repetitive compulsion, as revisited by feminist theorists.[18] Freud's hypothesis of a "compulsion to repeat" (*Wiederholungszwang*)—whose elaboration itself coincides historically with the double formation of English modernism between 1908 and 1924—attempts to come to terms with the problem of "traumatic neurosis" foregrounded at the beginning of *Beyond the Pleasure Principle* (1920) by "the terrible war which has just ended" (*"Der schreckliche, eben jetzt abgelaufene Krieg"*).[19] The problem of memory, or rather memory *loss*, illustrated by the "great number" of instances of shell shock from the war, becomes a fundamental feature of Freud's elaboration of the psychic "economy"—from which will emerge, for example, both the popular psychological picture of ego and id and its contested counterimage in the critique of the American ego-ideal and the Lacanian account of subject formation.

For Ford, too, who himself suffered the effects of being shelled in Becourt-Becordel in July 1916, the experience of wartime trauma was decisive in reshaping his well-established preoccupation with the problem of memory. Whatever the psychological effects on Ford personally, the experience becomes an organizing feature of his postwar fiction (notably the series of novels entitled *Parade's End*) and—most significantly for our concerns here—his own reminiscences of involvement in the literary avant-garde, beginning with his memorial to Conrad.[20] In this way, the formation of English modernism we are tracking around *the transatlantic review*'s doubling and repetition of *The English Review* follows a specifically Ford-ian variation of the Freud-ian *Wiederholungszwang*.

The reissue of *The Nature of a Crime*, an otherwise negligible story, foregrounds the way Ford invests in the figure of Conrad the wider predicament of modernist memory. Although with its suggestively German pseudonym (an anagrammatical combination of the names of Ford and Conrad), and its suggestive twinning of concealed sexual and financial affairs, it might appear to fit the imaginative concerns of the high modernist moment, a moment of widespread financial bankruptcy throughout Europe, exploited, for example, by Thomas Mann and André Gide, whose work seems oddly evoked, respectively, in the pseudonym Aschendrof, echoing the Aschenbach of Mann's *Der Tod in Venedig*, and in the story's theme of financial fraud, anticipating Gide's *Les faux-monnayeurs*. The story's financial motif is made more interesting for the suggestive contrast it implies between the failing economic ventures of Ford's two reviews and what Bourdieu styles "the anti-economic economy of pure art" ("*cet univers économique proprement anti-économique*")[21] that might be seen to inform the symbolic economy with which Ford seeks to invest the artistic aims of his own collaboration with Conrad.

As indicated by Ford's editorial citation from Conrad's letter authorizing publication, the story serves as a pretext to recall the spirit of *The English Review* in launching the first issue of the *the transatlantic review*. The prefatory comments by Conrad and Ford, which Ford published in the August issue of the review, reiterate this connection (Conrad writes that "what impresses me most is the amount this fragment contains of the...atmosphere of the time...when the *English Review* was founded"[22]). Yet Ford's insistence on returning to the scene of this collaboration reveals something else besides. In his own prefatory comments, Ford claims he had forgotten all about the collaboration: "the details of its birth and its attendant circumstances remain for me completely forgotten, a dark, blind-spot on the brain."[23] Some pages later, he continues: "Eventually I had to admit the, as it were, dead fact. And, having admitted that to myself, and my Colaborator [*sic*] having corroborated it, I was at once possessed by a sort of morbid craving to get the story re-published in a definitive and acknowledged form."[24] One might say a great deal about what this disavowal and "morbid craving" show in terms of the "curious affair" of the Ford–Conrad romance—there is surely here a complex literary, psychological, and sexual economy, made all the more symbolic by the shrill reaction from Conrad's guardian figures against what they took to be Ford's opportunism in exaggerating the nature of the Ford–Conrad collaboration. Ford's own explanation for the "dark, blind-spot on the brain" ascribes this psychic economy to an amnesia, clearly the result of that experience of shell shock during the war (in July 1916) that provided the imaginative pretext for the Tietjens novels, the first of which Ford was serializing in *the transatlantic review:*

> At a given point in my life I forgot, literally, all the books I had ever written; but, if nowadays I re-read one of them, though I possess next to none and have re-read few, nearly all the phrases come back startlingly to my memory and I see glimpses of Kent, of Sussex, of Carcassone—of New York, even; and fragments of furniture, mirrors, who knows what?[25]

This "blind spot" of memory, intervening between *The English Review* and *the transatlantic review,* organizes the Fordian economy of *Wiederholungszwang* with which Ford promotes a repetitive formation of English modernism. At stake in the symbolic economy of Ford's mismanaged affairs is not only the reputation of individual authors but also the reputations of those various literary and cultural traditions to which all three authors avowed (or disavowed) affiliation, reputations inscribed in the "English" and "transatlantic" titles of the two reviews.

Re-Citing Conrad in Modernist Memory

In staging his reissue of *The Nature of a Crime* around a forgetting, Ford is engaged in another form of repetition—the repetition of whole passages of text, paradoxically *from memory*—which becomes central for the book-length memorial, *Joseph Conrad: A Personal Remembrance,* to emerge from *the transatlantic review.* Ford's "blind spot" with respect to *The Nature of a Crime* provides an occasion for Ford to recount how, having forgotten "all the books I had ever written," he is nonetheless endowed with a striking power of memory. The qualification that he possesses next to none of his own books and has reread few of them, draws all the more attention to the compulsive repetition with which he continually returns to passages from the work of his collaboration with Conrad. This act of citing passages from memory becomes the hallmark of the completed Conrad memorial, and an essential feature of Ford's most important (and most influential) account of the Conrad–Ford method of searching for the *mot juste*.

The adjacency of location and citation—the remembered passage evoking the location of composition—creates an "impressionist" principle of distortion that remains central to Ford's claims for the modernism of Conrad's "conquest of a language" and "conspiracy against a literature."[26] In his introductory comments to *The Nature of a Crime*, this principle is used to claim authority for distinguishing the difference between passages written by Ford and passages written by Conrad—something Ford began doing already in an essay from 1911 in *The English Review*, repeated in an early issue of *the transatlantic review* in republishing selected passages from their first collaboration, *Romance*, and resumed as a premise of the memorial. The distinction claims authority, however, in a double sense: first, by retrospectively claiming a textual authority for the previously published "analysis"; and second, by prospectively claiming, for this Proustian reading memory, the authority to identify "the phrases exactly as they stand" on the basis of their collaborative practice of "read[ing] one passage or another aloud for purposes of correction."[27] Necessarily doubled by the moment of its composition and that of its rereading, the remembered passage of text, for Ford, thus becomes the citation of a recitation.

In evaluating Ford's Conrad memorial, it is difficult to determine whether to give priority to Ford's remembrance of the collaborative process of recitation, or to Ford's impressionist interpretation of the printed passage of text. This ambiguity informs the central confusion of narrative subject by which "the writer," as Ford designates himself, assumes first-hand knowledge of the experiences told over and over again by Conrad before they were transcribed into the form of the published text of Conrad's work. That principle of confusion, already elaborated in the discussion of *The Nature of a Crime*, is taken a step further in the *Remembrance*: "When he talked on such occasions he was like his 'The Mirror of the Sea.' Indeed, a great part of his 'The Mirror of the Sea' was just his talk which the writer took down in a shorthand of his own extemporising, recalling to Conrad, who was then in a state of great depression, various passages of his own relating."[28] This kind of assertion seems to justify the critical responses it provoked from Jessie Conrad and Edward Garnett. It was labeled "that detestable book"[29] by Conrad's widow, whose letter to the *Times Literary Supplement* set the tone of hostility that informs many later scholarly assessments of Conrad's collaboration with Ford. And it was criticized by Edward Garnett, who wrote "In the magic name of 'impressionism' a man can magnify, distort, or suppress facts and aspects to his own glorification."[30] Ford seems to give himself an extraordinary authority over Conrad's texts. On the basis of some claimed prior "recitation," Ford can claim authoritative knowledge and experience in citing a passage from Conrad—even to the extent of embellishing and supplementing Conrad's stories with anecdotes of his own. Ford's method suffers from the ambiguity of its own logic: any claim he makes about Conrad is likely to seem a retrospective distortion; his "remembrance" can only be an "impressionist" fiction, a "novel."

The double bind of Ford's recollections of Conrad, however, presents a further, more troubling offense. Ford enacts a problem of memory as the necessary condition for any critical reading of Conrad. This is not a problem of claiming a prior recitation of the cited passage; it concerns, rather, the problem of memory rehearsed in every characteristically Conradian passage of literature, each of "those famous passages" Woolf writes about, including the passage Jean Rhys cites in *After Leaving Mr. Mackenzie*. He is citing the problem of citing Conrad. In Ford's account, priority is given to the linguistic coordinates of the French passages of literature (above all, from Flaubert) on which both he and Conrad modeled both the specific cadence of their own sentences and the ideal of their shared goal to write "Absolute Prose."[31] The claim that Conrad's "conquest of a language" and "conspiracy against a literature" took the form of translating passages of French literature into English might at first appear the least likely way to promote the prestige of Conrad's writing, inviting the charge of a form of plagiarism (that Ford, more precisely, and referring to his own practice, calls "pastiche").[32] Ford's repeated emphasis, however, both in citing Conrad and citing their own collaborative recitation of Conradian passages nonetheless insists on a close attention to the individual passage of text that helped canonize Conrad at the heart of English modernism.

Ford is, in a number of ways, though, repeating Conrad's own attempt to situate the problem of memory in his own writing. In the opening to *A Personal Record,* the reminiscences Conrad wrote for Ford's *English Review,* Conrad indulges in "the pleasant fancy" that he began writing the tenth chapter of *Almayer's Folly* under "the shade of old Flaubert" (*PR,* 3); and in the second paragraph cites the opening line of that chapter ("'It has set at last,' said Nina to her mother, pointing to the hills behind which the sun had sunk" [*PR,* 3]). Conrad's is more complicated a linking of Flaubert with the passage he cites than Ford's embellishment on this invocation in the beginning of his *Remembrance,* where Ford claims "the first words of Conrad's first book were penciled on the flyleaves and margins of 'Madame Bovary.'"[33] Ford condenses and displaces the complex multiplicity of cultural and linguistic coordinates within which Conrad attempts to situate the "sunset in Malayan Isles" evoked by "Almayer's romantic daughter" in a setting "far removed" from the "commercial and yet romantic town" of Rouen under the "shade" of that "last of the Romantics," Flaubert. In some respects, though, Ford's repetition of Conrad's invocation of Flaubert gives clearer linguistic precision to the problem of cultural memory Conrad underlines by linking, with the word *romantic,* the southern "Malayan" setting of the passage with the northern French location where it was written. The complex question of relations among all the various coordinates invoked by Conrad are reduced, in Ford's repetition, to an economy of relation between French and English that anticipates the account to come of that collaborative practice of translation work and stylistic attention to the *mot juste* in the creation of the "New Form"[34] and the shared ambition to "write Absolute Prose."[35]

Ford's lengthy discussion of Conrad's choice of the word *azure* in a passage from "Youth" is noteworthy. Presented as a more complex example of Conrad's "translating directly from the French in his mind," it recapitulates the lengthy earlier accounts of the collaborative process by which the "writer" (Ford) and Conrad worked together in pursuit of "Absolute Prose":

> The writer remembers Conrad spending nearly a whole day over one word in two or three sentences of proofs for the Blackwood volume called "Youth." It was two words, perhaps—serene and azure. Certainly it was azure. 'And she crawled on, do or die, in the serene weather. The sky was a miracle of purity, a miracle of azure.' Conrad said, a*zure,* the writer *ay*sure—or more exactly *ay*syeh. This worried Conrad a good deal since he wanted a*zure* for his cadence. He read the sentence over and over again to see how it sounded.[36]

The difference in pronunciation might seem to make little difference to the effect of the printed word, except, of course, to suggest Conrad's own doubts about the choice of words, and thus to enable Ford to discuss Conrad's effort to use "only such words as are found in the normal English vernacular."[37] Whether *azure* can be said to be "normal English vernacular" is something that occupies Ford for several pages, involving a discussion of the likely "conversational vocabulary" of the narrator, Marlow (whom Ford impressionistically spells "Marlowe" throughout), who would be using the word. Toward the end of Ford's discussion, he cites the "whole passage of 'Youth' under consideration," with the emphatic qualification, "the writer is quoting from memory, but as far as this passage is concerned he is fairly ready to back his memory against the printed page."[38]

Challenging the reader to verify his text against that of Conrad's, Ford engages in a characteristically provocative critical game, repeated in the Preface where he emphasizes "all the quotations but two have been left unverified, coming from the writer's memory. It is the impression of a writer who avowed himself an impressionist. Where the writer's memory has proved to be at fault over a detail afterwards out of curiosity looked up, the writer has allowed the fault to remain on the page."[39] If this was just the kind of game of "hide and seek"[40] that Edward Garnett failed to appreciate in his critical review, it is worth noting that Ford's impressionist mistakes are not without critical purpose. The consistently misspelled "Marlowe," for example, may be given authoritative justification by turning to Conrad's own text—in "Youth: A Narrative," the story that first introduces Marlow, we read: "Marlow (at least I think that is how he spelt his name)" (*Y*, 3). What concerns Ford, indeed, in the lengthy discussion of the word *azure*, is the difference between the English of Marlow's oral storytelling and the English of the printed page, on which the studied simplicity of Conrad's "Youth" itself depends.

The overall effect of this citation—like Ford's compulsive reprinting of Conradian passages in the pages of *the transatlantic review*—is to consecrate the stylistic achievement of Conrad's writing, to mark off those passages that are uniquely Conradian (as Ford graphically does in using italics to distinguish Conrad's writing from his own, or "the writer's," in the select passages reprinted from *Romance*), and to demonstrate the work of producing "Absolute Prose" from a painstaking process of translating between French and English in search of *le mot juste*. What Ford does in drawing attention to the way the word *azure* works in this passage might indeed be compared to later attempts to define the modernist effects of Conrad's style—Fredric Jameson's analysis, for example, of Conrad's "'impressionist' will to style";[41] or Edward Said's various attempts to explain "the extraordinary care [Conrad] took with the way his narratives are delivered."[42] Ford's early promotion of the formalist modernism of Conrad's work drew attention to the French modernist ideal written into the Conradian passage of literature, the Flaubertian ideal of (as Jameson puts it) "creat[ing] a decoding machinery which does not have its object external to itself but present within the system";[43] or the Mallarmé ideal of *l'oeuvre pur* to which Said refers.[44]

It is the very distortion of Ford's memory, and the insistence on his own presence at the scene of writing, that helps establish the mythology of an English modernism translating into English the ideals of a French modernism modeled on a Flaubert or Mallarmé. The cited passage from "Youth" is revealing in this regard not only for the slight textual distortions introduced by Ford's memory but also because it reveals a constitutive distortion of memory within the passage itself that is a part of what Jameson and Said attempt to theorize in defining the difference in Conrad's repetition of Flaubert's modernism. For Jameson, Conrad's "aestheticizing strategy" follows the attention to language as pure style to produce the Flaubertian "nonrealization of the image"[45]—the sky, the sea, the ship—but then goes on to reinvest that image with another form of realism, or reality effect: in short (and to single out the most essential feature of Jameson's argument as it concerns "such 'purer' descriptive passages"[46] depicting the sea) "the sea is both a strategy of containment and a place of real business."[47] The description of the sea, in the passage Ford cites, is the scene of a labor that is both an exercise in pure style (choosing words, creating the "English" of Conrad's "Absolute Prose") and an account of the "romance" of English merchant marine seafaring labor. (Ford describes this as "almost the perfection of sea writing of its type."[48])

Said's argument, in the essay "Conrad: the Presentation of Narrative," is especially revealing in light of Ford's practice of citing Conrad throughout *Joseph Conrad: A Personal Remembrance*, because the distorting element Said finds introduced into *l'oeuvre pur* is "that intransigent remnant of the writer's identity that is not amenable to language"—that is, as he puts it later, "Conrad's autobiographical presence," which Said usefully describes as "distributed" through "each tale" "in numerous roles: first as the person to whom events happened, as speaker, as listener, then finally as author who at one moment presents narrative, negates it by pretending it is speech, then negates that (in letters during the throes of composition) by denouncing its difficulties, then negates even that (late in his career) by sounding like Everyone's Favorite Old Novelist."[49] What is striking about this formulation is how easily it can be transposed into a description of how Ford impersonates that "autobiographical presence" both in the general "pastiche" of his biographical portrait of Conrad and, more particularly, in his description of the oral recitations that preceded the writing of the passages of text he then cites. On one hand, this clarifies how successfully Ford is able to insinuate himself as that "autobiographical presence" distorting the pure autonomy of a text that effaces all trace of its author. On the other hand, in the distortion introduced through Ford's distinction between "the writer" and Conrad as author, Ford reveals how complex an effect of linguistic, literary, and cultural distinction is that "autobiographical presence" Said outlines for us (and implicitly, himself, theorizes by recourse to Freud's notion of a *Wiederholungszwang*: "Perhaps this was Conrad's way of escaping the debilitating consequences of repression and the compulsion of the pleasure principle"[50]).

Both Jameson and Said follow Ford in presenting Conrad as attempting to translate into English the formal purity of French modernism, its "Absolute Prose" (Ford), its "practice of style" (Jameson), and "*l'oeuvre pur*" (Said). This illuminates the repetitive formation of English modernism not only in suggesting, generally and historically, that English modernism follows French modernism, but also, and more fundamentally, in creating a distinction within the texts of English modernism that preserves the purity of the original French modernist "practice of style" over against its

English repetition. This distinction might be explained as a further extension of French modernism in terms of Bourdieu's theory of "cultural capital" generally, as well as the more particular attention he gives to the distinctions within successive avant-garde factions in the formation of the "genesis and structure" of French modernism as a "literary field." But Ford's distorted and distorting memory of Conrad calls attention to a material practice of citing, and recitation, that lodges this French ideal at the center of English modernism both as "linguistic capital" and as "symbolic capital." What Ford does in drawing attention to the word *azure* in the passage from "Youth" is to give that word a sort of exuberant surplus value that both repeats the French modernist ideal of "Absolute Prose" and distorts it by rehearsing Conrad's struggle to make English words fit the pattern of that French modernist ideal.

The distortion of what Said calls the "autobiographical presence" in Conrad's texts has its counterpart, then, in Ford's "fiction biography"[51] (as Garnett styled it), but both are grounded, in the passage cited from "Youth," in what Conrad himself described as the "feat of memory" (*Y*, xi) by which Marlow renders a version of Conrad's experience on board the *Palestine*. The problem of memory here is what Jameson ascribes to the relation between ideology and form—the relation between the work of seafaring represented by the narrative and the labor of writing itself. Jameson's formulation—"the sea is both a strategy of containment and a place of real business"—usefully foregrounds an apparently trivial pun on the word *passage*—the sea passage, the passage of literature—whose ambiguity of reference turns the autonomy of the modernist text toward a linguistic and literary problem of cultural memory. Any descriptive sea passage, such as the one Ford cites from "Youth," can be read as a mimetic representation of Conrad's experiences as a sailor or as a self-referential exercise in style. Recognizing that each passage is both at once, the problem of memory presented by the Conradian passage is the difficulty of determining which takes priority over the other.

"Youth: A Narrative" is perhaps the most economical of all Conrad's stories in its ability to make the sea passage stage the problem of remembering and forgetting of older literary tropes of sea journeys. In this elementary exercise in how "narrative" displaces the object ("youth") it seeks to retrieve in memory, Conrad is able to turn his own experience aboard the *Palestine* into Marlow's account of the *Judea*'s doomed efforts to reach Bangkok before its burning cargo of coal entirely consumes both itself and the ship. Less important than the displacement of Conrad's own personal experiences is the displacement of cultural memory enacted in Marlow's narrative performance. Registered in a pattern of splitting names in two, beginning with Marlow's name itself ("Marlow, or at least I think that's how he spelled his name") and extending to a string of names referred to in Marlow's yarn telling ("Wilmer, Wilcox—some name like that"; "his name was Mahon but he insisted that it should be pronounced Mann"; "a woman's name, Miranda or Melissa—or some such thing"), this displacement of names is most fully realized in the "words written" on the stern of the ship—"*Judea*. London. Do or Die" (*Y*, 12)—whose legend will disappear as the ship sinks: "The unconsumed stern was the last to sink; but the paint had gone, had cracked, had peeled off, and there were no letters, there was no word, no stubborn device that was like her soul, to flash at the rising sun her creed and her name" (*Y*, 35). The split already written into the ship's legend—"*Judea*" and "London"—anticipates the way the story rehearses Marlow's simple memory of lost "youth," his first glimpse of "the East," as a constitutive problem of cultural and historical memory. The Marlow of "Youth" enables Conrad to narrate this as a specifically English problem of remembering and forgetting of cultural origins.

Marlow as narrator enables Conrad, too, to reformulate the problem of a specifically Malay cultural memory that defined the projected novel sequence with which Conrad began his literary career (as discussed in the previous chapter). "Youth" deliberately simplifies the geographical and cultural details with which Conrad had evoked the imagined Malay communities of the Borneo settings of *Almayer's Folly* and *An Outcast of the Islands*. All such details are elided from the memory of the "East" to which Marlow arrives at the end of the story. The vagueness of "Youth's" Malay setting, especially by contrast to the wealth of geographical, cultural, and historical references about the entire Malay Archipelago given in "Karain: A Memory" (published the year before "Youth") might in part be attributed to Conrad's conscious adjustment to an English readership unable to distinguish between the Dutch-controlled island Malay settings of Conrad's fiction and the British-controlled areas of peninsular Malaysia, including Singapore and the Straits Settlements. Conrad's very first literary award (The Academy's award for *Tales of Unrest*) praised Conrad (citing a passage from "Karain: A Memory") for having "annexed the Malay Peninsula for us."[52] The family romance of Conrad's Malay fiction had, from the start, played on the difference between British and Dutch interests in the Malay Archipelago—the English Lingard is a father figure for both Almayer and Willems, the two Dutch "outcasts" of the "islands." Whereas the romance of Conrad's Malay trilogy looked back to an earlier historical moment before the consolidation of separate British and Dutch spheres of territorial control, the shift in Conrad's investment in a romance of Malay politics represented by "Youth's" simplification may in part be explained in terms of the consolidation of those territorial Dutch and British colonial differences that would ultimately produce the postcolonial nation-states of Indonesia and Malaysia.

Marlow's ironic perspective resolves the problem of historical vision on which the Lingard trilogy hinges by enacting a deliberate forgetting of the piratical seafaring ethos that is the shared, contested romance of Malay and English history on which the Malay trilogy is premised. At the same time, the controlled irony of Marlow's distortion of cultural memory redistributes the distinctive features of the earlier family romance of Malay politics in other ways. The "differend" of a contested English and Malay genealogy, which we traced in the previous chapter's reading of the Malay trilogy, gets reinscribed as Marlow's more specifically English problem of remembering and forgetting. The "feat of memory" with which Conrad is able to retell the story of his own shipwreck arrival at Bangka involves a studied ambiguity over whether Marlow arrives in Dutch-controlled or British-controlled Malay territory. This geographical difference inscribes an important "differend" into the ambiguous vagueness of Marlow's "East" that is matched in the linguistic register of the voice that, mistaking Marlow's boat for a shore boat, curses him with "outlandish, angry words, mixed with words and even whole sentences of good English, less strange but even more surprising" (*Y*, 39).

This last example momentarily calls attention to the multilinguistic diversity and multiracial conflict involved in the colonial contest over Malay waters, but it is just this "heteroglossia" and interracial contact that Conrad organizes into what Guerard described as the "surface charm"[53] of "Youth." In an earlier rehearsal of this problem of remembering and forgetting Malay culture and history, "Karain: A Memory," Conrad thematizes this as the differend of the "memory" in the subtitle—as I have explored (repeatedly) elsewhere, this presents a fundamental ambiguity of cultural and historical memory, referring both to the memory of the English narrator (a precursor of Marlow) and that of the title character, Karain, haunted by a memory of betrayal, guilt, and exile, narrated as the story's tale within a tale.[54] If Conrad's entire career might be described as a turning away from the Lingard trilogy's investment in Malay culture and history, this forgetting of Malay history only serves to inscribe the Malay "differend" all the more powerfully into the generating features of the Conradian narrative. So, in the title of *Lord Jim*, the English "Lord" is premised on an ultimately unfathomable differend over the linguistic translation from the Malay *tuan*.

The economy of forgetting with which Conrad turns to Marlow to condense and displace the geographical and historical coordinates of the Malay trilogy is repeated, albeit within the Ford-ian symbolic economy, in the distortion of memory introduced by Ford's addition of an *e* to the spelling of Marlow's name. This combines the distinction of a French linguistic-literary ideal with the literary capital implied by an allusion to Christopher Marlowe.

If Ford's distorted spelling is in some respects licensed by the text of "Youth" itself, it adds the claim of a literary affinity, or lineage, that seems to belong much more to Ford's biographical fantasy than to the Conradian passages he repeatedly cites. This fantasy is improvised early in the *Remembrance,* in a quite deliberate distortion of impressionist biography: "He was a gentleman-adventurer who had sailed with Drake. Elizabethan: it was that that he was."[55] This fantasy is itself a repetition of the fantasy developed in his 1911 essay for *The English Review:* "I have thought very often that Conrad is an Elizabethan."[56] If in this earlier essay Ford spells Conrad's Marlow correctly, that is perhaps because the association with his Elizabethan literary namesake is made explicit, reinforced with pastiche quotations that graft Conrad onto Marlowe in a miniature fantasy of literary lineage:

> And can you not imagine one of [Conrad's] Arab sheiks, or Marlow, that tremendous old man of the sea, or even the teacher-narrator of *Under Western Eyes,* gazing upon the face of some woman who had caused a great deal of trouble in some obscure quarter of the world and saying reflectively: "Was that the face that launched a thousand ships and burned the palm leaf towns of Parabang?"[57]

Ford's later memorial to Conrad in *the transatlantic review* might be read as a repetition on a larger scale of this distorted pastiche quotation from Marlowe's *Doctor Faustus.* To some extent, moreover, the repetitive formation of English modernism might be revealed in this Ford-ian distortion of memory, begun in the pages of *The English Review* (begun, indeed, as a pastiche of Conrad's own reminiscences in the first issues of *The English Review*) and repeated in the pages of *the transatlantic review.* It encodes a distorted genealogy of cultural memory that repeats, albeit with Fordian variations, the distorted genealogy of cultural memory implicit already in Marlow's narrative of Conrad's text.

Above all, Ford's pastiche attempts to recapitulate the imaginative investment Conrad's fiction places in Malay culture. Relocating the Helen of Marlowe's *Doctor Faustus* to "the palm leaf towns of Parabang" Ford performs a daring, if not entirely successful, flight of critical fancy in attempting to weave the Malay setting of Conrad's fiction into an established English literary lineage. Woolf's allusion to Helen is much more successful in capturing and criticizing the "beauty" of Conrad's prose because of the twist with which she turns Helen's classical image into the problem the reader faces: "One opens his pages and feels as Helen must have felt when she looked in her glass." But Woolf's image, though also invested in the question of reading genealogies of modern cultural memory, excludes the investment in Malay culture that Ford's fantasy attempts to remember, in however distorted a form (as, for example, in the distorted English pronunciation of the Malay place name, Palembang—"Parabang").

The 1924 *Remembrance* elaborates more fully on this cultural investment, turning an improvised fantasy of gold prospecting in "Palembang" (now spelled in the standard way) into an extended analogy for his collaboration with Conrad:

> Think of setting out from Stamford-le-Hope, a safe harbour where at least there was contact with ships, estuaries, tideways, islands, into an unknown hinterland of savage and unknown populations, of bare downs, out of sight of the refuge of the sea, to persuade an unknown wielder of the pen, the finest stylist in England, to surrender his liberty to a sailing partnership—to surrender too his glamorous "subject," for all the world as if you had adventured into the hinterlands behind Palembang to ask some one only just known to give up to you for joint working the secret of one of those mysterious creeks where gold is found. An adventure like that of "Victory" itself.... And then to insult the owner of the creek with groans, sighs, O God's, contortions.[58]

The analogy works, on a number of levels, as a pastiche of Conrad. Suggesting the extended comparison between the Romans in Britain and Europeans in Africa from the beginning of "Heart of Darkness," it also alludes to that core plot element of the Malay, or Lingard trilogy, whereby Lingard's discovery of gold prospects in a Borneo (rather than a Sumatran) river crystallizes a deluded set of partnerships. Ford's displacement of the Bornean onto a Sumatran setting, and his reference to *Victory* rather than the Lingard trilogy, belong to the impressionist distortion and pastiche, effectively condensing an array of allusions to Conrad's work into the scene of Ford's own unique Conradian Malay fantasy. As with the misspelling of Marlow, Ford's composite portrait of Conrad as an Elizabethan "gentleman-adventurer" prospecting in Palembang effects a temporal-historical distortion that evokes an economy of modernist collaboration tied to a history of modern European economic and political exploitation.

The analogy is extended throughout the *Remembrance* fusing together an account of Ford's collaboration with Conrad and commenting on the Malay themes that preoccupied Conrad throughout his career. In the process, Ford offers a distorted, but nonetheless revealing reflection on the problematic memory of Malay culture and history in Conrad's work itself. Although Ford's distorted memory in many respects erases the specificity of Conrad's Malay fiction, in other respects Ford's distortions foreground the significance of the Malay settings. So, for example, Ford's distorted memory of Conrad inscribing the "first words" of *Almayer's Folly* into the "flyleaves and margins" of *Madame Bovary* foregrounds a linguistic association not only between the French of Flaubert and the English of Conrad's modernism but also the Malay language that frames the "first words" of *Almayer's Folly* ("Kaspar! Makan!").

In particular, Ford draws on the theme of cross-cultural betrayal that runs through many of Conrad's Malay tales. Drawing attention to a moment when he let down Conrad during their collaboration on *Romance*, Ford writes "So the writer failed Conrad as any other King Tom always fails any Malay Prince."[59] The vagueness of the reference to "any" King Tom or Malay Prince suggests a blurring of different plots. Ford might be referring to the situation of *Almayer's Folly* or to that of *The Rescue*. Lingard's failure to back up his political investment in Malay plots constitutes the core theme of the trilogy; but a similar motif of betrayal runs through *Lord Jim*. Heavily invested in the motif of memory itself, this English betrayal of Malay allies structures Conrad's entire career around the problem of finishing the Lingard trilogy. Implicit in the very first work, this thematic problem of the memory of English investments in Malay history, culture, and politics defines also the key stages of Conrad's adjustment of his language, style, and narrative form, as illustrated most notably by "Karain: A Memory" and "Youth: A Narrative."

Ford also associates the English betrayal of Malay allies with Conrad's own betrayal of the principles of French modernist "Absolute Prose." Toward the end of the memorial, Ford characterizes Conrad's "conquest of a language" (and, implicitly, his "conspiracy against a literature") as a betrayal:

> In later years Conrad achieved a certain fluency and a great limpidity of language. He then regretted that for him all the romance of writing was gone.... [H]e made tributes to the glory of the English language, by implication contemning the tongue that Flaubert used. This struck the writer, at that time in a state of exhausted depression, as unforgivable—as the very betrayal of Dain by Tom Lingard.... Perhaps it was that.[60]

Ford is not entirely precise about when Conrad betrayed the shared goal of writing "Absolute Prose" modeled on French modernist ideals, but that lack of precision is matched by the analogy to Tom Lingard's betrayal of "Dain," which impressionistically confuses the Balinese prince, Dain Maroola, of *Almayer's Folly* (whom Lingard betrays only at a remove) with the Buginese-Malay prince Hassim, of *The Rescue*, and perhaps also the Dain Waris of *Lord Jim*. The confusion may be intended to cover over the fact that Conrad had, early on, made "tributes to the glory of the English language"; although it is also worth noting that those "tributes" may be traced back to the reminiscences Conrad wrote for *The English Review*, and more especially to the final installment, which marked the breakup with Ford that accompanied Ford's loss of managerial control over the *Review* itself. Within the economy of

Ford's characteristically distorted memory of this "betrayal," however, what is especially revealing is the investment placed on linking the modernist prestige of Flaubert's "tongue" with the political romance of Conrad's Malay characters. This suggests an underlying connection between the linguistic and literary capital of French and the symbolic capital of Malay. Each constitutes, as it were, the conspiratorial matrix behind that "conquest of a language" and "conspiracy against a literature" by which Conrad, in Ford's eyes, forges a new English modernism.

Here, Ford's *Remembrance* might be seen again to repeat Conrad's *A Personal Record*. In the Author's Note, Conrad, too, links the linguistic significance of French to the importance of his imaginative investment in Malay history and culture. Conrad devotes the first part of the Note to correcting the "erroneous" "impression of my having exercised a choice between the two languages, French and English, both foreign to me" (*PR*, iii). The lengthy denial that he "exercised a deliberate choice between French and English"—in many ways an extension of the circuitous evasion of autobiography that characterizes all of Conrad's reminiscences—is nonetheless revealing in the way it stages this correction as a mock diplomatic standoff between himself and Sir High Clifford, the former administrator and future Governor of Britain's Malay territories. Although the dispute is clearly presented as a dispute between friends, the mock diplomatic language performs a scene of contest with colonial authority that simultaneously regulates a difference between English and French and dramatizes a difference between Clifford's and Conrad's "knowledge" of Malays. It is a particularly striking instance of the "differend" of a shared and contested English and Malay history. Although the language of diplomatic correction Conrad adopts suggests precisely the legal resolution of differences—"what in diplomatic language is called 'rectification'" (*PR*, v)—the "rectification" of Clifford's comment about Conrad's choice of French over English is preceded by a difference not so easily resolved by the (simultaneously French and English) word *rectification*—namely, the difference between Clifford's and Conrad's respective claims to "knowledge" about Malays. The particular definition of *rectification*[61] as a term used to redefine territorial boundaries following political disputes is especially interesting in light of the territorial difference between the region of Clifford's administrative authority—the British controlled Malay settlements ("Malaysia")—and the Dutch East Indies territories in which almost all of Conrad's Malay fiction is set. This is precisely the difference that "Youth" deliberately masks in omitting to name the place of Marlow's arrival. It is also a part of the deliberate poetics of misnaming and displacement by which all of Conrad's work enacts a remembering and forgetting of the geography, history, and politics of its imagined Malay communities.[62]

Consecrating English modernism around the memory of Conrad, Ford repeats this fundamental problem of remembering and forgetting—the "differend" of Conrad's Malay cultural memory—that defines the overall trajectory of Conrad's career. Ford repeats this, moreover, as the problem of English modernist memory inherent in the practice of citing literary passages of "Absolute Prose." The linguistic and literary capital of a French modernist ideal written into Conrad's search for *le mot juste* inscribes into each passage of Conrad's English prose a symbolic economy of remembering and forgetting Malay culture and history.

Jean Rhys and the Transatlantic Modernism of Ford's *the transatlantic review*

What Ford does with the colonial scene of Conrad's Malay settings is matched, in a number of respects, by his promotion of Rhys, first in the pages of *the transatlantic review* and then in his introduction to her first collection of stories, *The Left Bank and Other Stories*. While Conrad's Malay settings constitute a defining ambiguity in Ford's memory of Conrad's English modernism, Rhys's Caribbean background plays an analogous role in Ford's promotion of her place within the new "transatlantic" coordinates of the modernist program taking shape in *the transatlantic review*. Initially, Ford appears unable to situate Rhys within the cultural horizons of *the transatlantic review*. When she is first introduced by the pseudonym "Jean Rhys" in Ford's editorial, her name is the only name not prefaced by the title "Miss," "Mrs," or "Mr." Whether accidental, whether the result of uncertainty about her marital status, or whether some unconscious expression of Ford's feelings about her, the name stands out. Later in the same editorial, her name does not figure at all in Ford's descriptions about the cultural coordinates of the largely American "new movement" of young writers published in the review.

Rhys scholars have often faulted Ford for misrecognizing Rhys's Caribbean background[63]—most notably, in finding a combined class and racial bias in Ford's comment, in his Preface to her first collection of stories, that "coming from the Antilles," she has "a terrifying insight and a terrific—an almost lurid!—passion for stating the case of the underdog."[64] Yet Ford's difficulty in placing Rhys symptomizes a question of cultural perspective written into the "transatlantic" title of the review. Ford would later attempt to describe the international community of artists descending on him in Paris as "like a riot in the Tower of Babel"—"The beings that bore down on me... were of the most unimaginable colours, races and tongues. There were at least two Japanese, two negroes—one of whom had a real literary talent—a Mexican vaquero in costume,

Finns, Swedes, French, Rumanians."[65] From this heterogeneity of cultural perspectives, Ford would repeatedly forge a much more narrowly articulated Anglo-American transatlantic community of writers—as when he writes, in the editorial just mentioned, of a movement stirring "all over the Anglo Saxon World from the West Middle West of the United States to the West Middle West of the London suburbs."[66]

Ford's "transatlantic" modernism thus seems to register a blindness to the black Atlantic and Creole modernisms traced by critics such as Antonio Benítez-Rojo, Édouard Glissant, and Paul Gilroy, among others. To the extent that Ford's difficulty in placing Jean Rhys's "Antillean" background confirms such a view, it nonetheless also emphasizes the way Ford's "transatlantic" modernism might retrospectively be understood as having crystallized around just such a blind spot. Like that "dark, blind-spot on the brain" by which Ford characterizes his amnesia about the circumstances of his collaboration with Conrad over *The Nature of a Crime*, Ford's "transatlantic" designation foregrounds an ambiguous priority of cultural memory. On the one hand, Ford's Anglo-American transatlantic modernism has not yet recognized in Rhys those transatlantic Creole and Afro-Caribbean crossings that will surface in *Wide Sargasso Sea*. On the other hand, it seems to have forgotten the coordinates of his own collaborative affair with Conrad over *Romance*. Rather than accusing Ford of distorting the cultural memory of "transatlantic" modernism, I want to suggest Ford here provides a diagnosis of the symbolic economy of English modernism. Ford's faulty memory registers the faultlines between overlapping formations of transnational modernism.

"Vienne," the story published in *the transatlantic review* under the inaugural pseudonym, Jean Rhys, provides a revealing first glimpse of that literary style, linguistic voice, and cultural perspective we now associate with the Rhys of *Wide Sargasso Sea*. One thing that stands out, by contrast to the transatlantic cultural crossings that have made *Wide Sargasso Sea* so paradigmatic a postcolonial text since its publication in 1966, is the lack of virtually any trace of a Caribbean, West Indian cultural perspective informing the story as it appeared in 1924. The story offers three short sketches of life in Vienna around 1921, and is based on Rhys's own experience of living in Vienna while her husband, Jean Lenglet, was secretary to the Japanese delegation of the Interallied Commission overseeing the disarmament of Austria. "Vienne" recalls the postwar milieu of a city that had once been the capital of the Austro-Hungarian Empire. The story's international perspective is in this respect typical of the European cosmopolitanism that informs Ford's *transatlantic review*. The title foregrounds a cosmopolitan English "French" over an elided Austrian German cultural-historical perspective ("Vienne" gets translated, in the second sentence, into "Vienna," but the German Wien is elided altogether). Rhys's title, and the imagined community it momentarily evokes, exemplifies the linguistic milieu of Ford's review, which was based in Paris and which sought to internationalize what Ford called the "Anglo-Saxondom" of his English-speaking American and British readership. With rather striking linguistic precision, moreover, Rhys's "Vienne" gives literary form to the postwar bankruptcy of European financial and cultural capital that preoccupied so many transatlantic modernists like Pound, Eliot, and Joyce.

Here, too, is a paradigmatic modernist riddle of cultural memory. From the title's French name, "Vienne," unfolds an impressionistic personal remembrance of things past:

> Funny how it's slipped away, Vienne. Nothing left but a few snapshots—
> Not a friend, not a pretty frock—nothing left of Vienna.[67]

The disproportion between the scale of personal and historical loss registered in that "nothing left of Vienna" is calibrated through the effect of translating "Vienne" into "Vienna." What emerges from the ever so slight difference produced in this translation effect is an unexpected priority of cultural memory that gives shape to the story's narrative perspective: nostalgically attached to personal memories of postwar Vienna in 1921, the narrative voice seems to know nothing of an older Vienna—which is nonetheless all the more powerfully evoked. It remains ultimately ambiguous which is the more important register of cultural memory, the personal memory of Vienna in 1921, or the historical memory of the old cultural capital of prewar Central Europe.

The question of identity embedded in this first story's problem of cultural memory anticipates the way Rhys's early stories and novels develop miniature studies in the cultural capital of modernist memory. One of the striking things about Rhys's first published story is the linguistic economy with which it produces a distinctively *English* accent. This linguistic economy might be reduced to the effect of two words: *dam*—as in the phrases "a dam good judge"; and "It was dam cold for golf"; and *rum*—as in "Married to a barber. Rum"; and "a rum Viennese." Mixing cosmopolitan French phrases ("She gave me the *songe bleu*") with such colloquial English traits, Rhys creates a narrative perspective that captures a crisis in European consciousness in the naïve accents of an English voice. Such translation effects recall the practice of translating between English and French that Ford discusses in his remembrance of Conrad. It was just this practice of translation that formed the basis of the "affair" of Rhys's apprenticeship with Ford.[68]

Rhys's story creates its English narrative voice through a deliberately displaced deployment of French, as is thematized in the middle vignette (which was deleted from all later versions of the story): "He talked French, and though my French was improving there were blanks."[69] "Blanks" aptly describes the gap between French and English produced by the translation work of style Ford fostered in Conrad and Rhys—indeed, all too aptly, since the word's association, through the French, with "whiteness" makes it an overdetermined word, one that is charged with a problem of racial identity.[70] One need only think of the Conradian "blank spaces" on the map; or the resonance of the word in Rhys's *Wide Sargasso Sea*. This is not to say that the translation work of Ford's collaborative affairs with Conrad and Rhys is simply a matter of white racial identity. Whiteness, rather, is inscribed around a similar ambiguity of cultural memory as that inscribed in Rhys's "Vienne." The relation between Francophone and Anglophone linguistic registers, for both Conrad and Rhys, always traverses a problem of white racial identity (most evident in the French Belgian context of Conrad's "Heart of Darkness" and the Creole West Indian context Rhys's *Wide Sargasso Sea*); but "whiteness" constitutes a loss of identity, or amnesia, from which then proceeds the narrative remembrance of things lost: in larger narrative terms, for Conrad the rescue work of searching for a lost European cultural identity in the Malay Archipelago; for Rhys the remembrance of a lost Creole or Caribbean past.[71]

The economy with which Rhys uses English words invites a reconsideration of the way Ford describes his collaboration with Conrad in search of *le mot juste*. The two words *dam* and *rum*, from "Vienne," are very different from the words *azure* and *serene*, over which Conrad and Ford agonized. But their effect, as markers of an English accent, resolves what Ford presents in the *Remembrance* as the Conradian problem with English—the fact that "no English word is a word...no English word has clean edges....Thus, all English prose is blurred."[72] This predicament of English (as much a predicament of linguistic as of literary capital) became the principle by which Ford measured elsewhere, on the one hand, the discipline of Hemingway's prose (in overcoming that "curse of English prose...that English words have double effects"[73]) and, at another extreme, the "huge prodigality" of Joyce's ability to make good on "the associations that, like burrs, cling undetachable to every English word."[74] Ford's lengthy account of Conrad's translation work on the word *azure* is revealing, in this respect, because, although he at first seems to be suggesting that Conrad sought the discipline of a Hemingway ("his whole endeavour was given to using only such words as are found in the normal English vernacular"[75]), the word *azure* cannot, after all, be detached from those Joycean associative "burrs" conveyed in Ford's mock transposition of their different pronunciations.

The economy with which Rhys's "Vienne" creates the English accent of its narrative voice through a displacement of French ("blanks") and a foregrounding of singular English words (*dam* and *rum*) suggests a studied distance from standard English that might, in part, be a result of the elocution lessons she took at the Royal Academy of Dramatic Art.[76] This distance from standard English, however, has an important, established place within the development of English modernism. As Hugh Kenner points out in *The Pound Era*, and as Michael North has elaborated more recently in *The Dialect of Modernism*, the formation of Anglo-American modernism, from the 1880s to the 1920s, coincides with the making of the *O.E.D.*, that vast collaborative undertaking to produce a New English Dictionary on Historical Principles that might stabilize, within historical context, the contemporary meaning of English words.[77]

Following the work of Tony Crowley and others, North has shown how the *O.E.D.* took shape around a set of intense debates (both in England and in America) over "standard English," debates that coincide with the career of Joseph Conrad. The linguistic capital of English constitutes the shared, if contested field of collaborative work occupied by the modernist projects of Ford, Conrad, Rhys, and the *O.E.D.* collaborators. This collaborative work of agonizing over English words emphasizes the way the "Englishness" of English words acquires the kind of ambiguous priority of cultural memory written into the English word *Vienna* in Rhys's "Vienne." So, the word *rum* might, after all, signal the Caribbean perspective I earlier suggested was almost wholly absent in this story. To the extent that we might hear a West Indian association in the word, however, this accentuates the peculiar Englishness of the word all the more, implying a difference between the story's English narrative voice and whatever Caribbean cultural perspective we might ascribe to its author—whose ear might well be attuned to some of the etymological ironies of the English word. Might Rhys have known of the disagreements amongst etymologists over whether the word *rum* originated in the West or the East Indies?[78]

Azure offers a still more revealing case. Showing an apparent colonial bias, the *O.E.D.* defines the word as "*originally*" meaning "of a deep intense blue" and "*now* usually of a soft clear bright blue, as in the sky of our more northern latitudes." This colonial bias of presuming a readership identifying with "our more northern latitudes" introduces a curious distortion into the very "historical principles" on which the *O.E.D.* sought to trace the evolution of the English language. Ford's lengthy discussion of Conrad's use of the word may do little to specify whether Conrad's *azure* carries an archaic or a contemporary semantic charge—whether, in the terms of the *O.E.D.*, it is the word used to describe the sky of "our more northern latitudes" or the sky of, as it were, "their" more southern latitudes. The passage from "Youth" that Ford cites from memory—indeed, the whole narrative passage of the *Judea*'s English crew from

London to the "East"—stages the process of remembering and forgetting of cultural origins that regulates the use, poetic or vernacular, of English words. *Azure*—whose etymology the *O.E.D.* traces back to a characteristically mistaken transposition from the Arabic, metonymically linked to "lapis lazuli"—posits, in a word, the problematic priority of European cultural memory that is rehearsed over the course of "Youth: A Narrative": does Marlow's journey recall, or obliterate the signs of Europe's old Orientalist obsessions? Rhys repeats this problematic ambiguity of "English" cultural and historical memory with still more effective linguistic economy.

At stake in Ford's collaborative affairs with Conrad and Rhys is the linguistic capital of "English," along with the cultural capital of "Englishness"—both of which are evoked in the name of Ford's *English Review* (whose title Ford credited to Conrad's "Youth"ful sense of ironic naming[79]), in the "transatlantic" coordinates of *the transatlantic review*, and in Ford's distorted memory of Conrad's Malay and Rhys's Caribbean settings. In his Preface to the collection of short stories, *The Left Bank*, Ford writes about Rhys's rejection of his own editorial advice:

> I tried—for I am for ever meddling with the young!—very hard to induce the author of the *Left Bank* to introduce some sort of topography of that region [i.e., the "Left Bank" of Paris], bit by bit, into her sketches—in the cunning way in which it would have been done by Flaubert or Maupassant, or by Mr Conrad 'getting in' the East in innumerable short stories from *Almayer* to the *Rescue*. ... But would she do it? No! With cold deliberation, once her attention was called to the matter, she eliminated even such two or three words of descriptive matter as had crept into her work.[80]

Couched in that characteristic contrast between an older generation of modernists and the newer generation (Rhys is here classed as part of "French youth"), Ford's account suggestively links Rhys's rejection of the Conradian "descriptive passage" to a problem of "topography." Ford continues, as follows, quoting from one of three stories in *The Left Bank* that refer to the Antilles, "Mixing Cocktails," which is the only one of the three in which Rhys directly describes the scene of her Dominican childhood (and this is the only quotation Ford offers in his long introduction):

> So she hands you the Antilles with its sea and sky—"the loveliest, deepest sea in the world—the Caribbean!"—the effect of landscape on the emotions and passions of a child being so penetrative, but lets Montparnasse, or London, or Vienna go.[81]

As a judgment of Rhys's failure to evoke the "Left Bank" location of her stories, Ford's representation of Rhys is bound to look questionable. If one sees in this Ford's devaluation of Rhys's Caribbean background, then it reveals the Eurocentrism of Ford's "transatlantic" modernism. If, by contrast, one sees in this Ford's overvaluation of an exotic "Antillean" perspective, then it reveals the Eurocentrism of Ford's Anglo-American primitivist modernism. It is possible, though, to see in Ford's impressionist reading of Rhys's prose a logic of misrecognized cultural backgrounds that makes Ford precisely the figure able to lodge both Conrad and Rhys at the heart of "English" and "transatlantic" modernism.

Although Ford misquotes the passage from "Mixing Cocktails," his recollection of the passage from memory nonetheless reveals a closer attention to the logic of Rhys's story than one might initially imagine. Here, again, Ford's practice of citing passages from memory constitutes a revealing mode of modernist critical and creative practice. Ford's citation of the passage from Rhys reiterates the double translation effect of Rhys's own naming of the region that Ford identifies as the "Antilles." While in the two stories that precede and follow "Mixing Cocktails," Rhys also uses the French name "the Antilles," in "Mixing Cocktails" itself—the story from which Ford quotes—the region is named "the West Indies." This English translation of "the Antilles" is articulated in the voice of the narrator's "English aunt": "The English aunt gazes and exclaims at intervals: 'The colours...How exquisite!...Extraordinary that so few people should visit the West Indies....That *sea*....Could anything be more lovely?'" Immediately following this is the passage Ford (mis)quotes, in which another name—the Caribbean—is used in counterpoint to the touristic perspective of the "English aunt": "It is a purple sea with a sky to match it. The Caribbean. The deepest, the loveliest in the world" (CS, 37).

Ford's memory of this passage displaces the story's English articulation of "the West Indies," but this calls attention to a split between the Francophone and Anglophone registers of "the Antilles" and "the Caribbean" that captures a creolizing logic underwriting the fundamental problem of memory posed by the story.[82] Moreover, in the context of the collection of stories as a whole, the problem of the first-person narrator's childhood memory of the "Antilles" of times past articulates, as a creolizing Francophone/Anglophone split, the problematic priority of cultural memory registered in the difference between *Vienne* and *Vienna*, the French and English names for the capital city of a lost European past. Is Rhys's reading of the cultural capital of Europe premised on a prior Creole linguistic, literary, and cultural consciousness, or is that Creole consciousness shaped by the capital cities of Europe? Legible already in the title of the early story "Again the Antilles," this problematic priority of Creole memory comes to shape the overall trajectory of Rhys's work and the way it has been critically received.

Fittingly, some of the memories that shaped the successive versions "Vienne" (in 1924, expanded for the 1927 publication of *The Left Bank*)[83] appear in the late, fragmentary story "Temps Perdi" (1968), which attempts to fit together memories of a life in England and Vienna and Rhys's visit to Dominica during the 1930s. Explaining the name of the estate Temps Perdi, she writes "'Temps Perdi' is Creole patois and does not mean, poetically, lost or forgotten time, but, matter-of-factly, wasted time, lost labour" (*CS*, 267). Characteristically, this "Creole patois" definition complicates any reading, even as it invites such a reading, of Rhys's career as a writerly search for a lost Caribbean space of childhood. In the logic of Ford's misrecognition of Rhys's Caribbean perspective, Ford lays the groundwork for a reading of Rhys's search for "Caribbean" things past. Something similar might be said for the logic of Ford's misrecognition of Conrad's Malay perspective. In each case, Ford's impressionist reading enacts a problem of naming, misrecognized cultural backgrounds, and cultural memory embodied in the "transatlantic" and "English" affiliations of his two reviews. This problem of memory, inscribed in each individual passage of literature as a characteristic modernist practice of citation, defines the repetitive formation of English modernism.

Reading Modernist Memory

Ford Madox Ford represents for English modernism, then, a sort of objective correlative for the memory of Europe's lost cultural capital and the repeated attempt to shore up its fragments in the symbolic economy of "Absolute Prose." This Fordian economy of mismanaged cultural capital is what Rhys herself once captured, impressionistically, in her cubist portrait of Ford as the fictional Heidler from *Quartet*: "Marya thought: 'He looks exactly like a picture of Queen Victoria'" (*Q*, 114). Rhys's distorted caricature of Ford as Heidler might provide a counterpart to Ford's caricature memory of Conrad as "*homo europeaus sapiens*, attuned to the late sixteenth century."[84] Within the context of *Quartet*, this image makes sense as much as a problem of pictoral, realist perspective, as a problem of cultural capital. The issue it raises—the imposture of "English"ness, as mediated through the reading of a grotesquely distorted icon of British imperial sovereignty—forms a revealing counterpoint to the artistic, historical, and cultural distortion of Ford's portrait of Conrad as Elizabethan gentleman adventurer. Just as Ford's portrait captures a certain truth about Conrad's narrative aims and methods—a truth condensed in the way Ford spells Conrad's Marlow "Marlowe"—Rhys's oblique literary portrait of Ford captures a truth about those "English" cultural claims Ford made for his own literary endeavors.

Rereading the symbolic economy of Ford's English modernism from the perspective of Rhys's miniature studies in reading modernist memory, we might now return to consider how the Conrad passage Rhys cites in *After Leaving Mr. Mackenzie* situates the linguistic and literary coordinates of the Ford-ian field of English modernism. Like those other miniature studies, its place in the novel suggests a studied framing of the problem of reading, but here focused on the specifically literary passage. The passage of text is read as if it were an act like looking into a mirror, Norah seeing her own "slavery" in the description of a "slave" in Conrad's novel:

> She picked up the book lying on her bed-table—*Almayer's Folly*—and had begun to read:
>> The slave had no hope, and knew of no change. She knew of no other sky, no other water, no other forest, no other world, no other life. She had no wish, no hope, no love.... The absence of pain and hunger was her happiness, and when she felt unhappy she was tired, more than usual, after the day's labour.
>
> Then she had got up and looked at herself in the glass. (*AL*, 103)

This act of reading stands in contrast to the problem of reading with which the main character, Julia, has been introduced at the very outset of the novel. Julia's unsettled state of mind (after having "parted from Mr. Mackenzie" as it is put in the first line, echoing the novel's title) is established in her relation to the interior furnishings of her Paris hotel room, whose descriptive features get reorganized around her response to "an unframed oil-painting of a half empty bottle of red wine, a knife, and a piece of Gruyère cheese, signed 'J. Grykho, 1923.' It had probably been left in payment of a debt" (*AL*, 10). Julia's reading of this painting establishes a problem of realistic, or mimetic, representation as the premise for the novel's narrative interest (for example, in the significance of what happened "after leaving Mr. Mackenzie"). Her first reading of the painting is, as it were, literal: "Every object in the picture was slightly distorted and full of obscure meaning." Then, "unable to avoid looking at it," she cannot decide whether it is any "good"—establishing a standard of aesthetic judgment on which our own reading of interiority (both interiority of social space and of psychological identity) depends:

> But really she hated the picture. It shared, with the colour of the plush sofa, a certain depressing quality. The picture and the sofa were linked in her mind. The picture was more alarming in its perversion and the sofa the more dismal. The picture stood for the idea, the spirit, and the sofa stood for the act. (*AL*, 11)

This is a characteristic example of the way Rhys's narratives are premised on a problem of reading modernism. Set against the later instance of Julia's sister's reading of Conrad, this initial reading of the economic field of artistic modernism in Paris in the 1920s (the "Left Bank" scene of her first collection of stories) frames, in advance, around the French modernist field of Bourdieu's analysis, a literary field of English modernism designated by the passage from Conrad's *Almayer's Folly*.

In what sense, then, does this contrast between the French scene of Julia's reading of the painting and Norah's reading of the Conradian passage reproduce the split Francophone/Anglophone axis that organizes so much of her work around the problematic priority of a Creole memory? In fact, the citation from Conrad is organized around a problem of memory, and specifically the failing memory of the mother. Shortly after this passage, Julia will be described as "remembering the time when she had woven innumerable romances about her mother's childhood in South America" (*AL*, 105). Is this a condensed reference to the Creole family romance of Jean Rhys's own childhood memories?

The problem of memory, for Julia—which at this moment in the narrative gets figured around the crisis of her mother's imminent death, suggesting the entire problem of the narrative be considered as a case study of mourning or melancholia—is fundamental for organizing the ambiguity of the narrative's coordinates around a loss that at first seems to be figured as the loss of dependence on a man, the Mr. Mackenzie of the title. The ambiguity of the title is only fully revealed at the end of the novel, when Julia meets Mr. Mackenzie one final time, suggesting that the title might signal either that Julia never "gets over" the affair with Mr. Mackenzie, or that the narrative enacts the process by which she does "get over" that affair. The narrative's underlying concern is to delineate the ways in which the "affair" with Mr. Mackenzie was, from the very beginning, something rather different from the sort of sexual "affair" it is taken for. Put one way, the memory of that affair, and the compulsion to organize narrative in temporal relation to it, might be interpreted as the willed forgetting of something else: the death of the mother, the disintegration of the family, a loss of self. The narrative logic moves toward an articulation of all these problems as a constitutive temporal problem of memory—"The last time you were happy about nothing, the first time you were afraid about nothing. Which came first?" (*AL*, 160).

This problem of the priority of memories, for which the ambiguity of the title will become the organizing motif, is anticipated at the very beginning of the novel, in a passage that follows from, and further complicates the problem of reading outlined above:

> She found pleasure in memories, as an old woman might have done. Her mind was a confusion of memory and imagination. It was always places that she thought of, not people. She would lie thinking of the dark shadows of houses in a street white with sunshine; or of trees with slender black branches and young green leaves, like the trees of a London square in spring; or of a dark-purple sea, the sea of a chromo or of some tropical country that she had never seen. (*AL,* 12)

This last image—the description of a sea ("a dark-purple sea")—stands out in Rhys's work as a whole because it simultaneously recalls and displaces the strong autobiographical pull of her own Caribbean childhood memories of Dominica, present in three of her earliest stories ("Trio," "Mixing Cocktails," and "Again the Antilles" from *The Left Bank*), and predominant in her final, unfinished autobiography. As a marker of Julia Martin's indeterminate social background, the image consolidates that problem of reading with which her psychology and character is introduced: the imagined sea is robbed of any of that aura of authenticity ascribed to personal memory, once described as "the sea of a chromo" (that is, a chromolithograph), or of some "tropical country she had never seen." This antitrope of memory, as it were, anticipates the later fragmentary recollection of childhood once it is intimated that such a description might be an attempt to evoke not her own memory of place, but that of her mother's.

The memory of the mother, in *After Leaving Mr. Mackenzie*, is of course split between Julia and Norah, and it is perhaps for this reason that the cited passage from Conrad plays so interesting a role in the texture of the novel. It provides, indeed, a rather precise counterpart to Julia's image of the "dark-purple sea"—a descriptive passage, however, that is also a sort of antitrope of memory, or, more simply, the antitrope of trope: "She knew of *no other sky, no other water, no other forest, no other world, no other life*" (my emphasis). Again, simplifying the problem of Norah's reading of this passage a good deal, one might nonetheless argue that this passage is presented, in its reductive mimetic narcissism, as a reflection of Norah's willed refusal of any such "other" perspective—and that, mimetically, Norah's own self-consciousness identifies with this imagined "slave's" perspective as the zero point of perspective, as it were. In a sort of arrest and reversal of the Hegelian master–slave dialectic, Norah constitutes her white middle-class English sense of identity around this extreme representation of enslavement in a tropical country.

Rhys might be seen to offer a miniature reading of Conrad's tropical descriptions by singling out the passage that seems to embody the blindspot around which they are constituted. As an excerpt, a collage piece, the passage is framed as "literary"—as a piece of literature for reading (whether "light" or "serious" depends on the psychology of Norah, of course—and, recalling Bourdieu's point, translated into the English context, we might insist on the interdependence of both). It is in this sense, as the trope for literary description, that the passage marks an aesthetic certainty: a certainty of nonmemory around which then the problems of memory discussed above get articulated. If the Conrad passage might be taken as Rhys's own compulsion to repeat the formation of English modernism, it demonstrates the problematic priority of memory at the heart of that repetitive formation: a problematic priority of memory that reduplicates, in the reader's difficulty in prioritizing the relation between Julia's and Norah's perspectives, the questions of identity and identification rehearsed in the novel's hierarchy of reading effects. It is not simply a matter of the ambiguity as to whether Norah does or does not identify with the Siamese slave of Conrad's novel. Around that extreme arrest of the Hegelian dialectic, the passage organizes a multiplying set of *misrecognitions* of identity, all of which replicate the ambiguous priority of memory embedded in the narcissistic construction of a white middle-class English "reading" memory (of either sister)—whereby there is no certain *prior* experience, or memory, preceding the mass-mediated forms of modern representation (the "chromo"lithograph of a sea; the literary depiction of a slave's consciousness). The only certainty is the whiteness, or blankness, of memory itself. In this sense, then, Rhys offers, around the split perspectives of the two sisters and in the double negation of their memories of the mother, a reading of English modernism as the compulsion to repeat an impossibility of white middle-class English identity.

PART II

Creole Modernism

4

JEAN RHYS'S FRANCOPHONE ENGLISH AND THE CREOLE "IMPASSE" OF MODERNITY

In this chapter, I return to the problem posed by Jean Rhys's memory of Creole things past to consider how it illuminates a more general question about the creolization of modernism and modernity. What kind of priority is given to the cultural memory of a Creole linguistic and cultural past in Rhys's work? Is her work organized from the very first by an attempt to recapture a lost childhood sense of Creole identity, or does this only later, and notably with the writing of *Wide Sargasso Sea* in the late 1950s and 1960s, come to define the predicament that had faced the protagonists of her first four novels in the metropolitan capitals of London and Paris? This is, in part, a question of the changing meaning of the term *Creole* itself, which I consider in the next chapter. It is also, however, a problem informing the historical coordinates of modernism and modernity. To what extent is the English modernism we have traced in the previous chapter premised on a Creole modernism? Is the repetitive formation of the first also a reactive formation against the second? To what extent is European modernity premised on a linguistic and cultural process of "creolization" and transculturation?

To explore these questions, I examine here the last of Rhys's interwar novels, *Good Morning, Midnight* (1938), whose Parisian setting revisits the urban settings of her earlier work. Enabling a review of all of Rhys's work between 1924 and 1938 as an extended study of the streets and interiors of metropolitan modernity, *Good Morning, Midnight* also stands in revealing counterpoint to Walter Benjamin's extended study of European modernity in *The Arcades Project* (*Das Passagen-Werk*) begun in 1927 (the year Rhys's *The Left Bank and Other Stories* appeared) and remaining incomplete with his death in 1940. In *Good Morning, Midnight*, Rhys characterizes the dilemma of all her female protagonists and narrators as an "impasse." In its literal and its figurative meanings, this "impasse" also describes the problem of modernity Walter Benjamin grasped in the material history of the Parisian arcades—those streets turned into covered malls that constituted, for Benjamin, the historical embodiment of one era (the bourgeoisie housed in private interiors) dreaming the next (the masses turning private into public space). In examining the correspondence between each writer's genealogy of modernity, I argue that Benjamin's projected *Arcades Project* illuminates, and is illuminated by, the problematic place of a Creole perspective in Rhys's work from this period. The correspondence between the "impasse" of Rhys's Creole consciousness and the Benjaminian "standstill of dialectics" ("*Dialektik im Stillstand*")[1] reveals, in turn, I argue, the impossibility of white racial identity that constitutes the "blank"ness of memory and modernity we have already begun to trace in the repetitive formation of English modernism.

To develop this argument, I organize the chapter around a comparison between *Good Morning, Midnight* and Conrad's *The Shadow-Line* (1917), a novel from the later period of Conrad's writing career, in which he revisits the Conradian trope of the sea passage in much the same way that Rhys revisits her own tropes of metropolitan streets and interiors.[2] Reading Rhys's *Good Morning, Midnight* alongside Walter Benjamin's *Arcades Project* (and its own fleeting reference to Conrad's *The Shadow-Line*), this chapter examines the shared problem of modernism and modernity that links the geography of interior space in Benjamin's arcades, Conrad's sea passages, and Rhys's urban topography.

Anterior Interiors
The First-Person Narrators of *Good Morning, Midnight* and *The Shadow-Line*

Conrad's *The Shadow-Line* and Rhys's *Good Morning, Midnight* both emphasize first-person narrators in ways that invite attention to the biographical circumstances of each author's experience of cultural and racial identity: for Conrad, the experience of refashioning himself from a Polish gentleman into an English sailor within the racial hierarchies of British imperial administration of overseas commercial trade; for Rhys, the experience of a West Indian–born immigrant woman moving in the avant-garde artistic circles of metropolitan European capitals.[3] Yet each work constitutes its first-person narrative perspective around moments of self-recognition that seem, rather, to erase those authorial experiences of cultural-geographical difference. The narrator of *The Shadow-Line* finds himself identified as the "right man" (*SL*, 31) for appointment to "first command" (*SL*, 88)—accepted, culturally and racially, as "one of us" (to use the loaded phrase from *Lord Jim*). The narrator of *Good Morning, Midnight*, too, finds herself identified as entirely English, although here the shock of being identified as an "English tourist" (*GM*, 34) and the "Englishwoman" (*GM*, 41) produces a very different effect. English identity, entirely unproblematic for Conrad's, is entirely problematic for Rhys's narrator.

What helps make each effect uncanny is the recursive structure of a first-person narrative revisiting the scene of experiences already treated in prior narratives. Conrad's experience of "first command" aboard the *Otago* in 1888 had provided material for a number of prior stories, including portions of *Lord Jim* and "The End of the Tether" and the whole of "The Secret Sharer." Rhys's narrative looks back on a number of experiences drawn from her own life (her short-lived marriage to Jean Lenglet; the death of her newborn son) already touched on in previous work ("Learning to Be a Mother"; *Quartet*). While neither narrative directly acknowledges this autobiographical dimension, their effects are felt in the way each revisits a prior geography of experience. In *Good Morning, Midnight*, an urban topography of cafés, streets, and rooms coordinates the relation between the narrator's past and present existence. In *The Shadow-Line*, the coordinates of the ship's navigation out from the shadow of the Island of Koh-ring in the Gulf of Siam, and past the latitude of 8° 20´, marks the difference between before and after "the first passage of my first command" (*SL*, 88). This emphasis on urban geography and seafaring cartography, respectively, returns each writer to privileged tropes from their earlier work.

The Shadow-Line repeats one of the most elementary exercises of "Conradian" style: the invocation of geographical knowledge as the privileged form of experience. Geographical knowledge, for Conrad, and especially as applied to seafaring navigation, is privileged both as the experience of mastery, with English hegemony over commercial worldwide sea-trading routes, and as the mastery of that experience, transcribed into narrative form. Both are balanced in that early model of the Marlow sea yarn, "Youth: A Narrative" (1898), whose youthful voyage out East recapitulates as personal experience an entire history of navigational exploration and discovery. *The Shadow-Line* revisits that story's relation between youth and experience, inscribing its version of professional apprenticeship in the suggestively navigational image of the title's "shadow-line" between youth and experience ("one perceives ahead a shadow-line warning one that the region of early youth, too, must be left behind" [*SL*, 3]).

It is the literal and figurative limitations set by geographical knowledge that distinguish the Conradian vocation of narrative style, and that situate Conrad at the inauguration of a specifically

English modernist moment.⁴ "Youth," for example, invokes a history of geographical exploration only to emphasize its erasure in the lived experience of the *Judea*'s fated voyage. Perhaps the most famous formulation is the "blank space" on the map of Africa in "Heart of Darkness": the imagined place of adventure for Marlow which, already at the outset of his narrative, "had become a place of darkness" (*Y*, 52). This example remains a touchstone for the modernist rupture in the grand narrative claims of enlightened European geography and history. Conrad's "blank space" invokes, but then undermines, that principle of what Michel de Certeau outlines as the "scriptural economy" (*"l'économie scripturaire"*) of Enlightenment history in which writing "consists in constructing, on its own, blank space—the page—a text that has power over the exteriority from which it has first been isolated" (*"Je désigne par écriture l'activité concrète qui consiste sur un espace propre, la page, à construire un texte qui a pouvoir sur l'extériorité dont il a d'abord été isolé"*).⁵ Conrad's fiction privileges geography not to revive the "scriptural enterprise" (*"l'entreprise scripturaire"*)⁶ of a *Robinson Crusoe*, but to sound out its referential limits—what we have come to recognize as the structural breakdown of literary realism and the emergence of a self-referential modernism in which (to cite again de Certeau) "there is no entry or exit for writing, but only the endless play of its fabrications" (*"Ces fictions romanesques ou iconiques racontent qu'il n'y a, pour l'écriture, ni entrée ni sortie, mais seulement l'interminable jeu de ses fabrications"*).⁷ If neither Conrad nor Rhys practice the kind of clear break from realism that Michel de Certeau associates with the "theoretical fictions" of Jarry, Roussel, and Duchamp, topographical descriptions in each are nonetheless premised on the same fundamental disjuncture of writing and geography de Certeau ascribes to the modernist break from the "scriptural economy" of the "the modern West" (*"de l'Occident modern"*).⁸ Simultaneously, places of real social experience and literary *topoi*—the sea, in Conrad, and the city streets, in Rhys—define the self-referential double-bind of topography in European literary modernism.

Walter Benjamin finds both sides of this double-bind of topography in the Parisian arcades, most especially in Baudelaire's poetry, where "the images of women and death are permeated by a third, that of Paris. The Paris of his poems is a submerged city—its topographical formation, the old deserted bed of the Seine" (*"Es ist das Einmalige der Dichtung von Baudelaire, daß die Bilder des Weibs und des Todes sich in einem dritten durchdringen, dem von Paris. Das Paris seiner Gedichte ist eine versunkene Stadt und mehr unterseeisch als unterirdisch"*).⁹ The poetry of Baudelaire's "submerged city" underscores a revealingly gendered logic chiasmatically linking the streets in Rhys and the sea in Conrad to articulate what Benjamin calls the "dream image" (*Traumbild*) of modernity. Essential to all three is the economy with which the street passage and the sea passage is inscribed in the literary passage of text (*le passage* in French, *die Stelle* in German).[10]

The "Impasse" of *Good Morning, Midnight*

Good Morning, Midnight formulates this double-bind in the figure of the "impasse" that confronts the narrator, Sasha Jansen, in the opening pages of her narrative. Inaugurating the novel's extended deconstruction of an expected relation between interior and exterior spaces, the novel opens by turning the inanimate room into a speaking subject: "'Quite like old times,' the room says. 'Yes? No?'" (*GM*, 9). What follows is a description that moves from the interior to the exterior topography of this oddly objectified speaking subject:

> There are two beds, a big one for madame and a smaller one on the opposite side for monsieur. The wash-basin is shut off by a curtain. It is a large room, the smell of cheap hotels faint, almost imperceptible. The street outside is narrow, cobble-stoned, going sharply uphill and ending in a flight of steps. What they call an impasse. (*GM*, 9)

Describing the blocked-off street outside her hotel room, this feature of Parisian street architecture also figuratively evokes the "impasse" of Sasha's social position, trapped by cultural alienation, relative poverty, and sexual dependence. The ambiguity of this interior/exterior relation—the final sentence might refer either to the "street outside" or to the overall situation of the "room"—locates, physically and psychologically, the narrating person who appears in the very next line ("I have been here five days"), and whose narrative, told in the present tense, will return to the "impasse" of this interior/exterior relation of "room" to "street." Both as a realistic description of a social space and as a figurative problem of reading social space, this "impasse" inaugurates a network of images (streets, passages, corridors, closed entrances, blocked exits) that characterize both interior space and the interior monologue in which Sasha Jansen's experiences are narrated throughout *Good Morning, Midnight*.

As a number of commentators have remarked, the word *impasse* figuratively encapsulates the predicament of almost all of Rhys's female protagonists.[11] Connecting room and street in a word that undoes the separation of interior private and exterior public space, the "impasse" delineates the experience Rhys's protagonists are bound to repeat in finding themselves trapped in the double-bind of private and public metropolitan social space, whether in Paris (Marya Zelli in *Quartet*) or in London (Anna Morgan in *Voyage in the Dark*) or both (Julia Martin in *After Leaving Mr. Mackenzie* and Sasha Jansen in *Good Morning, Midnight*). Moreover, the word *impasse,* while initially describing a Parisian topography, turns out to refer also to a *London* topography. The fact that the physical, architectural sense of the word is far more commonly an English word alerts us to the possibility that the Parisian "impasse" described at the beginning of the narrative conceals the thought of another, London topography—namely, the "room just off the Gray's Inn Road" (*GM,* 44), which is Sasha's home in London from which this Parisian vacation is a temporary escape.

In its characteristic juxtaposition of Paris and London experiences, *Good Morning, Midnight* reiterates but also complicates, in turn, the dialectical relation between rooms and streets that Benjamin traces in the poetry of Baudelaire. Sasha Jansen, Rhys's female *flâneuse,* retraces the logic of Baudelaire's *flâneur,* as Benjamin does, too, in light of the Paris of the 1920s and 1930s, and on the eve of the Second World War.[12] In the 1939 exposé of "Paris, Capital of the Nineteenth Century," Benjamin writes (in the passage cited at the end of the last section): "Baudelaire's rebellion is always that of the asocial man: it is at an impasse. The only sexual communion of his life was with a prostitute" (*"Ce qui n'empêche que la rebellion de Baudelaire ait toujours gardé le caractère de l'homme asocial: elle est sans issue. La seule communauté sexuelle dans sa vie, il l'a réalisée avec une prostituée"*).[13] Sasha's "impasse," too, is figured in sexual terms. The figure of the prostitute ("saleswoman and wares in one" [*"die Verkäuferin und Ware in einem"*] in Benjamin's earlier formulation[14]) is, indeed, much more typically the norm of female experience for Rhys's narrator-protagonists, who are more at home in the public space of the streets than the privacy of interior bourgeois space. Sasha flees the oppressive space of a private room of one's own in London to wander as a female *flâneuse* through the public spaces of Paris, but only ultimately to find that the difference between Paris and London compounds the oppressive experience of impoverished urban life and marginalized cultural identity.

As with the *flâneur,* the city is, for Sasha, "now a landscape, now a room," with the relation between "rooms" and "streets" heightening—but at the same time exposing—the phantasmagoria, or bourgeois illusion of a separate private interior space insulated from the place of work and social labor. Sasha's first extended memory—the recollection of her short-lived job as *vendeuse* in a clothing store—enacts Benjamin's insight that "department stores," "the last precincts" of the *flâneur,* "put *flânerie* to work for profit."[15] The recollection of her quitting her position as clothing-store receptionist consolidates the image of the "impasse" by association with the extended description of the labyrinthine maze of rooms, passages, and corridors in which she finds herself trapped. Even after she has quit—a moment of temporary release "out in the Avenue Marigny, with my month's pay...and the air so sweet"—the claustrophobic interior space of the shop with its "passages that don't lead anywhere" (*GM*, 25) becomes a metaphor for her exclusion from employment (following a description of her failure as guide for American Express): "The passages will never lead anywhere, the doors will always be shut" (*GM*, 31).

Her physical entrapment is also linguistic. The loss of her job is the result of miscommunication with the store's English boss, precipitated by her attempt at humor in replying to the question, "And how many languages do you speak?" Thinking that the question is "a joke," perhaps because both she and the English boss are English speakers in a French-speaking environment, she responds by saying she speaks only "one" language (*GM*, 19). The confusion escalates later when she is unable to understand the word *caisse* as pronounced by the boss whom she dubs, in her interior monologue, "Mr. Blank." Sasha's linguistic predicament recalls the problem outlined by Jacques Derrida in *Monolingualism of the Other*, in which the only language one knows—in Derrida's example, French—is not considered to be one's own. Rhys redoubles that predicament by creating a narrative voice perfectly fluent in, yet culturally excluded from, both French and English. Sasha's humorous claim to be able to speak only "one" language comes to enact, in earnest, the predicament of Derrida's statement, "I only have one language, yet it is not mine" ("*Oui, je n'ai qu'une langue, or ce n'est pas la mienne*").[16]

The logic of what Derrida calls the "monolingualism of the other" ("*le monolinguisme de l'autre*") is marked, in a more precise sense, by Rhys's use of the word *impasse*, whose grammatical and rhetorical ambiguity is governed by a doubly monolingual French and English register of meaning. Derrida, like Rhys, alludes to the rhetorical meaning of the French word *impasse*. As Rachel Bowlby points out, "In rhetoric, an 'impasse' defines a structure where the proposition includes assumptions which are contrary to those of the addressee, who is thus unable either to reply according to the same terms, or to deny something on which s/he has not been directly challenged."[17] *Good Morning, Midnight*, Bowlby further argues, "is structured like a rhetorical impasse, too, since all its positive terms are already excluded with the force of impossibility."[18] The novel's early designation of "What they call an impasse" establishes the linguistic and spatial premise of its interior monologue. An apparently sharp difference between "their" (French or English) and "our" (French or English) meaning is erased to produce a single language (the "English" of Rhys's Anglo-French translation effects). This English might be described as a monolingualism of French and English. Each constitutes, in their ascription of "monolingualism" to the other, a double-bind of untranslatability (what makes Sasha unable to communicate with her English boss). This turns

Derrida's "impassable, *indisputable*" ("*indépassable,* incontestable")[19] proposition into a predicament that is simultaneously linguistic, rhetorical, and spatial. Interior monologue and interior space are both constituted around the logic of the "impasse."[20]

The "Impasse" of Jean Rhys's Creole Consciousness

In what sense does the "impasse" of interior monologue and interior space register a specifically Creole consciousness? Arguably, the novel that most rigorously excludes any alternative to the consciousness of one trapped in a European metropolitan capital, *Good Morning, Midnight* may offer the most characteristic form of a Creole narrative consciousness in Rhys's work as a whole. The double-bind with which its narrative voice articulates the "impasse" of a "monolingualism" of metropolitan European consciousness registers all the more powerfully those traces of a Francophone and Anglophone Creole past that appear throughout Rhys's work of the 1920s and 1930s and that will come to dominate the later work of *Wide Sargasso Sea*. As with the first-person narrators of "Vienne" (1924; revised for the 1927 collection of stories) and the first published novel, *Quartet* (1929), and as with the main protagonist in *After Leaving Mr. Mackenzie* (1931), Sasha's background is left deliberately uncertain. This studied ambiguity of cultural background follows a pattern of deliberate omission, a marked forgetting of the past, anchored in that stylistic practice we have already discussed in the use of the Conrad passage in *After Leaving Mr. Mackenzie.* In deliberately suspending, if not erasing, the memory of a fixed cultural past, Rhys reformulates the "blank" memory of Ford's English modernism. In a linguistic and cultural sense, this "blank" is neither French nor English (in a metropolitan sense), neither Francophone nor Anglophone (in a Creole sense); it is an impossibility of both white middle-class and white Creole identity. In this sense it might be considered the counterpart both to the "impassable, *indisputable*" logic of Derridean "monolingualism" and also to the cultural logic of an "impasse" that forms an important precedent for Derrida[21]: the "impasse" with which Édouard Glissant introduces his *Discours antillais* (*Caribbean Discourse*): how, given the "present impasse" of the "dead-end" situation of Martinique, to realize the process of "creolization" or "Relation."[22]

The "impasse" of the first-person narrative voice of *Good Morning, Midnight* recapitulates the Francophone English experiments in narrative voice that have characterized Rhys's work up until this moment. In all these texts there is always a possibility that the European scene of translation between French and English is underwritten by a Caribbean subtext, a Francophone-Anglophone axis of translation. The problematic priority of cultural memory embedded in individual English words—*dam, rum, Vienna,* or even *impasse*—registers the ambiguity of narrative consciousness organizing each of these Rhys texts; an ambiguity of memory anchored in the aesthetic certainty of nonmemory articulated by the fetishized literary passage, as we explored in our discussion of Rhys's citation from Conrad's *Almayer's Folly* in *After Leaving Mr. Mackenzie*. Although *Good Morning, Midnight* is organized, too, around a literary passage (the title's citation from Emily Dickinson's poem), what anchors the ambiguity of memory for this novel's narrative consciousness is not a passage of literary text so much as the displaced passage of text through song.

In the middle of the novel, a memory is evoked by a gramophone recording of "some béguine music, Martinique music":

The gramophone is grinding out "Maladie d'amour, maladie de la jeunesse...."

I am lying in a hammock looking up into the branches of a tree. The sound of the sea advances and retreats as if a door were being opened and shut. All day there has been a fierce wind blowing, but at sunset it drops. The hills look like clouds and the clouds like fantastic hills.

Pain of love,
Pain of youth,
Walk away from me,
Keep away from me,
Don't want to see you
No more, no more....

Then we talk about Negro music and about various boîtes in Montparnasse. (*GM*, 92)

Read as a memory of some moment in Sasha's past life, the present-tense description of "lying in a hammock looking up into the branches of a tree" seems much more positively the sort of Antillean memory that surfaces in the trio of stories from *The Left Bank and Other Stories* than the negative formulation of Julia Martin's imagined memory, in *After Leaving Mr. Mackenzie,* of "the sea of a chromo or of some tropical country that she had never seen."

One thing that makes the description stand out, after all, is its isolation from the other kinds of experience recounted by the present-tense narrative voice. The memory is connected neither with the moment of the anecdote that supplies the memory of the gramophone recording ("This is late October, 1937"), nor with the Parisian hotel room to which this second part of the novel will inevitably return (and specifically, in the concluding paragraph's "This damned room—it's saturated with the past....It's all the rooms I've ever slept in, all the streets I've ever walked in....Rooms, streets, streets, rooms...." [*GM*, 109]). The singularity of the memory makes it seem privileged in a way that would support its interpretation as a clue to the lost memory around which the narrative as a whole seems to be constructed.

In the very beginning of the novel, the problem of this buried memory already implied by the temporal and spatial narrative coordinates of the "impasse" is picked up in an account of Sasha's response to "a sad song" hummed and tapped out by a woman at an adjacent table in the café. The song, "Gloomy Sunday," precipitates a memory that leads Sasha into a breakdown of crying, symptom of the melancholic state that marks the present tense of narrative consciousness. In this first vignette, Sasha's pre-history is abbreviated to suggest a presumed suicide attempt: "Saved, rescued, fished-up, half-drowned, out of the deep river, dry clothes, hair shampooed and set. Nobody would know I had ever been in it. Except, of course, that there always remains something" (*GM*, 10). Whether this "remainder" refers to the trace of the Seine experience itself (which does recur throughout the narrative) or what led up to the suicide attempt, the "something" that remains echoes the problem of memory provoked by the song. As Sasha says, first to the woman and his American friend to explain her crying fit, and then to the waiter on returning from the *lavabo*, "It was something I remembered" (*GM*, 10, 11).

Does the later description of "lying in a hammock" recall this "something...remembered" or the "something" remaining? And, if so, does it suggest a lost Antillean memory as the clue to the narrative's melancholic formation? The role of song in precipitating the problem of memory is crucial in each case, and might be seen as a structural constant throughout Rhys's work. "Gloomy Sunday"—the song whose score the woman at the next table is reading, humming, and tapping—is all the more interesting for foregrounding the Francophone English register of the novel's grasp of cultural phenomena. Called "Gloomy Sunday" in the first instance, the song is briefly recalled later with the words *Sombre dimanche* (*GM*, 16). This ambiguity—ambiguity in the sense that one cannot immediately, or perhaps ever, decide whether Sasha thinks of the song in French or in English; or whether the initial conversation has been translated into the "English" of the narrative discourse, a discourse which then itself reproduces the "monolingualism" of "impasse"—is echoed in the song that precipitates the possible Antillean memory of the middle of the novel. Before the memory itself, the song is rendered in French: "The gramophone is grinding out 'Maladie d'amour, maladie de la jeunesse'" (*GM*, 92); but following the descriptive memory, the lines are translated into English: "Pain of love,/Pain of youth,/Walk away from me,/Keep away from me,/Don't want to see you/No more, no more" (*GM*, 93).

What makes the process of translation implied in this example so interesting is not simply the rendering of the French lyrics into English but, rather, the possible translation of cultural associations suggested by the "béguine music, Martinique music." It is, after all, the cultural associations that seem to govern the singularity of that memory of lying in a hammock produced by the process of translation. That memory, or problem of memory, emerges from a material dislocation of culture and identity that seems best explained by Fernando Ortiz's improvisation of the concept of "transculturation" in *Cuban Counterpoint:* "the word *transculturation* better expresses the different phases of the process of transition from one culture to another because this does not consist merely in acquiring another culture, which is what the English word *acculturation* really implies, but the process also necessarily involves the loss or uprooting of a previous culture, which could be defined as a deculturation. In addition it carries the idea of the consequent creation of new cultural phenomena."[23] The set of associations provoked by the song triggers the same crying fit described at the beginning of the novel, there explained by the statement "It was something I remembered," and here recalled as follows: "I am talking away, quite calmly and sedately, when there it is again—tears in my eyes, tears rolling down my face. (Saved, rescued, but not quite so good as new....)" (*GM*, 93).

The set of transcultural associations developed here suggests that the translation work of Rhys's Francophone English might be less a matter of language (French into English) than a matter of translation across media—an attempt to convey the effect of that "béguine music, Martinique music" and the cultural milieu that leads to the talk of "Negro music" and "the Cuban Cabin in Montmartre." The voice of this distinctive narrative consciousness emerges, then, around a response to those "forms of communication" (*modes de la communication*) Glissant describes as characteristic of the "practice of cultural creolization" (*pratique de métissage*).[24] Drawing on Glissant, Paul Gilroy explores "the possible commonality of post-slave, black cultural forms"[25] inscribed in the patterns of language and music forming a diasporic "black Atlantic" experience. Rhys's narrative voice is indeed haunted by this experience; and, more specifically, by the elusive archive of that "practice of diaspora" that Brent Hayes Edwards analyzes in the work of transnational black artists in Paris in the 1920s and 1930s.[26] All of her interwar texts—and above all *Good Morning, Midnight—*seem attuned to these "practices of cultural creolization" generally and more specifically to the expressive modes of translation across media, especially in musical recordings, that make up the "black Atlantic" experience in Gilroy's sense or the archival traces of "black internationalism" in Edwards's sense. Yet if Rhys's Francophone English is haunted by the traces of this historically specific moment of transatlantic black diasporic modernism in the Paris of the interwar period, the narrative consciousness it shapes is simultaneously excluded from and even defined against that experience.

As with the Conrad citation in *After Leaving Mr. Mackenzie*, the lyrics of the "Martinique song" give cultural perspective to the narrative voice, not so much through the meaning of the words themselves but, rather, through the problem of translation across the mass-mediated form of gramophone recording. *Good Morning, Midnight* emphasizes the importance of a nonverbal, nonliterary medium of experience from the start: the image of the gramophone itself marks the "gap" of memory around which the present-tense narrative discourse forms. As we read in the opening section: "The thing is to have a programme, not to leave anything to chance—no gaps. No trailing around aimlessly with cheap gramophone records starting up in your head, no 'Here this happened, here that happened.' Above all, no crying in public, no crying at all if I can help it" (*GM*, 15). The "gramophone record...in my head" (*GM*, 17), concatenated by the end of the novel with the cinematic image of "my film-mind" (*GM*, 176), specifies, in terms of the mass mediation of cultural forms, the constitution of that "damned voice in my head" (*GM*, 187) that is the voice of narrative discourse. If, as Elaine Savory points out, the descriptive memory prompted by the "Martinique music" is "a sure code of the coastline of Dominica" for "those familiar with Rhys texts,"[27] the problem of ascribing to Sasha an "inheritance of the memory of that island" encounters an equally familiar problem from Rhys's texts. Like Julia Martin's thought of "a dark-purple sea" from *After Leaving Mr. Mackenzie*, the descriptive experience of "lying in a hammock," listening to the "sound of the sea" and looking at the hills and the clouds, suggests, indeed, Rhys's personal memory of Dominica, embedded as the miniature genetic code for narrative. In the later novel that memory is not quite so rigorously negated by the forms of mass media that turn Julia Martin's memory into "the sea of a chromo or of some tropical country that she had never seen." Yet the care with which that memory is embedded in *Good Morning, Midnight* gives it something of the same isolated and framing function as the Conrad citation in the earlier novel. To the extent that the Conrad passage provided, as we have seen, something like the certainty of non-memory, the frozen trope of the literary passage around which the narrative constitutes its reading of English modernism as the impossibility of white middle-class identity, this descriptive moment offers a revealing counterpart, providing readers "familiar with Rhys texts," in Savory's terms, a certainty of lost memory.

Taken as the telling clue of lost memory, the certain point of Sasha's relation to Rhys's autobiographical relation to her own childhood memories, the description itself might all the more effectively be read as a negation of that Creole perspective that critics (and I include myself here) have invested in Rhys's texts. On the one hand, the miniature description seems to transcend the terms of the narrative "impasse" we have already outlined: the image of the "hammock" dispels the deadlocked relation of interior to exterior that defines Sasha's compromised social position as a woman whose "market value" is constituted by the relation between bedroom and street. And the prose of the passage seems to dispense with the spatial, metaphorical, and metonymic logic of the rest of the narrative: the simile of the second sentence marks a release from the oppressive space of interior passages—"as if a door were being opened and shut"—leading, according to a logic not seen elsewhere in the novel, to a sentence entirely given over to natural description: "All day there has been a fierce wind blowing, but at sunset it drops." Finally, the descriptive passage concludes with a rhetorical flourish, a chiasmatic description that substitutes one natural exterior reality ("hills") with another ("clouds") in a "fantastic" romance of pure description. According to such a reading, then, the Creole landscape description creates a refuge from the "impasse" of Sasha's oppressive imprisonment within the metropolitan social space of that exemplary capital of Europe, Paris.

Yet what enables one, after all, to designate this experience as Creole is the cliché of "lying in a hammock"—a cliché satirically condensed, for example, by Flaubert's definition of *creole* in the *Dictionary of Received Ideas:* "CREOLE. Lives in a hammock" ("*Créole. Vit dans un hamac*").[28] If one imagines that the descriptive passage is written by someone conscious of that stereotype—and Rhys's overall career can be characterized as a long apprenticeship in the art of unearthing the Creole of modern French and English literature—then the descriptive "code" might embody the very impossibility of ascribing to Sasha, or to any fictional character like Sasha, an authentic memory of some West Indian, Caribbean, Antillean Creole past. This might be thought of in sentimental terms (the terms suggested by the lyrics of the song): Rhys's lived sense of her childhood in Dominica cannot find fictional form except through the devaluation of a stereotype. Or, it might be figured in more formal terms as the most economical use of the trope of the Creole in Rhys's work: as a marker, not of the excluded cultural outside of Europe, but precisely as the most central literary cliché governing European modernism and its relation to mass-mediated consumer forms.

Within the context of *Good Morning, Midnight*, this Creole memory stands in narrative apposition to the "very sad story" told by the Jewish painter, Serge, about the woman from Martinique in London, whose crying he could not console: "She was crying because she was at the end of everything. There was that sound in her sobbing which is quite unmistakable—like certain music...and she started a long story, speaking sometimes in French, sometimes in English, when of course I couldn't understand her very well" (*GM*, 95–96). As a number of critics[29] have discussed, it is really this story that offers the submerged Caribbean or West Indian counterpoint to

Sasha's claustrophobic sense of "impasse." Yet to the extent that Sasha identifies with this experience of being victimized by the cruelty not only of society at large but also by the sympathy of friends—the racism of the one being compounded by the sympathetic misunderstanding of the other—it turns, after all, on an impossibility of identification. When, at the outset of the story, Sasha recognizes an immediate affinity—"'Exactly like me,' I say"—the painter contradicts, "No, no...Not like you at all....She wasn't a white woman. She was a half-Negro—a mulatto" (*GM*, 95).

If this story reproduces the general dilemma of Rhys's characters' consciousness of their white racial identity through a longing to be black, it makes of the possibility of a white Creole consciousness within the matrix of racialized European modernity the key to that problematic invisibility, or unlocatability signaled by the word *blank*. In this sense, it is the submerged secret identification between the displaced memory of a *white* Creole experience in Paris and the *nonwhite* Creole experience of displacement in London that makes the singularity of Sasha's recollection of some completely other landscape the privileged passage. The ambiguity of racial identity and identification this adds to the already ambiguous consciousness of a Creole perspective (that is, either negated as stereotype or affirmed beyond the stereotype) might be explained in terms of the core trope of literariness that governs Rhys's overall reading of modernism.

We have already discussed how, in *After Leaving Mr. Mackenzie*, the Conrad citation anchors the repetitive formation of an "English" literary modernism. The stereotype of the Creole in *Good Morning, Midnight* recalls the way English literary modernism follows French modernism in a receding history of literary imitations whose genealogical priorities are held in suspended animation in Rhys's Francophone English and the linguistic, literary, and cultural meaning of its "impasse." The elusive place of a Creole consciousness in this genealogical embedding of literary modernisms is marked, in *Good Morning, Midnight,* in the title's citation from the Emily Dickinson poem given in the epigraph. Itself a miniature reading of that poem's inversion of the heliotrope, set off from the unfolding consciousness of the fictional Sasha, the title draws unusual authority from a tradition of women's writing in a double process of simultaneously reiterating its tropological movement—loosely speaking, to create the atmosphere of a "voyage in the dark"—and investing its universal literary trope with the problematic racial lines of demarcation that surface in the doubling of the Creole hammock memory and the "very sad story" of the Martinique woman who is unable to appear "except after dark" (*GM*, 96).

Considered as a prefiguration of what Rhys famously will do with the stereotype of the Creole in Charlotte Brontë's *Jane Eyre*, the location of the "impasse" of a Creole consciousness within literary precedents (and the precedence of literature) is characterized less by finding a (white or black) Creole consciousness in literary tradition than by finding the impasse of a Creole consciousness (neither white nor black) in the *loss* or *disappearance* of literary tradition in the mass-mediated forms of cultural production. In this sense the title's isolation of the line from the Dickinson poem stands in determinate relation to the lyrics of the songs in *Good Morning, Midnight* ("Bloody Sunday"/ "Sombre dimanche" and "Maladie d'amour"/ "Pain of love"), which themselves mark the verbal form of a memory registered as lost in translation across a variety of media, and whose disturbance produces the "gramophone record" and "film-mind" of that novel's narrative discourse. This deadlocked dialectical relation between a lost Creole memory and its reproduction in mass-mediated form shapes, then, the "impasse" of Sasha's narrative consciousness in *Good Morning, Midnight*. It recapitulates, too, the distinctive shape of narrative consciousness in Rhys's earlier texts, as is revealed by a brief survey of *The Left Bank and Other Stories* (1927), *Quartet* (1929), and *Voyage in the Dark* (1934).

The Left Bank and Other Stories

The Left Bank and Other Stories presents the first articulation of a Creole narrative consciousness in Rhys's work, in the three stories—"Trio," "Mixing Cocktails," and "Again the Antilles"—that form a sequence at the center of the collection. The relation of each story in sequence constitutes something of a puzzle within the collection as a whole, suggesting a narrative "I" that might unify all the stories of *The Left Bank* yet at the same time binding the three stories together in a way that none of the others are bound together and so, in fact, isolating them as if to frame the "Left Bank" setting of the collection. The point of connection among these "Antillean" stories is marked by the overdetermined logic of the final sentence (and also paragraph) of "Trio": "It was because these were my compatriots that in that Montparnasse restaurant I remembered the Antilles" (*CS*, 35). The sentence seems more direct a claim for an Antillean past than any of the semi-autobiographical moments in Jean Rhys's published work, from "Vienne" to *Good Morning, Midnight*.

The peculiar logic of this "compatriot" identity is full of possible ironies. Most prominent, perhaps, is the question of racial identity highlighted by the narrator's emphasis on the "very black" man, the "coffee-coloured" woman and the girl with "evidently much white blood in her veins" (*CS*, 34). Does calling these people "compatriots" constitute a Creole family romance of identification, or, on the contrary, an ironic disavowal of racial identification? Does this register a claim, or ironic disavowal, of shared national identity between people from French-controlled Martinique and someone from

British-controlled Dominica? If the "compatriotism" they share is, in fact, an *ex*patriotism, does this expatriate Parisian identity not precede the fact of their respective, and contrasting, expatriate experiences? What the story produces is a claim to memory—"I remembered the Antilles"—but a memory that remains as yet unrelated. In the sequential logic of the trio of stories (that might or might not borrow the first story's title to unify them), it is certainly possible to assume that the story that follows, "Mixing Cocktails," constitutes the rendering of that memory of the Antilles provoked by the presence of the narrator's "compatriots" in the Parisian café. That connection, indeed, might explain the narrative logic connecting those fragments of Antillean memories that surface in the later novels. This imagined sense of another community, Antillean compatriotism in counterpoint to European cosmopolitanism, may then frame the narrative perspective on the "Left Bank" scene of the European metropole.

Yet the very elements that go toward the making of such a unified narrative perspective dictate its fragmentation. The story that follows, "Mixing Cocktails," constitutes its unique childhood memory of Dominica—the prototype of the miniature landscape descriptions that haunt the later novels—around a fairly explicit dismantling of the narrative first person. The "I" of the first sentence gives way to the "you" of the second paragraph. By the time the story turns to the familiar landscape description—complete with the stereotype of "Lying in the hammock" that will resurface in *Good Morning, Midnight*—the first- and second-person narrative has declined to "one" to produce the familiar troping of heliotropism as dream-image:

> Lying in the hammock, swinging cautiously for the ropes creaked, one dreamt.... The morning dream was the best—very early, before the sun was properly up. (*CS*, 36)

In the middle of the story, in the moment we discussed in the previous chapter in terms of the Rhys-ian formation of the "English" accent of narrative voice, the grammatical declension of first to second person is reversed, so that the "English aunt" (even before she has been introduced as such) takes the position of the first person and the narrative first person is displaced to "you":

> I am speaking to you; do you not hear? You must break yourself of your habit of never listening. You have such an absent-minded expression. Try not to look vague. (*CS*, 37)

This disruption of narrative person turns on the English aunt's interdiction against "worshipping the sun"—"One was not to sit in the sun. One had been told not to be in the sun.... One would one day regret freckles" (*CS*, 37)—linking the Creole stereotypes of "lying in the hammock" and fears of racial degeneration and intermixture with the central trope of literary description. Complicated, too, with the associations of the "mixing cocktails" (according to Thomas[30] a code for racial intermixture), the story constitutes a Creole consciousness around an unravelling of grammatical persons, leaving the seemingly definitive statement from the previous story—"I remembered the Antilles"—suspended around the fractal possibilities of the third-person plural "our" floated, in parenthesis, toward the end of the story: "our cocktails, in the West Indies, are drunk frothing...." That linguistic split between the "Antilles" of the Montparnasse café and the "West Indies" of the English aunt's articulation marks only one of the fractures by which Rhys's Francophone English introduces the overseas colonial axis into the European scene of the Left Bank.

The final story in this trio reveals in what sense this Creole consciousness both fixes and unfixes the narrative consciousness of the collection as a whole around the disputed passage of English literature (discussed in chapter 1). "Again the Antilles"—again the title refers both to itself and to its place in the trio of stories—establishes the terms for a "compatriotism" of identity in the space of the printed English word (Chaucer's lines cited in the Dominican newspaper) by contrast to the spoken French Creole of "Trio." This simultaneously undoes any unified "compatriotism" of Antillean perspective and constitutes in that impossibly fractal perspective the *literary* consciousness around which the entire collection of stories can no longer be grouped. The dispute over the authority of the passage of English literature foregrounds the literary consciousness of that shared, if contested English literary tradition (within which the line from Chaucer would make recognizable sense) and the literate consciousness of a community of newspaper readers following the debate over Chaucer in the *Dominica Herald and Leeward Islands Gazette*. This momentarily imagined community of contest over racial identity, literary authority, and inter-island Caribbean social relations also constitutes, momentarily, that narrative perspective whose loss Rhys traces around the eclipsed dominance of the medium of print literacy. To the extent that the *Dominica Herald and Leeward Islands Gazette* specifies a Creole consciousness repeatedly invoked and repeatedly negated, it marks, as archaic counterpoint, the rather different space of reading and writing with which Rhys's own work engages. Already split between the Chaucerian vernacular of English literature and the print capitalism of the English-language newspaper, this Creole consciousness is the displaced origin of a literariness eclipsed by the mass-mediated forms of modernity.

Quartet

Rhys's first published novel, *Quartet,* marks this loss of literary tradition under the mass-mediated forms of modernity around the impossibility of recapturing a Creole past. In its opening scene, which reconfigures the "Left Bank" of her collection of stories as the social setting of what will lead to Marya Zelli's own "impasse," the sound of a song prompts a "melancholy pleasure" that will be the keynote to this character's identity crisis:

> The drone of a concertina sounded from the courtyard of the studio. The man was really trying to play "Yes, we have no bananas." But it was an unrecognizable version, and listening to it gave Marya the same feeling of melancholy pleasure as she had when walking along the shadowed side of one of those narrow streets full of shabby *parfumeries,* second-hand book-stalls, cheap hat-shops, bars frequented by gaily-painted ladies and loud-voiced men, midwives' premises. (*Q*, 7–8)

There is perhaps no ground on which to claim this forms any kind of "code" for Rhys's West Indian past, except that the words of the song and possibly their musical associations constitute a distant metonymic connection with the general region of the Caribbean—and thus the only reference at all in this novel. What the passage emphasizes is the distortion effected by the concertina version—the rendering "unrecognizable" of what is, then, presumably a familiar tune. This relation of the familiar to the unrecognizable is connected to the "melancholy pleasure" of the *flâneuse,* providing a revealing, if fleetingly positive, vision of what will become the "impasse" of *Good Morning, Midnight*—namely, the "pleasure" of walking the streets.

This illusory freedom of female consciousness (whose logic will be revealed, over the course of the novel, as the mirror image of the husband's imprisonment for fraud) stands in counterpoint to the illusory respectability of bourgeois domestic comfort into which Marya will be inducted as a member of the Heidler household (first as female model for Lois's painting, then as her husband's mistress). This "quartet" of relations (the façade of European middle-class society) is sustained by a complex of mutual misrecognitions refined into the first sustained version of Rhys's Francophone English. When addressed in the streets of St. Michel and Montparnasse by "very shabby" youths "in unknown and spitting tongues," Marya "would smile in a distant manner and answer in English: 'I'm very sorry; I don't understand what you are saying'" (*Q*, 5)—a version of "monolingualism" that deploys the postures of English-ness against the insinuations of a heterogeneity of "French" meanings. This Francophone English produces the novel's extended study of the hypocrisies of a modern "English" pretense of detachment from the crisis of European modernity. If the French streets constitute the scene of revelation for English hypocrisies, however, it is by insisting only on the imposture of English or French, each mimicking the other, without appeal to a knowledge, or "recognition" of what makes the one turn to the other. This may be because what Rhys leaves out of the equation is precisely the professional role of the writer in the "Left Bank" scene of artistic collaboration and exploitation.

Voyage in the Dark

Voyage in the Dark provides perhaps the most economical Francophone English displacement of literary consciousness in the puzzle of its protagonist's name, Anna, whose claim on the reader's sense of narrative consciousness emerges from an anagram of the Zola novel, *Nana*. Before we learn her name, we read:

> I was lying on the sofa, reading *Nana*. It was a paper-covered book with a coloured picture of a stout woman brandishing a wine-glass. She was sitting on the knee of a bald-headed man in evening dress. The print was very small, and the endless procession of words gave me a curious feeling—sad, excited and frightened. It wasn't what I was reading, it was the look of the dark, blurred words going on endlessly that gave me that feeling. (V, 9)

Characteristically for Rhys, it is not merely the allusive set of references to Zola's novel that invites the reader to consider possible contrasts and parallels between Anna's journey into lower middle-class prostitution and Zola's classic portrait of the decadence of the Second Empire in the figure of the high-class prostitute, Nana. As with the complex hierarchy of reading effects that precede the literary citation of the Conrad passage in *After Leaving Mr. Mackenzie*, this description of the "feeling" of reading disrupts the expected order of literary effects (what Barthes characterized as the "readerly" relation to classical texts[31]), refusing precisely that commonsense distinction between what is inside and what is outside of a text for which Derrida's practice of "deconstruction" has become so well known. The effect this description has on the construction of narrative voice lies at the heart of Rhys's most recognized claims to literary recognition—from the adoption of her own pseudonym, to the reimagining of Charlotte Brontë's Bertha Mason as Antoinette Cosway. In its inaugurating displacement and reconstitution of literary form around the identification of narrative consciousness, however, it reconstitutes the printed page—"the endless procession of words"; "the look of the dark, blurred words going on endlessly"—as an extension, or reiteration, of that place of experience, or feeling, designated in the opening of the novel—"It was as if a curtain had fallen...It was almost like being born again"—and that is most easily glossed, simply, as "England," whose towns and streets form a close parallel to the "endless procession of words": "You were perpetually moving to another place which was perpetually the same" (*V*, 8).

What makes *Voyage in the Dark* the most extended elaboration of a Creole narrative consciousness in Rhys's work up to *Wide Sargasso Sea* is its attempt (foreshadowing that later novel) to organize narrative around the transatlantic "voyage" from the West Indies to England evoked in the opening page of the novel. Anna Morgan—more so than any of the other fictional "Rhys" women—most fully seems to mirror the journey of Jean Rhys (or, rather, Gwen Williams, as she would then have been called) from Dominica to England. In organizing narrative around a series of recurring memories of the West Indian world she has left, *Voyage in the Dark* would thus seem to provide the fullest exposition of the problem of Antillean memory, thematizing it, moreover, around the dominant trope of the "voyage." The trope underscores the problematic status of that memory, which remains suspended between the parallel "voyages" of the remembered departure from home and the nightmare journey in the "dark"ness of England. In this sense, *Voyage in the Dark* anticipates the "impasse" of *Good Morning, Midnight*—even to the extent that the Francophone English resonance of "voyage" figures a similar impossibility of cultural relation of priority.

As the reference to *Nana* illustrates, Rhys develops the translation work of Francophone English to much the same effect—indeed, "the look of the dark, blurred words going on endlessly" might be explained, in part, as an effect of the opacity of an Anglophone reading of the French text. The difference, of course, is that the Francophone English narrative voice is furnished with a West Indian background, foregrounding a difference between metropolitan and colonial English scenes that should govern such narrative differences as, for example, between Anna's descent into prostitution and Nana's ascent as prostitute. What is all the more important about this alternative deployment of Francophone English, however, is that this very difference is what is called into question. From the very beginning of the novel, the word *difference* itself—a word whose French and English resonance offers a more banal "monolingualism" of Francophone English than *impasse*—defines what will ultimately constitute the impossibility of distinguishing the Creole from the English narrative perspective. Initially suggesting the difference between the West Indies and England, the word begins and ends as a term defining a "difference" applied to the feeling of being in England, or, more precisely, "it": "Sometimes it was as if I were back there and as if England were a dream. At other times England was the real thing and out there was the dream, but I could never fit them together" (*V*, 8).

Thus the Francophone English of *Voyage in the Dark* reframes the metropolitan Paris/London axis of English "monolingualism" onto a West Indian Anglophone/Francophone colonial axis of linguistic and cultural identity. Yet even as it does this, it moves toward the logic of the "impasse" of Creole consciousness realized in *Good Morning, Midnight*. One of the first, and strongest, "Antillean" memories of the novel—to which Rhys would return many years later in her own unfinished "autobiography" *Smile Please*—reveals the movement of this "monolingualism." Articulating that longing to be black that is at the heart of the "impasse" of Rhys's Creole consciousness, Anna's recollection of her nurse Francine recalls a song. This song supplies the memory that seems to be the absent cause of all those various other "Rhys women"—the memory, that is, of departure from home:

> She used to sing:
>   *Adieu, sweetheart, adieu*
>   *Salt beef and sardines too,*
>   *And all good times I leave behind,*
>   *Adieu, sweetheart, adieu*
> That was her only English song.
>   –It was when I looked back from the boat and saw the lights of the town bobbing up and down that was the first time I really knew I was going. Uncle Bob said well you're off now and I turned my head so that nobody would see me crying—it ran down my face and splashed into the sea like the rain was splashing—Adieu sweetheart adieu— And I watched the lights heaving up and down. (*V*, 31–2)

The word *adieu* from Francine's "only English song" reproduces a similar translation-problem to that of the word *impasse:* a word that is both French and English. Here, of course, the "English" is underwritten by a French patois, and that Creole perspective written into the Francophone English of the narrative discourse becomes inextricable from the recurrent memories of Anna Morgan's West Indian past. (The word *procession*, linking the "Corpus Christi processions" mentioned in the first paragraph of the novel and the "endless procession of words" in *Nana*, provides a good example of this.) Anchored in the thematic of racial identification—Anna's disavowal of whiteness—this Creole perspective, embedded in the experience of another's relation to English, forms the linguistic trace of an anterior Creole cultural identity and identification (an expanded version of what Rhys does with the erasure of a Creole narrative perspective in the story "Mixing Cocktails"). Anna's memories recall the hostility of her Aunt Hester (like the "English aunt" of "Mixing Cocktails") to Francine. In a scene that describes a classic coming-of-age experience of first menstruation, Anna recalls the different attitudes of her aunt and

Francine—attitudes that construct contrasting, opposed cultural traditions, anticipating the antagonism between Rochester and Christophine in *Wide Sargasso Sea*. Hester's English Victorian conceptions of wit, of literature ("the bookshelf with Walter Scott and a lot of old Longmans' Magazines" [*V*, 70]) and of word games ("Who did Hall Caine? Dorothea Baird" [*V*, 71]) are counterposed with Francine's "ritual" enjoyment of food, her singing and "'beating tambou lé-lé,'" and her storytelling ("Sometimes she told me stories, and at the start of the story she had to say 'Timm, timm,' and I had to answer 'Bois sèche'" [*V*, 71]).

The parallel narrative unfolding of Anna's "voyage" in the dark and the compulsion to repeat memories of her childhood past—mirrored according to a logic of "illness" (the bodily experience of maturation, and the experience of pregnancy and abortion)—culminates in a return to the memory of the Corpus Christi carnival during the concluding, short part of the novel. This apparent recovery of Creole things past constitutes and is constituted by a turn away from, as much as a turn toward, the cultural matrix of those memories. This is the problem of Creole narrative consciousness reduced in the stereotyped trope of "lying in the hammock" from "Mixing Cocktails" and *Good Morning, Midnight* that binds together the impossibility of racial identity and commodified, mass-produced cultural memory. Rather than seeing the Creole perspective of the novel emerge in the contrast between a deathly English and a celebratory carnival culture, its most important trace might be felt in the advertising image that arrests the movement of narrative implied in the literary trope of "voyage"—and its Francophone English counterpart in the "adieu" of Francine's "only English song"—in the dialectical image of commodification: "salt beef," "sardines" and above all "Biscuits Like Mother Makes, as Fresh in the Tropics as in the Motherland, Packed in Airtight Tins" (*V*, 149).

The resemblance between Rhys's genealogies of mass-mediated modernity and Benjamin's *Arcades Project* is interesting not merely for adding a colonial dimension that might seem lacking in Benjamin. On the contrary, what emerges from the problematic impasse of a Creole consciousness is precisely the same set of concerns, converging on the dialectical images of "streets" and "prostitutes": the same focus on the shock effect of experience within a logic of commodification, mass-mediated material culture, and social space. In Benjamin's theory of the "trace" and comments on "interiors," we can discern something of the scope of this recognition that the genealogy of bourgeois white male privilege encounters the shock of its impossible Creole origins. Benjamin's arguments are relevant not so much to allow a reading of Rhys's literary projects, as to illustrate the shared concern each writer has for collecting the material traces of a history that dissolves the "literary" as such—into so many "passages," "citations," "traces."

The Shock of Racial Profiles and the Trace of Creole Culture

Sasha Jansen's encounter with Mr. Blank in *Good Morning, Midnight* contrasts with the memory of successful employment that inaugurates Conrad's *The Shadow-Line*. Although Conrad's novel opens, too, with an abrupt resignation, the "rash" action of having "chucked my berth" (*SL*, 4) on a steamship is prelude to an extended account of the narrator's unexpected appointment as first in command of a sailing ship. These contrasting experiences of losing and acquiring employment, respectively, emphasize, all the more, the difference between Rhys's narrative of female entrapment in an urban topography of city streets and hotel rooms and Conrad's narrative of masculine adventure on the open seas. Yet the very success of Conrad's narrator in gaining employment hinges on an experience of estrangement similar to that of Sasha's encounter with Mr. Blank. This experience is what Benjamin notes in his passing reference to *The Shadow-Line* in the Konvolut entitled "The Interior, the Trace" (*Das Interieur, die Spur*). Benjamin transcribes the narrator's reflections after having received the miraculous commission from the Harbor Master, Captain Ellis: "I was, in common with the other seamen of the port, merely a subject for official writing, filling up forms with all the artificial superiority of a man of pen and ink to the men who grapple with the realities outside the consecrated walls of official buildings."[32]

For Benjamin this passage illustrates "the theory of the trace," and he comments: "Knowledge of human nature, such as the senior employee could acquire through practice, ceases to be decisive" (*"Menschenkenntnis wie der erfahrene Beamte sie wohl durch Übung gewinnen konnte, ist nicht länger etwas Entscheidendes"*).[33] Comparing Conrad's narrator's encounter with the Harbor Master and Sasha's encounter with Mr. Blank, both might be taken as instances of this diminishment of practical knowledge, the elision of experience from the official judgment of an employee. This makes each contrasting experience of acquiring and losing employment structurally the same, both experienced (or rather remembered) as moments of administrative, workplace misrecognition. In each case, the shock of misrecognition consolidates that odd displacement of racial and cultural difference, by which interior narrative monologue establishes itself as entirely English, in contrast to the biographical circumstances of Conrad's Polish and Rhys's West Indian backgrounds.

This displacement might in part be explained by Benjamin's argument that, at the turn of the century, "the real center of gravity of living space is transferred to the office" (*"Um diese Zeit verlagert der wirkliche Schwerpunkt des Lebensraumes sich ins Büro"*).[34] Both Sasha and Conrad's narrator experience the contradictions of living and office space. Sasha finds herself literally and figuratively both enclosed by and excluded from the space of the clothing shop, whose "modernized" reconstruction of "a very old house—two old houses" (*GM*, 25) has resulted in the shop's labyrinthine structure of "passages that don't lead anywhere" (*GM*, 25). Conrad's narrator finds himself miraculously invited to enter—and then appointed to command—official administrative space, as represented successively by the Harbor Office, the Officers' Home, and the interior space of the captain's cabin. In both cases, the contradictions of living and office space define the coordinates of the narrator's retrospective interior monologue.

In the case of Sasha, her own personal investment in the clothing store is defined by a fetishistic consumer attraction to one particular dress, stored in the fitting room to which she retreats in her "nightmare" experience of misunderstanding the English boss. Its cost (four hundred francs) defines what she identifies as her "market value" in the interior dialogue she conducts with Mr. Blank: "So you have the right to pay me four hundred francs a month, to lodge me in a small, dark room" (*GM*, 29). Following the extended memory of this past incident, the discovery that her own hotel room costs twice as much as the "four hundred francs a month" offered to another client leads to the reflection that her appearance as "English tourist" "shows that I have ended as a successful woman, anyway, however I may have started. One look at me and the prices go up" (*GM*, 34). The memory of her earlier attachment to the four-hundred-franc dress defines the contradictory logic of her confinement to the work space of the shop for the sake of her *flâneuse* enjoyment of wandering the streets. The later reflection confirms this as part of the logic of the "impasse" of her present situation: "And when the Exhibition is pulled down and the tourists have departed, where shall I be? In the other room, of course—the one just off Gray's Inn Road, as usual trying to drink myself to death" (*GM*, 34). This early allusion to the Paris International Exposition of 1937 (held between May and November) dates the narrative present tense of the narrator's trip to Paris, determining, too, the temporal and geographical coordinates of its interior monologue according to a tourist economy that overdetermines the contradictory spatial logic of the "impasse" of her hotel room with the living space ("the other room") of her everyday London lodgings.[35]

The opening pages of *The Shadow-Line*, too, focus on a series of interior spaces. The first is the "immaculate interior" of the Harbor Office, "a lofty, big, cool, white room, where the screened light of day glowed serenely. Everybody in it—the officials, the public—was in white. Only the heavy polished desks gleamed darkly in a central avenue, and some papers lying on them were blue. Enormous punkahs sent from on high a gentle draught through the immaculate interior" (*SL*, 7). Over against this embodiment of colonial officialdom is the "Chief Steward's" room—"a strange room to find in the tropics" (*SL*, 9), which seems an exaggerated attempt to sustain the illusion of private bourgeois interiority against the "immaculate" whiteness of colonial administrative work. It seems the very image of Benjamin's description of the way the "interior" emphasizes "traces." What makes it "strange" is precisely its "abundance of covers and protectors, liners and cases," as Benjamin describes the interior, "on which the traces of objects of everyday use are imprinted" (*"Man ersinnt Überzüge und Schoner, Futterals und Etuis in Fülle, in denen die Spuren der alltäglichen Gebrauchsgegenstände sich abdrücken"*).[36] Conrad describes the room as follows:

> The fellow had hung enormously ample, dusty, cheap lace curtains over his windows, which were shut. Piles of cardboard boxes, such as milliners and dressmakers use in Europe, cumbered the corners; and by some means he had procured for himself the sort of furniture that might have come out of a respectable parlour in the East End of London—a horsehair sofa, arm-chairs of the same. I glimpsed grimy antimacassars scattered over that horrid upholstery, which was awe-inspiring, insomuch that one could not guess what mysterious accident, need, or fancy had collected it there. (*SL*, 9)

This image of misplaced, petit-bourgeois European domesticity stands in dialectical opposition to the official space of colonial administrative business: the complementary, if enigmatic and secret private living space, next to the "immaculate interior" of the Harbor Office. Caught between the unpalatable intimations of the Chief Steward (who is scheming to give to another what will become the narrator's command) and the equally distasteful "supremacy of pen and ink" (*SL*, 29) of colonial administration—between the Officers' Home and the Harbor Office—the narrator's dilemma is several times figured in an impossible choice between "work" and "home"; between the decent job he has just quit and a domestic arrangement that he disavows ("This is not a marriage story" [*SL*, 4]). These contradictions are resolved, however, in the space of the captain's cabin. Its decorative interior balances the extremes of domesticity and official business, reconfiguring a topographical relation of interior to exterior space around an implied proper organization of the space of a ship: "The mahogany table under the skylight shone in the twilight like a dark pool of water. The sideboard, surmounted by a wide looking-glass in an ormolu frame, had a marble top. It bore a pair of silver-plated lamps and some other pieces—obviously a harbour display. The saloon itself was panelled in two kinds of wood in the excellent, simple taste prevailing when the ship was built" (*SL*, 52).

While for Conrad it is the social and physical "command" of interior and exterior space that organizes narrative, for Rhys it is the "impasse" of a relation between interior and exterior that coordinates the first-person narrator. Despite the very different social experiences in each, both constitute this spatial dialectic through an excess of emphasis on the first-person narrator. This excess may be linked to the way each narrative revisits memories drawn on in prior literary work. What is notable, however, is that this excessive return to a prior scene of autobiographical fiction constitutes the narrative first person around the material traces of *another* person's prior experience of interiority. In an obvious sense, both narrators encounter interiors that have been inhabited by others: for Rhys, the hotel room; for Conrad, the captain's cabin. In both narratives, though, a prior story embedded within the narrative calls attention to a particular other experience of interiority. Halfway through *Good Morning, Midnight*, on visiting the studio of a Russian painter from whom she will buy a painting of a banjo player, Sasha listens to the painter's "very sad story" of a Martinique woman living in London who is afraid to go out in the streets during the day: "She told me she hadn't been out, except after dark, for two years" (*GM*, 96). This Martinique woman's story recapitulates, in miniature, Sasha Jansen's own story, offering a glimpse of her existence in that "other room," Sasha's London room. The experience of extreme racial estrangement recapitulates the Anglo-French monolingualism of the other and provides a revealing counterpoint to the dialectical relation between room and street figured by Sasha Jansen's "impasse"—an "impasse" whose Parisian topography has its London scene; and whose temporal narrative form (as captured in the title's rhetorical mode of address "Good Morning, Midnight") inverts, too, the usual tropological relation of room and street—the room not usually figured as the refuge from day; the street not usually the place of greeting at night.

In *The Shadow-Line*, the prior story of another's cultural and racial experience is, more centrally, that of the narrator's predecessor, the violin-playing former captain demonized by the first mate, Burns, who insists that his ghost haunts the ship, figuring the ship's passage across latitude 8° 20′ as a trial of exorcism. Though not Creole in the cultural-linguistic sense that undergirds Rhys's work, the story of the captain's affair with a woman in Haiphong introduces a domestic economy of relations whose cultural-racial coding translates many of the same Creole stereotypes from the West to the East Indies. The documentary evidence of the captain's relationship with a woman is a photograph, "that amazing human document," as the narrator describes it, displaying the captain "with his hands reposing on his knees, bald, squat, grey, bristly, recalling a wild boar somehow; and by his side towered an awful, mature, white female with rapacious nostrils and a cheaply ill-omened stare in her enormous eyes" (*SL*, 59). Conrad's handling of this story might be explained by the way his mastery of its basic gothic narrative elements resolves the dialectical relation between private and public interior space: the spectral qualities of a former bourgeois interior space (the captain's cabin) are managed by the practical business of navigation—and that exorcism is performed by turning the haunted spot of the captain's grave (latitude 8° 20´) into a simple matter of cartography.

These prior stories both involve a domestic economy crucially different from that of the first-person narrator. In Rhys's novel, the Martinique woman is living with a Frenchman: "It seemed that she stayed with him because she didn't know where else to go, and he stayed with her because he liked the way she cooked" (*GM*, 96). Recalling the spatial arrangement scripted by the Parisian hotel room's "two beds, a big one for madame and a smaller one on the opposite side for monsieur" (*GM*, 9), but standing in contrast to Sasha's solitary confinement, on an income of "two-pound-ten every Tuesday," in "a room off the Gray's Inn Road" (*GM*, 42), this inner story reformulates the "impasse" of sexual relations in terms of a bourgeois economy of domestic relations—or rather, in terms of the impossibility of such a domestic economy. The Russian painter's story foregrounds an estrangement of national and racial identification at the heart of what might otherwise seem the regulating norm of everyday domestic arrangements. This reveals how interior monologue is constituted around an "impasse" of white racial identification: not the impasse of the "Martiniquaise" of this inner story, but the impasse of that *white* identity that is defined against it. It is around this impossibility of racial identity that the narrative constitutes the topography of interior space. This structure recalls the most famous of all of Jean Rhys's works, *Wide Sargasso Sea*, whose celebrated rereading of *Jane Eyre* calls attention to an anterior Creole experience (the madwoman in the attic) that is the repressed truth of the English domestic interior.

A similar impossibility of white racial identity is at work in Conrad's narrative. Generally, the circumstances of the narrator's appointment to his first command emphasize a difference between the mixed racial populations of the Harbor and of the ship he abandoned, on the one hand, and, on the other, the all-white crew of his first command. Benjamin's choice of passages from Conrad is revealing in this regard because it registers a shock of white racial classification in the narrator's surprise at being chosen to command the ship. The problem of white racial classification is announced early on, around the inexplicable event of the narrator's "throw"ing up his "berth":

[According to Captain Giles's "deeper philosophy"] things out East were made easy for white men. That was all right. The difficulty was to go on keeping white, and some of the nice boys did not know how.

> He gave me a searching look, and in a benevolent, heavy-uncle manner asked point blank:
> 'Why did you throw up your berth?' (*SL*, 14)

What the opening to *The Shadow-Line* captures, more so than just about any other Conrad novel, is the extent to which this "difficulty" of "go[ing] on keeping white" forms part of the alienating experience of being inducted into the administrative bureaucracy of the British merchant service. Yet what this passage identifies is not so much the shock of *losing* one's racial identity, the fear of "going native" (as so many interpretations of "Heart of Darkness" would have it); rather, what is traced here is the shock of being classified as white in the first place. That, at any rate, is one of the implications of the opening *mise-en-scène* of the novella, which begins with the "rash action" of "throwing up a job for no reason" (*SL*, 4). It is this ambiguous avowal or disavowal of a white "berth" that sets the stage for the administrative question raised in Benjamin's passage.

This moment of white racial identification is, moreover, itself underwritten by a prior fantasy that, especially in light of Rhys's work, might be read as a Creole fantasy (or family romance, as we shall discuss in the next chapter). As with Rhys, what makes this a fantasy of impossible white racial identity is the fact that it constitutes the Creole experience as an impossibility of recognized "white" *female* racial identity: the "awful, mature white female" of the photograph, about whom the narrator goes on to say:

> She was disguised in some semi-oriental, vulgar, fancy costume. She resembled a low-class medium or one of those women who tell fortunes by cards for half-a-crown. And yet she was striking. A professional sorceress from the slums.... I noticed that she was holding some musical instrument—guitar or mandoline—in her hand. Perhaps that was the secret of her sortilege." (*SL*, 59)

The cluster of associations evoked by this photograph offer a suggestive combination of racial stereotypes and references to the form of East Indies opera discussed in chapter 2. Although this set of white Creole associations is certainly displaced—exorcised, one might say—in the narrator's recounting of the sea passage across the "shadow-line" of the Gulf of Siam, the photograph (and the photographic medium itself) invokes a lost sense of private bourgeois domestic interior space. The narrator disposes of this experience, as he disposes of the photograph itself ("I even threw it overboard later" [*SL*, 59]), but not without leaving a trace of this creolized white woman's experience in the otherwise entirely homosocial and homoerotic economy of relations on board the ship.

In both *The Shadow-Line* and *Good Morning, Midnight*, these anterior Creole experiences of white racial identity generate the first-person narrative perspective around a doubling and repetition of interior space and interior monologue. As indicated by Walter Benjamin's analysis of the antithetical relation of "living space" to "the place of work," the navigation of sea passages, for Conrad, and the "impasse" of a relation between hotel rooms and city streets, for Rhys, constitute the double-bind of an interior that refers both to a real social experience of geographical space and again only to the "blank space" of its self-referential "scriptural economy." The word *blank* itself, throughout Conrad and Rhys, and according to the logic of Anglo-French "monolingualism of the other" (through association with the French *blanc*), always carries the suggestion of a white racial identity. We see this in the rhetorical gesture with which Rhys has Sasha call her boss "Mr. Blank"; and we see this, too, in *The Shadow-Line*, when the narrator considers "that rather blank side of the situation I had created for myself by leaving suddenly my very satisfactory employment" (*SL*, 18). Each encounter with official administration registers this impossibility of white racial identification in a "blank" space that disrupts, in characteristic modernist fashion, what Michel de Certeau calls the "scriptural economy" of Enlightenment history.

The passage Benjamin cites from Conrad's *The Shadow-Line* is all the more interesting for the way it accidentally identifies an effect of impossible white identification at the heart of that experience of alienation for which the passage is presumably chosen. Benjamin's citation, in fact, splices together two different passages: the narrator's encounter with Captain Ellis, the "Harbor Master" who appoints him to his "first command," and the head shipping master who, even more awed by the narrator's unexpectedly exalted appointment, sees him off in "a short but effusive passage of leave-taking" (*SL*, 34). The difference between the Harbor Master and the head shipping master is deliberately marked in Conrad's text by the insinuation of a racial difference: the latter "had a Scottish name, but his complexion was of a rich olive hue" (*SL*, 29). It is by no means clear how Benjamin may have read this passage himself. Does he mistake the half-caste shipping master for the racially superior Captain Ellis—or vice versa?[37] Does his "theory of the trace"—the theoretical complement to the analysis of the "interior"—hinge on the priority of a *white* or a *mixed racial* recognition of the narrator's Englishness? In the main part of the passage he cites, the narrator's uncanny self-recognition as the "right man" for "command" is constituted by the recognition of others—namely, the shipping master, and all the other various mixed racial employees of the Harbor Office: "To that mixed white, brown, and yellow portion of mankind, out abroad on their own affairs, I presented the appearance of a man walking rather sedately" (*SL*, 35).

The ambiguity of Benjamin's reading of the passage he cites thus recapitulates the problem of spatial reference that constitutes the uncanny interior monologue of first person narrative in both *The Shadow-Line* and *Good Morning, Midnight*.

What Benjamin's *Arcades Project* has perhaps most in common with the concerns of Conrad's *The Shadow-Line* and Rhys's *Good Morning, Midnight* is precisely that ambiguity of reading inscribed in the literary economy of the individual passage of text. For Conrad and Rhys that ambiguity manifests itself in the uncanny reiteration of interior space and interior monologue. For Benjamin the transcription of each of the vast array of passages that constitute the *Arcades Project* aims at grasping "the ambiguity attending the social relationships and products" of the bourgeois epoch, "the law of dialectics seen at a standstill" ("*Zweideutigkeit ist die bildliche Erscheinung der Dialektik, das Gesetz der Dialektik im Stillstand*").[38] It is in this sense, then, that all three writers' attention to modernist form constitutes the literary passage as the trace of an eclipsed bourgeois ideal of interior social space. That lost ideal, in all three cases, constitutes the impossibility of white racial identity around a prior Creole bourgeois experience.

5

CREOLE LEGACIES IN RHYS'S *WIDE SARGASSO SEA* AND PRAMOEDYA'S *THIS EARTH OF MANKIND*

In March of 1958, outlining the novel that would become *Wide Sargasso Sea,* Jean Rhys wrote to Francis Wyndham about her difficulties in finding a title: "I have no title yet. 'The First Mrs Rochester' is not right. Nor, of course is 'Creole.' That has a different meaning now."[1] This comment on the changed meaning of the word *Creole* reiterates the problematic priority of cultural memory we have already found at the heart of Rhys's response to English modernism. If it gives priority to an older, lost colonial meaning of *Creole,* her comment foregrounds at the same time the "different meaning" it has for the emerging, postcolonial present, in March 1958. Both meanings shape *Wide Sargasso Sea.* Although she rejected "Creole" as a title for the novel, the historical and linguistic problem of definition resonates throughout, troubling successive readings in ways that have made the novel a canonical point of reference for the contested understanding of colonial and postcolonial meanings of the term. Confirming the influence of Creole modernism on postcolonial readings of English literary traditions—*Wide Sargasso Sea* has become a touchstone for such postcolonial reevaluations—the critical compulsion to return repeatedly to *Wide Sargasso Sea* also raises the suspicion that the novel itself, and critical readings (like my own here), repeat the reactive formation against Creole modernism that constitutes part of the repetitive formation of English modernism discussed in part I of this study. As I explore in this chapter, comparing Rhys's use of the stereotype of the Creole heiress with Pramoedya's use of a remarkably similar stereotype in *This Earth of Mankind, Wide Sargasso Sea* stages the problematic relation between a lost, colonial meaning and an emerging, postcolonial meaning attached to the "Creole" subject matter of her novel.

Although it is by no means clear what precisely Rhys's letter understands by this "different meaning," at least part of the difference may be explained in terms of a shift in emphasis from a demographic to a linguistic meaning. As Denise de Caires Narain argues, in an attempt to intervene in the disagreement between Kamau Brathwaite and Peter Hulme over the credibility of Rhys's representations of Creole characters in *Wide Sargasso Sea*, the word *Creole* "is now predominantly used to refer to the demotic speech of West Indians (in all its island/mainland variants), rather than to refer to those Europeans born in the West Indies (such as Jean Rhys)."[2] Already in the late 1950s, this newer meaning had acquired much of the complex combination of linguistic, literary, and political resonances that would lead to the theories of "creolization" elaborated in the 1970s by Brathwaite and Glissant. If we consider the extent to which Jean Rhys was writing *Wide Sargasso Sea* at just the moment when a transnational, translinguistic Creole modernism was taking shape, we might well ask how Rhys responds to such an emergent Creole modernism. Why does she return to the nineteenth-century stereotype of the Creole heiress at this historical conjuncture, as the twentieth-century idea of a linguistic and cultural Creole continuum of Caribbean identity is taking shape?[3]

The debates between Hulme and Brathwaite during the mid-1990s anticipate the deep divisions that continue to characterize the critical reception of Rhys's writing.[4] As the "Helen of our wars" (Brathwaite's evocative phrase for her contested place within Caribbean writing), Rhys has also become something of a canonical point of reference for the unresolved debates over theories of race, hybridity, and *créolité* by which Creole modernism, generally speaking, has influenced criticism well beyond Caribbean literary studies, shaping the influential contours of postcolonial studies. Mary Lou Emery's recent *Modernism, the Visual, and Caribbean Literature* finds no difficulty situating Rhys alongside Claude McKay as part of a transformative project of "Caribbean modernism" that developed as early as 1930.[5] By contrast, Carolyn Vellenga Berman's extended study of the figure of the Creole woman in nineteenth-century domestic fiction, *Creole Crossings*, puts Rhys's *Wide Sargasso Sea* in the company of "white supremacist redefinitions of 'Creole' in the late nineteenth century."[6] Both Emery and Berman situate Rhys at the center of extended, important studies of what I am calling "Creole modernism," although Emery sees Rhys as participating in discourses of decolonization while Berman sees Rhys reacting against those discourses.[7]

Berman's study is especially important in tracing the colonial meaning of "Creole"—and in particular the figure of the Creole woman (specified in Rhys's letter)—as a key motif running through nineteenth-century transatlantic domestic fiction. Aligning Rhys's account of the "different meaning" attached to the word *Creole* with that of the *O.E.D.* definition, Berman argues that Rhys retrospectively racializes a term that was "at its core a non-racial category,"[8] applicable to Creoles of color as easily as to white Creoles. This "anachronistic projection of a modern racial binary"[9] is graphically illustrated in the *O.E.D.*'s attempt to give priority to the "now usually = *creole white*" definition (a) over the "now less usually = *creole negro*" definition (b), incidentally eliding altogether the possibility of a mixed racial definition. Arguably, however, it is precisely this problem of meaning that Rhys's *Wide Sargasso Sea* unearths with the contested legacy of the figure of the Creole woman, or heiress. To examine this anachronism—which is both philological and literary—I propose to consider the contested Creole legacy left by Rhys's *Wide Sargasso Sea* alongside the "creole beauty" (*TE*, 205) ("*kreol kecantikan*" [*BM*, 200]) and its legacy in Pramoedya Ananta Toer's *This Earth of Mankind*. Comparing the troubling shifts in the meaning of the term "Creole" registered in Rhys's novel with the apparently entirely different usage of the term within the Indonesian context of Pramoedya's *This Earth of Mankind,* I hope to show how both novels situate the stereotype of the Creole heiress as the linguistic and literary point of contest over genealogies of modernism and modernity.

The Creole Heiress

Both *Wide Sargasso Sea* and *This Earth of Mankind* seem to give priority to the nineteenth-century stereotype of the Creole heiress over the late-twentieth-century interest in linguistic and cultural "creolization" characteristic of the Creole modernism that emerges from Caribbean writing in the 1950s and forms one of the primary foundations for postcolonial theories of hybridity. Rhys emphasizes the fascination for such a stereotype at the outset of Part Two, when she introduces the unnamed Rochester narrative voice through his obsession with the look of Antoinette's facial—and racial—features—above all, her eyes:

> I watched her critically. She wore a tricorne hat which became her. At least it shadowed her eyes which are too large and can be disconcerting. She never blinks at all it seems to me. Long, sad, dark alien eyes. Creole of pure English descent she may be, but they are not English or European either. And when did I notice all this about my wife Antoinette? (*WSS,* 39)

This initial description of Antoinette's "Creole" features is a precise but also precariously balanced rewriting of the image of the Creole to emerge from the combined allure and repulsion with which Rochester describes his first impressions of Bertha Mason in *Jane Eyre*. Above all, the balancing of the physical signs of Antoinette's racial inheritance—"pure English" but then again "not

English or European either"—is overdetermined by the manner in which Rochester's assessment here, as retrospectively in the account from *Jane Eyre*, concerns the "bargain" of the marriage. Throughout Part Two the implications of this twinning of racial and financial legacies will unfold in an account that simultaneously plots the consolidation of, and dissects, the nineteenth-century English stereotype of the West Indian Creole heiress.

In order to assess in what ways this return to the nineteenth-century stereotype of the Creole constitutes a response to the linguistic-literary formation of Creole modernism, we might contrast this inaugural objectification of Antoinette's Creole look with the objectification of the "creole beauty" (*TE*, 205) ("*kreol kecantikan*" [*BM*, 200]) of Annelies in *This Earth of Mankind*. This objectification is inaugurated early in the novel, well before the phrase "creole beauty" surfaces, midway through the novel, in repeated formulations that emphasize its function as a particular, and particularly literary stereotype. Minke's very first description of Annelies reveals a fascination for the fetish of her racialized appearance analogous to the example from *Wide Sargasso Sea*:

> In front of us stood a girl, white-skinned, refined, European face, hair and eyes of a Native. And those eyes, those shining eyes! ("Like a pair of morning stars," I called them in my notes.) (*TE*, 25)
>
> *Suasana baru menggantikan: di depan kami berdiri seorang gadis berkulit putih, halus, berwajah Eropa, berambut dan bermata Pribumi. Dan mata itu, mata berkilauan itu seperti sepasang kejora; dan bibirnya tersenyum meruntuhkan iman.* (*BM*, 12)[10]

There are a number of obvious contrasts between Minke's instant fascination for Annelies's looks and Rochester's initial description of the "disconcerting" aspect of Antoinette's looks. Many of these contrasts, however, only confirm the sense in which each elaborates on the same stereotype of "creole beauty." "Creole beauty" is the formulation that appears later in *This Earth of Mankind* when the poetic simile describing her eyes—"like a pair of morning stars" ("*seperti sepasang kejora*")—is repeated as part of a more extended literary topos.

Although Rochester at first appears more repelled than attracted by Antoinette's eyes, it soon becomes apparent that this very dynamic of repulsion and attraction is determined by a similar stereotype of Creole beauty to that in *This Earth of Mankind*. In his first attempt at a letter to his father, Rochester imagines writing "I have sold my soul or you have sold it, and after all is it such a bad bargain? The girl is thought to be beautiful, she is beautiful. And yet..." (*WSS*, 41). This sequence—"thought to be beautiful"; "is beautiful"; "And yet"—constitutes the core dynamic of Rochester's troubled response to the reputed beauty of the Creole heiress, a response which, as this passage makes clear, involves a complex imbrication of public and private evaluations of the economic, social, and cultural transactions involved with the "bargain" of marriage to a Creole heiress. It echoes the opening of Part Two—"So it was all over, the advance and retreat, the doubts and hesitations" (*WSS*, 38).

Over the course of Part Two, the narrative traces the troubled combination of repulsion and attraction with which Rochester responds to Antoinette, and to everything she embodies for him, producing his final judgment on her madness—a judgment that consolidates not only the general type of the "mad Creole" discussed in Rhys's 1958 letter cited above but also "that particular mad Creole"—that is, the Bertha Mason character of *Jane Eyre*. One of the things that make this so compelling a reading of nineteenth-century English usage of the term *Creole* is its ability to show the inner logic connecting two apparently contradictory definitions: the Creole of pure white descent and the Creole of mixed descent. Both come together in the prestige, and suspicion of the prestige, attached to the family lineage of the white Creole heiress. One key axis of the plot of the arranged marriage between Rochester and Bertha Mason, as Jean Rhys reconstructs it from *Jane Eyre*, is Rochester's growing suspicion about Antoinette's family background. The inherited madness that Rochester projects onto Antoinette, and in the emblematic form of the name Bertha, is simultaneously figured as the inherited madness of a pure white heritage and as the product of her mixed racial family background.

A similar combination of seemingly contradictory racial stereotypes figures the mental breakdown of Annelies in *This Earth of Mankind*, although here the primary sense of Annelies's "creole" identity would appear to be the opposite from that of Antoinette: while the latter is presented first as a Creole of pure white descent, the former is first presented as a Creole of mixed racial descent. The contrast emphasizes Rhys's investment in a white Creole identity, by contrast to Pramoedya's investment in the mixture of Annelies's racial characteristics. This racial investment is crucial in shaping what Peter Hulme has called the "creole family romance" by which Rhys screens out a whole history of anti-colonial struggle in order to re-inscribe the coordinates of Bertha Mason's family history in *Jane Eyre* within a condensed and displaced version of her own white Creole family history.[11] A similar kind of racial investment might be seen at work in shaping what emerges, in counterpoint to *Wide Sargasso Sea*, as the Creole family romance of the Buru tetralogy. Each Creole family romance appears to stand in striking opposition the one to the other: the one to produce a white Creole identity distinct from both a metropolitan English national identity and distinct from black or mixed Creole ancestry; the other to produce a mixed Creole identity whose primary identification will be for the native (*pribumi*) over against the white side of the family line. The problems of racial identification embedded in each Creole family romance may certainly be linked to autobiographical considerations that would help sharpen the contrast between the nostalgic colonial racism shaping Rhys's work and the anti-colonial critique of racism shaping Pramoedya's work.[12] What is more interesting and important, however, in assessing the significance of both these Creole family romances for the mid-twentieth-century moment of decolonization, is that they both grasp the problem of racial identity and identification as a fundamental problem of delusion, a pathology of identity that recalls the "vicious circle" of "dual narcissism" of black–white relations Frantz Fanon set out to break in *Black Skin, White Masks*.[13] There is a structural and historical relation between the delusional pure white Creole perspective of *Wide Sargasso Sea* and the delusional mixed racial Creole perspective of *This Earth of Mankind*. What each shares is the problem of reading the racial features of the Creole (the appearance of the racial fetish, whether that of the pure white or that of the mixed racial features).

In both novels, it is the outside (non-Creole) perspective that consolidates this delusional moment of recognition, something emphasized all the more by the obsessive fascination with eyes. In *Wide Sargasso Sea*, this objectification of the Creole enables Rhys to reconfigure the motivating problem of narrative perspective informing almost all of her previous first-person narrators—namely, the ambiguous priority of cultural perspective, or background, embodied by, and written into the names, of such figures as Marya Zelli, Anna Morgan, Julia Martin, and Sasha Jansen. So effective is this reconfiguration, indeed, that it is difficult not to read all of those characters in light of *Wide Sargasso Sea*, and to characterize Rhys's motivating narrative dynamic as one dominated by the problem of Creole perspective. What such a retrospective rereading misses, however, is the extent to which the Creole perspective in Rhys can never emerge as anything but a delusional identity, and as seen from an outside, non-Creole perspective. If *Wide Sargasso Sea* most clearly identifies a Creole cultural problematic underlying all of Rhys's work, it does so as a matter of negative identification. Neither the Creole status of the nineteenth-century white Creole heiress nor the flexibility of a twentieth-century Creole linguistic-literary space offers the originary ground, or primary form of identification. In this sense, and within the logic of her own narrative fiction, the form of her literary affiliation with an emerging Creole modernism in the 1950s and 1960s describes a revealing negative dialectic. Caught between the two different meanings of the term *Creole*, as articulated in the letter cited above, her novel's failure to affiliate with a contemporary, emergent Caribbean creole-linguistic continuum is itself grasped in the failure of affiliation embodied in Antoinette's Creole family romance—a failure of affiliation powerfully imagined at the very heart of English literary traditions. Paradoxically, then, the very excess of her identification with English literary tradition marks both her distance from the Creole modernism of Caribbean writing and the defining role of her work in illuminating how fundamentally Creole modernism reshapes English literary tradition in light of twentieth-century developments in Caribbean writing.

The significance of this delusional moment of Creole recognition in *Wide Sargasso Sea* may be measured against the corresponding emphasis Pramoedya's Buru quartet places on a delusional Creole recognition in the formation of Indonesian modernism. As with *Wide Sargasso Sea*, this moment of Creole recognition is most fully embodied from the perspective of the madwoman—in the final section of *Wide Sargasso Sea* when Antoinette becomes the Bertha Mason character from *Jane Eyre*; and in the concluding moments of *This Earth of Mankind*, when Annelies attempts to define the terms of her deportation to Europe. We shall need to return to the problem posed by each of those attempts to present the psychological state of the Creole. As with *Wide Sargasso Sea*, however, that final moment is premised on an outsider's grasp—in the case of *This Earth of Mankind*, of course, that of the narrator, Minke.

As with *Wide Sargasso Sea*, Minke's outsider status vis-à-vis Annelies's "creole beauty" is emphasized. The term "creole beauty" first surfaces at the point when Dr. Martinet, in his attempts to diagnose Annelies's mental breakdown, gives to Minke the responsibility of psychiatric doctor that he has up until then himself only reluctantly assumed ("I'm not a psychologist" [*TE*, 204]; "*Maaf. Aku bukan ahlijiwa*" [*BM*, 199]). "And I—an outsider, just an acquaintance—must I also accept some responsibility for her just because of her beauty? Creole beauty" (*TE*, 205) ("*Dan aku—seorang luaran, seorang kenalan sahaja—kini harus ikut bertanggungjawab hanya karena kecantikannya semata. Kecantikan kreol*" [*BM*, 200]). The appearance of the term *kreol* almost as a matter of psychiatric diagnosis certainly deserves closer consideration. One thing it reinforces, however, is the sense in which Minke's "outsider" status quite clearly sets the cultural meaning of that term *creole* (or *kreol*) at a much farther distance from the Caribbean coordinates of Rhys's sense of the term. On the one hand, one might emphasize the extent to which it is a generalized, cosmopolitan stereotype—a multicultural ideal, illusion, or rather pathology. This is suggested a page later when Minke invokes the names of Alexander the Great and Napoleon: "Alexander the Great, Napoleon, all would fall to their knees to gain your love" (*TE*, 206) ("*Iskandar Zulkornain, Napoleon, pun akan berlutut memohon kasihmu*" [*BM*, 201]). Here the meaning of the term *kreol* would appear to extend well beyond the sense that predominates in English—namely, a designation for those born in the Americas, and most especially in the Caribbean.

The delusion of universality and geographic specificity, however, is built into this first enunciation of the term *creole* in a particularly striking way. Minke asks: "Where else on this earth of mankind could one discover such perfect Creole beauty, such a beautifully harmonious form?" (*TE*, 206) ("*Kecantikan kreol yang sempurna, dalam keserasian bentuk seperti yang aku hadapi sekarang ini, di mana dapat ditemukan lagi di tempat lain di atas bumi manusia ini?*" [*BM*, 201]). It is this question that leads to the flight of excessive poetic fancy that consolidates the trope of "Creole beauty" all at once as the touching, slightly self-mocking, but also tragic recognition of Minke's own pathological attachment to Annelies, as lover, apprentice-psychiatrist, and husband-to-be:

> Her eyes blinked so slowly. Yet her beauty was still profound, greater than all the combined and individual meanings to be found in the treasuries of the languages. She was a gift from Allah, without equal, unique. And she was mine alone.
>
> "Arise and awaken, Flower of Surabaya! Do you not know? Alexander the Great, Napoleon, all would fall to their knees to gain your love. To touch your skin they would sacrifice their nations, their people. Awaken, My Flower, because the world is a lesser place without you," and without knowing it I was kissing her on the lips, and then became fully conscious of what I was doing. (*TE*, 206)
>
> *Kedipan matanya begitu lambat. Namun kecantikannya tetap agung, lebih agung daripada segala perbuatan yang pernah dilakukan orang, lebih kaya daripada semua dan seluruh makna yang terkandung dalam perbendaharaan bahasa. Ia adalah karunia Allah tiada duanya, satu-satunya. Dan dia hanya untukku.*
>
> "*Bangun dan sadar, kau, Puspita Surabaya! Apa kau tak tahu? Iskandar Zulkornain, Napoleon, pun akan berlutut memohon kasihmu? Bahwa untuk dapat menyentuh kulitmu mereka akan bersedia mengurbankan seluruh bangsa dan negerinya? Bangun, Puspitaku, karena kehidupan ini merugi tanpa kesaksianmu,*" *dan tanpa setahuku telah kukecup bibirnya dalam keadaan sepenuh sadarku.* (*BM*, 201)

The stereotyped excess here makes for a number of difficulties in translation, reading, and commentary. In particular, given the number of different literary traditions converging here (Malay, Javanese, European), there is a sort of aesthetic and cultural surplus for which no amount of expertise in Indonesian studies can account. The *tone* is difficult to evaluate. Is it excessively and unselfconsciously trapped in sexist, cultural stereotyping (as Clifford Geertz judges of the Buru tetralogy in general[14])? Or is the excess its self-conscious manipulation of stereotype, as might rather be suggested by the philological consciousness betrayed in the formulation "richer than all the combined and individual meanings to be found in the treasuries of the languages" (*"lebih kaya daripada semua dan seluruh makna yang terkandung dalam perbendaharaan bahasa"*). This is a part of that aesthetic problem of operatic taste traced at the beginning of our study. A little later, indeed, the trope of "Creole beauty" is specifically associated with an operatic aesthetic, when Magda Peters visits the Mellema family and finds Annelies "like an Italian prima donna" (*TE*, 227) (*"seperti primadonna Italia"* [*BM*, 222]).

In this way, the comparison between the Creole stereotype in *This Earth of Mankind* and *Wide Sargasso Sea* calls attention to the possibility that the generic and aesthetic distortion of opera, this space of literary estrangement for Conrad's English modernism and Pramoedya's Indonesian modernism, respectively, might be seen to constitute, in longer historical perspective, the Creole modernism to which both Conrad and Pramoedya respond—each at opposite ends of the twentieth century, and from opposite sides of the social and political experience of colonialism and decolonization. Pramoedya's use of the term *Creole* itself points to a literary precursor that both confirms this suggestion and might help illuminate its relevance for the relation between *This Earth of Mankind* and *Wide Sargasso Sea*. Louis Couperus's 1900 novel *De Stille Kracht* (*The Hidden Force*) constitutes an important touchstone within Dutch literature both for the literary trope of the Creole and for the sociological significance of that trope within Dutch East Indies colonial society.

For Couperus, indeed, the stereotype of the "milky white Creole" (*"deze melkblanke kreole"*),[15] as embodied in the character of Léonie, figures the decadence of Dutch East Indies colonial society. At the beginning of the novel, she is introduced as possessing "the languid dignity of women born in Java, daughters of European parents on both sides" (*"mit die loome statigheid van in Indië geboren vrouwen, dochters van geheel Europeesche ouders"*).[16] This mark of family distinction, however, is compromised both by the fact that she arrives as a divorcee and stepmother—in other words, a *former* Creole heiress—and by the ambiguity of her racially marked, Creole white physical appearance:

> She had something that attracted attention at once. It was because of her white skin, her creamy complexion, her very light blond hair, her strange gray eyes, which were sometimes narrowed a little and always held an ambiguous expression.[17]
>
> *Zie had iets, waarnaar men dadelijk keek. Het was om haar blanke vel, haar teint van melk, haar heel licht blond haar, hare oogen, vreemd grauw, soms even geknepen en altijd met een uitdrukking van dubbelzinnigheid.*[18]

Echoing the terms of Rochester's attempt to pin down the "disconcerting" look of Antoinette in *Wide Sargasso Sea*, but displacing the ambiguity of the look onto a description of the way she walks, the narrative concludes its initial portrait of Léonie, turning her character into a synecdoche for creole East Indies society: "Yet though she looked very European, it may have been her leisurely walk, that languid dignity that was the only Indies characteristic that distinguished her from a woman newly arrived from Holland" ("*en in hare zeer Europeesche verschijning was misschien alleen die langzame pas, die loome statigheid de Indische nuance, dat, wat haar onderscheidde van een vrouw, pas uit Holland*").[19] During the course of the novel, however, this "languid dignity" undergoes a process of decadent dissolution. Only ten pages later, it becomes "the loitering gait and swinging hips peculiar to the Creole" ("*met haar sleeppas van heupwiegelende kreole*");[20] and by the middle of the novel she has become the "milky white Creole" ("*deze melkblanke kreole*"),[21] whose decadent sensuality desires both Theo, her husband's pure European son, and Addy, his illegitimate mixed-race son—she "wanted to taste" the "difference between the white-skinned Dutch type, which had only slightly been influenced by the Indies, and Addy's wild, animal type" ("*zij wilde proeven het verschil van hun beider mannebekoring; dat even ver-Indo'schte Hollandsche blond-en-blanke, en het wilde-dierachtige van Addy*").[22] By the end of the novel, her "milky white Creole languour" ("*melkblanke kreole-loomheid*")[23] gets transformed into the stereotype of the mad Creole woman, as registered in Addy's recoil from her toward the end of the novel:

> Something in her words and in her voice struck him: a crazy hysteria, which he had never noticed before, when she had always been the quietly passionate mistress, her eyes half closed.... Something in her repelled him. He loved the soft, pliant surrender of her caresses, the smiling indolence that she used to display, but not these half-crazed eyes and purple mouth which seemed ready to bite.[24]
>
> *Hij zag haar aan: iets in hare woorden, in hare stem deed hem opzien, een hysterische gedetraqueerdheid, die hem vroeger nooit was opgevallen, toen zij altijd geweest was de stil hartstochtelijke minnares, de oogen half gesloten... Iets stuitte hem van haar af: hij hield van het lenige en weeke en meêgeven van liefkoozing, met iets indolents en glimlachends— zooals zij vroeger geweest was:—niet van deze half krankzinnige oogen en purpuren mond, gereed om te bijten.*[25]

This demonization of the figure of the Creole white woman suggests a common literary trope shared across the variety of national, linguistic, and cultural traditions within which both Jean Rhys and Pramoedya Ananta Toer are working. It is possible to explain the convergence of these various traditions on this stereotype in terms of a discursive shift, in the Foucauldian sense, from the politics of alliance to an analytics of blood.[26] The Creole heiress, in this regard, becomes the point of reference for an eclipsed, older politics of alliance; her racialized objectification and demonization as mad woman constitutes the emergence of a racism born of new biopolitical discourses.

Such a view is especially useful in light of the comparative sociological perspective underscored by Couperus's novel. While Rhys deploys the stereotype of the Creole heiress through recourse to the specific sociological context of Caribbean society, Pramoedya deploys it through that of Dutch East Indies society. There are, to be sure, important material cultural analogies to be noted between the colonial plantation culture in the West Indies and that of the East Indies—in both cases, the collapse of a Creole, landholding social elite is the sociological premise for a transitional late-colonial state formation. The question, though, is the extent to which that comparative global cultural framework precedes, or follows, the formation of the literary stereotype of the Creole heiress. If Couperus's work suggests the priority of the literary stereotype, it illuminates the extent to which that very stereotype has long served as a way of regulating, through aesthetic categories, those perceptions of social and racial heritage. This may be why Rhys turns to the Creole family romance at the heart of English literary traditions, and why Pramoedya turns to the Creole family romance in the formative moment of an emergent Indonesian literary tradition.

Creole Family Romances

The delusional moment of Creole recognition, in both *Wide Sargasso Sea* and *This Earth of Mankind*, inaugurates, then, a specifically Creole family romance. The Freudian formulation of a "family romance" (*Familienroman*) is useful here precisely insofar as it foregrounds the model of reading stories in distinguishing (ultimately) the "family romance" as a phase of normal fantasy for the child growing up, on the one hand, and signaling a neurotic distortion in the adult, on the other.[27] The Freudian family romance comes to be regulated according to a particular model of reading— namely, the Freudian reading of Oedipus—but the core problem of piecing together the "family background" in order to determine psychological disorders retains something of the profoundly problematic question of determining what is normative, what is pathological (something that Françoise Vergès indicates is the shaping problem of priority in the development of the "family romance" model). Both *Wide Sargasso Sea* and *This Earth of Mankind* grasp this problem of priority embedded in their respective Creole family romances as a problem of reading (at root, the problem of negotiating the passage into literacy), and it is this problem of reading the Creole legacy that illuminates each work's relation to the linguistic-literary formation of Creole modernism.

Following the cue of Freud's formulation of the *Familienroman*, with its allusive reference to *novel* (*Roman*) form, the Creole family romance might, in each case, best be grasped as a problem of narrative form. Both *Wide Sargasso Sea* and *This Earth of Mankind* invest the psychological breakdown of their Creole characters around a problematic relation to the very kind of novel form with which each is itself arguably obsessed. Antoinette's madness, in Part Three of *Wide Sargasso Sea,* is figured in her claustrophobic enclosure within the pages of Charlotte Brontë's *Jane Eyre*. Annelies's declining condition, too, is figured in her inability to relate to the European stories Minke reads to her: "Come now, begin a beautiful story. One better than Stevenson's *Treasure Island* or *Kidnapped*, more beautiful than Dickens's *Our Mutual Friend.* Those stories don't speak, Mas" (*TE,* 236) ("*Ayoh, mulai saja cerita yang indah. Lebih bagus dari* Pulau Emas *dan* Terculik-nya*Stevenson itu, lebih indah dari* Sahabat Karib *Dickens. Cerita-cerita itu tidak bersuara, Mas*" [*BM,* 230]). A key feature of each narrative is the parallel between the enforced "return" of the Creole to Europe and the feared enclosure within European novel form. This narrative formula dictates the core problem of *Nachträglichkeit* around which the Creole family romance is elaborated: the Cosway family romance retrospectively unfolded as prequel to the Bertha Mason of Charlotte Brontë's *Jane Eyre;* and Minke's mourning for the loss of Annelies, which constitutes the narrative point of departure for the notes on which the novel is based: "In the beginning I wrote these short notes during a period of mourning: She had left me, who could tell if only for a while or forever?" (*TE,* 15) ("*Pada mulanya catatan pendek ini aku tulis dalam masa berkabung: dia telah tinggalkan aku, entah untuk sementara entah tidak*" [*BM,* 1]). It is, indeed, the structural importance of this narrative formula that foregrounds the importance of the Creole family romance for each author. This is underscored by Peter Hulme's use of the term "creole family romance" to refer to Jean Rhys's own retrospective reconstruction, and displacement, of her family's "Creole" lineage in *Wide Sargasso Sea*. Hulme seeks to bring meticulous material attention to the historical details excluded from the novel's family romance to demonstrate the extent to which that fiction—or "romance"—displaces the historical realities of English colonial politics following the moment of the novel. This approach yields crucial information, although its most intriguing contribution may in fact be to compel us to return to the terms of the novel's logic of misnaming and displacement in the construction of its own fictional Creole family romance. Such a romance (and whatever pathology we ascribe to it) belongs less to the biography of the author (Ella Gwendoline Rees Williams) than it does to the

English literary tradition whose continuity or discontinuity is invoked by her name (Jean Rhys).

Minke's Creole family romance may have a less obvious biographical, or autobiographical significance. Nonetheless, given the fact that the Buru tetralogy as a whole bears witness to the national trauma of 1965, and Pramoedya's deportation with thousands of other political prisoners to the penal island colony of Buru, it is important to consider in what sense this retrospectively formulated narrative emphasis on Minke's melancholic loss of the "creole beauty" relates to the traumatic experiences of 1965. As we shall explore more fully in the chapter to follow, it is Annelies's mother, the Nyai Ontosoroh, who stands as the figure of testimony. To the extent that she comes to embody the ideals of revolutionary Indonesian anti-colonial nationalism, however, it is the traumatic loss of her daughter—and the Creole family romance that this retrospectively crystallizes for Minke and for the overall narrative shape of the Buru quartet—that consolidates Nyai Ontosoroh as the heroic and tragic figure of Indonesian nationalism.

The different manner in which these two novels plot the Creole woman's enforced "return" to Europe as itself a movement into madness and delusion might be seen to enact a kind of chiasmatic mirroring of the colonial and postcolonial variations of the colonial family romance. In the plot of *This Earth of Mankind*, the colonial law courts refuse to recognize any Native family claims on Annelies—neither those of her mother, who, as a native Nyai, has already lost legal maternity over her children in having them recognized as the legal children of their European father; nor those of her husband, Minke, since the standing of Islamic marriage law is not recognized by the colonial Christian legal system. The courts grant legal guardianship over Annelies to Mellema's Dutch wife and son Maurits, and Annelies is essentially deported, against her will, to Holland. In this way Minke's Creole family romance constitutes the utopian afterimage of a rude awakening to the realities of colonial legislation and its repressive force. By comparison to the plot of *Wide Sargasso Sea*, it is striking to note the extent to which the mixed racial ideal of "creole beauty" that embodies this utopian afterimage is negated by the imposition of a white identity legislated by the courts.

The terms of this dispossession of Annelies's native heritage are made explicit in a way that also reflects, in a chiasmatic reversal and in contrasting comparative cultural perspective, the legal dispossession that accompanies Antoinette's return to her husband's estate in England. The question of legality, property, and ownership at the center of the court battle with which *This Earth of Mankind* ends concerns the Mellema estate. Not until the end of *Child of All Nations* will this estate finally be appropriated from Nyai. Symbolically it is already clear, however, that the legal battle over Annelies constitutes the emergence of a Manichean struggle between colonized and colonizer. In this struggle, the Creole heiress figures an erasure of native claims to property and rights; it becomes, indeed, the trope for transforming such claims into those of a European legacy.

If Minke's Creole family romance emerges, retrospectively, as the melancholic loss entailed by the systematic dispossession of native rights with the *mise-en-scène* of the colonial contest, Antoinette's creole family romance emerges, also, as a melancholic loss, but from the retrospective narrative perspective of the dispossessing colonizer, the Rochester figure in Part Two of *Wide Sargasso Sea*. There is an obvious simplicity in viewing the one (*This Earth of Mankind*) as narrating the perspective of the colonized, whereas the other (*Wide Sargasso Sea*) narrates the perspective of the colonizer. Such a Fanonian perspective is, in fact, invited by the shared narrative trajectory of the Creole woman's racialized and gendered objectification and contestation. Yet this very simplification underscores the extent to which the Creole family romance, both for the colonized and for the colonizer, in a Fanon-like Manichean contrast, remains the romance of an *outsider*. This is, indeed, the sense in which it marks a racialized pathology in the Freudian formation of the "family romance": as a fiction that survives the normal fantasies of childhood adjustment, the Creole family romance constitutes the sign of a pathological attachment: Minke's melancholic attachment to the memory of Annelies (which constitutes the narrative *mise-en-scène*, and aesthetic *mise-en-abyme* for the entire quartet); Rochester's obsessive attachment to Antoinette's Creole family background, a fantasy condensed, displaced, and encrypted in the name Bertha.

Most readings of *Wide Sargasso Sea* consider Rochester's renaming of Antoinette a violent erasure of her West Indian cultural identity, the imposition of an English name in place of the French first name she shares with her mother and as a sign of her mother's Martinique background.[28] Compelling though this reading certainly is, it tends to give priority to the power of rejection over that of Rochester's initial attraction. Both sides of Rochester's response need to be considered in order to recognize in what sense the novel's Creole family romance is shaped at least as much through the English first-person narrative perspective of Part Two as it is through that of Antoinette's first-person narrative voice. When Rochester comes to impose the name "Bertha" on Antoinette, it signals all at once his attraction and repulsion. If this English-sounding name displaces the mother's French name ("He has found out it was my mother's name" [*WSS*, 68]), it symptomatically reveals what Rochester suspects she has inherited from her mother. "Bertha" is the name that both conceals and betrays the paranoid knowledge with which Rochester (projecting his own madness onto Antoinette) has constructed his own romance of Antoinette's Creole family.

In its attempt to contain the madness associated with the mother's name, it also reveals the complex of further associations embedded in Rochester's observations about his wife's "long, sad, dark alien eyes." It is the entire chain of these associations—the racialized identity that is neither English nor European; the possibility of illegitimate relations within the extended Cosway family; and, in particular as relayed through Daniel Cosway who claims to be one of those relations, the secret of the mother's madness—that constitutes the confirmation of the stereotype of the Creole madwoman for Rochester, in a way not unlike the progressive unraveling of the "languid dignity" of Couperus's creole into the "crazy hysteria" of her final appearance. Yet it is just this movement, consolidating the stereotype of Creole madwoman, that crystallizes, too, Rochester's Creole family romance on which his own paranoid pathology hinges. Each stage in the fulfillment of the "bargain" of the marriage transaction betrays his own investment in the very fantasy of a Creole family romance that he would appear, in the end, violently to be rejecting. At the very outset, even although he seems inwardly to rebel against the monetary terms of the arranged marriage, he persuades Antoinette to set aside her own misgivings on the basis of personal "trust" as opposed to the public, monetary "bargain" ("I'll trust you if you'll trust me. Is that a bargain?" [*WSS*, 47]). Already, indeed, this contrast between a public and private economy of relations has revealed a psychic dependence on the Creole family romance that no amount of financial compensation can accommodate. In the first imaginary letter to his father, Rochester's financial and psychic accounting of the marriage transaction yields the conclusion: "I have sold my soul or you have sold it, and after all is it such a bad bargain? The girl is thought to be beautiful, she is beautiful. And yet..." (*WSS*, 41). Rochester is quick to dispense with the financial accounting of the bargain (the "thirty thousand pounds"), but he will never come to terms with his obsession for Antoinette's Creole beauty.

Rochester's dependence on his Creole family romance becomes clearest where it is most destructive—in the act of sleeping with Amélie; and in his confrontation with Christophine. Each of these scenes demonstrates the manner in which he breaks up her relationship with the domestic servants. But it is in the process of destroying her own identity, and the affiliations on which it depends, that his own paranoid dependence on those very affiliations emerge: his desire for Amélie reduplicates the racialized fascination, attraction and repulsion, he exhibits toward Antoinette; his antagonism toward Christophine, giving fullest expression to his rejection of Antoinette's Creole cultural world, also defines the extent to which he has come to depend on a paranoid knowledge of that world—its obeah and patois in particular—to control (or rather fuel) his own pathology through an oppressive patriarchal control of others.

It is in plotting the crystallization of this paranoid knowledge that Rhys formulates, around Rochester's Creole family romance, a relation between the "different meaning[s]" of "Creole" elaborated in her 1958 letter: between the nineteenth-century stereotype of the Creole and the twentieth-century sense of a Creole linguistic and cultural continuum. The novel's own dependence on obeah as a key element of plotting, and its occasional, strategic use of patois to give linguistic-literary texture to the West Indian world that attracts and repels Rochester must be read both in relation to the new political, linguistic, and cultural sense of "creolization" emerging at the time Rhys was writing and as part of longstanding stereotypes of the Creole, especially nineteenth-century literary stereotypes and not necessarily even those specific to the West Indies (as demonstrated by Couperus's East Indies "creole" Léonie, whose dissolution is also ascribed to the "hidden force" of native witchcraft).

Rochester's paranoid knowledge of obeah, for example, suggests an unresolved relation between the two (made all the more visible in Judith Raiskin's Norton Critical Edition, whose authoritative explanations of obeah, or "the creolized, syncretic religion" of "vodou,"[29] provide illuminating explanations for the love potion, or "poison," administered by Christophine; but whose cultural and scientific explanations only increase the effects of paranoid knowledge produced in Part Two). Obeah becomes the sign of his decisive turn against Antoinette's affiliations, but it also reveals the extent of what he has sought to learn about West Indian society before he breaks it up. It is a sign of how much he suspects he himself has been "creolized." And within the larger scope of the novel, it is a sign of how much English culture is grounded on a process of "creolization." Rochester's Creole family romance is all at once a retrospective illumination of the older sense of the term *Creole* and an examination of how this nineteenth-century English repressed Creole family romance reveals the process of "creolization," in the newer sense of the term, long at work in the formation of English culture.

This begins to emerge in the manner in which the dispute over obeah defines Antoinette's Creole identity according to a racial difference that is based on an ultimately undecideable linguistic question. The dispute between Rochester and Christophine over obeah—what forms the axis of plotting in Part Two, and what constitutes for Rochester the deciding *legal* issue—is not simply the question of whether or not Rochester was poisoned. This, already, might be said to constitute a *differend* in Lyotard's sense of the legal definition of this neologism, because what Rochester considers "poison" Antoinette considers a love potion. Christophine, however, introduces a distinction that complicates the love/hate symmetry of this trope of the love potion. Arguing that obeah is not meant for white people—"it's too strong for *béké*" (*WSS*, 92) (a phrase mimicked in Rochester's parenthetical thoughts)—Christophine introduces a Creole term for "white" (*béké*) that she then goes on to apply to the definition of Antoinette's identity in a way that recalls Rochester's earlier comment on Antoinette's eyes ("Creole of pure English descent she may be, but they are not English or European either"): "She is not *béké* like you, but she is *béké*, and not like us either" (*WSS*, 93). It is this patois restatement of the problem of Antoinette's Creole white identity that governs the more fundamental dispute between Rochester and Christophine—namely, whether it is Christophine or Rochester who is responsible for Antoinette's mental breakdown.

The critical debate over whether Christophine offers a subaltern perspective within the novel or, on the contrary, shores up a white Creole fantasy of the loyal and devoted *da* reduplicates the novel's own ambivalence, as registered in her patois voice, with regard to the emergent Creole modernism of the 1950s.[30] The fact that Rochester's own voice deliberately mimics her formulations, in the parenthetical rejoinders that punctuate the scene of their confrontation; the fact that these formulations, and notably the formulation about Antoinette as *béké*, double Rochester's earlier observations; and, finally, the fact that the novel's opening anticipates all these nuances in Christophine's initial patois formulation for the dilemma of creole beauty—"The Jamaican ladies had never approved of my mother, 'because she pretty like pretty self' Christophine said" (*WSS*, 9)—all this underscores the linguistic function of creole or patois in articulating a problem of Creole identity. What remains undecideable, however, is the extent to which it is the English or the Creole voice that frames this problem of identity.

As we have already seen, the parenthetical English mimicry of Creole phrases in the narrative voice of Part Two suggests something much more interesting than a mere heightening of the use of patois phrases for local color. As with the structure of Rochester's Creole family romance, the attempt to control the effects of Creole as a language become an organizing obsession within the novel's most English voice. All those moments of mimicry, and especially in the scene of confrontation with Christophine, provide ample illustrations of the effects of what Homi Bhabha has examined in terms of the ambivalence and hybridity of colonial mimicry.[31] To the extent that Bhabha's argument itself constitutes an elaboration on the linguistic model of "creolization" this is, after all, entirely to be expected. It is the thoroughgoing ambivalence of such mimicry that opens this model of "creolization" to the problems of identity that so notoriously attend it and subsequent theories of hybridity. The meaning of *Creole* is always bound to reduplicate that problem of its "different" meaning articulated in Rhys's 1958 letter. All the "different" meanings are registered when Christophine gives voice to the nineteenth-century stereotype of the Creole: "She is Creole girl, and she have the sun in her" (*WSS*, 95).

Within the earlier stages of Rochester's narrative, however, there is a scene of linguistic instruction in patois that illuminates in what sense the dominant English voice of the novel orients itself toward the coordinates of a Creole linguistic continuum. It is, notably, also a scene of seduction, Antoinette's attempt to seduce Rochester through teaching him patois songs, in the early days of their marriage and before her disastrous recourse to Christophine's obeah:

> All day she'd be like any other girl, smile at herself in her looking-glass (*do you like this scent?*), try to teach me her songs, for they haunted me.
> *Adieu foulard, adieu madras*, or *Ma belle ka di maman li*. My beautiful girl she said to her mother (*No it is not like that. Now listen. It is this way*). She'd be silent, or angry for no reason, and chatter to Christophine in patois. (*WSS*, 54)

This scene illuminates the linguistic core around which Rochester's Creole family romance crystallizes. Haunted, first, by the rich resonance of songs from Antoinette's mother's Francophone Creole background (including lyrics that emphasize the mother–daughter bond), Rochester is then drawn into the intricacies of translation, the impasse of a translation whose failure remains closed to the text (Rochester is, indeed, haunted by that failure or impasse of translation). Finally, patois is learned as a language ascribed to others, a language of the other: "chatter." This is the language Rochester learns enough to recognize, to internalize, but not to speak or fully understand. Designated patois it comes to define the limit of Rochester's paranoid knowledge of Antoinette's world, in a double sense, showing the limitations of that knowledge and imposing a limit on what Rochester can accept. So, in the confrontation with Christophine:

> She began to mutter to herself. Not in patois. I knew the sound of patois now.
> She's as mad as the other, I thought, and turned to the window. (*WSS*, 97)

Yet to the degree that Rochester sets this Francophone Creole patois as the limit, the point of rejection of the entire world of Antoinette's Creole affiliations, this proves also the core linguistic element of his own Creole family romance.

Crucially, this linguistic core is constituted as a *literary* effect. To explain this as the effect of a Creole oral tradition transcribed in print captures only part of the effect. The lines possess a haunting literariness because they register a hierarchy of relations between languages (French and English), between oral and written media, but a hierarchy whose order has become rearranged in being passed down as lines of poetic song. This derangement of language constitutes the linguistic aberration of the novel's English voice, its internalization of the mad maternal inheritance—as the inheritance of a linguistic madness, the poetic logic of those lines. Rochester's renaming of Bertha, rather than refusing this logic, in fact perpetuates it. Reflecting the same pathological attempt to control linguistic creolization that surfaces in his play on Francophone names (Antoinette's, but also Christophine's), the act of renaming Antoinette Bertha is also an attempt to manipulate the "creolization" of linguistic hierarchies. As Antoinette puts it, "that's obeah too" (*WSS*, 88). The name Bertha constitutes the specifically English investment in the fantasy of a Creole family romance, the shape of whose erotic desire is, at core, a linguistic aberration.

Minke's Creole family romance is also marked by a linguistic aberration that emerges in the exaggerated *literary* effect of Minke's repeated song of praise for Annelies's eyes "like a pair of morning stars." By contrast to the extreme misogyny exhibited in the reaction formation of Rochester's Creole family romance, Minke exaggerates, by contrast, his extreme attraction to Annelies, diagnosing it, indeed, in terms of the overall "philogyny" with which he characterizes his own romantic pathology. This initially comic self-diagnosis ("Oh, philogynist" [*TE*, 27]; "*Ahoi, philogynik*" [*BM*, 14]) assumes a more serious register at the moment when he is called on to assume the position of psychiatric doctor vis-à-vis Annelies as patient: "The result of my own actions as a philogynist" (*TE*, 205) ("*Akibat tingkah philogynikku sendiri*" [*BM*, 200]). Annelies's breakdown is ultimately attributable to a specific traumatic incident—the incestuous rape by her brother—but this family "secret" only foregrounds all the more the complex aetiology of racial identification and antipathy (hatred of whites and exclusive identification with her native mother) that Dr. Martinet has been attempting to unravel. Crystallizing around this problem of racial conflict within the psyche, the "creole beauty" that signals the formation of Minke's Creole family romance also constitutes the novel's ambivalent historical portrait of the emerging science of psychoanalysis or psychiatry.

The sense of "responsibility" awakened in Minke by this "creole beauty" stands in striking contrast, of course, to Rochester's response in *Wide Sargasso Sea*. Each might be read, however, as capturing two sides of the general discourse over the psychology of racism during the 1950s—most notably as embodied in the work of Frantz Fanon. These debates—Césaire, Mannoni, Fanon—constitute a crucial discursive precursor for theories of "creolization" and are themselves inseparable from the literary phenomenon of Creole modernism. Neither Rhys nor Pramoedya can directly be placed within this discursive framework; but nor can either be separated from its decisive role in the history of decolonization. The prominence given to the ambivalent position of psychoanalysis or psychiatry, in *This Earth of Mankind*, calls attention to the aberrant philological root of this "Creole" moment in the overall experience of decolonization.

If the effects of obeah constitute the physical, spiritual, and cultural sign of the Creole family romance that simultaneously binds Antoinette and Rochester together and forever separates them in tragic misrecognition of each one's dependence on the other, the corresponding sign in *This Earth of Mankind* is the odd image of the "palakia tree seed" (*TE*, 180) ("*sebuah biji palakia*" [*BM*, 175]) with which Minke describes the onset of a headache in the chapters that concern his awakening sense of responsibility for Annelies's "creole beauty." There is no obvious explanation for this word *palakia*, which does not appear in Indonesian or Javanese dictionaries. The English translation suggests an indigenous kind of tree, signaling perhaps Minke's inability to extricate himself from Javanese forms of superstition. Without a fuller philological accounting of the reference, however, it is perhaps premature to read it as a part of the network of analogous references to superstitious charms and poisons that accompany the practice of obeah in *Wide Sargasso Sea* and, more directly related, the "hidden force" of native witchcraft and Islamic plots associated with the decadence of the "creole" woman in Couperus's novel. At most, one might recognize its function in positing a binary opposition between indigenous and European cures: when the headache image first appears, Minke thinks of the new invention of aspirin, imagining it might cure him better than the brown-onion vinegar concoction, and leading to the thought of the Indies as "a country that can do nothing but wait upon the products of Europe" (*TE*, 180) ("*negeri yang hanya dapat menunggu-nunggu hasil kerja Eropa*" [*BM*, 175]).

Signaling what we earlier described as the moment of Creole delusion, the madness that Minke and Annelies each briefly shares, this image yokes together material and spiritual, physical and psychic processes. Suggestively capturing Minke's own conflicted sense of himself—as Javanese noble devoted to European enlightenment ideals—this image also suggests the possibility of a specific physical disorder, such as the Burmese syphilis passed onto Robert Mellema by the Japanese prostitute (which suggests in turn a possible explanation for the biological infertility Minke discovers in himself in *Footsteps*).[32] Its brief appearance suggests, however, only a temporary disorder, one that momentarily effects a disturbance in a range of hierarchies and contrasts—not unlike that set of hierarchies disrupted by the linguistic effects of Rochester's "obeah" of naming. The form of intoxication associated with it, moreover, is related to the literary excess that produces his song of praise, suggesting, too, that it may have a specifically literary and philological provenance. If so, it is a characteristically syncretic provenance, alluding perhaps both to an indigenous tree and to the tree of life and knowledge in the shared biblical books of Judaism, Christianity, and Islam. This "palakia tree seed" offers an aberration of the word, a philological derangement that is the corresponding moment of crystallization of Minke's Creole family romance to Rochester's in *Wide Sargasso Sea*.

At the risk of classifying and thus missing the full polylinguistic, polysemantic play of this "palakia tree" (*sebuah palakia*), one might speculate that Pramoedya here is playing on the Javanese penchant for mysticism that will form the basis for Minke's critical formulation of "Javanism" in *Footsteps*. Although this "palakia tree" may be related to one of those indigenous trees classified under the genus *Palaquium*—and highly valued by Europeans; indeed, through a process of transplantation producing the vast rubber estates that fueled the globalizing economy over the turn of the century[33]—the word *palakia* in fact seems to elude any of the many classifying systems of European philology and science. One of these, however, suggests the term may be linked to complicated astrological predictions for children. Walter William Skeat, in his *Malay Magic* (1900), refers to the "casting up (*palak* or *falakiah*)" of the "numerical values of the letters of both parents' names."[34] It points to a linguistic core, but one that signals a linguistic "creolization" process whose "nation language" (to borrow Brathwaite's formulation) is the emerging linguistic-literary formation of *bahasa Indonesia*.

If, for Rochester, the moment of linguistic aberration enforces a paranoid pathology, for Minke it has a rather different effect. Although his Creole family romance is part of a retrospective formation of melancholic tragic recognition, the disruption of linguistic-literary hierarchies proves liberating in important and decisive ways. The grounds for this have already been established early in the novel, in a linguistic effect more immediately accessible to an English reader than the obscure, as yet unexplained allusion to the palakia tree. Minke's own name constitutes an internalized racialized taunt thrown at him by his Dutch teacher, then adopted by his family in a further twist to the initial humiliation. The full story of this inaugural scene of naming, however, emerges as a potentially idealized resolution to the oppressive systems of *both* Javanese modes of address *and* the colonial European system of family names, when Annelies accepts the name precisely as a sign of his merely native identity, concluding "Minke is a good name" (*TE*, 40) ("*Nama Minke juga bagus*" [*BM*, 29]). Minke, however, never can tell Annelies the full story of his name's origins in a racial epithet ("I've never told anyone what I thought, not even Annelies" [*TE*, 40]; "*Juga pada Annelies bagian ini tak pernah kuceritakan padanya*" [*BM*, 29]). Annelies's acceptance of the name is an idealized, imaginary resolution of what remains part of the vicious circle of internalized racism and "double consciousness." Nonetheless, in the momentarily utopian derangement of the hierarchy of traditional Javanese and the patriarchal structure of colonial European naming systems, the creolized English form of Minke (as a Dutch half-articulation of the English word *monkey*) stands as a sort of liberating version of Rochester's oppressive imposition of the name Bertha.

Creole Literary Passages

Much of the literary power of *Wide Sargasso Sea*—what makes it all at once a part of the creative ferment of Caribbean literary reformulations of tradition in the 1950s and 1960s; and what makes it stand apart from that Creole modernism as the belated repetition of an earlier English modernism—is concentrated in Part Three and the manner in which it executes the logic of the entire book's inexorable movement toward re-imagining the precise coordinates of the character of Bertha Mason in Charlotte Brontë's *Jane Eyre*. As an evocation of extreme mental disorder, the book already powerfully resonates in the age of psychiatry and schizophrenia. As an evocation of the deracinated, displaced—unplaceable—former "colonial" settler returned to the "mother" country, the book resonates powerfully also, and all the more so in being twinned with the rewriting of the feminist classic. It is the relation between these concerns that emerges as most powerful, from the logic with which the novel demonstrates that they have all along haunted the pages of the much-read Victorian novel. If there is something permanently disturbing about the creolization of literary tradition, it is that the fetish of racial identity and the fetish of literary identity share the same fate.

The Creole legacy Rhys imagines in *Wide Sargasso Sea* cannot overcome the "impasse" of consciousness in her earlier works. It does, however, resituate that "impasse" (and its repetitive reformulation of the ambiguities of English modernism) according to the literary and linguistic coordinates of the Creole. "Creole," for Rhys, as we have explored taking our cue from her 1958 letter, means both a particular kind of figure (albeit one whose social identity has become lost to view) and something different, something more akin to the emerging theories of "creolization" that shape the linguistic-literary formation of Creole modernism. As imagined in *Wide Sargasso Sea*, this problem of Creole legacy is the problem of a literary legacy. Paradoxically, to the extent that this views the ensemble of Creole cultural traditions from an *outside* perspective, Rhys's work must be viewed as part of (if also a contested part of) twentieth-century Caribbean writing that has enacted a decisive displacement of literary traditions and the relation between different traditions. The paradox is both cultural, marking her distance from and relation to Creole traditions, and literary, marking her insistence on Creole literary form at the heart of the canonically English text of *Jane Eyre*. But to the extent that *Wide Sargasso Sea* also attempts to grasp the *inside* perspective of a particular Creole—the madwoman in the attic of *Jane Eyre*—the problem of identity, literary and racial identity, remains unresolved. Above all, it remains a problem for reading.

PART III

Indonesian Modernism

6

THE VANISHING GENRE OF THE *NYAI* NARRATIVE
Reading Genealogies of English and Indonesian Modernism

In this chapter, I examine how the figure of the *nyai* (Indonesian concubine, mistress, or house servant) stands at the traumatic core of transnational literary modernism linking the overlapping formations of English, Creole, and Indonesian modernism we have been tracing through the comparative study of Joseph Conrad, Jean Rhys, and Pramoedya Ananta Toer. In order to retrace the origins of Indonesian nationalism, Pramoedya turned to the genre of the *nyai* narrative, whose appearance and disappearance during the turn of the century encapsulates the range of problems of reading what Pramoedya called "pre-Indonesian" literature. What Pramoedya's novels illuminate about the appearance and disappearance of *nyai* narrative form during the turn of the century prompts examination of the importance of this genre for the work of Joseph Conrad and the trace it leaves in the formation of English literary modernism. Governed neither by the marriage system of European colonizers nor by the customs of the colonized, the status of the *nyai* constitutes a challenge to social and legal conceptions of domestic relations within an international perspective. The formation and disappearance of *nyai* narrative form poses this question of international domestic arrangements as the shared problem of reading genealogies of English and Indonesian literary modernism.

The historical emergence of Indonesian nationalism in Pramoedya's Buru tetralogy is structured around the device of two distinct, opposed narrative perspectives: that of Minke (based on the historical proto-nationalist, Tirto Adi Suryo), who recounts the early awakening of anti-colonial nationalism in the first three volumes; and that of his adversary, the secret police agent, Pangemanann, who takes over the fourth volume to narrate Minke's arrest and exile, the confiscation of his manuscripts, and the subversion of his political organizations. This narrative device is framed in turn by the figure of Nyai Ontosoroh, who, from the start, appears as the very type of heroic anti-colonial nationalism. The story of her being sold as *nyai* into concubinage with a Dutch *tuan*, her subsequent rise to the level of overseer of her master's agricultural estate, and the fate of her daughter, taken from her by the Dutch courts and sent to Europe, form the substance of the first novel, *This Earth of Mankind*. Described as Minke's "unofficial teacher" (*TE*, 111) ("*seorang guru tidak resmi*" [*BM*, 105]) and "spiritual mother" (*H*, 351–52) ("*ibu rohani*" [*RK*, 352]), she reappears throughout each of the following three novels until, at the very end of the final volume, she is given possession of the manuscripts on which all four novels have been based. It is difficult not to read her character as a utopian prefiguration of the ideals of Indonesian nationalism. At the same time, however, she embodies those ideals for a readership that has witnessed their violent reversal in the traumatic events of 1965, when an alleged communist coup provided the pretext for the persecution, arrest, and massacre of countless communists and communist "sympathizers" that accompanied the fall of Sukarno, Indonesia's first president, and the rise of Suharto's "New Order" regime.[1] As Pramoedya explained in 1995, "As a woman who stood up, alone, to the injustices of Dutch colonialism, she was a character who provided a model of resistance and courage for my fellow prisoners to look up to, so that their spirit would not be demoralized by the killings and the cruelties witnessed in the camps."[2]

The genre of the *nyai* tale helps explain how Pramoedya is able to combine into a single character this unusual combination of revolutionary anti-colonialism and testimonial to postcolonial state oppression. The number of *nyai* narratives to appear in Dutch and Malay between the 1880s and 1920s suggests the emergence of a literary genre premised on a crossover between the otherwise sharply divided worlds of colonizer and colonized within turn-of-the-century Dutch East Indies. Written by a variety of figures—Dutch women immigrants, Indies-born men from various ethnic backgrounds, Dutch male modernist writers, and forerunners of Indonesia's anti-colonial nationalist movement—the genre virtually disappeared in the second decade of the twentieth century. Nyai Ontosoroh's story only partially fits the pattern of this turn-of-the-century melodramatic literary genre that crossed over languages (Dutch and Malay) and different media (print, drama, and film). But her story stands as a complex and powerful reminder of and commentary on a genre that disappeared once the colonial-regulated Malay-language literary press, Balai Pustaka, founded in 1908, began promoting a wide range of books that became the institutional point of reference for subsequent accounts of Indonesian literary modernism. D. A. Rinkes, the colonial official who monitored Tirto Adi Suryo's political activities (as Pangemanann monitors Minke's), also presided, as director of Balai Pustaka from 1917, over the disappearance of *nyai* narratives from the officially sponsored dissemination of Malay-language literature.[3]

The genre of the *nyai* narrative is closely related to the colonial phenomenon of *nyai* concubinage itself, a particular feature of Dutch East Indies social life related to—and symptomatic of— what Ann Stoler has described as "the dominant domestic arrangement in colonial cultures through the early twentieth century."[4] If the disappearance of the *nyai* tale as literary genre may be related to the passing away of a particular form of colonial domestic arrangement, Pramoedya's return to this form is by no means a complacent celebration of what has been overcome in the passage out of colonialism. Far from celebrating its eclipse, the Buru tetralogy returns to the particular social, literary, and linguistic economy of the *nyai's* experience as an unresolved problem for the present, recalling both the utopian ideals of Indonesian nationalism and bearing witness to their loss. In this sense, the *nyai* tale is a genre that embodies trauma. Reflecting on the traumatic core of Indonesian modernism, Pramoedya's return to the genre of the *nyai* narrative reflects, in turn, on a traumatic core of early twentieth-century transnational modernism.

Defining the *Nyai*

In her landmark study of Dutch East Indies colonial society, Jean Taylor describes the status of the *nyai* to emerge following the abolition of slavery in 1860 and from the longstanding practice of colonial concubinage:

> In the VOC centuries [during the rule of the Dutch East Indies Company], men had made free with the Asian slave women of their households. After 1860, however, there was no more domestic slavery. Men living in concubinage now sought their companions among the free population of the Indonesian villages. The woman selected assumed management of the European's household and staff, a position that gave rise to the common colonial euphemism for concubine, "housekeeper." It became customary for the concubine to exchange her colored or indigo kebaya for a white one and to adopt slippers, the clothing symbolizing her new status and passage from the Indonesian to the halfway world of a bachelor-centered Indies society.[5]

This description offers a condensed historical image of the figure of the *nyai*. Although Taylor here uses the Dutch term "housekeeper" (*huishoudster*), rather than *nyai*, the Dutch colonial usage suggests, nonetheless, the complex semantic force of euphemism and cross-cultural translation embedded in the adaptation of the Javanese word *nyai*, an initially respectful form of address to women.[6] *Nyai* comes to name what the Dutch *huishoudster* euphemistically avoids, as suggested in *This Earth of Mankind* by Minke's early reaction to the family of Nyai Ontosoroh, in reflections that offer an alternative historical image to set in counterpoint to Taylor's image of the *nyai*:

> Not only Mrs. Telinga [Minke's landlady] and I knew, but it felt as if the whole world knew, that such indeed was the moral level of the families of nyais: low, dirty, without culture, moved only by lust. They were the families of prostitutes; they were people without character, destined to sink into nothingness, leaving no trace.... All social classes had passed judgment on the Nyai, as well as all races: Native, European, Chinese, Arab. (*TE,* 54)
>
> Bukan hanya Mevrouw Télinga atau aku, rasanya siapa pun tahu, begitulah tingkat susila keluarga nyai-nyai: rendah, jorok, tanpa kebudayaan, perhatiannya hanya pada soal-soal berahi semata. Mereka hanya keluarga pelacur, manusia tanpa pribadi, dikodratkan akan tenggelam dalam ketiadaan tanpa bekas.... Semua lapisan kehidupan menghukum keluarga nyai-nyai; juga semua bangsa: Pribumi, Eropa, Tionghoa, Arab. (*BM,* 44)

There is clearly a multiplicity of social and linguistic perspectives at work in the adaptation of the term *nyai* to define the status of a native "concubine," "housekeeper," or "mistress" in a colonial Dutch East Indies household. The specifically Javanese form of respectful address changes considerably in translation into the euphemistic, pejorative and disrespectful colonial "judgment" on the *nyai*. It becomes an international coinage, an effect of what Bakhtin calls "heteroglossia," caught, as the *nyai* herself is, between the world of native Javanese family values and the multiracial, international economy of colonial domestic affairs.[7]

The extreme antinomy of respectability and disrepute built into this international coinage is embodied in Nyai Ontosoroh's lived experience, as retold in the first half of *This Earth of Mankind*. The educated, wealthy, and powerful overseer of an agricultural estate at the time Minke meets her, Sanikem weighs her European middle-class sense of independence and privilege against the humiliation of having been sold into slavery. The experience of abject shame in being sold by her father colors all of the later stages of the narrative, as encapsulated in her refusal to forgive her parents and her insistence on an absolute break with the past: "Let the past be severed from the present. The wounds to my pride and self-respect still haven't healed. If I remember how I was so humiliatingly sold" (*TE,* 94) ("*Biar putus semua yang sudah-sudah. Luka terhadap kebanggaan dan hargadiri tak juga mau hilang. Bila teringat kembali bagaimana hina aku dijual*" [*BM,* 87]). This humiliation is inscribed into the formula with which she loses her given Javanese name Sanikem and assumes the title *nyai:* "As soon as I regained consciousness [following the moment when Mellema first sleeps with her], I knew I was no longer the Sanikem of the previous day. I'd become a real nyai.... And the name Sanikem disappeared forever" (*TE,* 87); ("*Begitu aku siuman kembali, kuketahui aku bukan si Sanikem yang kemarin. Aku telah jadi nyai yang sesungguhnya.... Dan nama Sanikem hilang untuk selama-lamanya*" [*BM,* 79]). Her insistence thereafter on the title Nyai accentuates the contradictory position she occupies under colonial modernity as the housekeeper and mother of a modern bourgeois family, who has herself rejected her Javanese past while still, in the eyes of the law, the kept native slave of a colonial *tuan*.

The contradictory economy of this form of domestic partnership underlies the stereotype of the *nyai* that emerged from the circulation of stories about *nyais* during the turn of the century. Taylor's historical account of late colonial concubinage is itself based on her study of one important set of such stories—namely, stories written between the 1870s and 1910s by Dutch women, mostly new arrivals in the Indies following the lifting of restrictions on immigration in 1870. The didactic purpose infusing these women's stories, sometimes explicitly sympathizing with the plight of the abandoned *nyai* and more often anxious over the fate of her children, provides for Taylor an important historical record. The conflict between European marriage form and the form of cohabitation between a European *tuan* and a native *nyai* licensed by Dutch colonial society produced problems that were quite specific to late Dutch East Indies colonial society—above all, concerning the legitimacy of children born into either form of domestic arrangement, and hence the legal definition of "European" identity. Yet as Ann Stoler has extensively argued, these problems—leading up to the Mixed Marriage Act of 1898—form part of a much wider set of interlocking policies in the colonies and in Europe seeking to insulate the bourgeois family from the economic, affective, and legal bonds linking native servants with European children.[8] More obviously on display in the earlier stories by Dutch women, these problems fundamentally shape the stereotype of the *nyai* in the work of the more celebrated male Dutch writers P. A. Daum and Louis Couperus.

The social significance of the term *nyai* emerges not just from the contending moral and social perspectives of stories circulated in Dutch. Crucial both for the linguistic definition of the term and for any evaluation of the *nyai* narrative as a genre are the stories about *nyais* published in Malay. As Pramoedya writes, introducing three such tales written by the historical model for Minke, Tirto Adi Suryo, "Stories concerning the interracial makeup of life in the Indies, written in lingua franca Malay during the 19th century and at the beginning of the 20th century, were dominated by nyai narratives" ("*Cerita-cerita tentang kehidupan inter-rasial di Hindia dalam Melayu lingua-franca dari abad 19 dan sekitar awal abad 20 didominasi oleh cerita tentang nyai-nyai*").[9] Besides the various tales about *nyai*s published by Tirto Adi Suryo,[10] Pramoedya also discusses (both in his biographical study of Tirto, *Sang Pemula*, and in his anthology of "pre-Indonesian literature," *Tempo Doeloe*) stories about *nyai* by F. Wiggers, H. Kommer, G. Francis, and Hadji Moekti. Of all of these, however, one story stands out as the almost definitive example of *nyai* narrative form: *Nyai Dasima*, originally published by G. Francis in 1896. Early in *This Earth of Mankind* it is singled out as a particularly important index of the genre, when Nyai Ontosoroh recommends the book to Minke as a model of European-style writing in Malay: "Francis wrote *Nyai Dasima*, a truly European-style novel. But in Malay. I've got the book. Perhaps you'd like to study it" (*TE*, 110); ("*Francis, Nyo, dia telah menulis Nyai Dasima, benar-benar dengan cara Eropa. Hanya berbahasa Melayu. Ada padaku buku itu. Barangkali kau suka mempelajarinya*" [*BM*, 104]).

Clearly an important text for Pramoedya's Buru quartet—one that Pramoedya anthologizes as an inaugural text for Indonesian literary modernism—part of the riddle of its repeated appearance in the Buru quartet is the fact that there are very few allusions to the substance of the story itself. *Nyai Dasima* remains—even up until the end of the tetralogy—a book that appears (as it does first to Minke) yet to be read. Arguably, *Nyai Dasima* is so well known that its story may be taken as a given. As Pramoedya discusses in *Tempo Doeloe*, the 1896 version published by Francis was followed by retellings of the same story in Sundanese verse (by O. S. Tjiang, 1897) and in Dutch (by Manusama, 1926). There were also numerous folk play and folk opera versions (according to James Siegel, one company staged the play at least 127 times), and as many as three screen adaptations (1929, 1930, and 1970).[11] It is, indeed, the one notable *nyai* story to have outlived the disappearance of the genre.

As a number of critical commentaries have shown, although there are important variations from one version to another, the basic plot remains remarkably similar: the heroine, Dasima, the *nyai* of an Englishman, Tuan W., is persuaded to leave both her *tuan* and their daughter to marry a native man, Samiun, the villain responsible for Dasima's brutal murder.[12] *Nyai Dasima* offers something rather different from the Dutch stereotype of the *nyai* as, to cite Taylor, "seducer of hapless European men by means of potions and magic, and popularly suspect as prone to take revenge on a rival or new bride through poison."[13] Incidentally, this is the stereotype against which Minke first measures Nyai Ontosoroh, viewing her as "a sorceress" (*TE*, 52) ("*dukun sihir*" [*BM*, 42]) casting a "spell" (*TE*, 51) over him ("*Nyai kurasakan telah menyihir kesedaranku*" [*BM*, 41]) and employing "black magic" (*TE*, 53) ("*guna-guna*" [*BM*, 43]). *Nyai Dasima* reconfigures this "image of the concubine possessed by evil and cunning" into the image of a victimized heroine, an image that remains, according to Taylor, "unvarying" in each version: "the *nyai* is ever faithful, patient, suffering."[14] Rather than reversing Dutch stereotypes, however, *Nyai Dasima* redistributes many of the same stock elements (notably, spells and black magic) into a melodrama of stereotypes—above all the stereotypes of the hypocritically pious Moslem villain and the benign but absent paternal English *tuan*. Dasima's fraught position as victim, between the Englishman Tuan W and the native Samiun, gives exemplary narrative and dramatic form to the precarious social position of all the various *nyai*s of *nyai* stories, which typically present the *nyai* as trapped between native Javanese or Islamic and European or Christian family structures and values.

This international contest of perspectives comes to the foreground in one of the few substantive references to the plot of *Nyai Dasima* in the Buru tetralogy. In the publicity preceding the trial investigation into the murder of Nyai Onsotoroh's *tuan*, newspaper reports in the Dutch-language press refer to the character of Nyai Dasima in an attempt to discredit Dr. Martinet's expressions of sympathy for Nyai Ontosoroh:

> [T]he Dutch-language press in their own way and style rejected Dr. Martinet's sympathy, which was directed at one who was only a Native woman, and a concubine, too, who perhaps was not even clear of any wrong-doing in the case. There have been many proven cases of nyais conspiring with outsiders to murder their masters. The motives: lust and wealth. In the nineteenth century alone, there could be listed at least five nyais who had gone to the gallows. Even the character Nyai Dasima, of the popular Malay novel, could have carried out the same crime, had not her master, Edward Williams, been such a wise person. The paper closed its piece with the suggestion that Nyai Ontosoroh be investigated more thoroughly. (*TE*, 277–78)
>
> *Maka koran-koran kolonial berbahasa Belanda dengan cara dan gayanya sendiri tidak membenarkan sympati sang Dokter yang ditujukan hanya pada seorang wanita Pribumi, gundik pula, yang boleh jadi belum tentu bersih dari perkara. Sudah banyak berbukti nyai-nyai bersekongkol dengan orang luar untuk membunuh tuannya. Motif: kemesuman dan harta. Dalam abad sembilanbelas ini saja, kata sebuah koran, dapat dicatat paling tidak lima orang nyai telah naik ke tiang gantungan. Boleh jadi Nyai Dasima bisa melakukan kejahatan yang sama sekiranya Tuan Edward Williams bukan seorang arif bijaksana. Walhasil: penutupnya pembunuhan juga. Hanya bukan Edward Williams yang jadi kurban—Dasima sendiri. Koran itu munutup dengan saran agar mengusut Nyai Ontosoroh lebih teliti.* (*BM*, 272)

Even as it refers to details of *Nyai Dasima* that are presumed to be familiar to its readership, the Dutch-language newspaper redirects those details to confirm the typicality of a very different kind of *nyai* narrative, the story of those stereotypically cunning *nyai*s conspiring to kill their *tuan*s. This international contest of perspectives suggests in what sense *Nyai Dasima* appears as a familiar story not yet read. Presuming a shared (Dutch and Malay) reading experience, the story stands as the index for a whole range of *nyai* stories because it epitomizes an unresolved set of profound differences over how to read the story of a *nyai*.

The *Nyai* as Disappearing Subaltern Figure

The structure of the Buru tetralogy is framed by this unresolved set of differences, beginning with the contrast between the fiction of Nyai Ontosoroh's real experience and the historical allusion to the fictional Nyai Dasima, and extending to the host of allusions to turn-of-the-century *nyai* narratives that haunt the whole tetralogy. In his introduction to *Tempo Doeloe*, Pramoedya comments on a problem of reading that attends all the texts of what he calls "*sastra pra*-Indonesia" [pre-Indonesian literature]: "What is published here has not yet for certain been read, but what is read here has already for certain been published" ("*Ada penerbitan memang belum tentu ada pembaca, tetapi ada pembaca sudah tentu ada penerbitan*").[15] This almost aphoristic formulation for a readership of "pre-Indonesian" texts suggests in what sense the literary form of the *nyai* narrative is foundational for his reconstruction of early Indonesian anti-colonial nationalism. The Dutch-language newspaper references to *Nyai Dasima* in *This Earth of Mankind* provide a revealing index for that uncertainty of readership that, as Pramoedya goes on to explain in *Tempo Doeloe*, concerns the specific conditions of print distribution and circulation for turn-of-the-century Malay-language publications. Although the actual readership for such publications may have been quite small, they reached a much wider audience through reading circles (people who, though unable to read, paid to have newspapers and stories read to them) and also through dramatic performances (above all, through the form of East Indies opera or *Komedi Stamboul*, discussed in chapter 2). *Nyai Dasima* provides a common point of reference for a wide range of people, from various social and ethnic backgrounds, all of them, as it were, not-yet-Malay-language readers. This includes not only the implied Dutch-language readers of the newspaper reports that assume familiarity with a Malay-language story but also the implied Malay-language auditors to whom that story might have been read or performed as part of the repertoire of East Indies opera. It is this as-yet-unformed readership that constitutes the problem of how to read the *nyai*'s story.

James Siegel builds on this linguistic strand to Pramoedya's argument in his discussion of the compulsion to retell the story of *Nyai Dasima*. The persistent retelling of this story, Siegel argues, represents a set of unresolved contests over a language (*lingua franca* Malay) that has not yet become Indonesian (*bahasa Indonesia*). According to this reading, *Nyai Dasima* in all her various manifestations represents the "ghost" of the turn-of-the-century print medium of *lingua franca* Malay: "She is the ghost of "pre-Indonesian" as Pramoedya Ananta Toer called the *lingua franca*, and she continues to haunt the language that never fully replaced it, the national language, Indonesian. She illuminates the nonarrival of language, which is to say its continuous failed attempts to convey something."[16] The sense in which this *lingua franca* "failed" stands in revealing contrast to Benedict Anderson's celebrated emphasis on the success with which *bahasa Indonesia* provided a vehicle for imagining Indonesian anti-colonial nationalism (and so in turn the paradigmatic model for his argument about the medium of print in the rise and spread of nationalism in *Imagined Communities*).[17] Rather than arguing opposed positions, Anderson and Siegel may be read as looking at two sides of the same phenomenon: what Pramoedya articulates in terms of the uncertain question of readership for what was certainly published over the turn of the century; and what his Buru quartet captures, alternatively, in the figures of Nyai Dasima and Nyai Ontosoroh.

Both for the not-yet-Indonesian readers of the turn of the century and for contemporary readers of Pramoedya's Buru quartet, the contradictory social position of the *nyai* constitutes an ongoing challenge of reading across hierarchies of race, religion, and gender. This recalls Gayatri Spivak's influential argument about giving voice to subaltern Third World women's perspectives. If the power of Nyai's narrative gives voice to the subordinate social position of the *nyai* in late colonial society, it is a voice that can emerge only refracted through the perspectives of others: her oral testimony is relayed through the voice of her daughter, whose retelling is transcribed in turn into the written record of Minke's notes. Neither Nyai Dasima nor Nyai Ontosoroh can simply be identified as subaltern figures. Each comes to occupy an elite middle-class social position: Dasima's narrative describes the loss of such a social position; Sanikem's narrative describes the embattled acquisition of such a social position. Both are more obviously concerned with middle-class preoccupations. Yet it is in the *transitional* social movement of their stories—whether through the upward mobility of Nyai Ontosoroh from slave to mistress or the downward mobility of Dasima from Tuan W.'s mistress to Samiun's subordinate wife— that the *nyai* appears in narrative form. What Pramoedya's Buru tetralogy illuminates is that this is not only the effect of an individual's changing from one social position to another. It is also, and more fundamentally, an effect of the way in which the social status of the *nyai* registers the volatility of relations between different social positions. It is in this sense that the *nyai* fits Ranajit Guha's definition of the "subaltern classes" (which Spivak offers as a corrective to the generalized adoption of the term *subaltern* in academic postcolonial studies[18]) as comprising *"the demographic difference between the total Indian population and all those whom we have described as 'elite.'"*[19] What Nyai Ontosoroh and Nyai Dasima *share*, indeed, is the space of just such a "demographic difference." The social position of the *nyai* appears in narrative form as a vanishing figure, the story of her disappearance revealing the "demographic difference" between the "elite" classes and the "total" Indies population. This is, then, the problem of how to read the story of a *nyai*, a subaltern reading effect produced by the genre of the *nyai* narrative.

This subaltern reading effect is related to the critical dilemma outlined by Laurie Sears, who, in the introduction to a collection of essays on representations of femininity in contemporary Indonesia, asks whether Spivak's "evocative image of the third-world woman" can leave no more than "traces or blurred images." She proposes that it is possible to "reveal the many faces of the 'feminine,' without arguing that our representations are authentic ones," so long as one interrogates (and Sears cites Judith Butler here) "what the theoretical move that establishes foundations *authorizes,* and what precisely it excludes or forecloses."[20] This last injunction is especially important for the case of the Buru tetralogy, which lays claim to a dissident reading of the foundational moment of Indonesian anti-colonial nationalism. It does so by foregrounding the ways in which *nyai* narrative form emerges as an unresolved set of questions about the social status of the *nyai* that retrospectively determines our understanding of the literary foundations of Indonesian modernism, the linguistic foundations of *bahasa Indonesia,* and the political foundations of Indonesian anti-colonial nationalism.

Besides the historical text of *Nyai Dasima*, and behind Pramoedya's fictional reconstruction of the experience of Nyai Ontosoroh, there exists a whole range of *nyai* figures that haunt the Buru tetralogy as "traces and blurred images" of lost or forgotten texts. The historical Tirto Adi Suryo wrote a number of narratives about *nyai*s, which Pramoedya discusses in *Sang Pemula*. He cites C. W. Watson's description of an early story concerning "the faithful Sundanese" Nyai Mina[21] and discusses two later stories by Tirto that appeared in *Medan Prijaji: Cerita Nyai Ratna* (1909; republished in *Sang Pemula*) and *Nyai Permana* (1911–1912). He also discusses a number of other *nyai* narratives serialized in Tirto's

Medan Prijaji, including F. Wiggers's *Dari Boedak Sampe Djadi Radja,* H. Kommer's *Tjerita Njai Paina* (both anthologized in *Tempo Doeloe*), and Hadji Moekti's *Hikajat Siti Mariah* (which Pramoedya reprinted in a volume on its own).

As with *Nyai Dasima,* there is no simple way of reading allusions to these narratives against their historical counterparts. Minke's first *nyai* narrative, for example, does not correspond with any of the known texts published by the historical Tirto. Elements from Kommer's *Njai Paina* surface in the story of Surati, as told in *Child of All Nations:* Surati, like Paina in Kommer's tale, is forced to become the *nyai* of an exploitative Dutch plantation overseer; and both exact revenge by contracting smallpox and passing on the disease to their *tuan.* Yet such historical allusions create effects of uncanny repetition, accompanied by a proliferation of differences between the variety of *nyai* narratives retold or referred to. The accumulation of repeated references to *nyai* tales creates a sort of constantly changing kaleidoscopic distortion of narrative form, as each repetition marks a difference in a reader's sense of the *nyai* narrative pattern. This inscribes a disappearing subaltern reading effect of *nyai* narrative form into the texture of the Buru quartet as a whole, which is premised on the gap between the texts published during the turn of the century and Pramoedya's imaginative reconstruction of the historical moment that produced them.

It is just this gap that generates the narrative device of the secret police agent Pangemanann, a fictional persona who embodies the link between D. A. Rinkes's work of monitoring Tirto's political activities and Rinke's later work as director of the Malay-language literary press Balai Pustaka.[22] Pangemanann's name itself has a ghostly relation to the historical F. D. J. Pangemanann, author of two of the stories republished in *Tempo Doeloe* (*Tjerita Rossina* and *Tjerita Si Tjonat*); and who introduces himself to Minke, in *Footsteps,* not only as an avid reader of the Malay-language fiction published by Minke's *Medan* but also as a potential writer himself. When he takes over as first-person narrator of the fourth volume of the tetralogy, he embodies in fictional form a particularly powerful version of that historical problem of readership Pramoedya poses about the "pre-Indonesian" texts anthologized in *Tempo Doeloe.* The effect of having the first three volumes read, edited, and (re)arranged by Pangemanann, and then delivered to Nyai Ontosoroh, consolidates in fictional form the historical record of Pramoedya's research. In *Sang Pemula* it is the historical evidence of secret letters from D. A. Rinkes that shows how the bankruptcy of Tirto's newspaper *Medan Prijaji* and the breakup of his political organization *Sarekat Islam* resulted from the systematic work of discrediting Tirto's name, infiltrating his organizations, and prosecuting his exile. Making Pangemanann the secret agent responsible for this police work, Pramoedya emphasizes the gaps in the historical record exposed by Rinkes's letters. While *Sang Pemula* provides the documentation to explain those gaps, the Buru tetralogy creates a heightened consciousness of what has been lost or erased from historical record. *Nyai* narratives, part of the historical documentation in *Sang Pemula,* signal, in the Buru tetralogy, a more troubling absence of historical documentation, framing the entire tetralogy through Pangemanann's delivery of all the manuscripts to Nyai Ontosoroh, and enclosing the whole within the space of an open-ended subaltern *nyai* reading effect.

The emphasis on Nyai Ontosoroh as the privileged future reader brings together two different moments of rupture in historical documentation: the destruction of Tirto's work of the 1910s and the destruction of Pramoedya's historical research into that work in the 1960s. This double rupture is marked by the tetralogy's allusion to *Nyai Permana*, published in some of the last volumes of *Medan Prijaji* before it was closed down, those volumes themselves being among the documents lost when Pramoedya's house was ransacked during his arrest in 1965.[23] In the Buru tetralogy, the text of *Nyai Permana*, although included in the notebooks confiscated by Pangemanann, drops out of the picture entirely when Pangemanann returns Minke's manuscripts to Nyai Ontosoroh. This lost text illuminates an important shift in Pramoedya's emphasis on *nyai* narratives. Before 1965, he describes the literary depiction of the *nyai* as a social and political question of class transition. In *Realisme-Sosialis dan Sastra Indonesia,* the recently published version of notes for a seminar he taught in 1963, *Nyai Permana* is singled out as an example of fiction that shows the formation of a new class, which, while not yet crystallized into the class struggle between bourgeois and proletariat, constitutes the clearest, most dialectically significant emergence of a literary "socialist-realism" within the Indonesian context. Tirto's *Nyai Permana* falls into the period of what he calls *"sastra dalam penjadian* atau *sastra gatra"* [literature under construction or formative literature], a crucial stage in the development of a "modernism" that is not simply an off-shoot of European modernism, but that, rooted in the linguistic emergence of *bahasa Indonesia,* prefigures the formation of a socially and politically engaged, "socialist-realist" Indonesian modernism.[24] In this argument, the *nyai* constitutes a transitional figure in terms of both social modernity and literary modernism.

In the wake of 1965, however, *Nyai Permana* comes to signal a missing link in genealogies of Indonesian literary modernism. The genre of the *nyai* narrative now marks a rupture in the development of "pre-Indonesian" literature. In *Sang Pemula,* Pramoedya's discussion of the by then lost text of *Nyai Permana* emphasizes the way Tirto's depiction of the *nyai*'s unusual economic position was far ahead of his time in promoting the legal rights of women. *Nyai Permana* illuminates an affinity between Tirto's proto-nationalist agenda and that of the celebrated feminist Kartini: "I wrote the story myself. I based it on real events but mixed in things reflecting the dreams of the girl from Jepara [i.e., Kartini], especially about the rights that must be possessed by women—the right of a woman to divorce her husband, for example. Such a right should not lie only with the husband, who can then get rid of his wife whenever he likes" (*F*, 424) ("*Cerita ini tulisanku sendiri, suatu kejadian sesungguhnya yang aku padukan dengan impian gadis Jepara tentang hak-hak yang semestinya dimiliki oleh kaum wanita, yakni: hak untuk meminta cerai dari suami. Bukan pria saja yang boleh menceraikan istri setiap waktu ia suka*" [*J*, 422–23]). Telling the story of a *nyai*'s free choice to leave her *tuan*, Minke uses the *nyai* narrative (as did Tirto) to promote domestic-partner rights acknowledged neither by the European legal system nor by the traditional Javanese family structure.

This use of *nyai* narrative form to promote women's rights, however, marks only a potential, unrealized part of Tirto's political agenda, underscoring what was foreclosed with the subversion of Tirto's press. As Pramoedya discusses in *Sang Pemula,* the collapse of *Medan Prijaji* led to the collapse of Tirto's other publications associated with this feminist agenda, including notably the journal *Poetri Hindia*. Indeed, as part of the ultimately successful campaign to discredit Tirto, G. Francis, author of *Nyai Dasima*, attacked Tirto's journalistic standards, renaming *Poetri Hindia* with a strikingly pejorative use of the term *nyai: Njai Hindia*.[25] The closing down of Tirto's press ended the only media circulating such ideas about women's rights—and, in the case of *Poetri Hindia,* one of the only places where writing by native women had begun to appear. *Nyai Permana,* in this sense, stands for a future Malay-language reading (and writing) that never took place. *Nyai Permana* crucially supplements the text of *Nyai Dasima* as an index of the vanishing genre of the *nyai* tale, linking it materially and historically to the destruction of the proto-nationalist Malay language press that preceded the formation of the colonial-regulated Malay-language literary press, Balai Pustaka. By extension, too, then, the genre of the *nyai* narrative becomes the literary form of an interrupted reading process: an unresolved problem of social modernity—the status of women within an international economy of domestic labor and partnership—registered as a foundational problem of Indonesian literary modernism.

This is what the figure of Nyai Ontsoroh embodies in fictional form. *Nyai Dasima* appears as a text yet to be read, registering the transitional turn-of-the-century genre of the *nyai* narrative. *Nyai Permana* appears as the text of a lost space of reading, registering the vanishing of the genre of the *nyai* narrative as the uncanny, displaced literary-linguistic social space of reading in the Buru tetralogy. The material effects of this collective erasure of *nyai* stories, fictional and real, makes Nyai Ontosoroh stand testimony to the appearance and disappearance of *nyai* narrative form as an effect of the foreclosure on subaltern perspectives both in the late colonial period and for the postcolonial present of New Order Indonesia.

The Appearance of the *Nyai* in English Modernism

Before returning to consider how the Buru tetralogy presents the historical disappearance of *nyai* narrative form as part of the structure of its own narrative closure, I want to consider how the work of Joseph Conrad emerges in counterpoint to the genre of the *nyai* narrative.[26] The specifically English figure of Tuan W. in *Nyai Dasima* already suggests a possible relation between genealogies of Indonesian and English literary modernism. This English *tuan*, variously identified as "Edward W." (in G. Francis's and also O. S. Tjiang's Malay texts) or "Edward Williams" (in the later Dutch version by Manusama), ties the story to the historical moment of the British Interregnum, when Stamford Raffles temporarily took over governance of the East Indies following the defeat of Napoleon. This claim to historical fact, as James Siegel has discussed, is by no means incidental to the special linguistic and literary circumstances of the story's appearance at a particular moment in the transnational emergence of Malay as a print medium open to a multi-ethnic Indies readership: when, as Siegel puts it, "works designed for one group—Chinese, 'native,' European, Arab—were read by all."[27] Whatever the reason may be for this displacement of the more usually Dutch figures of the *tuan*s found in other *nyai* narratives, it establishes an interesting set of fictional and historical correspondences with the paternal role of the English Tom Lingard, who presides over the Malay colonial family romances with which Conrad began his literary career.

In Conrad's first two novels, *Almayer's Folly* (1895) and *An Outcast of the Islands* (1896), Tom Lingard oversees the domestic affairs of the Dutch protagonists—Almayer's ill-fated marriage in the first and Willems's disastrous extra-marital affair in the second—in ways that reproduce a number of the same social anxieties embedded in the Dutch narratives about *nyai*s. *Almayer's Folly*, in particular, reconfigures concerns both for the children of mixed parents and, albeit in the figure of the married Mrs. Almayer, the negative stereotype of the cunning *nyai*. This is suggestively confirmed by an early review of the novel in *The Straits Times*, which combines the sort of sympathetic anxiety for Almayer's "half-caste" daughter, Nina, that one might expect from Dutch female *nyai* narratives, with a fascinated disgust for Mrs. Almayer that fits the Dutch male stereotype of the cunning and evil *nyai*. The review sums up the novel as an accurate depiction of "the miserable results of a mixed marriage under existing social conditions."[28]

More revealing still is the spirited response from a subscriber to the *Straits Times* who argues that neither the reviewer nor Conrad demonstrates an understanding of "Dutch Indian Society" by dwelling "so deeply on the social disabilities of the results of mixed marriages."[29] This Anglophone contest over the respectability of "mixed marriages" mirrors Dutch debates over the acceptability of *nyai–tuan* cohabitation. The gap between these two writers' views of what is and is not acceptable in the Dutch East Indies might be measured against Hanneke Ming's argument that "while on many occasions a mixed marriage was socially unacceptable, in everyday life an unofficial spouse was outwardly treated with the same respect as a legal one."[30]

Just such a contest of Dutch and English perspectives is already embedded in Conrad's manipulation of the colonial family romance of his Malay fiction. It is only because of Lingard's insistence that Almayer marries the Sulu girl Lingard has rescued from a pirate ship, in what one otherwise might have expected to take the form of a more characteristic *nyai* arrangement. "Mrs. Almayer"—she has no other name in the text—constitutes, indeed, a sort of defiant and spirited negation of the colonial status of the *nyai*: "You know, Kaspar, I am your wife! Your own Christian wife after your own Blanda [Dutch] law!" (*AF*, 40). In adjusting these characteristically East Indies problems of domestic respectability to his English readership, Conrad appropriates the question of English reputation within the shared and contested space of Malay, Dutch, and English sensibilities. Viewed this way, one can recognize how Conrad's interest in tracing a genealogy of intertwined English and Malay histories led him to reformulate the extreme contest over reputation found at the core of *nyai* narratives. Conrad translates this into a contest over the reputation attached to the figure of the English *tuan*.

Lord Jim illustrates how that core concern for the specific colonial meaning of *tuan* emerges from an elision of reference to the specific colonial meaning of *nyai*. At the heart of the romance plot of *Lord Jim* is, after all, a kind of *nyai* narrative, the story of Jim's relationship with Jewel—"We have heard so many such stories," Marlow says as preface, and "Apparently it is a story very much like the others" (*LJ*, 275). As with the matrix of family plots in his earlier Malay tales, it seems to be the figure of the *nyai*'s daughter (Nina, in *Almayer's Folly*) that is the focus. Introducing "the story of his love," however, Marlow foregrounds what, for the Conradian narrative, constitutes the foreclosed, buried figure of the *nyai*: "Apparently it is a story very much like the others: for me, however, there is visible in its background the melancholy figure of a woman, the shadow of a cruel wisdom buried in a lonely grave, looking on wistfully, helplessly, with sealed lips" (*LJ*, 275–76). The buried figure is Jewel's mother, whose grave Jim tends with "an espousal of memory and affection" that defines, for Marlow, his "romantic conscience" (*LJ*, 276). Describing the family circumstances that led to Jewel's mother's marriage to "the unspeakable Cornelius," Marlow briefly outlines the cryptic form of *Lord Jim*'s inner *nyai* tale:

> How the poor woman had come to marry the awful little Malacca Portuguese—after the separation from the father of her girl—and how that separation had been brought about, whether by death, which can be sometimes merciful, or by the merciless pressure of conventions, is a mystery to me. From the little which Stein (who knew so many stories) had let drop in my hearing, I am convinced that she was no ordinary woman. Her own father had been a white; a high official; one of the brilliantly endowed men who are not dull enough to nurse a success, and whose careers so often end under a cloud. I suppose she too must have lacked the saving dullness—and her career ended in Patusan. (*LJ*, 276)

"After the separation from the father of her girl"—the odd syntax of this detail already suggests a reconfiguration of a key element in the *nyai* tale, the crucial moment in which the white *tuan* leaves his *nyai* and whatever offspring there may be (*Nyai Dasima* is unusual in its exaggerated emphasis on the English *tuan*'s remaining with his daughter). "How that separation was brought about"—this, of course, the substance of the *nyai* tale, distinguishes one *nyai* tale from another, the one constant being the inevitable separation of *tuan* and *nyai*. Leaving this a mystery, Marlow forecloses on the *nyai* narrative, although not without leaving two possible versions: separation by death or convention. The elusive reference to "the merciless pressure of conventions" is the most explicit allusion to that set of questions concerning the social acceptability of mixed marriages with which his own first novel was received in the Anglophone Malay press—the most explicit allusion, then, to that disputed and contradictory set of legal rulings about mixed marriage, race relations, and the definition of "European," around which the *nyai* emerges as a key figure of social, literary, and linguistic transformation.

The retelling of this story reveals the rudiments of a *nyai* tale, the distinctive features of its erasure, and the shape of its cryptic imprint on the overall structure of *Lord Jim*. Buried at the heart of *Lord Jim*, it constitutes a sort of inverted genetic code for the overall narrative. If the "white official" whose "career" ends "under a cloud" suggests the first half of Jim's story, the extraordinary woman whose "career ended in Patusan" anticipates its second half. The problem of entitlement involved in discriminating the various nuances of translating *tuan* as "Lord" ("They called him

Tuan Jim: as one might say—Lord Jim" [*LJ*, 5]) inscribes into the novel's title an inverted English image of *nyai* narrative form.

This erasure of the *nyai*, both as literary figure and as a question of international domestic arrangements, has been consolidated in successive readings of Conrad as a canonical point of reference for English modernism. Rhys's citation from Conrad's *Almayer's Folly* in *After Leaving Mr Mackenzie*, as we have already discussed, provides a particularly revealing example, staging the literary passage as an entirely problematic space of reading: an English woman reading a male modernist representation of a slave woman's subaltern consciousness. The citation occurs when Norah, the sister of the main character, Julia, picks up "the book lying on her bed-table—*Almayer's Folly*—and had begun to read" (*AL*, 103). The text then cites the following passage:

> The slave had no hope, and knew of no change. She knew of no other sky, no other water, no other forest, no other world, no other life. She had no wish, no hope, no love.... The absence of pain and hunger was her happiness, and when she felt unhappy she was tired, more than usual, after the day's labour. (*AL*, 103)[31]

Rhys neither names the figure of Conrad's novel, Taminah, an apparently peripheral character and in the most subordinate of subaltern class positions; nor does she provide any indication of the novel's social or cultural setting. This foregrounds all the more the subaltern reading effect already inscribed in Conrad's novel.

Taminah's character serves as an index in each novel, albeit in different ways, for the extreme differences in racial, national, class, and other forms of social identities that comprise the communal totality toward which each novel gestures: once again a "subaltern" figure in that more precise definition of the term developed by the Subaltern Studies historians, as the "demographic difference between the total...population and all those...described as 'elite'." In *Almayer's Folly* this subaltern effect is already explicable in terms of the double difference in social status between Almayer's daughter, Nina, and the slave, Taminah, marked by the latter's initial description as "Siamese" and as a "slave": from the most subordinate class, by contrast to Nina's elevated class position, she is nonetheless accorded a national and racial status ("Siamese") denied to Nina by the "contempt" she is shown for her "mixed blood" (*AF*, 42).[32] This doubling of and difference between the two female characters, incidentally, might illuminate the colonial politics of sexuality and gender that will get displaced in the masculine construction of Conrad's celebrated "secret sharer" motif: what each of these women secretly share is a political identification with and desire for the Balinese male hero, Dain Maroola, organizing resistance against Dutch colonialism. This political identification,

The Vanishing Genre of the Nyai Narrative 169

moreover, has an interesting resonance with Pramoedya's own reading of *Almayer's Folly*, whose plot he once succinctly summarized as "the story about a Balinese prince who is smuggling guns to organize resistance against Dutch colonial rule."[33]

The contrast between the two sisters in Rhys's novel complicates any attempt to read her citation of Conrad as, in anything but a negative dialectical sense, the articulation of an unconscious political sisterhood of anti-colonial political identification. Such a reading seems as belabored as that of Norah's improbable identification of her own form of domestic "slaving" with the "slave" of *Almayer's Folly*. Yet it is indeed the problematic labor of reading that Jean Rhys's citation foregrounds, linking the avant-garde scene of reading English modernism, itself complicated by the ambiguous priority of a relation to Creole modernism, with the interrupted space of reading *nyai* narratives in Indonesian modernism.

There is a curious riddle to the nationally and racially marked "Siamese" identity of Taminah, since Conrad seems to have chosen a Javanese-sounding name (*tuminah* can mean "patient, calm, and careful" in Javanese) for a Siamese character living in Borneo. Neither the details of this odd misnaming and displacement of his Malay setting, nor their elision in Rhys's citation, allows us to read Taminah as a *nyai* figure precisely. Both as a matter of social representation, and as a matter of plot, however, Taminah does figure the foreclosure on a subaltern perspective that is the hallmark of the genre of the *nyai* narrative. In Conrad's novel, Taminah's knowledge of Nina's secret romance places her at the heart of the novel's *Nyai Dasima*-like melodramatic plotting of contested Arab, Dutch, and Malay perspectives.[34] In Rhys's novel, the cited literary passage registers the elision of her story as just that sort of displaced literary-linguistic social space of reading that emerges, in Pramoedya's Buru tetralogy, in the gaps between the well-known story of *Nyai Dasima*, the lost text of *Nyai Permana*, and the character of Nyai Ontosoroh. In each of these very different social and literary contexts, the space of reading articulates a problematic and unresolved relation between an international economy of literary reading and an international economy of domestic labor. In this sense, the *nyai* tale haunts not only the early moments of what Pramoedya calls "pre-Indonesian" literature; as a form that symptomizes an ongoing social, literary, and linguistic foreclosure of subaltern perspectives, the genre also haunts the early roots of twentieth-century transnational modernism.

The social and historical significance of the position of the *nyai* points, then, to an international economy of domestic relations that leaves its mark both on the form and on the content of English modernism—shaping a crucial part of what Fredric Jameson has examined (using *Lord Jim* as prime example) as the "political unconscious" of European "high modernism."[35] This is not, however, to say simply that Pramoedya's work restores a subaltern perspective that has been repressed in the formation of European and transatlantic modernism. Pramoedya's return to the genre of the *nyai* narrative indicates a much closer affinity between the linguistic-literary formations of English and Indonesian modernism. For each, the subaltern *nyai* perspective constitutes the problematic modernity of international domestic arrangements as a secretly shared political unconscious.

The Transnational Matrix of Indonesian Modernism

The international context of this foreclosure on subaltern perspectives is formally emphasized, in the Buru tetralogy, by the novel's final gesture of delivering to Nyai Ontosoroh "manuscripts that are by right yours, the writings of Raden Mas Minke, your beloved son" (*H*, 359) ("*naskah-naskah yang memang menjadi hakmu, tulisan R. M. Minke, anakmu kekasih*" [*RK*, 359]). Controlled by the device of the split narrative consciousness of Pangemanann's troubled (Menadonese Catholic) conscience, this attempt to atone for what has been done to Minke leads to a revealing set of foreclosures on the subaltern reading effect of *nyai* narrative form. These are emblematized by the gesture with which, erasing the title of Nyai, he delivers the manuscripts to "Madame Sanikem Le Boucq." Pangemanann has earlier revealed that, in his own reading of Minke's manuscripts, he reads the story of Nyai Ontosoroh as that of the "change from the Native way of thinking to the European way of thinking":

> I took out the manuscript of *This Earth of Mankind* and was about to start reading it again for the umpteenth time. Long pencil strokes in the margin on some pages indicated the passages that I had to reread. These were all about the change from the Native way of thinking to the European way of thinking. The different ways that the change made itself felt, the transformations in tastes and views. And it always came back to Sanikem. (*H*, 277)
>
> *Aku ambil naskah* Bumi Manusia *dan mulai hendak membacanya untuk kesekian kali. Garis-garis pinsil panjang-panjang pada pinggiran halaman adalah tanda-tanda yang menunjukkan bagian yang harus aku perhatikan: peralihan dari cara berfikir Pribumi pada cara berfikir Eropa, bentuk-bentuk pernyataannya, penggeseran selera dan pandangan. Dan selalu intinya adalah Sanikem.* (*RK*, 276)

Here the literary passage performs an exemplary foreclosure of the "Native" (*Pribumi*) perspective. Attempting to substitute this modernizing imperative of transition from "Native" to "European" for the dilemma of transition from Sanikem and Nyai, Pangemanann elides the title of Nyai altogether.

Yet the very emphasis with which Pangemanann defines the passage from native to European way of thinking as the hermeneutic key to his reading of Minke's manuscripts reveals the unstable reading effect generated by the spectral *nyai* perspective on which he seeks to foreclose. Whether or not his reading reflects the "transformations" described in Minke's notes, the problem of a transition from native to European thinking does indeed reflect his own narrative consciousness as a native Menadonese with an elite French education (and a good training in *explication de texte*). Indeed, not only is each rereading of the passage from native to European refracted through his own hybrid Menadonese, French, and Catholic Christian perspective. Insofar as these are passages taken from Minke's notes, it is also a reading refracted, as with Annelies's retelling of Nyai Ontosoroh's story, through Minke's perspective. In marking the importance of Sanikem's "transformation" from native to European, Pangemanann, on the one hand, seeks to displace the arrested dialectic of Minke's anti-colonial consciousness and, in the same gesture, succeeds in underscoring the gap between that awakening consciousness and his own troubled conscience. The figure of the *nyai* embodies this gap—and hence is simultaneously invoked and erased in Pangemanann's symptomatic emphasis that "it always came back to Sanikem."

Pangemanann can only reiterate the contradictory logic of naming that characterizes the traumatic kernel of Sanikem's humiliation in becoming a *nyai*. So, too, in his final attempt at foreclosure, when he delivers Minke's manuscripts over to "Madame Sanikem le Boucq." Turning Sanikem into the Christian name of a married, European woman, this final gesture only reiterates the repressive logic of naming, identity, and legal status embedded in the traumatic core of *nyai* narrative form. "Sanikem," the name given originally by her Javanese father, has now, according to the logic of transformation from native to European, assumed its "proper" Christian place in a European order of names. The exaggerated emphasis on names calls attention to the legal significance of what we have called, following Spivak, the "foreclosure" on subaltern perspectives. The language of "right" and legacy that suffuses his discourse suggests a final accounting and last judgment both in a religious Christian sense and also in the legal sense of leaving a will or legacy. Even as he submits himself to the "judgment" of Sanikem, the language of right and rights with which he surrenders the manuscripts suggests that he has been compelled to forfeit his right to redeem the estate he claims to be leaving as legacy. He has, in this sense, already "foreclosed" on his estate, that "house of glass" that signifies both the metaphorical power he has accumulated of becoming the eyes of the state and the additional sense that emerges from his appropriation of Minke's own house—as well, of course, as that more material and specific documentary sense in which his notes, *House of Glass* (*Rumah Kaca*), are themselves the criminal, but state-sanctioned theft of Minke's notes.

According to the formulaic modernism of Pangemanann's reading of the transition from native to European, Sanikem's "Native" experience is sublated into a "European way of thinking," her status as *nyai* made respectable through a marriage that confers on her the title of "Madame"—and it is to this Europeanized "judgment" that Pangemanann submits both Minke's notes and evaluation of his own conduct. More revealing still, Pangemanann's attempted foreclosure on the *nyai*'s subaltern perspective is foregrounded by a further instance of foreclosure. Just before delivering the manuscripts to Sanikem, Pangemanann leaves another legacy. Remembering Minke's act of giving his maid "everything he owned," Pangemanann does the same for his maid: "I am writing a letter for you, Tjeu. I am giving you everything I own" (*H*, 358) ("*Akan kubikinkan surat untukmu, Tjeu, semua milikku ini kuserahkan padamu*" [*RK*, 359]). The legacy of Minke's manuscripts is preceded, then, by a legacy that forecloses already on that final act of foreclosure. The importance of this double act of foreclosure is underscored by the fact that the maid appears, and is named, at precisely the moment when Pangemanann articulates the interpretive logic of transition from native to European thinking by which his narrative attempts to foreclose on all its various "native" informants.

The appearance of this housemaid is precipitated by a lengthy meditation on names and naming, provoked by the example of Sanikem, that leads Pangemanann to ask after the housemaid's name: "'What is your name, tell me.' 'Tuminah, Tuan'" (*H*, 278) ("*Siapa namamu sebenarnya?*" "*Tuminah, Tuan*" [*RK*, 277]). The last in a series of named women (all of whose names supplement, for Pangemanann, the forgotten name of Minke's mother), Tuminah embodies the tetralogy's closing subaltern female perspective: "And here, beside me now, there was Tuminah, illiterate, from a village, understanding only the language of her mother. She has never read a book in all her life. Her education consists only of the legends of the Mahabarata and the Ramayana and the village superstitions. And she had given to me everything she knew about kindness. And she had in fact given herself as well" (*H*, 281) ("*Dan di dekatku sendiri sekarang seorang Tuminah—buta huruf, dari kampung, hanya tahu bahasa ibunya. Tak pernah membaca buku seumur hidupnya. Hanya dididik oleh dongengan Mahabarata dan Ramayana, Pancatantra lisan dan tahyul kampungnya. Dan dia telah berikan segala yang pernah diketahui tentang kebajikan kepadaku. Juga memberikan dirinya sendiri*" [*RK*, 280]).

I will resist speculating on whether Pramoedya's Tuminah might constitute a citation from Conrad's *Almayer's Folly*, resituating the coordinates of his Taminah within those of the Buru quartet. The similarity of names, however, suggests a relation between the problematic economy of reading itself and an international economy of domestic relations. Tuminah and Taminah occupy a shared space of reading across the colonial hierarchies of race, religion, and gender. The shared space, moreover, is the subaltern reading effect of *nyai* narrative form. Tuminah's status as domestic servant, her illiteracy, and her marginalized relation to *lingua franca* Malay ("even her Malay was still full of Sundanese words" [*H*, 281]; "*bahasa Melayunya pun tercampur terlalu banyak bahasa Sunda*" [*RK*, 280]) all figure what Pangemanann has just characterized as "the Native way of thinking," and, too, the subaltern female position as Gayatri Spivak characterizes its necessary relation to the "great texts."[36] The coda Tuminah provides to Pangemanann's narrative might alternatively be described as a disavowal of *nyai* narrative form or as itself a truncated *nyai* narrative. Pangemanann seems to go out of his way to disavow anything more than a relation of master to servant, but these very disavowals (such as asking whether she has a husband, and later urging her to find herself a husband) already hint at a closer kind of relationship, or rather dependency, as imagined in the last phrase in the citation above: "And she had in fact given herself as well."

It is precisely the terms of the relation of master to servant, moreover, that suggest how Tuminah fills the contradictory social position marked by the status of *nyai*. Originally a paid domestic servant in the service of the Pangemanann family, she has not been paid since his wife's departure for her native France, serving in her absence as mistress of the house—that is, overseeing the management of the household. It is this domestic arrangement that likely leads to Pangemanann's repeated disavowals. By the same token, it is just this international economy of domestic relations that defines the social position of *nyai* as the ambiguous sign of respectability, or disrepute, for middle-class families. Tuminah's appearance at the very end of the narrative thus confirms the attempt to foreclose on those very questions of racial identity and class position that constitute the legacy that Pangemanann has appropriated from Minke.

This is the legacy left by the uncanny disappearance of *nyai* narrative form at the beginning of the twentieth century. In arguing that this is a legacy that belongs to both Indonesian and English modernism, I have foregrounded the problem of reading that is an essential feature of the genre and its material and historical importance for genealogies of literary modernism. Yet this literary form registers a social trauma that also escapes the descriptive power of literary analysis. As Stoler notes discussing interviews she and Karen Strassler conducted with Javanese women and men who worked as domestic servants during the late colonial period, the *nyai* narrative constituted a "hidden story": "Merely to state that one had worked in a Dutch home was to invoke such plots, to stir suspicion, to suggest a hidden story. Even to acknowledge having known women who were 'kept' or sexually assaulted was to risk being tainted oneself."[37] Stoler and Strassler reveal in what sense this "hidden story" is both bound to and exceeds the bounds of a literary genre. As Pramoedya's Buru tetralogy illustrates, the genre registers these traumatic social forms through a linguistic trauma, through untranslatable elements (*nyai, tuan, Taminah*) that nonetheless come to form the shared literary and linguistic points of reference for a matrix of transnational modernisms during the turn of the century. Pramoedya's Buru tetralogy registers the continuing literary-historical relevance of this vanishing genre by revealing in what sense it constitutes a traumatic core for the problem of reading genealogies of transnational modernism.

7

DECOLONIZING TRADITION
Pramoedya's Indonesian Modernism

The work that Pramoedya produced between 1965 and 1979, during the period of his detention and then internment in the remote penal island colony of Buru, stands as an extraordinary historical testimony. It stands testament not only to the sufferings and losses of those who were deported to Buru following the events of 1965, as recorded most notably in the two-volume set of prison memoirs, *Nyanyi Sunyi Seorang Bisu*, partially translated into English as *The Mute's Soliloquy*. In the Buru tetralogy, Pramoedya also provided an enduring literary-historical record of the period of anti-colonial national awakening during the turn of the century. In addition, Pramoedya wrote two more large-scale historical works of fiction: *Arus Balik*, set in the sixteenth century, and *Arok Dedes*, set in the thirteenth century. Despite the extraordinary historical scope of all these works, it is for the *gaps* in historical memory that the work of Buru stands as a towering achievement, a crucial testament to the unfinished process of decolonization in the twentieth century. As we have already begun to explore in the previous chapter, it is these gaps in the historical record that structure the Buru tetralogy and shape the historical significance of Pramoedya's genealogy of the linguistic-literary formation of Indonesian modernism. In this chapter, I explore how these gaps in the historical record form the basis for a genealogy of Indonesian modernism that extends throughout all of the work of Buru and that constitutes a powerful model for decolonizing tradition.

In a 1992 essay "My Apologies, in the Name of Experience" (*"Ma'af: Atas Nama Pengalaman"*), Pramoedya discusses at length the historical ambition of the work he undertook on Buru. Emphasizing that he is a writer, not a historian—"it is not the materials of history that I examine, but its spirit" *("jadi bukan materi-materi historis yang kukaji, tetapi semangat-semangatnya")*—he explains: "I began deliberately with the theme of Indonesia's National Awakening—which, while limited regionally and nationally, nonetheless remains part of the world and of humanity. Step by step I am writing to the roots of its history, [in a body of work] that for the moment is not ready to be published or perhaps may never be published" ("*Sengaja kuawali dengan thema Kebangkitan Nasional Indonesia—yang walau terbatas di bidang regional dan nasional namun tetap bagian dari dunia dan umat manusia—setapak demi setapak juga kutulis pada akar historinya, yang untuk sementara ini belum siap terbit, atau mungkin tidak akan bisa terbit*").[1] This process of writing "step by step" (*setapak demi setapak*) to the "roots" (*akar*) of the history of Indonesian nationalism clearly refers to the main historical focus of the Buru tetralogy on the period of "Indonesia's National Awakening."[2] It also refers, however, to the process at work in Pramoedya's decision to write about earlier historical periods—the sixteenth-century setting of *Arus Balik* and the thirteenth-century setting of *Arok Dedes*. The "roots" of Indonesian nationalism—which the tetralogy already traces back to the formation of "pre-Indonesian" literature, as we have seen—reach far back, indeed. It is notable, too, that Pramoedya emphasizes that it is an unfinished, incomplete process, referring to "a body of work that has yet to be, or may never be published"—alluding not only to the two historical novels not yet published in 1992 (*Arus Balik* was published in 1995, *Arok Dedes* in 1999), but also to the work lost forever (the last two volumes of the trilogy *The Girl from the Coast* [*Gadis Pantai*], for example, and *A Preliminary Study of the History of the Indonesian Language* [*Studi Percobaan tentang Sejarah Bahasa Indonesia*], both mentioned later in the same essay).

This work of "writing to the roots" of Indonesian nationalism is a guiding principle of the genealogy of Indonesian literary modernism that we explored in the previous chapter. The gaps in historical documentation revealed by the missing texts of *nyai* tales that haunt the Buru tetralogy present a problem of reading that, though specific to "pre-Indonesian" literature, calls attention to a more general problem of reading genealogies of transnational modernism. In this chapter, I examine how Pramoedya turns the gaps in historical documentation, including the personal losses incurred during the events of 1965, into a resource for decolonizing literary and cultural traditions. In the fragmentary form of the prison notes, *Nyanyi Sunyi Seorang Bisu*, we find a principle of genealogy at work that is all at once personal and literary, familial and historical, filiative and affiliative.

This principle of genealogy emerges from a problem of composition—the sheer difficulty of composing the notes under the conditions of Buru prison camp—that is also linked to that traditional Malay and Javanese principle of composition Henk Maier traces around the semantic resonance of the two words *baca* ("reading") and *karang* ("composition").³ As revealed, above all, in the section devoted to the memory of his mother (*Karangan Bunga pada Kakinya;* "Flowers for Mother") and his father (*Mata Rantai;* "One Link in a Chain"), the prison notes show how Pramoedya turns these traditional forms of reading and composition into a resource for historical documentation and a decolonizing of tradition. This work of decolonizing tradition shapes the revolutionary family romance that has informed his work from the very start, and that becomes especially pronounced in the longer historical fiction composed on Buru: the Buru tetralogy, *Arus Balik,* and *Arok Dedes.* A reading of the revolutionary family romance shaping these last two works enables us to reconsider the implications of our reading of Conrad's colonial English-Malay family romance and Rhys's Creole family romance. Different and distinct though all three family romances certainly are, the genealogies of reading transnational modernism embedded in each are illuminated by the principle of genealogy at the heart of Pramoedya's revolutionary family romance. Pramoedya's principle of genealogy makes the fragment of literary text—remembered, composed in oral or written form, or simply registered as missing—the point of reference for an ongoing decolonization of multiple literary and historical traditions.

Lingkaran Setan
The "Vicious Circle" of History and the Rescue Work of Buru

Writing back to the "roots" of Indonesian nationalism means confronting what Pramoedya repeatedly calls a "vicious circle" (*lingkaran setan*).⁴ This phrase recurs throughout the work of Buru, and it reveals something important both about the challenge facing him in organizing the prison notes as a whole and the way he turns that challenge into a resource. Its most obvious referent is the bloody massacres and political repression that occurred in the wake of the aborted military coup of September 1965. This "vicious circle" undoes history, reversing the revolutionary history of Indonesia's struggle for independence and destroying Pramoedya's own efforts to document the prehistory of anti-colonial nationalism. So, in a letter to one of his daughters from the second volume of *Nyanyi Sunyi Seorang Bisu*, we read: "As I write here, all I can ask is when will this vicious and blood-filled circle end?" (*MS*, 254) (*Hanya satu, Et, kapan kita berhenti mengulang dalam lingkaran setan yang selalu berdarah ini?* [*NS* II, 171]). And in the third section of the first volume, "Watching *Wayang* for the Last Time" ("*Terakhir Kali Nonton Wayang*"), which elaborates on this trope more fully than elsewhere, we read: "For sure we are already an old country caught in the vicious circle of our dance: from out of the open door of colonialism and into the open door of postcolonialism, how many times must we be baptized in blood?" ("*Memang sudah menjadi bangsa tua yang selalu kiprah dalam lingkaran setan: dari pintu terbuka kolonial, ke pintu terbuka pasca-kolonial berapa kali permandian darah?*" [*NS* I, 37]).

The fragmentary form of the notes as a whole might be explained in terms of this "vicious circle." Whether writing letters to his children, documenting the conditions on Buru, or reflecting on his own life and work, Pramoedya finds himself caught in a "mute's soliloquy," as the English edition translates the Indonesian *Nyanyi Sunyi Seorang Bisu* (literally: the silent song of a deaf-mute), condemned to a laborious form of repetition and recomposition that seeks to remember both what was lost in 1965—including the historical documentation of the losses of earlier historical moments—and the losses he and his fellow prisoners faced in the prison camps. Although many of the notes are dated (most from 1976 or later), some of them (like the entire first section) are undated and were likely composed before he was given permission to write (in 1973).[5] Perhaps written down once, destroyed either by the authorities or by Pramoedya himself for his own safety, and then recomposed at a later date, first in spoken form to his fellow prisoners, then written down later, every section of the notes—indeed, each individual passage—bears the mark of a laborious rescue work of memory, both personal and historical. Each passage of the prison notes registers a version of the question from the opening section that haunts all of the notes: "Is it possible to take from a man his right to speak to himself?" (*MS*, 13) ("*siapa yang bisa rampas hak untuk berdialog dengan diri sendiri*" [*NS* I, 6]). Posed in relation to "everything" he lost "following the events of 1965," the question resonates throughout the prison notes, at times carrying the defiant force of a rhetorical question answered in the very act of asking, and at times assuming the force of a real question, as yet unanswered—as, for example, when we read, in a passage from which the English title takes its cue, "I have lost my voice. Were I able to sing, would anyone hear this mute's soliloquy?" (*MS*, 342).[6] Each passage of the prison notes is bound to repeat a variation of the question: "When will this vicious and blood-filled circle end?"

At the same time, each variation of the question seeks to turn the ongoing experience of loss into a critical resource for breaking that "vicious circle." Reflecting on the experiences recorded in the prison notes, Pramoedya again uses the phrase in "My Apologies, in the Name of Experience," linking it to the effort to write to the "roots" of Indonesian nationalism and tying it to his critique of "Javanism":

In detention for fourteen years and two months, stripped of everything altogether, I reflected on all this past experience from underneath the military boot that trampled on me. It all became clearer, that all of this was nothing but a material experience, a sort of historical vicious circle of *"kampung"* civilization and culture without reorientation inward, or outward either.

Dalam penahanan selama 14 tahun 2 bulan, terampas dari semua dan segala, semua pengalaman yang telah lalu aku renungkan dari bawah larsa militer yang menginjakku. Semua menjadi lebih jelas, bahwa semua itu hanya pengalaman alamiah belaka, suatu lingkaran setan histori dari peradaban dan budaya 'kampung' tanpa reorientasi ke dalam atau pun ke luar.[7]

This deliberately offensive characterization of his own Javanese background as a *kampung* civilization and culture is a more pronounced variation on the critique of "Javanism" one finds in the Buru quartet. Reconstructing Indonesian history is impossible without confronting, and "reorienting" the "historical vicious circle" of Javanese "civilization and culture." As he puts it later in the same essay, referring to his rewriting of the Javanese legend of Arok, this "vicious circle" "can only be broken by a reevaluation of it, *Verlichting, Aufklaerung,* that produces the creativity to break through its own ceiling" (*"lingkaran setan, yang hanya bisa diputuskan oleh reevaluasi atasnya, Verlichting, Aufklarung, yang menghasilkan kreativitas yang menjebol plafonnya sendiri"*).[8] Pramoedya's trope of the "vicious circle" does something more complicated and more interesting than pose, as binary opposites, a traditionally Javanese mystical vision of the circularity of history over against a modern European spirit of enlightenment. Both sides of this formulation might rather be seen as linked in the "reorientation" of the "historical vicious circle" "be it from within or from without" (*"ke dalam atau pun ke luar"*). The double (Dutch and German) linguistic register with which Pramoedya articulates the European coordinates of Enlightenment already suggest how the emergence of a specifically Indonesian modernism necessarily involves a displacement and reevaluation of European models of Enlightenment.

Most immediately, however, each repeated variation of the trope of the "vicious circle" effects a deliberate estrangement from within Javanese tradition. This characteristic feature of Pramoedya's critique of "Javanism" is often accompanied by an offensiveness for which then an "apology" (*ma'af*) is issued—as in the title of the essay "My Apologies"—although the apology only seems to underscore the offense in a sort of rhetorical vicious circle of apology and offense. Minke's critique of "Javanism," in *Footsteps,* appears with just such an apology: "Excuse me for using the term Javanism. Perhaps it offends some people" (*F,* 374) (*"Maafkan aku, bila kugunakan kata javanisme, yang mungkin tidak simpatik"* [*J,* 372]). In one of the later sections of the first volume of prison notes, entitled "Final Release" (*"Pembebasan Pertama"*), a similar, extended version of this emerges in the response Pramoedya records himself having given to a visiting journalist who asked him his views on the "psyche" of the Indonesian people. Echoing passages from "A Farewell to Wayang," Pramoedya here turns to an example from Joseph Conrad to effect an estrangement of the dominant Javanese hegemony over Indonesia:

> Official literature turns to prophesy to lick the boots of the authorities, the gods on the top of the earth. And why would it not be so? It's proven, because it's always been the case with writing. The gods can recruit by means of the men of letters in order to justify and legitimate the power of these authorities. Isn't that the problem of our inheritance up to the present? With the result that the psyche of the Indonesian people at large is that of the slave, and a corrupt slave, at that. Perhaps we should not be offended by what that Polish-born sailor-turned-writer wrote about the Javanese people: that everyone, from beggars to kings, is a slave. Only he didn't add that word corrupt.
>
> *Sastra resmi berfaal megelus-elus tungkai para penguasa, dewa di atas bumi. Dan apa yang tidak? Dan berbukti, karena diabadikan dalam tulisan. Para dewa pun dikerahkan oleh para pujangga untuk membenarkan dan mengabsahkan kekuasaan yang berkuasa. Kan terwariskan sampai sekarang? Walhasil psyché umum orang Indonesia adalah budak, dan budak yang korup. Jangan sakit hati kalau seorang pengarang-pelaut kelahiran Polandia menamakan orang Jawa itu, dari pengemis sampai rajanya budak. Hanya dia tidak tambahkan dengan kata korup.* (*NS* I, 183)

Here, the example—a passage recalled from Conrad's "Karain: A Memory" to which Pramoedya also alludes in his biography of Tirto Adi Suryo—is cited as a counterbalance against "official" Javanese literature. It recalls Minke's critique of "the literature of Java," especially the "*Mahabharata* and *Bharatayuddha*," "great epics" that "had become obstacles to the people's advancement" (*F,* 373) ("*Pandangan salah tentang keturunan dan darah sudah begitu berakar dalam literatur dan kehidupan Jawa. Mengibakan.* Ramayana *dan* Mahabharata *tak meninggalkan pegangan bagaimana memasuki dunia modern. Epos-epos besar itu kini telah jadi beban penghambat*" [*J,* 370]). It recalls, too, Pramoedya's criticism, in "My Apologies," of the "power of this dominating, massive education" ("*Kekuatan pendidikan yang dominan dan massal*") passed down "through oral and written literature, drama, music, song" ("*melalui sastra, lisan dan tulisan, pangguan, musik dan nyanyian*") and above all "carried [by] passages from the Mahabharata" ("*yang membawakan cuplikan-cuplikan dari Mahabharata*").[9]

This deliberately offensive estrangement of Javanese literature, culture, and civilization creates an alien genealogy of literary form—turning to the Conrad passage as a way of overturning the "official literature" of Java. In order to evaluate how this principle of alien genealogy is developed throughout the notes, and as a principle that underlies the historical fiction, too, it is important to recognize the extent to which it proceeds "from within" Javanese linguistic and literary traditions. As we have already discussed, in the second chapter, the narrative form of the Buru tetralogy is structured on a *mise-en-abyme* of Minke's aesthetic taste for gamelan music, whose seductive charm Pramoedya associates (both there and in the section "A Farewell to Wayang") with what (in *This Earth of Mankind*) is described as the "vicious circle" of its repeated, polyphonic musical form ("your people will drown forever in the overflow of repeated tones and vicious circles" [TE, 194]; "*seorang Jawa pun akan muncul, hanya akan tenggelam terus dalam curahan nada-nada ulangan dan lingkaran setan*" [BM, 189]). As we shall discuss in a moment, Pramoedya's genealogy proceeds from a deeply personal and familial Javanese genealogy. Here, we might note a formally significant contrast between what Pramoedya does in singling out the "dominating" effect of the passages from the *Mahabharata* and what he does in citing the Conrad passage. In the first case, the passage of literature is a touchstone for tradition; in the second, it provides a point of reference for contesting tradition (*terwariskan*).

If this already suggests a double movement of critique from within and without (*ke dalam atau pun ke luar*), both examples might also be read as an estrangement of tradition using traditional forms of reading, recitation, and composition. Henk Maier's account of the "acts of commemoration and differentiation"[10] that weave together *baca* (reading or recitation) and *karang* (composition, or arrangement) might be found in both cases, and in a way that complicates our sense of what is and is not Javanese about each passage of literature. Of course, the form of reading, recitation, and commemoration that occupies Pramoedya in the prison notes should be distinguished from the tales and stories that Maier is discussing. The passages he cites (*baca*) must all be from memory, given the conditions of his internment; and the process of arranging the prison notes (*karang*) does not exactly produce the "fragrant garlands—or bouquets—of words"[11] Maier refers to. Yet in this sense the literary association of the word *soliloquy* used in the title of the English translation (*The Mute's Soliloquy*) does capture the way the notes repeatedly return to forms of poetic and literary practice from which the writer is exiled. This, too, is part of the vicious circle, as suggested by the Indonesian title, whose "affective tonality," as Goenawan Mohamad points out,[12] alludes to Amir Hamzah's 1937 collection of poems, *Nyanyi Sunyi* (*Songs of*

Solitude), often cited as providing a bridge between the old Malay poetic conventions of the past and the modern style of the poetry written in the new Indonesian language.

Allusions like this, along with the vast repertoire of references to a whole range of texts that he had read, researched, or himself written before 1965, make the prison notes a remarkable rescue work of memory and documentation in which, however, the passage of literature is neither a touchstone for tradition nor a contestation of tradition, but rather a gap between traditions. It is these gaps—like the *nyai* narratives discussed in the previous chapter—that provide the occasion for a commemoration and composition that writes to the roots of Indonesian nationalism. The clearest gap is the one that divides Pramoedya from his Indonesian readership and turns his "mute's soliloquy" into the dissident voice of a writer more likely to be read outside than within Indonesia. This is an exile and estrangement of Pramoedya's own voice that is intimately related to the "vicious circle" echoed politically in the question "Is it possible to take from a man his right to speak to himself?" and in a literary sense in the thought "I have lost my voice. Were I able to sing, would anyone hear this mute's soliloquy?"

Pramoedya turns the vicious circle of these questions into a far-reaching genealogy of Indonesian history. For example, in the opening section, whose Indonesian title Rudolf Mrázek reads as an allusion to Soetan Sjahrir's letters from exile, Pramoedya recalls with a personal and historical bitterness those who had been exiled before him, revisiting and repeating the passages of earlier Indonesian nationalists and forerunners of nationalism, at the same time commemorating the gaps and breaks that constitute the interrupted history of Indonesian nationalism. In this opening section, it is striking that the first extended motif of singing is prompted, not by allusion to Amir Hamzah, but by the English words of a song: "During the Revolution when I was being held by the Dutch in Bukitduri Prison, I memorized a Negro spiritual, the first line of which went *'There's a happy land somewhere...'*—a symbolic promise for every person's future" (*MS*, 7) ("*Dulu, di penjara Bukitduri, pernah aku belajar menyanyi lagu yang dibuka dengan kalimat* There's a happy land somewhere—*lambang hari depan untuk setiap orang*" [*NS* I, 2]). Clearly outside the orbit of Javanese tradition, this example nonetheless introduces the Javanese term—*pesangon* ("separation pay," or *vade mecum*, or "provisions")—that best articulates what it is that the rescue work of the notes seeks to remember in collecting those passages of remembered words, songs, and texts that form the basis for all the notes from Buru.

The phrase "vicious circle" itself, moreover, suggests that there is already something intimately foreign at the heart of Javanese culture: *lingkaran setan* means literally "satanic circle," embedding a double Islamic and Christian religious resonance in a trope repeatedly used to imply a pre-Islamic, pre-Christian religious and cultural historical frame of reference. Most often, the trope is used to describe the world of Javanese *wayang* (in the Buru tetralogy, in *Arus Balik*, and in "A Farewell to Wayang"); or to the thirteenth-century Hindu-Javanese religious and cultural context of the legend of Arok, which Pramoedya used as the basis for *Arok Dedes* (both "A Farewell to Wayang" and the later essay "My Apologies" explicitly refer to Arok in developing the trope of the "vicious circle"). The "reevaluation" required to break the "vicious circle" of Javanese culture and civilization, then, demands a "reevaluation" on both (or rather all) sides—a simultaneously "inward" and "outward" reorientation of "*kampung* civilization and culture."

Some five years before the events of 1965, in response to repressive laws forbidding Chinese Indonesians from conducting trade outside the cities, Pramoedya wrote a set of letters, published in book form in 1960 under the title *Hoakiau di Indonesia* (*The Chinese in Indonesia*), in which he sought to expose the racial, economic, and cultural fallacies shaping the anti-Chinese measures. (For this, he was imprisoned without trial for a year.)[13] In the course of the argument, Pramoedya developed a far-reaching historical survey of Indonesia that placed Chinese Indonesians at the center of Indonesia's national, political, economic, and cultural identity. Anticipating not only the scope of the Buru tetralogy (and its insights into the government manipulation of anti-Chinese resentments) but also the historical grasp of sixteenth-century Indonesia in *Arus Balik*, Pramoedya constructs out of the extreme forms of racial alienation distorting Indonesian politics at that time an improvised genealogy of Indonesian history. It is notable that he adopts, both personally and rhetorically, a form of what Maier calls "playing relatives." Pramoedya argues, at one point, that he cannot deny he himself has Chinese blood flowing in him; and framed his letters in a deliberate gesture of both friendship and relation to his Chinese interlocutor: "Let us shake hands here. We will not forget anything that has happened in our lives, and we will pass on our notes to our descendants, to history" (*CI*, 238) ("*Terimalah jabatan tanganku. Kita tidak bakal lupakan apapun dalam hidup kita ini, dan kita akan sampaikan catatan kita pada anak-cucu kita, pada sejarah*" [*HI*, 278]).

In the third letter of *Hoakiau di Indonesia*, Pramoedya anticipates, too, the trope of the "vicious circle" that recurs so frequently in the work of Buru. Its formulation here—which, so far as I have been able to ascertain, appears to be the first formulation of this trope in Pramoedya's work—reveals more clearly than elsewhere the intimate estrangement of alien genealogies implied in Pramoedya's own genealogy and critique. The letter begins with a curious invocation of the "atmosphere of Christmas" (*suasana Natal*)—already an interesting, deliberate estrangement of the dominant Islamic cultural context of Pramoedya's readership. It is followed by another odd twist, writing (in a letter addressed to Hs-y, but published originally in journal form) "my heart feels truly moved to be able to speak with my own soul" (*"sungguh mengharukan rasanya di hati dapat bicara dengan nurani sendiri"*)—adding a phrase that has, as Sumit Mandal points out, uncanny echoes in the prison notes: "There is not a force on this earth that can stop a person from speaking with his own soul" (*CI*, 93) (*"Tak ada suatu kekuatan di atas bumi ini yang dapat melarang orang bicara dengan nuraninya sendiri"* [*HI*, 81]).[14] Here, we might identify this articulation of the voice of the writer (he identifies himself in the next sentence as such) as itself a part of that alien, estranging genealogy, a deliberate displacement of the coordinates of the writer's more usual relations. This "soul"-searching estrangement of the expected coordinates of this Indonesian writer's identity is tied to "this Hoakiau problem" that "attracts[s] and disturb[s] my soul so much"; and, at the end of the opening paragraph, is in large part explained by a deliberate filiative and affiliative relation to those designated as the aliens within Indonesia: "I prefer being friends with the peoples of all countries, and...I could not deny if it were said that it is possible I also have Chinese blood flowing in me" (*CI*, 93) (*"perasaan kemanusiaanku tersinggung...dan...aku tidak bisa membantah bila dikatakan ada juga darah Tionghoa mengalir dalam tubuhku"* [*HI*, 81]).

At the end of this letter, then, Pramoedya returns to the initial coordinates of the opening to sum up his disturbance with and opposition to the scapegoating of Chinese: "One round after another of finding scapegoats until finally common sense itself becomes the scapegoat" (*CI*, 116) (*"Gegeran demi gegeran, sampai mungkin sekali otak waras bakal jadi kurban gegeran"* [*HI*, 110]). The "scapegoat" (*kurban*) perhaps already suggests the common (if contested) Islamic and Christian (originally of course Hebrew) story of Abraham's sacrifice. Arguing against the further provocations of the campaign against the Chinese, he writes "People will just get dizzy, caught up in a never-ending devil's circle, whether or not there is even a devil around" (*CI*, 116) (*"Orang hanya berpusing-pusing dalam lingkaran setan—tanpa atau dengan sang setan itu sendiri"* [*HI*, 110]). As the final clause underlines, the specifically religious sense of this Christian, Islamic formulation is less important than the complex of cultural relations embedded in the metaphor. A pungent metaphor for the intimate resentments of the shared, contested roots of the dominant monotheisms, this "vicious circle" of scapegoating extends to all sides of Indonesia's national identity ("whether or not there is even a devil around"). In this way, it anticipates the terms with which Pramoedya will attempt to break the "vicious circle" of 1965 through an extended practice of alien genealogy.

"Mata Rantai"
>> The Genealogical Link as Break

In "One Link in a Chain" ("Mata Rantai"), the section that introduces the second volume of the Indonesian and Dutch editions of the notes, Pramoedya begins a set of reflections about his father by appealing to the scientific laws of genetic inheritance: "The point is that each and every person is a link in the chain connecting one person with the most-recently-born representative of the human species. The connection between these links is entirely biological, unlike other human links, which hold mysteries that can never be fully explained, not through rational thought, feelings, or intellect" (*MS*, 103) ("*Maka setiap orang, sekiranya tidak mandul atau tidak punah sebelum dewasa, akan menduduki tempatnya sebagai mata rantai, penghubung manusia awal dengan manusia akhir. Kaitan antara satu mata dengan yang lain memang bersifat biologis semata. Tetapi kaitan manusiawinya mengandung rahasia mistis yang tak-kan habis-habis diterangkan, dan setiap kali menantang akal, perasaan dan pikiran manusia untuk menjawabnya, melahirkan ilmu dan filsafat, juga tidak habis-habisnya*" [*NS* II, 2]). This unbreakable genetic link introduces the root formula—"one link in a chain" (*mata rantai*)—not only for his own genealogical link to his father but also for a tracing of the genealogy of Indonesian nationalism, especially around the Boedi Oetomo movement in which his father participated.

The contrast between "biological" and "other" links gives a clue to how Pramoedya turns the scientific theory of genes toward a principle of genealogical critique. Whereas the "generational bonds" ("*hubungan generasi*") form an "endless chain corresponding with the law of genetics" ("*suatu jajaran mata rantai yang kait-mengait tak habis-habisnya, juga dengan hukum warisan yang berkait-kaitan*") those other links "can be severed by a break in tradition" ("*mungkin putus karena putusnya tradisi*") (*MS*, 103, 104; *NS* II, 2). Although it is not immediately apparent from the way Pramoedya develops this in "Mata Rantai," the unbreakable link of genetic theory provides the critical perspective from which to theorize "breaks" in tradition. Pramoedya's contrast might be compared with the contrast Edward Said makes between "natural filiation" and "affiliation," the former grounded in the biological process of generation, the latter constituting a "compensatory order" that repeats the patterns of the former at the level of social institutions—what Pramoedya calls the "more 'human' terms" "culture," "civilization" and "tradition."[15] In this sense, Pramoedya's distinctions have important affinities with the emergence of a "critical consciousness" that Said traces to a general crisis in nineteenth-century European human sciences prompted by the scientific problem posed by a search for origins.

Pramoedya's concerns might, in some respects, appear to be quite different from Said's. Indeed, his focus on the bonds of "natural filiation" is prompted by a rather striking and immediate human concern in Buru exile, cut off from any contact with his children: "In the biological chain I am the link between my parents and my children. This is the one that is irrevocable and cannot be broken, differing, let us say, from a social link, which can be severed by a break in tradition—between myself and my children, for example, because I have not had the opportunity to communicate with them in their adolescent and young-adult years" (*MS*, 104) ("*Dan aku hanya satu mata rantai antara orangtuaku dengan anak-anakku. Jelas: aku tidak mati muda, juga tidak mandul. Kaitan itu tak terbantahkan. Namun ada kaitan manusiawi dan social yang mungkin putus karena putusnya tradisi: aku belum pernah bergaul dengan mereka pada masa remaja dan dewasanya. Tradisi itu belum bisa terancam putus*" [*NS* II, 2]). Cut off from his children, he sets himself the task of attempting to fill in the "gaps of information" (*menjembatani kekurangan ini*) in the "picture" (*gambaran*) that "other people" (*orang-orang lain*) will tell them about "their father" and "the link between them and my parents, the generation above me" (*MS*, 104). If, on the one hand, this appears to follow Said's point that writers need to compensate for the "failed idea or possibility of filiation,"[16] it is notable that Pramoedya lays such emphasis on the *filiative* order, as if finding there—rather than turning to "affiliation"—the compensation for the broken communication between himself and his children. Given the sharpness of the critique of "Javanism" we see elsewhere, it is even more notable that he emphasizes his need to fulfil his obligation, as father toward his children and as a son toward his parents, as a "link in the chain" (*mata rantai*) of successive generations.

This principle of directly *filiative* obligation toward his Javanese lineage leaves its mark on just about all the prison notes, whether or not he is directly addressing his children. It is especially prominent in the two sections devoted to memories of his father and mother, respectively, "One Link in a Chain" ("Mata Rantai") and "Flowers for Mother" ("Karangan Bunga pada Kakinya"). In these sections in particular it is possible to see Pramoedya turning a filial devotion to Javanese genealogy inside out, as it were, to form the principle for a more radical kind of genealogy able to confront the gaps and breaks in history and equipped to break the "vicious circle" of Javanese tradition. The seeming contradiction involved with this critique of "Javanism" from within is perhaps clearest in Pramoedya's memories of his father, "a man," he reflects in "Mata Rantai," "who detested feudalism yet held Javanese culture in high esteem and never raised his voice against Javanese feudal culture" (*MS*, 105) ("*Ia seorang liberal dan javanis sekaligus, tidak melakukan ibadah, pecinta kebudayaan Jawa, pembenci feodalisme, tetapi tanpa disa-*

darinya juga tidak berkeberatan terhadap kebudayaan feudal Jawa" [*NS* II, 4]). The conflict between his father's "high esteem" for Javanese culture and his detestation of its "feudal" features emerge in a passage in which Pramoedya explains the origin of his own given name: "I was born on February 6, 1925, and my father, a Javanese who had a near-mystical feeling about words, named me Pramoedya. Reflecting the revolutionary spirit of the time, the name was constructed from the phrase '*Yang Pertama di Medan*' or 'First on the Battlefield'" (*MS*, 107) ("*Kalau pada 6 Februari 1925 anak mereka yang pertama lahir, sebagai orang Jawa yang selalu mencari arti pada setiap nama, dinamai anak Pramoedya. Menurut pengertiannya, nama itu berarti 'Yang Pertama di Medan,' sesuai dengan pergolakan pada waktunya*" [*NS* II, 5]). Missing from the English-language edition, *The Mute's Soliloquy*, the passage continues:

> Whether this is the correct Javanese etymology, I don't know. He himself went so far as to change his own name. An opponent of feudalism, with a firm break he cast off the "Mas" in front of his personal name, leaving: Toer.
> The blacked-out mark over "Mas" on his old-fashioned blue-painted name-plaque summoned a great many, far-reaching contemplations.
> *Benar tidaknya menurut bahasa Jawa, aku tak tahu. Ia sendiri pun telah timbang-timbang namanya sendiri. Sebagai pembenci feodalisme, dengan putusan yang kukuh ia buang Mas pada nama pribadinya, tinggal: Toer.*
> *Blok hitam pada Mas pada papan nama bercat biru itu untuk waktu lama telah memanggil renungan-renungan yang panjang.* (*NS* II, 5)

This memory of his father's act of erasing the honorific title "Mas" is perhaps the most economical image of Pramoedya's effort to honor the memory of his father's Javanese heritage while at the same time recalling his place in history as "a nationalist who gave his full support to the independence movement" (*MS*, 123) ("*ia adalah seorang pejuang gerakan kemerdekaan*" [*NS* II, 31]). It provides, too, a succinct formulation for the principle of Pramoedya's own genealogy of Indonesian nationalism, one he is able to write into the authorial identity of his family name "Toer": a writing that seeks to erase the hierarchies of feudal Javanese culture while leaving the mark of that erasure as a sign of the revolutionary legacy of Indonesian nationalism.

Indeed, in ways that clearly do not always translate easily into English, all of the notes collected under the heading of "Mata Rantai" reveal forms of that constant interplay between Javanese and Indonesian that Benedict Anderson has discussed in terms of Pramoedya's use of the Indonesian language as a means to "cross swords with his Javanese heritage."[17] This section shows a number of revealing affinities with the formal example of the memoirs, *Kenang-Kenangan,* written by Soetomo, the founder of Boedi Oetomo. Soetomo has a much more prominent place in "One Link in the Chain" than the English edition would suggest, since the numerous allusions to him are entirely dropped from the translation. The most notable of these is the comment that, when his father took on the task of reorganizing the local branch of Boedi Oetomo, "he took over all the functions of Dr. Soetomo of Blora, except the position of Doctor" (*"Ia gantikan semua jabatan Dokter Soetomo di Blora, kecuali sebagai dokter"* [NS II, 4]). Soetomo was, as Benedict Anderson puts it, "the first prominent Indonesian to write something like an autobiography, the well-known *Kenang-Kenangan*—a title that can be translated as Memoirs, but is really better rendered as Memories."[18]

The formal significance of Soetomo's *Kenang-Kenangan* (1934) might be ascribed to the way Soetomo refashions Javanese conceptions of genealogy and descent to suit the contemporary, nationalist moment of the 1930s. Anderson's essay on the memoirs, indeed, suggests that they might stand as a model for the emergence of Indonesian modernism—providing in the realm of prose what Amir Hamzah's *Nyanyi Sunyi* provided in the realm of poetry. Soetomo's prefatory note to his readers reads:

> The Javanese saying *Kacang, mangsa ninggal lanjaran* means that each descendant will always inherit some characteristics of his progenitors. With this in mind, readers can readily discover my true character through my descriptions of the nature and character of each ancestor. Since both my grandfather and my father have been dead for twenty years, including their stories has raised no objections from those of their former colleagues who are still alive. This discussion of my ancestors also might benefit numerous persons. The tracing of Javanese genealogies is sometimes difficult because Javanese rarely have surnames. Since my genealogy reaches back into antiquity, its publication will provide a great many people with the opportunity of tracing their own origins.[19]

Anderson's reading of the memoirs sees this modern transposition of Javanese genealogies into a twentieth-century Indonesian context in terms of a foreshadowing of the "nationalist solution" to the problem of tradition—to abbreviate his argument considerably, "imitating one's forefathers by not imitating them. Being a good Javanese by becoming a good Indonesian."[20]

Clearly Pramoedya's relationship with Javanese traditions is less accommodating, as we have begun to see, and as Anderson has shown extensively. It is this model, however, that might allow us to recognize a deeper shaping impulse than would otherwise be available to an English reader, behind Pramoedya's own transposition of Javanese genealogies. One revealing example of the kind of way in which Pramoedya *departs* from Soetomo's presentation of his own genealogy as one of interest to the readers because it "reaches back into antiquity," reminds us, again, of the double edge of the title "Mata Rantai," or "One Link in a Chain." At the very beginning of the section, having noted that his father was born in 1897, the son of a mosque official (*naib*), he goes on to write: "There are still approximately twenty more links in the chain above that. But there's no use in talking about that genealogy/family tree [*silsilah*]" (*"Masih ada barang dua puluh mata rantai lagi di atasnya. Tetapi tak ada guna bicara tentang silsilah"* [*NS* II, 3]).

This emphasis on only *one* of the links in the chain of that genealogy (to borrow the emphasis given in the English translation) foregrounds the extent to which, as in the previous description of his father as not only the founder of a family but also the originator of a "tradition," Pramoedya's improvisation on the customs and practices of Javanese genealogy is deliberatively selective. To the extent that Soetomo's memoirs might offer a model, it is in their attempt to articulate a sense of "tradition"—but for Pramoedya the concept of "tradition" is one that emphasizes the revolutionary break from the past that is also *aware* of the past. The concept of tradition Anderson characterizes Soetomo as seeking—one that, corresponding with the nationalist solution of the 1920s and 1930s, could show how to be a good Javanese by being a good Indonesian—fits the temperament and historical moment with which Pramoedya is mostly concerned in "One Link in a Chain": the moment of "National Awakening" following 1908; the moment of "Boedi Oetomo"; and the moment immediately following the time period of the Buru tetralogy. To the extent that Pramoedya, too, attempts to articulate a sense of "tradition," it is one that goes a step further than Soetomo's to conceive a *revolutionary* nationalist tradition.

Here, the importance of Pramoedya's opening emphasis on *filiation*, on the unbreakable links of genetic laws, may become clearer, since the very filiative act of Javanese genealogy serves to identify those *breaks* in history that constitute Pramoedya's grasp of Indonesian modernism, as discussed in the previous chapter. In "Mata Rantai," the most striking and emblematic break is the appearance of the name Toer, with which his recollections proper begin: "Toer is the name of my father, founder of the Toer family. It is an odd name—not at all 'Javanese'—and in the 1950s, when the name first began to become known nationally through my published works, it stirred numerous questions about its origins, especially among those who knew that its bearer was ethnic Javanese. But in the 1920s and 1930s it was a familiar name in the social and political life of the small town of Blora" (*MS*, 104) (*"Ayahku, Toer, adalah pendiri keluarga Toer. Pada tahun 1950 waktu nama ini muncul di depan umum melalui tulisan-tulisanku, orang merasai kejanggalannya. Apalagi setelah mengetahui itu nama keluarga orang Jawa. Sebenarnya tidak perlu betul, karena nama itu sudah bermunculan dalam tahun-tahun dua puluhan dan tiga puluhan. Juga bukan asing dalam kehidupan sosial dan politik di kota kecil Blora."* [*NS* II, 3]). Pramoedya thus opens his recollections proper by tracing the "odd name" that did not sound at all Javanese in the 1950s back to the 1920s in order to show the intimate estrangement that signals both a link and a break, a link to his Javanese father and to his father's break from the tradition of using the honorific *Mas*.

This combined genealogy and critique stands not only within the tradition marked by Soetomo's memoirs; it also has key affinities with the forms of critical genealogy to emerge from what Said identifies as the repetition of filiation and affiliation in the nineteenth century (including, one might add, Said's own form of secular criticism). Said lists philology as one of the disciplines among others within which this "critical consciousness" may be found. In some respects, however, philology is the dominant discipline—governing, for example, Nietzsche's influential variation on this same pattern, to which the word "genealogy" is indeed attached. According to Foucault, in "Nietzsche, Genealogy, History": "Genealogy is gray, meticulous, and patiently documentary. It operates on a field of entangled and confused parchments, on documents that have been scratched over and recopied many times" (*"La généalogie est grise; elle est méticuleuse et patiemment documentaire. Elle travaille sur des parchemins embrouillés, grates, plusieurs fois récits"*).[21] Especially in light of the conditions under which Pramoedya composed all of the work of Buru, this appears to stand in striking contrast to the work of genealogy Pramoedya undertakes. Yet precisely this contrast—the wealth of documents available to Foucault's Nietzschean genealogist, the corresponding lack of documents in the prison camps of Buru—calls attention to the shared focus on philology. Although Pramoedya's genealogy takes place in the absence of documents, it is just that absence that looms large as the "field of entangled and confused parchments" and "documents that have been scratched over and recopied many times." Pramoedya's genealogy is "patiently documentary," too, but it operates in a field of memory that is constantly retracing gaps in historical documentation. The crossed-out honorific that gives Pramoedya the strange-sounding Javanese name Toer links the moment of the father's involvement in the nationalist movement of the 1920s with the moment of the son's rise as an Indonesian writer in the 1950s. If these are based on "links" in the genetic "chain," they also point to breaks in history and Pramoedya's patient genealogy attempts to mark those breaks: in a personal sense, attempting to reconstruct the experiences of his parents' generation; and in a historical sense, situating those experiences within the coordinates of the historical moment usually taken to be the beginning of the nationalist movement. Both sets of experience are premised on the loss of documentary evidence that Pramoedya attempts to re-mark for the present—in this sense, "Mata Rantai" is not simply a personal variation on the historical themes Pramoedya will take up in the Buru tetralogy; the specific memories of his father's successive attempts to establish and sustain the schools of the Boedi Oetomo movement—and the successive failures—form part of the memory work by which the Buru tetralogy traces back to the "roots" of the period of "National Awakening"—and finds a break, a rupture, and indeed an erasure of documents.

If the memory work of Pramoedya's notes documents the loss of documents—notably, for example, the destruction of the sequels to *The Girl from the Coast* (*Gadis Pantai*) about Pramoedya's parents' generation—it is also patiently philological in another sense. Although Pramoedya does not imitate Soetomo's model of Javanese genealogy, and although Pramoedya does not imitate his father's "near-mystical feeling about words," he does allude to these, registering them, documenting them, and even playing with them in a literary and linguistic sense that deserves some attention. "Mata Rantai" opens with an allusion to the same Javanese proverb with which Soetomo prefaces his *Kenang-Kenangan*—prefacing, indeed, the whole discussion of genetic theory and genealogy with a kind of comparative linguistic, philological, and literary comment on "proverbs" and "aphorisms." In the beginning of the English-language edition, this emerges from the juxtaposition of two proverbs, one Dutch ("The apple falls not far from the tree" [*de appel valt niet ver van den boom*]) and the other the Javanese proverb Soetomo refers to: "*Kacang ora ninggalake lanjarane*," translated "A string bean doesn't break free from its vine." Pramoedya proceeds to explain, introducing the "genetic theories" (or "genetic laws," *hukum warisan*, a phrase that might perhaps also be translated "laws of tradition") that provide the basis for his genealogy: "What this means is that a child will not differ greatly from his parents. Long before Mendel was born and the secret of chromosomes was discovered, agrarian communities had developed their own genetic theories, ones based on the mystery of blood" (*MS*, 103) ("*Artinya: anak takkan jauh dari orangtuanya. Rumus kebijaksanaan petani tentang hukum warisan sebelum Mendel dilahirkan, sebelum diketahui tentang rahasia kromosom dan sebangsanya, rahasia darah*" [*NS* II, 1–2]).

Offering these two proverbs as instances of the way in which the scientific theory of "genetic laws" was anticipated by folk wisdom, Pramoedya introduces a comparative linguistic and literary frame of reference that has important consequences for the genealogy to come. As with the formulation from "My Apologies," in which Pramoedya writes that the "vicious circle" of Javanese culture and civilization can be broken only through "reevaluation," adding *Verlichting, Aufklärung* to mark a double Dutch and German linguistic register for the sort of "enlightenment" that would help break the "vicious circle" of tradition, there is, here too, an important interplay of different linguistic contexts informing our evaluation of the critical weight of different "genetic theories." There is a similar doubling of Dutch and German linguistic registers, since the original Indonesian adds a German version immediately following the Dutch proverb (*"Atau Jerman:* Der Apfel fällt nicht weit vom der [*sic*] Stamm" [*NS* II, 1]).

The Indonesian edition makes still clearer the comparative linguistic and literary frame of reference for this genealogical model. Before citing the Javanese, Dutch, and German proverbs, Pramoedya opens the section with still another "saying":

> It is certainly possible to find something offensive about the saying: every person is descended from farmers. But it's not clear if this insult would be felt by ancestors of nomads, hunters, or sheep herding peoples, who perhaps aren't so far from the ancestors of farmers after all.
> *Memang ada saja yang sakit hati bila dikatakan: setiap orang adalah keturunan petani. Belum tentu yang sakit hati itu keturunan nomad, pemburu atau penggembala domba, boleh jadi memang tidak lain dari keturunan petani.* (*NS* II, 1)

One thing this opening clarifies is the fact that the comparative Javanese, Dutch, and German linguistic and literary context with which Pramoedya introduces his Javanese genealogy is framed in turn by another linguistic-literary frame of reference. In spirit, we might describe this as Indonesian—or, to use Benedict Anderson's formulation, "revolutionary Malay"[22]—both for its leveling of social classes and for the fact that it is simply introduced by Pramoedya as a "saying" in the Indonesian of his own text. The simplest reading, indeed, of this opening is to take it as a saying that deflates all pretensions to elevated birth. Yet what is difficult to pinpoint about this opening—what makes it so difficult to translate, and evidently Willem Samuels felt it was wiser not to try translating it at all—is the problematic factor of whatever might be offensive, or insulting (*sakit hati*) about the saying. Difficult though this is to evaluate, Pramoedya's point emerges clearly enough from my questionable translation of the second sentence: it is not a simple matter to evaluate the degrees of resentment written into such a saying. Pramoedya makes this problem of offensiveness and resentment a crucial premise for any genealogy.

By contrast to the essay "My Apologies," Pramoedya's reflections on his own Javanese background, here in "Mata Rantai"—and also in the section devoted to memories of his mother, "Flowers for Mother" (to which we will return in a moment)—do not juxtapose

Javanese genealogy with so deliberately an offensive critique as that captured in the formulation "*kampung* civilization and culture." Any genealogy, however, is accompanied by that possibility of resentment and offense, the insinuation of a possibly alienating reminder about where one comes from. It is indeed this possibility that turns genealogy into a critique.

At the most personal level, this possibility gives the term *mata rantai* an ambiguous twist. If Pramoedya can open this section taking comfort in the thought that "In the biological chain I am the link between my parents and my children" (*MS*, 104), by the end of the section this remains an open question: "Am I a link that ties the links above me with those links below? That I do not know" (*MS*, 124) ("*Adakah aku sebagai mata rantai dan mata rantai di bawahku masih berkait-kaitan dengan yang di atasku? Aku belum tahu*" [*NS* II, 32]). This is an effect, in large part, of the ambiguous twist given to this formulation by its filiative and affiliative meanings—the biological "link" is "unbreakable," while the "social link" can be severed. But what splices these two meanings together—or rather, what insinuates the one into the other—is precisely the comparative literary and linguistic frame of reference with which the section as a whole begins. The root model of Pramoedya's genealogy is, indeed, a literary model, and one focused on proverbs and aphorisms passed down from ancient societies. The "genetic theories" encoded in proverbs and aphorisms simultaneously encode "the secret of chromosomes" discovered by Mendel and the "mystery of blood."

Here, we find a revealing echo of the comments from "My Apologies" and something of a countermodel to those "passages" of the *Mahabharata* passed down orally and in written form that inculcate Javanese "*kampung* civilization and culture." To the extent that Pramoedya's miniature genealogy of literary history at the beginning of "Mata Rantai" does stand in counterpoint to the genealogy of Javanese literary history at the beginning of "My Apologies," it might be more accurate to see each as the inverse of the same process. Each passage of literature—whether proverb, aphorism, or constantly cited classic text—has its mystical and its rational side. Looked at in this way, the key term *mata rantai* itself provides a revealing echo of the term *lingkaran setan*. Each passage of text might constitute a link, or a break, in the chain; each passage may also form a link in or a break from the vicious circle of tradition. Each passage in this sense is not so much the documentary record of either the "mystery" or the science of "blood"; each passage, rather (not unlike the way he cites Conrad, from memory), constitutes a *gap* in the historical record that needs to be reevaluated for how it links or breaks lineages and traditions.

Reconsidering what Pramoedya writes about the "passages" of the *Mahabharata* that inculcate Javanese "*kampung* civilization and culture," it is possible to recognize the same principle of genealogy and critique at work. When Pramoedya invokes the *Mahabharata* as a text that exemplifies the "vicious and blood-filled circle," he cites the expertise of an outsider: "It is clear, though, in line with the opinion of Cornell expert Ben Anderson, that at the climax of the *Mahabharata*, 'they bathe in the blood of their own brothers'" (*"Tentu saja tidak angka resmi bisa ditampilkan. Yang jelas, sejalan engan pendapat pakar Cornell, Ben Anderson, klimaks Mahabharata adalah 'mandi darah saudara-saudara sendiri'"*).[23] It is not clear, in fact, what passage he is citing from Anderson—and, as Alex Bardsley points out, the phrase has a power all of its own in Pramoedya's Indonesian rendition: "The sound of Pramoedya's phrase is as beautiful as the image is horrible: *mandi darah saudara-saudara sendiri.*"[24] But the effect of this reference is not to establish scholarly authority so much as to insist on a comparative literary and linguistic frame of reference, reevaluating from outside and from within that "vicious circle" of tradition. The passage Pramoedya cites from Anderson—and translates into an Indonesian phrase "as beautiful as the image is horrible"—works in much the same way as Pramoedya sets the proverbs and aphorisms to work in the opening of "Mata Rantai." All of them, indeed, encode ancient wisdom about blood, lineages, genealogies. If all of them are richly evocative (exuberant one might say) on the "mystery of blood," as Pramoedya puts it, that allusiveness, or richness, or "mystery" itself points to the gap each passage also represents: a gap between lineages, cultures, civilizations. When Pramoedya cites Anderson, it is not at all simply a matter of using a non-Javanese judgment to belittle Javanese pretensions.

The comparative literary and linguistic frame within which Pramoedya gathers together all of the fragmentary notes from Buru is simultaneously one cut off from his Indonesian readership, and one deeply enmeshed in the repetition, citation, and recitation of a long history of writing—storytelling that depends on the interplay of Javanese, but also Malay, not to mention Dutch or German or English, literature. One might note that the reference to Conrad in the prison notes recalls him as "that Polish-born sailor-turned-writer" (*"seorang pengarang-pelaut kelahiran Polandia"* [*NS* I, 183]), making him a touchstone for the cosmopolitan transnational writer even as the formulation elides his relation to a specifically English linguistic-literary tradition. The passage of literature is not the link or break in any one lineage. It is the link or break in the relation between literary and linguistic lineages. So, for example, when Pramoedya returns to the Javanese proverb, which may be as much an allusion to Soetomo's *Kenang-Kenangan* as to the ancient wisdom of Javanese culture and civilization, he emphasizes a riddle of alien genealogies inscribed within the Javanese original: *"Adakah kacang sudah meninggalkan* lanjaran-*nya?"* (*NS* II, 32). In the English this is translated as "Can a bean free itself from its vine?"—a question that preserves the full comparative literary and linguistic perspective of its relation to the Dutch and German proverbs alluded to in the question that immediately precedes it, "But can an apple fall far from its tree?" This is, of course, and to repeat, the open question—as much a real question as a rhetorical one—inscribed into every one of the passages from the prison notes, whose ambiguity joins both the somber assessment of the "vicious circle" of the events of 1965 and the affirmative effort to record his position as "one link in a chain" between his parents and his children. In italicizing part of the Javanese word for "vine," *lanjaran*nya, Pramoedya seems to draw attention to a pun in the two meanings of *lanjaran*, meaning both "bean pole, trellis" and "a child adopted in the hope of having one of one's own."[25] Whatever kind of linguistic "playing with relatives" may be embedded in the adopted child of this Javanese proverb, the combined filiative and affiliative philological play registered in Pramoedya's use of this, among other ancient proverbs, resonates strongly as a principle of alien genealogy Pramoedya puts to work in the family romance structures of his fiction.

Pramoedya's Revolutionary Family Romance

Before returning to consider how the form of this alien genealogy that emerges from the memories of Pramoedya's father in "One Link in a Chain" ("Mata Rantai") is repeated in a different register in the section devoted to memories of his mother in "Flowers for Mother" ("Karangan Bunga pada Kakinya"), we should briefly consider how it shapes the wider arc of what Pramoedya produced on Buru. This might in turn enable us to consider how the work of Buru as a whole has provided the comparative perspective from which we have been evaluating the overlapping and contested genealogies of reading transnational modernism embedded in Conrad's and Rhys's respective English and Creole family romances of reading. The picture of Pramoedya's parents that begins to emerge from these and other sections of the prison notes in some respects confirms and repeats the autobiographical sketches that had been Pramoedya's characteristic (and characteristically modernist) form of writing throughout the 1950s. One can only speculate how this picture might have been reshaped into a historical grasp of Indonesia during the 1910s and 1920s in the two sequels to *Gadis Pantai* (*The Girl from the Coast*) that were destroyed when his house was looted and his library and manuscripts were destroyed following his arrest in 1965. One can conclude, however, from the combined double portrait presented by "One Link in a Chain" and "Flowers for Mother" that it would not have been a continuous success story of national awakening from the moment of the founding of Boedi Oetomo in 1908 to the naming of Indonesia in 1922, and the formal establishment of the independence movement with the declaration of the Oath of Youth (Soempah Pemoeda) in 1928. That double portrait sketches the picture of a family pulled apart by the forces aligned against the nationalist movement of his father and the democratic ideals of his mother. Each fragment of this picture, however, is infused with a revolutionary family romance.

Already from the start of Pramoedya's career as a writer the features of this revolutionary family romance are recognizable—above all, in the two long works written in Bukitduri prison, *Perburuan* (*The Fugitive*) and *Keluarga Gerilya* (*The Guerrilla Family*). Both present families torn apart by war, betrayal, and impossible conflicts of loyalty during the revolutionary struggles for independence in the 1940s. Taken as touchstone representations of the independence struggle—the first focused on the resistance against the Japanese, the second concerned the guerrilla war against the Allied forces attempting to reestablish Dutch colonial control—it is notable that the conflicts with which each novel is most occupied are those within the respective families, rather than the conflict between opposed military sides. Each poses intractable dilemmas confronting families during revolutionary struggle and is driven, in a sense, as the title of *Keluarga Gerilya* suggestively formulates it, by an impossible contradiction between the bonds and loyalties of family relations and the revolutionary imperative to overturn social hierarchies of the existing social order. Both feature sons at odds with their fathers, and *Keluarga Gerilya* is notable for the narrative consciousness of a mother figure with a tragic knowledge of the intimate secrets and deadly betrayals that lead to the near total destruction of her family.

If the families of these early works are more truly caught up in revolution than the families that appear in the later work of Buru, the term "family romance" does not so clearly apply in the sense we used this term to compare the Creole family romances of Rhys's *Wide Sargasso Sea* and Pramoedya's Buru quartet in chapter 6. Even although they are self-consciously situated in relation both to traditional Javanese (*wayang*) and modern European (romance) forms of storytelling, and even although part of their revolutionary literary challenge concerns the characters' recognition of the relevance of contending (Javanese and European) models of family relations, these early works are not so clearly organized around the retrospective reconstruction of a family romance; nor do they foreground so clearly the specific questions of *reading* raised by the Freudian term *Familienroman* (with reference to the normal fantasies of a child who reads romances) and reinforced by the more classical script of the Oedipal complex.

These very questions come to the foreground in the work of Buru. Indeed, in "Flowers for Mother," introducing that "mystical bond between a mother and her child" (*MS*, 125) ("*ikatan mistis antara ibu dan anak*" [*NS* II, 46]) that must be recognized as "a product of the age before logic came to reign" (*MS*, 125–26) ("*orang dahulu pada jaman pra-logika itu*" [*NS* II, 46–7]), Pramoedya explicitly refers to the Freudian model of the Oedipal complex, characteristically resituating it within a comparative literary and linguistic frame of reference similar to the framing discussion of proverbs and aphorisms in "One Link in a Chain." Here, too, Pramoedya characteristically begins with the general Malay literary examples—*Malim Kundang* and *Dampo Awang*—before juxtaposing another set of three contrasting cultural examples; here, though, there is just one European example, "the Greek *Oedipus Rex*" followed by the "Javanese *Prabu Watu Gunung*, and the Sundanese *Sangkuriang*" (*MS*, 125–26) ("*dalam* Oedipus Rex *atau* Prabu Watu Gunung *dalam versi Jawa dan* Sangkuriang *dalam versi Sunda*" [*NS* II, 46–47]). Pramoedya goes on to situate his own work as a writer within this comparative world literary perspective:

> Each time I think of [my mother], especially when I'm trying to write, my mother is always vaguely present, hovering in my father's shadow. I suspect that the two-faced Oedipus complex, with a son loving his mother and hating his father, might very well be operating in my subconscious. (*MS*, 126)
>
> *Setiap kali aku mengenangkannya, apalagi mencoba menulis, selalu ibuku sebagai tokoh menjadi samar tak nyata terlindungi oleh bayang-bayang ayahku. Boleh jadi* oedipus-complex *yang bermuka dua, mencintai ibu dan membenci ayah, bekerja secara samar dan tidak sadar dalam diriku.* (*NS* II, 47)

Although it might be tempting to take this as a cue to read *Perburuan* and *Keluarga Gerilya* as the expression of this "two-faced Oedipus complex," it makes better sense, I think, to see in this Pramoedya's deliberately retrospective reconstruction of the "family romance" of his early childhood and as a foundation for his sense of authorship. As with the genealogy of literary lineages of reading and writing in "Mata Rantai," this, too, is the work of an alien genealogy. Together with the principle of genealogical reading developed there, this promises a retrospective grasp of the historical gaps represented by his parents' generation—in this sense, then, a revolutionary family romance that can account for, if not resolve, the lacunae, the gaps and breaks, that link the revolutionary moment of Indonesia's independence with what came before.

This revolutionary family romance does not, then, refer primarily to Pramoedya's depictions of families during revolutionary times (such as in his two first novellas, with their focus on the revolutionary independence struggle of 1945–47) but, rather, to the romance of *reading* a lineage of revolution. It is a revolutionary family romance of reading that emerges from a retrospective reconstruction of that twofold break in history and historical documentation on which the work of Buru is premised: the historical record of early Indonesian nationalism and "pre-Indonesian" literature, lost first in the colonial erasure of that history in the early twentieth century and lost again with the destruction in 1965 of Pramoedya's documentation of that earlier history. It is worth keeping in mind that these two moments of rupture in Pramoedya's genealogy of Indonesian modernism coincide historically with key moments in the formation, respectively, of Conrad's relation to English modernism and Rhys's relation to Creole modernism. This has already informed our contrapuntal readings of the Buru tetralogy alongside Rhys's *Wide Sargasso Sea* (written during the period Pramoedya was researching early Indonesian nationalism and published just after the events of 1965) and Conrad's Malay trilogy (written over the period Pramoedya variously describes as that of "pre-Indonesian" literature, "assimilative" literature, or the formative period of Indonesian modernism). As we explored in the previous chapter, the figure of the *nyai* constitutes a shared problem of reading, linking (and specifically in the Siamese slave Taminah from Conrad's *Almayer's Folly*) the family romances that structure Conrad's, Rhys's, and Pramoedya's respective genealogies of literary modernism. Before turning to consider how Pramoedya's revolutionary family romance shapes his two other large-scale historical works of fiction, we should briefly outline the contours of Pramoedya's revolutionary family romance as this has already emerged from our contrapuntal reading of the Buru tetralogy and the work of Conrad and Rhys.

Minke and Nyai Ontosoroh, who constitute the core of the Buru tetralogy's revolutionary family romance, present the two faces of what Pramoedya calls the "two-faced Oedipus complex" ("*jadi* Oedipus-complex *yang bermuka dua*") that "might very well be operating in my subconscious" (*MS*, 126) (*"bekerja secara samar dan tidak sadar dalam diriku"* [NS II, 47]). Minke, embodying the initiating moment of revolutionary nationalism, also represents the historical lacuna of a past revolutionary paternal legacy. Minke's discovery, in *Footsteps,* that he can never be a father because he is infertile offers a symbolic version of Pramoedya's own father's revolutionary past as a break with Javanese feudal tradition that is also the link connecting the figures of early twentieth-century forerunners of Indonesian nationalism (like Tirto Adi Suryo) with the revolutionary nationalism of the 1940s and 1950s. Nyai Ontosoroh, embodying the ideals of revolutionary nationalism sustained in the face of the traumatic reversals of 1965, figures the historical lacuna of a future matrix of revolutionary consciousness: a version of the idealized figure of Pramoedya's mother "always vaguely present, hovering in my father's shadow" (*MS,* 126) ("*sebagai tokoh menjadi samar tak nyata terlindungi oleh bayang-bayang ayahku*" [NS II, 47]). Each character embodies a different variation on the attempt to break from the "vicious circle" of Javanese "*kampung* culture and civilization." In Minke (as we explored in chapter 2), this "vicious circle" is registered in the aesthetic problem of operatic taste (recalling Pramoedya's father's attachment to and his mother's detachment from *wayang* and gamelan), as well as the entire political and cultural perspective of his Javanese *priyayi* worldview (which is that of Boedi Oetomo, the Javanese nationalist organization to which Pramoedya's father belonged). Not only does this problem of Javanese high cultural aesthetic inform every passage in the Buru tetralogy; to the extent that it situates the historical problem of a modern Javanese consciousness over the turn of the century, it also constitutes this as the same problem of aesthetic form, taste in opera, and modern consciousness that produces the ironic narrative perspective of Conrad's fiction. The vicious circle of Minke's split Javanese-European sensibility, a variation of the combination of offense and apology that characterizes Pramoedya's critique of Javanism, has its counterpart in the vicious circle of European racism and critique of that racism inaugurated in Conrad's first novel, *Almayer's Folly,* and invested in the ironic structure of Lingard's paternal supervision of all the various Malay colonial family romances throughout the Malay trilogy it took Conrad his entire career to complete.

Nyai Ontosoroh's willed estrangement from her Javanese roots embodies an apparently much sharper critique of feudal Javanese family values than with Minke; indeed, her insistence, even as mistress of the Mellema estate, on using the title *nyai* as a signifier of her status as bought slave recalls the unapologetic hard edge of Pramoedya's use of the passage from Conrad's "Karain: A Memory" to critique the mentality of the Javanese people: "everyone, from beggars to kings, is a slave." Not only does the contradictory social status of *nyai* constitute a revolutionary challenge to Javanese family values; as we have explored in chapter 6, the genre of the *nyai* narrative registers this revolutionary challenge as a problem of reading that precedes and underwrites the formation of Indonesian revolutionary nationalism. The genre of the *nyai* narrative that haunts the Buru tetralogy underwrites Minke's family romance, shaped by the contest of filiation and affiliation between his own family and Nyai's family, prominently featured in Minke's political choice of *bahasa Indonesia* (as urged by Nyai) rather than Javanese (as urged by his mother) as the medium for writing. If Nyai and Minke together form the core characters of the tetralogy's revolutionary family romance, it is a romance that ultimately poses but cannot resolve the gaps and breaks in a lineage of Indonesian nationalism. Minke's family romance, for example, as we have discussed in chapter 5, is structured by an impasse of racial recognition (the moment of racial "fetish," in Siegel's analysis) in the literary stereotype of Annelies's "Creole" beauty. Like the Creole family romance of Rhys's *Wide Sargasso Sea,* Minke's own Creole family romance engages a fierce and racialized contest over reading literary lineages. Rhys's *Wide Sargasso Sea* overlaps historically with the most immediate historical rupture—the coup of 1965—on which the Buru tetralogy is premised; and both belong to a postcolonial contest over the forms of racial identity and identification that have shaped and have also often been erased from the twentieth-century dominant forms of linguistic, literary, and cultural capital. The postcolonial contest registered in these "Creole" family romances necessarily demands a return to prior problems of reading, as we have seen in the way both Rhys and Pramoedya foreground passages from Conrad's work. As we have traced around the vanishing genre of the *nyai* narrative that haunts the Buru tetralogy, that work makes it impossible to separate the two historical moments of rupture—1965 (also the moment of Rhys's Creole modernism); and the turn of the century (also the moment of Conrad's English modernism)—for which Minke and Nyai, as fictional reconstructions of a lost history, present a revolutionary romance (and a politics) of reading.

The retrospective structure of Pramoedya's revolutionary family romance has, then, already revealed the shared historical moments of rupture that link the overlapping and contested alien genealogies of modernism informing Conrad's English–Malay family romance and Rhys's Creole family romance. Extending this to add a prospective reading of Pramoedya's other two epic historical novels, *Arus Balik* and *Arok Dedes,* we might grasp the broader historical scope within which Pramoedya's revolutionary family romance situates English and Creole genealogies of modernism and modernity.

Arus Balik ends with a genealogical riddle that embeds in its epic historical narrative a similar kind of principle of genealogy to the one Pramoedya builds around the Javanese proverb in "Mata Rantai." The historical moment the novel seeks to narrate is the reversal of power (the "turning tide" of the title) from the south (Java's Majapahit empire) to the north (with the arrival of the Portuguese). The proverbial riddle of the *malakama* fruit (*teka-teki buah si malakama*) will define the "vicious circle" of this historical moment it narrates in terms of a Javanese version of the "two-faced Oedipus complex." Here, an intimate estrangement of a Javanese genealogy works both from within and without, as it were. It sets the coordinates for an archipelago-wide historical vision that seeks to break from nostalgic evocations of the lost greatness of the Javanese Majapahit empire. At the same time, it reevaluates the converging influence of non-Javanese foreigners (Europeans and Arabs, in addition to Chinese) shaping modern Indonesia. The man of the people, loyal warrior, and leader, Wiranggaleng, who comes closest to being the epic hero of this novel advertised as "a maritime epic" (*sebuah epos maritim nusantara*),[26] sums up the double bind facing his army at the end of the novel. Caught between the invading Portuguese forces and betrayed by the leaders of Java's old Majapahit stronghold, Wiranggaleng's pyrrhic victory speech unfolds the logic of the title's metaphorical reversal of the current from south to north, concluding with a proverb that offers an analogous riddle of genealogy to those Pramoedya develops in the prison notes. The choice between taking up arms against the Javanese forces that betrayed them or against the encroaching Portuguese forces from the north, Wiranggaleng says, poses the "proverbial riddle of the *malakama* fruit: eat it and your mother dies; don't eat it and your father dies" ("*Itulah teka-teki buah si malakama, dimakan ibu mati, tidak dimakan bapak mati*").[27]

To the extent that Wiranggaleng himself is an epic father figure of sorts, his maritime exploits leave a double political legacy—split between those of his army that remain in the settlement on the Malay peninsula (a result of the doomed military exploit to retake Malacca) and those who return to Java (to face the proverbial riddle of the *malakama* fruit). These are legacies, one might note, that complicate the "epic" gesture of the narrative. Recalling the epic gestures of Conrad's Malay trilogy discussed in chapter 2, we see that *Arus Balik* presents a deliberate doubling of European and Malay narrative conventions, turning the reading conventions of each inside out to produce a problem of reading that deliberately questions the notion of an "epic" genealogy of a singular "maritime" imperial experience (whether that of an older Indonesian empire or that of a newer European world picture). The genealogy and critique with which Pramoedya meditates on this moment of reversal in Javanese and global power turns on another problem of paternal lineage: the problem of Wiranggaleng's stepson, Gelar, the son of Idayu, married to Wiranggaleng early in the novel in an idealized marriage union presented as a popular romance of the people. Gelar's biological father, however, is the Machiavellian Arab harbor master. As one of the main centers of narrative consciousness, this harbor master, or *shahbandar*—the same official position occupied by Babalatchi in Conrad's Malay trilogy—becomes a focal point for the reader's sense of the shifts and reversals of local and global political power. This grasp of the moment of Indonesia's "embrace of Islam" in the sixteenth century might be glossed with reference to comments Pramoedya makes in "My Apologies":

> The spread of this new religion was not accompanied by its civilization, as had been the case with Hinduism, because it was, practically, a side

effect of the chasing of Muslim traders from the sea-lanes by the power of the Christian West, a continuation of the expulsion of Arab power from the Iberian peninsula. One might say the spread of Islam was a side-effect of the international Pan-Islamic movement of the period.[28]

Penyebaran agama baru ini tidak disertai peradabannya sebagaimana halnya dengan hinduisme, karena praktis sebagai akibat sekunder dari terhalaunya para pedagang Islam dari jalur laut oleh kekuatan Barat yang Nasrani, kelanjutan dari penghalauan atas kekuasaan Arab di Semenanjung Iberia. Dapat dikatakan penyebaran Islam di Jawa adalah akibat sekunder dari gerakan Pan-Islamisme internasional pada jamannya.[29]

Arus Balik embodies this historical insight by making the harbor master the figure of an emerging new political consciousness; a fully Indonesian (archipelago-wide) consciousness, but one forged by the manipulation of others through a knowledge of the languages and cultures—Arab and European—coming from the north. In a revealing detail, it is the mesmerizing power of gamelan music and the dancing of the *wayang* performance that makes him determined to take Idayu for his own. The novel will end with a coda that recapitulates the novel's themes through the perspective of the product of this union, the son Gelar. Gelar, whom Wiranggaleng adopts, will be cursed and exiled (according to Javanese custom) for the murder of his biological father. In a melodramatic narrative acting out of the "two-faced Oedipus complex," Gelar's murderous repudiation of everything his father stands for results in his being banished from the Javanese world of his mother and stepfather. At the end of the novel the tormented guilty conscience represented by his conversion to Christianity figures Indonesia's "embrace of Islam" as the legacy of a double estrangement of Islam and Christianity, internalized as the working out—in a truly "vicious circle"—of the proverbial riddle of the *malakama* fruit.

Even so rudimentary an outline of the plotting of family lineages ought to indicate the novel's investment in genealogies of modern Indonesia—and specifically the ways in which Pramoedya turns a genealogy and critique of Javanese power (the fall of the Majapahit empire) into an ongoing genealogy and critique of Indonesian power. There is also at work in this novel, however, an analogous question of *reading* genealogies, or genealogies of *reading*, to the one that shapes the Buru tetralogy around the vanishing genre of the *nyai* narrative. The otherwise melodramatic plot of Gelar's murder of his Islamic father and conversion to Christianity is embedded, indeed, in a question of reading that, although fully orchestrated by the religious questions of contending senses of scripture, is more significantly rehearsed around the contending forms of written script. The harbor master's power—and hence the reader's sense of global political power—is significantly grounded in his command (or claim to command) of a particular set of languages and scripts, notably Javanese, Malay, Arabic, Portuguese, and Spanish. Foregrounding the role of translation in the competing forces of global and local power shaping the reversal of the current or backflow (*Arus Balik*) against Javanese hegemony, this also prepares for an important twist in the final coda that gives such prominence to the exiled, illegitimate son of the harbor master and Wiranggelang's wife, Idayu. The Oedipal murder retrospectively inscribes all of the Indonesian text of *Arus Balik* with the intimation of a genealogical contest or struggle over the romanized script of the novel itself. As with Pangemanann's Latin quotation from Roman Catholic scripture with which he concludes *House of Glass*, the concluding sections of *Arus Balik*, diaries from a Portuguese traveler, call attention to the romanized script in which the whole book has been written. Although not a direct comment on the shift from Arabic to romanized script in the writing of Malay manuscripts, it insinuates a material and aesthetic doubt that retrospectively recasts the whole novel, and most especially all the passages that concern the harbor master's perspective. That key figure of consciousness, embodying the reversals of power from south to north, is thus caught in the "vicious circle," or put under the murderous erasure of his son's split sense of Javanese and Islamic/Christian heritage. This recalls the effect of Pramoedya's earlier formulation, in *Hoakiau di Indonesia*, of the "vicious [satanic] circle" ("*lingkaran setan*"). It recapitulates on a thematic level what also materially opens each passage to multiple possibilities for reinterpretation and reevaluation.

This interrelation between reading, genealogies, and script lies at the heart of Pramoedya's revolutionary family romance. In the prison notes, and especially "Flowers for Mother," he documents the different scripts he learned from his father (Javanese, Dutch, Arabic), but there seems, in some respects, a notable absence of discussion of the significance of Malay—or, rather, that form of Malay that would emerge as the language of anti-colonial nationalism, *bahasa Indonesia*. In another respect, however, this very question lies at the center of every recollection and comment on languages and script. It is, indeed, this emerging language—and the revolutionary family romance of this tradition of reading and writing—that underwrites what we have discussed as the comparative literary and linguistic perspective of his genealogy and critique. When Pramoedya cites a "saying" without specifying the language (as in the beginning of "Mata Rantai") or refers to a tale or story without specifying that it is a Javanese, Sundanese, Greek, or Dutch tale, he is referring to—loosely speaking—a Malay, or as we might also say, a pre-Indonesian tale or story. In the picture that emerges of his parents from "Mata Rantai" and "Flowers for Mother," it is this language that is emerging, a language implicit in the interplay of all the languages, spoken and written, and all the scripts referred to in the fragmentary efforts to piece together the world of his childhood memory, a world in which a revolution was taking place, but also a world in which families were falling apart.

Although there is no simple formula for this revolutionary linguistic family romance, what he calls his own "two-faced Oedipus complex" does suggest a contrasting paternal and maternal grasp of languages and scripts. There is a tendency to associate the father with written, the mother with spoken language, but one key difference emerges in the suggestion that the mother did not read Javanese script. Rather, "My mother liked to read and could understand Javanese in Roman script, as well as Malay and Dutch" (*MS*, 128) ("*Ibuku seorang yang suka membaca majalah dan buku: Jawa, selama tidak berhuruf Jawa, Melayu dan Belanda*" [*NS* II, 50]). The idealized space of reading developed here—and written into the shape and form of the whole section "Flowers for Mother"—can be seen to prefigure the emergence of Indonesian as a revolutionary language able to undo the hierarchies of Javanese and open up to a heritage of world literature. The title of this section, "*Karangan Bunga pada Kakinya*," has an interestingly ambiguous play on the word *karangan*—literally "arrangement" and so "flower arrangement"; but it is also a term that means "composition" in a combined oral and written sense. As Henk Maier points out, the word evokes a tradition of Malay composition that is inseparable from oral forms of literary performance:

> Closely related to *baca* [reading, reading out loud, reciting, telling a tale (whether with or without a script)] and its connotations of memorable and, therefore, relevant knowledge is the term *karang*, which is usually translated as "compose," "put in order," formulate. *Baca* and *karang* are best described as being two aspects of the same activity, one moving backward, the other moving forward: *baca* refers to the activity of repeating letters or sounds, *karang* refers to the activity of arranging letters or sounds into fragrant garlands—or bouquets—of words, sentences, fragments. It should be obvious that it is hard to make a clear distinction between the two words: they comprise a new activity as much as a re-enactment, and everyone who is involved in the act of *baca* is also involved in the act of *karang*, and vice versa. Both are acts of commemoration and differentiation. *Baca* and *karang* are inseparable, interactive; they are two aspects of the same activity. Every creation of a garland is a repetition with a difference—and who would not feel melancholy and excitement at once in the awareness that so much is lost and gained in translating *baca* and *karang* as "read" and "compose," respectively?[30]

If this argument appears to link Pramoedya's work within a long and continuous tradition of Malay writing, it is important to note the attention Maier gives, throughout his survey of Malay writing, to the shift from an oral and manuscript culture of reading and composition to a culture of print texts. Maier is especially helpful in noting the ways in which this moment can be traced to different historical breakpoints, each one based on a forgetting of an earlier modern break from tradition. Nonetheless, the clearest shift is the one Pramoedya himself marks as "pre-Indonesian literature" over the turn of the century. This is the moment that James Siegel, following Pramoedya, describes in terms of the emergence of a Malay print culture open to readers from a variety of different literary and linguistic backgrounds.

Rather than eclipsing the oral and written tradition of Malay writing, however, Maier suggests that the transformation accompanying the emergence of this market in print texts might be conceived as opening those traditions to a still more exuberant form of "playing relatives." To conceive of the shift from Arabic Malay manuscripts to romanized print texts, then, only in terms of an ascendancy of European script and an accompanying hegemony of the colonial Dutch, would be to miss the variety of other languages and scripts converging on the market for Malay texts. During the turn of the century, this is the moment that produces the genre of the *nyai* narrative. In a number of important ways, this genre remains the most important problem of reading underwriting what we are considering Pramoedya's revolutionary family romance, now more specifically conceived in terms of the problem of reading genealogies of culture. Situated *between* cultures, indeed, the *nyai* narrative form—like the *nyai* herself, and the heteroglossic sense of the term itself—draws attention to the crucial *gaps* between lineages on which Pramoedya's Javanese genealogy and critique hinges. The revolutionary family romance is a romance of reading the literary passage, or fragment, as a revealing *gap* between languages, literatures, and cultures.

In Pramoedya's reflections on his parents in the prison notes, what is most contradictory is the place of Javanese, as language and script. As we have already seen, although Pramoedya's father "held Javanese culture in high regard," he "detested feudalism." Similarly, speaking of his mother, he writes that "her worldview" was "the Javanese worldview," although she does not read Javanese except in romanized script, does not draw on the Javanese classics for her storytelling, and is not drawn to the world of *wayang*. But there is also an extreme idealization, especially in a letter to his daughter, Et, telling her about her grandmother and telling her about the Indonesian revolution. Throughout this letter, he repeatedly links his mother simultaneously with the Indonesian revolution and the Javanese Hindu goddess, Pradnya Paramita:

> For me, she was a revolution on an individual scale, a woman who not only gave birth to her children, but who set down the ethical guidelines that her children would follow in life. Do not be surprised,

therefore, that when I look back at the past I see the Indonesian revolution embodied in the form of a woman—my mother, Pradnya Paramita, Hindu Goddess of the Most High Wisdom. (*MS*, 255)

Et, bagiku, ibuku adalah revolusi yang sangat individual, ibu yang bukan hanya melahirkan anak-anaknya, juga melahirkan kebajikan-kebajikan bagi nilai anaknya sebagai manusia. Karena itu jangan kau heran, bila aku menengok pada masa lalu, pada Revolusi Indonesia yang telah lewat, gambaran dalam batinku adalah Pradnya Paramita, ibuku. (*NS* II, 148)

The juxtaposition is in a number of ways striking, especially in light of the critique of Javanism and some of its more extreme forms, such as in the essay "My Apologies." Pramoedya's deliberately offensive characterization of Javanese "*kampung* civilization and culture"—especially, perhaps, the sarcastic description of the mobilization of the *Mahabharata* to "squeeze[e] the local deities down to mere '*kampung*' gods"—stands in striking contrast to this deliberately idealized vision of his mother as a Hindu goddess. In another passage, Pramoedya goes even further, constructing a quite explicit and deliberate model revolutionary family romance: "Had she lived some seven centuries ago, and had I been a king like Sri Kertanegara, she would have been enshrined, and I would have her worshipped as Pradnya Paramita, Hindu Goddess of the Most High Wisdom, like the obeisance of Kertanegara toward Queen Dedes." ("*Sekiranya ia hidup barang 7 abad yang lalu, dan sekiranya aku raja seperti Sri Kertanegara, ia pun akan aku candikan, dan aku persembahkan gelar Pradnya Paramita, Dewi Kebijaksanaan Tertinggi, yang dipersembahkan oleh Kertanegara pada Ken Dedes*" [*NS* II, 148].)

It is this extreme contrast, or antinomy—the "historical vicious circle" of "*kampung* culture and civilization" as epitomized in the "mythified" Javanese legend of Arok, by contrast with the image of the Indonesian revolution as embodied in the personification of his mother as Hindu goddess and likened to Queen Dedes—that seems to shape Pramoedya's investment in the rewriting of the Arok story in his novel *Arok Dedes*. According to Pramoedya's own account, again from "My Apologies," the aim was to free the story from the "cage of legend": "when I wrote the story *Arok and Dedes* in exile on Buru, I dressed them up with a new interpretation so they could come out of the cage of legend" ("*waktu kutulis kisah Arok dan Dedes dalam pengasingan di Buru, penampilannya aku persolek dengan tafsiran baru agar dapat keluar dari kerangkeng legenda*").[31] Indeed, quite explicitly Pramoedya associates this new "interpretation" of the familiar Javanese legend with a breaking of the "vicious circle":

> A fellow political prisoner—already I have forgotten his name—put the question [to me]: can the cycle of Arok not be replaced with a different

image? It can, and each person can create it for himself if he has the concern, interest, and will, as long as he does not forget the pattern of *"kampung"* civilization and culture, that self-same vicious circle, which can only be broken by a reevaluation of it, *Verlichting, Aufklaerung,* that produces the creativity to break through its own ceiling.

Seorang sesama tapol—sudah tak teringat olehku siapa namanya— mengajukan pertanyaan: apakah siklus Arok tidak bisa digantikan dengan gambaran lain? Bisa, dan setiap orang bisa membuatnya untuk dirinya sendiri bila punya perhatian, kepentingan dan kemauan, asal tidak melupakan pola peradaban dan budaya 'kampung' yang itu-itu juga, lingkaran setan, yang hanya bisa diputuskan oleh reevaluasi atasnya, Verlichting, Aufklarung, yang menghasilkan kreativitas yang menjebol plafonnya sendiri.[32]

If *Arok Dedes* seems to offer the most explicit—if allegorized, even fantasized—version of the revolutionary family romance whose fragmentary picture emerges in the prison notes, the novel also offers the most extended engagement with a specifically Javanese lineage, or genealogy, of reading—of *baca* and *karang*, in the senses Maier discusses.

The novel's specifically Javanese genealogy of reading thematizes the historical shift with which Pramoedya describes Arok's significance in "clos[ing] the era of Javanese Hinduism and [beginning] the era of Hindu Javanism."[33] Or, as he puts it in another letter to Et, from the prison notes, "Ken Arok...initiated the major historical shift in Java from a Hindu to an indigenous Javanese outlook" (*MS*, 251) (*"Dalam Abad ke-13 pun seorang paria yang mengawali babak Jawa-Hindu, meninggalkan Hindu-Jawa. Orang itu tak lain dari Ken Arok"* [*NS* II, 163]). Each formulation Pramoedya offers for this shift (and there are many comments on it scattered throughout the notes and in comments Pramoedya made following his release from prison) offers a slightly different variation on this vision of a turning point in history—the most economical formulation is given in "A Farewell to Wayang," the third section of the first volume of prison notes, his reflections on *wayang*: "*Revolusi Arok, pembuka kurun baru, dari Hindu-Jawa ke Jawa-Hindu*" (*NS* I, 39) [the Arok revolution, the opening of a new era, from Hindu-Java to Java-Hindu]. The chiasmatic formula "Hindu-Java/Java-Hindu" already suggests an underlying contradiction, or antinomy: above all, the sense in which the "revolution" of Arok may also be read as a "counterrevolution," prefiguring the counterrevolutionary coup d'état of Suharto in 1965. In the novel itself the chiasmatic formulation is figured as a matter of literature, language, and script: above all, and to simplify, the shift from Sanskrit (the classic script of Hindu culture and civilization) to Javanese (the classic script used to reshape the Hindu classics into "an indigenous Javanese outlook").

This linguistic, literary, and scriptural split already poses a seemingly contradictory contrast to Pramoedya's critique of "Javanism," since Javanese, in this context, is the linguistic and literary vehicle associated with the revolutionary undoing of the caste system of the older Hindu outlook. In a number of ways, Javanese in *Arok Dedes* functions the way Indonesian does for the twentieth century, while Sanskrit takes the place of the hierarchical structure of Javanese. This apparent reversal is part of the way the novel makes reversals of historical perspective a part of the reading process. To simplify the matter considerably, there are two main centers of narrative consciousness that embody this shift in linguistic-literary historical perspective: that of queen Dedes herself, the daughter of a Brahmin priest, for whom Sanskrit is the foundation of her sense of privileged cultural, religious, social, and racial nobility; and that of the slave girl Oti, whose place of origin is unknown, but who has learned to read parts of the Javanese translation and abbreviation of the *Mahabharata*.

Taken as touchstones of the two different scripts, Sanskrit and Javanese, these characters would appear to stand in revealing contrast, if not contradiction, to the comments we have seen Pramoedya make elsewhere: notably, in the idealization of his mother as the *revolutionary* figure of the Hindu goddess; and in his comments about the *counterrevolutionary* message carried by "passages from the *Mahabharata*" in its specifically Javanese form. Those comments seem to reverse the associations embedded in his rewriting of the Arok story. The image of his mother as Dedes seems to invest all the wrong associations—racial superiority, elite and esoteric literary knowledge, and mysticism—in what is presented as a revolutionary fantasy. The revolutionary consciousness of the rebellious slave girl Oti, on the other hand, is given a literary consciousness that Pramoedya, in "My Apologies" (and the essay on *wayang*) associates sarcastically with the mentality of a *"kampung"* civilization. In part this seeming dissonance at the heart of Pramoedya's grasp of the roots of Javanese language, literature, and culture might better be explained in a more extended reading of the novel and the transformation it plots in the consciousness of these two characters, in particular, and above all in the *gap* between them. Oti's relation to the "indigenous Javanese" version of the *Mahabharata* is already marked by her linguistic and ethnic marginality to Javanese culture (so that the historical formation of an "indigenous Javanese outlook" is seen to turn on a non-Javanese reading). Confronting Dedes's highly educated sense of refinement (represented by her Sanskrit literacy) with the leveling of class (represented by Javanese script), the novel precipitates a revolution in her sense of her Hindu outlook.

Pramoedya's rewriting of the Arok legend leaves these questions of revolutionary or counterrevolutionary consciousness open-ended. There is a "revolution" in the shift from the Hindu outlook to its indigenous Javanese form, but it leaves an open-ended legacy. Thematically, Dedes, who has become Arok's consort, but who must share Arok with another woman from the common people, faces the prospect of giving birth to a child conceived from the leader Dedes has toppled, Ametung, who had forcibly abducted her at the beginning of the novel. As with the shift from Arabic to romanized script, the implication of a shift from Sanskrit to Javanese outlooks—from Hindu-Java to Java-Hindu—carries with it the seeds of an internalized "vicious circle." One of the things that Pramoedya's "interpretation" of the Arok legend does is to leave out the most famous part of the story—the curse that the sword maker leaves to Arok's children. What substitutes for this is the "vicious circle" of the linguistic and literary reversal of Hindu-Java/Java-Hindu.

Arok Dedes figures this chiasmatic reversal of linguistic and literary perspective also in terms of an underlying problem of historical priority that recalls what happens in the reversals of Anglophone and Francophone registers, and spoken and written forms of Creole, in Rhys's work. This problem of historical priority is fundamental to the project of writing to the "roots" of Indonesian nationalism, to his genealogy and critique of "Javanism," and to the decolonizing of tradition that is part and parcel of his Indonesian modernism. What emerges in the course of each character's contested relation to different genealogies of Sanskrit and Javanese forms of language, script, and scripture is the dawning recognition that the shift from Sanskrit to Javanese forms *has already taken place*. The Javanese translation and adaptation of Sanskrit literature is, indeed, a part of the dismantling of the caste system and the abolition of slavery that is credited to—or blamed on—the eleventh-century King Erlangga. The events of *Arok Dedes,* then, are situated not only at some historical distance from a prior revolution; they take place, too, in the wake of the dismantling of those revolutionary reforms: slavery has been reintroduced; the caste system is returning, albeit in a different form. Thus, already within the historical horizon of *Arok Dedes* the characters experience the shift from "Hindu-Java to Java-Hindu" as the repetition of a struggle that has taken place a century before. Leaving this struggle unfinished by the end of the novel, Pramoedya takes us to the roots of a "vicious circle" to pose a version of the question repeatedly asked throughout the notes: "when will this vicious and blood-filled circle end?" At the same time, his genealogy and critique of Javanese *"kampung* civilization and culture" constitutes the repeated and continuing work of decolonizing tradition—the work of translating those reversals back and forth from Sanskrit to Javanese (as grasped in *Arok Dedes*), and then again (as grasped in *Arus Balik*) from Javanese to the standardizing scripts of Arabic to romanization. The long historical retrospect revealed in the structure of this revolutionary family romance is also implied in the linguistic and literary formation of twentieth-century Indonesian modernism, as grasped in the Buru tetralogy. It overlaps, too, with Conrad's engagement with the hegemony of standardized English at the beginning of the twentieth century; and Rhys's engagement with forms of creolized contest over standard English throughout the middle of the twentieth century. As Pramoedya's various formulations consistently suggest, the work of realizing the revolutionary potential of such linguistic-literary reversals of perspective remains unfinished. In the linguistic and literary articulation of his revolutionary family romance, this is what Pramoedya once described as the work of attempting to "transform" the "language of my mother"—the "wealth of Javanese with its many detailed nuances"—"in full into *bahasa Indonesia*" (*"bahasa Jawa adalah basa ibu saya. Kekayaan bahasa Jawa dengan nuansa-nuansanya yang rinci belum bisa saya gantikan sepenuhnya dengan bahasa Indonesia"*).[34]

Pesangon and Warisan
The "All-Round" Decolonizing of Tradition

In the section "Flowers for Mother," this work of transforming Javanese into Indonesian emerges as a repetition, but also a reversal of the problematic legacy of his father's Javanese tradition. If the Javanese of his father evokes the hierarchy of feudal relations that needs to be put under erasure—like the mark of the honorific *Mas* Pramoedya remembers his father blacking out on his name sign—the Javanese of his mother provides the model for a kind of storytelling, both spoken and written, committed to transforming not simply Javanese tradition but also all the forms of traditional hierarchies that intimately shape the estranging hierarchies of Javanese tradition (Hindu, Arab, European, Chinese, to mention only a select few groupings of tradition, each of which might figure complex contrapuntal "vicious circles" of their own).

One section of "Flowers for Mother," in particular, rehearses this revolutionary family romance of reading, writing, translation, and decolonization. In the passage discussed in the first chapter, where Pramoedya evokes the childhood memory of his mother's reading as an idealized space of world literature (beginning "My mother liked to read and could understand Javanese in Roman script, as well as Malay and Dutch" [*MS*, 128]; *"Ibuku seorang yang suka membaca majalah dan buku: Jawa, selama tidak berhuruf Jawa, Melayu dan Belanda"* [*NS* II, 50]), Pramoedya tells an anecdote about his mother that provides a model for his own writing. It is a model for Pramoedya's own practice of decolonizing tradition by gathering together passages of text that are neither simply the touchstones of tradition nor only the contestation of traditional hierarchies, but that constitute the concrete and material gaps linking different linguistic, literary, and cultural traditions. The anecdote itself offers a sort of personal variation of the saying "everyone is descended from farmers," since it concerns his mother's reaction against his own suggestion that he wanted to be a farmer when he grew up:

> "You're not made out to be a farmer," she immediately replied. "You're too lazy for that. You're a person who's meant to be free, an *all-round person.*" Later she told me the meaning of that foreign phrase. (*MS*, 128; translation slightly modified)
>
> "*Kau takkan cocok jadi petani. Untuk itu kau terlalu malas. Yang paling tepat kau sebaiknya jadi orang bebas, dan* all-round." (*NS* II, 49)

This anecdote leads to a further description, left out of the English translation, that gives an intimate insight into the practice of keeping a record of family traditions. The passage reads, in part:

> Probably this piece of advice only reached me once my father arranged one of those long compositions full of words of advice for children, for each person, and with names for each entry. And since I was the first-born child, I was mentioned the very earliest.... I found this command/advice confirmed on paper amongst the handwritten and typewritten manuscripts of my father. I took one copy from amongst these and concealed it for myself. These little words and sayings, spoken and written, part of the soul of my childhood, have become the concepts that today I keep in the foreground.
>
> *Boleh jadi pesannya itu disampaikan setelah ayahku menyusun satu karangan panjang, yang berisi pesanan-pesanan untuk anak-anaknya, seorang demi seorang, dengan disebutkan nama-namanya. Dan karena aku anak sulung, aku disebut paling dulu.... Aku temukan kertas pesan itu di antara tumpukan naskah tulisan atau tik-tikkan ayahku. Satu kopi di antaranya aku ambil dan kusembunyikan untuk diriku sendiri.*
>
> *Kata-kata yang sedikit itu, lisan dan tulisan, dalam jiwa kanak-kanakku telah menjadi konsep tentang hari depanku.* (*NS* II, 49–50)

Itself a miniature version of the family romance of reading genealogies of Javanese tradition that ties together the two sections of the prison notes we have been discussing in this chapter, the passage refers to something similar to the Javanese "family book" or arrangement (*karangan*) on which Soetomo's *Kenang-Kenangan* is modeled. In its combination of spoken and written, handwritten and typewritten forms, and in the combination of the mother's and the father's role in composing the book, it also provides a revealing instance of the family romance of reading and composition shaping Pramoedya's own sense of authorship.

Within this context it is revealing that the particular word given as an example of all "the little words and sayings" kept from childhood, includes his mother's use of the "foreign phrase" (*kata asing*) "all-round" as a qualifying description for "a person who's meant to be free." The sense in which this "foreign phrase" embeds an ideal of freedom within the passing on of a Javanese family's legacy serves as a revealing example of the sort of alien genealogy at work in Pramoedya's writing as a whole. The linguistic register of this word is by no means easy to pinpoint, however. In the introductory chapter I argued that this apparently English word might perhaps better be conceived as an Indonesian word. We might now more precisely read it as a word *between* languages, a word that promises an "all-round" decolonization of that hierarchy of languages within which it is embedded as the cultural form of a far-reaching estrangement of linguistic and literary traditions.

In order to summarize the double movement of Pramoedya's genealogy of Javanese and "all-round" decolonization of tradition, we might say that whereas "Mata Rantai" describes the imperative of Indonesian modernism to break from the "vicious circle" of Javanese tradition, as exemplified in the erasure of the honorific *Mas* in front of the family name Toer, "Flowers for Mother" describes the Indonesian modernism that is at the heart of Javanese forms of tradition. Two concepts of tradition run through the prison notes, and each might be taken as related to this double movement. There is the concept of legacy, *warisan*, linked to the official forms of literary tradition passed down, like the passages of the Javanese version of the *Mahabharata;* and then there is the wisdom of proverbs, aphorisms, "little words and sayings" passed down from parents to children. If the word *warisan* ("legacy," "inheritance") is associated with the first concept of tradition, the somewhat unusual word *pesangon* seems more attuned to the second concept of tradition. This is a word Pramoedya used as a metaphor for the teachings of his mother in an article from 1983 translated by Benedict Anderson who explains the term as follows: "*Pesangon,* from the Javanese *pasangan,* means literally 'travel money' or 'vademecum.'... Since there seems to be no comfortable English equivalent, and one striking feature of this text is Pramoedya's unusually explicit use of Javanese conceptions and traditions, I have left the word in the original."[35] This is also the word Pramoedya uses to describe his recourse to the first line of a "Negro spiritual" memorized during his first period of lengthy imprisonment in Bukitduri prison; it is a descriptive term, as we have already seen, for the rescue work of all the prison notes in their attempt to reconstruct a lost history through the arrangement of a whole set of passages of remembered words, songs, and texts. It is as *pesangon* that the passage, or fragment of literary text, works to call attention to the gaps between and links among linguistic, literary, and cultural traditions.

Conclusion

8

POSTCOLONIAL PHILOLOGY AND THE PASSAGE OF LITERATURE

> Because documents are more reliable, Meneer. They are more reliable than the mouths of their own authors.
>
> —Pramoedya, *House of Glass*

> *Soalnya memang kertas-kertas yang lebih bias dipercaya. Lebih bias dipercaya daripada mulut penulisnya sendiri.*
>
> —Pramoedya, *Rumah Kaca*

The work of Pramoedya Ananta Toer, I have argued in this study, provides an opportunity to reconsider transnational literary modernism; and specifically to grasp in what sense its cultural, historical, and political coordinates are defined by an ongoing process of decolonization. Pramoedya's genealogy of Indonesian modernism develops a practice of historical reading and writing that underlines the formative links between literary form, cultural tradition, and the politics of decolonization. This work of decolonizing tradition is also intimately linked to Pramoedya's attempts to document the significance for Indonesian anti-colonial nationalism of the linguistic and literary historical formation of *bahasa Indonesia*.

As we have already noted, the emergence of Indonesian as a paradigmatic language of anti-colonial nationalism stands in revealing historical counterpoint to that eminently colonial undertaking, the *Oxford English Dictionary*, begun during the mid-Victorian period and completed the same year Indonesian was adopted as the language of anti-colonial nationalism. In this final chapter, I offer some concluding reflections on the implications of these contrasting colonial and anti-colonial linguistic phenomena. In particular, I argue that, despite the sharp contrast between the *O.E.D.* and Pramoedya's documentation of *bahasa Indonesia*—the one a massive, encyclopedic work of linguistic, literary, and historical documentation; the other, an attempt to counterbalance successive attempts to destroy just such a monumental, encyclopedic effort of documentation— each stands as a testament to the same underlying problem of linguistic and literary form. This is the problem of the passage of literature we have found at the roots of English, Creole, and Indonesian literary modernisms.

As a practical and theoretical matter, the modernist emphasis on the individual passage of literature emerges in a turn from nineteenth-century European philology to twentieth-century literary criticism; from the comparative and historical linguistic principles of the first toward the formalist, synchronic linguistic principles of the second. The *O.E.D.* itself documents this turn in a number of ways. Launched in the mid-Victorian period and grounded in the principles of nineteenth-century comparative philology, it was not completed until 1928 (with a 1933 *Supplement*). Anticipating the dissolution of philology into the separate disciplines of "linguistics" and "literature," its own entry for "philology" (which appeared in 1906) tracks a revealing semantic shift, whereby the third, more specialized meaning—"science of language"—displaces the first, more general meaning—"love of learning and literature" (listed as "now rare"). Yet even as it documents the eclipse of the philological ideal on which it is itself built, the *O.E.D.* registers, in one of the illustrative citations for the first sense of philology, the ideal of philology as a "master science" for other disciplines. Seth Lerer has recently argued that the *O.E.D.* was "built, collaboratively, out of Victorian habits of reading."[1] Yet "more than coincidence," as Hugh Kenner argues in *The Pound Era,* links its growth and composition with the collaborative process of the English modernists, Joyce, Pound, and Eliot.[2] Whereas for nineteenth-century philology the textual fragment promised the scientific basis for a "master science" of human history as a whole, for literary modernism the individual passage of text becomes the fragmentary deposit of multiple, overlapping, and contested literary systems of culture.

What appears as the turn away from philology, however, also involves a return to philology, and this return to philology, everywhere present in a wide variety of twentieth-century critical approaches, is informed by a set of imperatives that have shaped a postcolonial philological approach to the literary and linguistic coordinates of the passage of literature. Schematically, these imperatives might be outlined as follows:

1. A suspicion of the historical priorities accorded by national languages
2. A reading of any passage of text as a dislocation (or tropological displacement) of material culture

3. An attention to the polylinguistic coordinates of words (an attention to the semiotic drift between linguistic, literary, and culture systems)

In what follows I will elaborate on these imperatives in order to draw some practical consequences for approaching texts in light of the preceding study. This is intended neither as a prescriptive methodology nor as a new theoretical program. It is itself, indeed, an attempt to return to philological principles that have long informed a wide range of work in both the theory and the practice of twentieth-century literature.

Edward Said's model of "contrapuntal analysis," one of the most prominent attempts to address the first of these imperatives (by setting the priorities of dominant European cultures in counterpoint with non-European cultural experiences), is premised on earlier comparative philological models (notably those of Auerbach and Spitzer, as discussed in chapter 2). The question of authority in evaluating any passage of text and its relation to culture (the problem posed by our second imperative) remains an unresolved question of traditional philology (especially European comparative philology). Vividly illustrated by Said's influential polemical critique of Orientalism, this unresolved question of traditional philology surfaces in many of the most powerful attempts to apply the tools of literary criticism to cultural study in general—for example, with the work of Walter Benjamin (touched on in chapter 4); and also that of Raymond Williams, whose *Keywords: A Vocabulary of Culture and Society* represents an especially revealing return to philological principles (and specifically those of the *O.E.D.*) in order to transform the traditional tools of literary criticism into a critical resource for cultural studies. If culture for Benjamin and Williams seems still very much located within metropolitan European space, each of their approaches registers far-reaching material dislocations of cultural capital, whether in the reading of Parisian arcades (Benjamin) or in reading the keywords of English culture and society. The issues raised by these critics (and the currents of theory they represent) have become still more relevant with the imperative to address the full diversity of linguistic and literary formations of human culture and society. Ironically, but fittingly, postcolonial theories that seek to break from the old Eurocentric models of comparative philology find themselves returning to certain key practical and theoretical problems confronted in the formation of nineteenth-century comparative philology: above all, the need for linguistic knowledge, authority, and precision in attending to the multiple linguistic and literary coordinates of the words studied in texts.

One important example of an attempt to theorize this critical, postcolonial return to older models of philology is the work of

Walter Mignolo, whose *Darker Side of the Renaissance* reevaluates the Renaissance from colonial American linguistic and cultural perspectives excluded from dominant Anglophone historical models of history. In order to conduct an analysis of what he calls "colonial semiosis," Mignolo explains, "I need philological procedures. Since I am dealing with colonial situations, however, I am not necessarily forced to carry on the ideological background attached to the methodological procedure itself. In fact, philology and comparatism should allow us to look at the European Renaissance by locating the understanding subject in the colonial peripheries."[3] The "new philology" Mignolo develops applies all three of the principles outlined above, but to a different set of overlapping cultural formations (counterpointing languages of the early colonial period in the Americas—Spanish, Portuguese, Quechua, Aymara, Nahuatl—against the dominant languages of the modern period, English, German, French). Different though this historical and geo-cultural focus is from our preceding study of English, Creole, and Indonesian modernisms, a similar philological insight emerges from Mignolo's argument to the one we have derived from Pramoedya's work of decolonizing tradition: the insight, in particular, as we explored in the previous chapter, into that palimpsest of different scripts—Sanskrit, Javanese, Arab, and Roman—that constitute the cultural capital of modern languages. Our three imperatives attempt to outline a critical reading of the reversals of historical perspective at work in producing any standardized modern script (whether, for example, English or Indonesian). These imperatives might alternatively be considered as variations on the two axioms that Mignolo draws from Ortega y Gasset, by way of A. L. Becker, in elaborating his model of "colonial semiosis": "The new philology to which I subscribe revolves around two axioms: (1) every word is exuberant, because it says more than intended; (2) every word is deficient, because it says less than expected."[4] What I call here "postcolonial philology" is intended generally as a description of the methodological and theoretical imperatives shaping literary study in the aftermath of decolonization. The three imperatives outlined above are suggested as a kind of philological checklist of points for reading a document like the *O.E.D.* in light of the overlapping concerns of English, Creole, and Indonesian modernisms.

Between Orientalism and Literary Criticism
The Imperatives of Postcolonial Philology

In the figure of the colonial archivist and Javanese specialist in Pramoedya's *House of Glass*, we encounter a revealing composite figure of nineteenth-century philology and Orientalism. His claim that "documents are more reliable...than the mouths of their own authors" represents a certain profession of faith in the philological grounding of his specialized study of Javanese. In the context of his discussions with the secret police agent, Pangemanann, the claim resonates with a distinct irony, since the "mouth" of the author of the first three volumes of the tetralogy has already been silenced. When the archivist lectures Pangemanann on what Javanese documents reveal about the Javanese people, it is a European expert on Javanese lecturing a Menadonese native with no knowledge of the Javanese language, in the absence of the Javanese character, Minke, whose first-person narrative perspective has been abruptly displaced by that of Pangemanann. The ironies will increase when Minke's documents are stolen and brought to the colonial archive for Pangemanann to study. One thing that is already illustrated by this situation, however, is the Orientalist presumption of nineteenth-century philology: that texts ("documents") construct the object of philological study—in this case, the Javanese language and people—far more reliably than the testimony of the people who are the subjects and speakers of the philologist's area of expertise.[5]

This underlying textual assumption is one of the key principles of comparative philology that gave scientific validity to the claims of philology in the nineteenth century as a "master science" for other disciplines. Comparative philology, developed by nineteenth-century German philologists into the comparative and historical study of the laws of linguistic change, stems from Sir William Jones's late eighteenth-century recognition of the shared linguistic roots of Sanskrit, Greek, and Latin. Providing the linguistic foundation for philology and giving scientific prestige to the study of Oriental languages and literatures, this cornerstone of nineteenth-century philology calls attention to the role of the Orientalist in shoring up European colonial authority and knowledge.[6] The narrower scholarly profile of the "Orientalist" who studies Oriental languages and texts is linked to the prestige of the master science of philology and so, in turn, to that wider sense of "Orientalism" that Edward Said has made so central a term for identifying the distorting and encompassing forms of European colonial knowledge and power.

The philological claims of the archivist in *House of Glass*, then, confront a certain suspicion; and this is much closer to the suspicious hermeneutic of a twentieth-century literary critic than the scientific claims of a nineteenth-century comparative philologist. Even as Pramoedya's dialogue underscores the connection between colonial and philological expertise—the European "Javanese expert" serving as scholarly advisor for the police official's efforts to become a "colonial expert"—the archivist's reliance on "documents" confronts a doubt about the reliability of such documentation. Although it by no means entirely discredits the authority of the archivist's "lectures" on Java, this doubt extends a suspicion on which the entire Buru tetralogy has so far turned. By this stage in the tetralogy the reader will likely hear the archivist's "lectures" with the same sort of "suspicion" with which Minke has listened to Europeans lecturing him on his own people, culture, and literature throughout the first three volumes. *House of Glass*, however, complicates this suspicion by investing it in the position of Pangemanann; and it is Pangemanann (not Minke) who gives us the profile of the twentieth-century literary critic over against that of the nineteenth-century philologist. When it comes to the key documents that are brought into the state archives—Minke's stolen notebooks—Pangemanann explicitly refers to his French training in close literary analysis, or *explication de texte*. If the European archivist depends on nineteenth-century Orientalist philology for special insight into the exercise of colonial power, Pangemanann's police work requires that he attend to the evidence of documents for which his French school training in "how to analyze a piece of writing" (*H*, 177) ("*menelaah sebuah tulisan*" [*RK*, 178]), with specific reference to an assignment to read Flaubert's *Un Coeur Simple*, provides the revealing model.

It is with this double twist, combining the suspect Orientalism of nineteenth-century philology with the suspicious hermeneutic of twentieth-century literary criticism, that the dialogue between archivist and secret police agent poses the question facing postcolonial philology: How can one adjudicate the reliability or credibility of documents? This dialogue poses, too, a miniature version of the problem of historical documentation in the Buru tetralogy as a whole. Premised on the attempt to reconstruct texts that have been destroyed, the Buru tetralogy gives special urgency to the reliability or trustworthiness of documents. Itself a part of the larger work of Pramoedya's attempts on Buru to record the experiences both of his fellow prisoners and of Indonesia's collective revolutionary history, so violently reversed in 1965, the Buru tetralogy is underwritten by an urgent testimonial imperative to archival truth. Yet like Pramoedya's "notes from Buru" (*catatan-catatan dari Buru*), smuggled out of Buru and collated later into the two-volume set of prison memoirs, the form of the Buru tetralogy is itself fragmentary, testifying, in the fiction of its documentary basis in Minke's notes, to a twofold destruction of historical documents (in the period of turn-of-the-century colonial Indonesia, and then again in the events of 1965). By taking us into the colonial state archives in the last of the four volumes of the Buru tetralogy, Pramoedya foregrounds this ongoing contest over historical documentation, posing again the questionable reliability of the Orientalist archive as a question for postcolonial philology.

In the figures of the Orientalist archivist Tuan L. and Assistant Police Commissioner Pangemanann, two kinds of philological premise confront each other: on the one hand, the comparative linguistic premise of nineteenth-century Orientalism; and, on the other, the analytical premise of twentieth-century literary criticism (informing all the various kinds of close reading of texts taught in schools). A similar confrontation of contending philological premises informs Edward Said's *Orientalism*. In his far-reaching and polemical critique of the way in which Orientalist scholarship has buttressed at least two centuries of European and American colonial and neo-colonial policies of territorial and cultural domination, Said drew attention to the continuing importance of the old generalist philological tradition for the twentieth century. Yet in order to appreciate the extent to which Said marks the beginnings of a postcolonial philology in the critique of Orientalism, it is important to emphasize Said's conflicted—indeed, contradictory—position vis-à-vis the nineteenth-century model of comparative philology that consolidated what Said analyzes as the discursive formation of Orientalism. On the one hand, his Foucauldian reading of Oriental textual scholarship is enabled by a distinctly postphilological, partly structuralist, but more precisely modernist theory of the "text"—developed, above all, in *Beginnings* and elaborated through *The World, the Text, and the Critic*, itself anticipated in his very first book on Joseph Conrad. On the other hand, what stands out in Said's continuous meditation on the modernist question of "the specific problematic of a text"[7] is the point of connection with the historical and linguistic practices of comparative philology. At the heart of Said's work, we might recognize a conflicted double movement: deploying a modernist theory of textuality against the Eurocentric universalism of nineteenth-century philology; but deploying that nineteenth-century European philological tradition against the isolating specialisms of modernist text-based literary criticism. Said's critical achievements may be seen to hinge on the same linguistic turn that has defined twentieth-century literary criticism, but his attempt to forge a "secular criticism" between Orientalism and literary criticism foregrounds the continuing significance of a historical and comparative philology in shaping the formalist "linguistic turn" that gives priority to the individual fragment of text held up for literary critical interpretation.[8]

The so-called linguistic turn[9] in literary theory, apparently premised on a *rejection* of the historical linguistic assumptions of nineteenth-century European philology, may also be conceived as a constant, repetitive *return* to those philological assumptions. Literary criticism throughout the twentieth century has been haunted by the lost coherence of the nineteenth-century "master science" of philology. Anglo-American summaries of literary theory in the second half of the twentieth century typically trace the starting point of literary theory to the eclipse of historical linguistics, with Ferdinand de Saussure's radical shift from diachronic to synchronic linguistics. This is what Foucault calls attention to in his discussion of the place of comparative philology in his archaeology of the human sciences. The discovery of comparative philology (the law of internal historical change in language) makes language into an object: "language began to fold in upon itself, to acquire its own density, to deploy a history, an objectivity, and laws of its own. It became one object of knowledge among others" (*"le langage se replie sur soi, acquiert son épaisseur propre, déploie une histoire, des lois et une objectivité qui n'appartiennent qu'à lui. Il est devenu un objet de la connaissance parmi tant d'autres"*).[10] Thus, according to the same process by which the human object of anthropology and psychiatry disappears as it gets constituted as the object of study, so, too, historical linguistics, even as it shapes itself as a possible "master science" of the human sciences, dissolves itself into the vanishing totality of its own object of study.

All three of the "compensations" Foucault lists for this paradoxical "demotion" of language "to the mere status of an object"—that it becomes the positivist medium of science; that it becomes the "modern form of criticism"; and that it enables the appearance of a new sense of the "literary"—suggest how nineteenth-century philology is inscribed into the linguistic turn of structuralist and post-structuralist theory. The last of the "compensations" Foucault lists, in particular, foregrounds the inner links between the emergence of literary modernism, the linguistic turn of theory, and the shadow cast by nineteenth-century philology:

> Finally, the last of the compensations for the demotion of language, the most important, and also the most unexpected, is the appearance of literature, of literature as such...the word is of recent date, as is also...the isolation of a particular language whose peculiar mode of being is 'literary.'...Literature is the contestation of philology (of which it is nevertheless the twin figure): it leads language back from grammar to the naked power of speech, and there it encounters the untamed, imperious being of words....At the moment when language, as spoken and scattered words, becomes an object of knowledge, we see it reappearing in a strictly opposite modality: a silent, cautious deposition of the word upon the whiteness of a piece of paper, where it can possess neither sound nor interlocutor, where it has nothing to say but itself, nothing to do but shine in the brightness of its being.[11]
>
> *Enfin la dernière des compensations au nivellement du langage, la plus importante, la plus inattendue aussi, c'est l'apparition de la littérature. De la littérature comme telle...le mot est de fraîche date, comme est récent aussi...l'isolement d'un langage singulier dont la modalité propre est d'être "littérature."...La littérature, c'est la contestation de la philologie (dont elle et pourtant la figure jumelle): elle ramène le langage de la grammaire au pouvoir dénudé de parler, et là elle rencontre l'être sauvage*

et impérieux des mots....Au moment où le langage, comme parole répandue, devient objet de connaissance, violà qu'il réapparaît sous une modalité strictement opposée: silencieuse, précautionneuse déposition du mot sur la blancheur d'un papier, où il ne peut avoir ni sonorité ni interlocuteur, où il n'a rien d'autre à dire que soi, rien d'autre à faire que scintiller dans l'éclat de son être.[12]

This last "compensation" explains perhaps best of all how it is that the isolated literary passage of text serves, in all three cases (for positivist linguistics, for critical exegesis, and for the "literary") as a sort of placeholder for that absent point of coherence of the "master science" of philology. As pure text, the practice of a writing without reference to anything but itself—this particular moment of turning the linguistic into the literary, for which the French term *écriture* seems uniquely appropriate—outlines the inner logic linking the opposed (but twinned) realms of comparative philology and literary criticism. The first isolates the universal laws of linguistic vowel and consonant change that connect and differentiate all languages throughout history. The second isolates the use of language in the act of breaking from anything but its own linguistic—which is to say "literary"—performance.

This turn from the laws of language to the "radical intransitivity" (*"une intransitivité radicale"*) of literature constitutes a foundational moment of literary modernism, ensuring a "ludic denial" (*"la dénégation ludique"*) of traditional values and enacting a "break" from "the whole definition of *genres*" (*"elle rompt avec toute définition de 'genres'"*).[13] Although Foucault's formulation might appear especially to evoke the features of a historically French literary avant-garde, his argument compels us to consider that, however classified (and both in its creative and critical manifestations), literary modernism is grounded in a break between its linguistic and its literary determinations. Whereas comparative philology insisted on the necessary, inner connection between the development of a language and the literature shaped by that language, the "radical intransitivity" of literary modernism follows only the formative laws of its own linguistic performance. This formal self-referentiality cannot, of course, entirely abolish the rules of grammar, nor does it even deny the laws of linguistic change on which comparative philology insisted. In fact, as Foucault's description implies, the modernist break internalizes all the more what comparative philology posited as the inner connection between the development of a language and the literature shaped by that language—there is, as it were, nothing but the perpetual linking of the linguistic to the literary, and the turning of language into literature. The moment comparative philology takes for its starting point—reading the text of literature as a manifestation of linguistic development—turns into the singular instance of a literary form creating language. The very *link* in the hermeneutic circle by which comparative philology derived the laws of language from the evidence of literature becomes the modernist *break* between linguistic and literary evidence. And what constitutes the turn from one to the other is, specifically and concretely, the passage of text—the literary evidence of linguistic development for philology, and the linguistic act of literature for modernism.

The dialogue between the archivist and Pangemanann enacts this linguistic turn generally in the contest and collaboration between the linguistic expertise of the one and the literary skills of the other. In some respects this might at first appear as the very inverse of Said's attempted negotiation of an oppositional position between Orientalism and literary criticism. It is, after all, in this collaboration that Minke's notes get stolen by the state. Between the Orientalist and amateur literary critic the text disappears. As we have been exploring in the preceding set of studies, however, it is the manner in which Pramoedya recaptures in fiction the loss of this historical record that enables an oppositional reading of the archive. Pramoedya's Indonesian modernism allows us to reconsider the terms of Said's efforts to formulate a "secular criticism," to reevaluate the contending demands of Orientalism and literary criticism, and to recognize why it is at the very moment when the object of traditional philological study disappears that the human, political, and historical stakes of reading become all the more critical.

If the archivist practices Orientalist philology while Pangemanann's police work employs literary analysis, neither position represents, simply, and in clear-cut distinction, the different premises of nineteenth-century philology, on the one hand, and twentieth-century literary criticism, on the other. Each constitutes, rather, a complex contest and collaboration between the demands of both. It is, indeed, in their combined work that we come to recognize the significance of the archives—specifically, what gets erased from the archive, under the double perspective of Tuan L.'s understanding of Javocentrism and Pangemanann's reading of Minke's notes. At the core of this example may be found an instance of what we explored in the last chapter as the double movement of genealogy and critique (genealogy of Indonesian modernism and critique of Javanism) by which Pramoedya enacts an ongoing decolonization of tradition. Our suspicion of the European archivist's comments on Javanese literature and the Javanese people must be weighed against our judgment of Pangemanann's police(d) reading of Minke's modern consciousness. In the absence of that traditional object of philological study—Javanese—and in the absence of the defining texts of Indonesian literary modernism, the reader is compelled to rely on a doubly unstable balance of perspectives. In the process, the entire Buru tetralogy comes to appear a kaleidoscopic set of unreliable passages whose very shape and survival are refracted through multiple distortions of reading.

The Postcolonial Philological Turn

The contest between the formalism of literary analysis and the linguistic expertise of Orientalism characteristically shapes a postcolonial philology; and these imperatives characteristically turn on the individual passage of text—that *link* or *break* between language and literature. Rather than forming a unified field of postcolonial philology, this contest over the individual fragment of text, the passage of literature, underscores a profound unevenness of effect in the way in which philological practices of the past impinge on the critical problems of the postcolonial present.

It is this unevenness that is the shared problem of postcolonial philology, and for which the individual passage of literature becomes the simultaneously linguistic and literary problem. Consider, for example, two contrasting examples from more or less obviously "postcolonial" literature written in English: Chinua Achebe's *Things Fall Apart* and V. S. Naipaul's *A House for Mr Biswas*. Achebe and Naipaul each position the story of their main protagonists in disproportionate relation to textual passages: Okonkwo's story, retrospectively cast in light of the question of how to dispose of the dead body, in relation to the "chapter" or "short paragraph" of the District Commissioner's imagined book; and Mohun Biswas's death, as presented in the novel's opening, in ironic relation to the possible manner in which it might be reported in the printed page of the newspaper for which he worked up until his being "sacked"—in the opening formulation of the novel—"ten weeks before he died." These are, in fact, complex figurations of the contest over the passage of printed text—in each, arguably, the idealized passage of *literary* text trumps the more general passage of text against which their deaths are reduced. But in both cases—each written on the eve of postcolonial national independence—the ironies and reversals involved in appropriating the medium of novelistic form in English entail forms of contest over the reading of text that enact a similar multiplication of philological premises as in our example from *House of Glass*.

The individual passage of literature, singled out as the site of a contest of authority, cannot itself provide a *locus classicus*, but presents, rather, the index of a fundamental and far-reaching dislocation of cultural reference. The now classical examples of the postcolonial novels cited above make the passage of literature the site of multiple dislocations of the historical, political, and linguistic coordinates on which they are premised. Achebe's *Things Fall Apart* famously foregrounds this in its title's citation of a passage from

Yeats's "The Second Coming," which simultaneously draws the reader into the canonical horizon of English literary modernism and reconstitutes the already complex textual coordinates of Yeats's poem within the cultural, religious, and poetic coordinates of the novel's disintegrating Igbo sense of imagined community. When, late in the novel, Obierika passes judgment on the fateful collision of Christian missionary values and Igbo customs, the dialogic force with which his words echo the title underscores the gaps between religious, poetic, and cultural traditions on which the very texture of the novel depends: "He has put a knife on the things that held us together and we have fallen apart."[14] Far from constituting an incidental effect of literary allusion, the calibrated citation and recitation of words from the passage of Yeats's poem reveals a deep-seated engagement with discrepant philological premises. The term postcolonial philology fits here because the passage of text demands an at least double estrangement, in which both the Igbo and the English emerge as foreign languages, the textual evidence of English or Igbo words ("things," "fallen apart") soliciting the kind of attention the philologist is trained to discern.

V. S. Naipaul captures this postcolonial philological imperative in another sense when, in the 1964 essay "Jasmine," he writes "To us, without a mythology, all literatures were foreign."[15] What precipitates the comment is an anecdote about an angry nationalist writer's protest against the imposition of the English language and the "alien mythology" of its literature, condensed in his objection to Wordsworth's "notorious poem about the daffodil": "A pretty little flower, no doubt; but we had never seen it. Could the poem have any meaning for us?" Rejecting the "superficial" prompting of the argument as "political," Naipaul argues that "it was really an expression of dissatisfaction at the emptiness of our own formless, unmade society."[16] This characteristic deflection of "political" motives already suggests a rather different kind of "expression of dissatisfaction" from what we find with Achebe, as perhaps most successfully embodied in the perspective of Ralph Singh, the disillusioned former politician and narrator of *The Mimic Men*. Faced with a related "postcolonial" condition—the narrator of Naipaul's *The Mimic Men* describes this as "the deep disorder" brought about by "the overthrow in three continents of established social organizations"[17]—Achebe and Naipaul respond in very different ways. What Ngũgĩ wa Thiong'o once called the "energy of the Okonkwos of the new literature who would rather die resisting than live on bent knees in a world which they could no longer define for themselves"[18] finds its inverted image in Naipaul's increasing political recoil from the energies of anti-colonial struggle.

Where the difference seems most striking—for example, Achebe's attack on Conrad's racism in "An Image of Africa" and Naipaul's embrace of "Conrad's Darkness" (essays both published in the mid-1970s)—one might also recognize a shared departure point: the contested passage of literary text, here specifically the racism, or "darkness" of the Conradian passage of literature. Achebe and Naipaul both have their eye on the isolated passage of Conradian text, although they appear to reach diametrically opposed positions on what the Conradian passage stands as an index to: for Achebe, the Conradian passage is a racist distortion of reality; for Naipaul, it is the accurate depiction of reality. The world of Conrad's "darkness," for Naipaul, is "my world, a world I recognize today";[19] for Achebe, it's quite the opposite. What each shares, even as they depart so radically on what they share, is a deep-seated concern for what Virginia Woolf characterized, already in 1924, as "those famous passages which it is becoming the habit to lift from their context and exhibit among other cut flowers of English prose."[20] The Conradian passage, for each, constitutes a particularly privileged site of the contest over language and tradition. The impasse of the Conradian passage, for Achebe, has its undeniable moments of greatness ("Even *Heart of Darkness* has its memorably good passages and moments: 'The reaches opened before us and closed behind, as if the forest had stepped leisurely across the water to bar the way for our return'"[21]); just as, for Naipaul, there are, undeniably, moments of "purple passage."[22]

This foregrounding of Conradian literary passages provides a version of that contest between linguistic and literary expertise outlined above and exemplified in the dialogue between Pangemanann and the colonial archivist. The unreliable overestimation of aesthetic judgment (appreciation for "memorably good passages" or criticism of "purple passages") holds in reserve another kind of evaluation that yields Achebe's and Naipaul's opposed evaluations of Conrad's depiction of reality. This evaluation is shaped by a shared imperative to bring more precision and authority to the cultural coordinates of the literary passage than aesthetic judgment can afford. If the posture of the literary critic's aesthetic judgment of the literary passage recalls the position of Pramoedya's Pangemanann, the more authoritative evaluation held in reserve recalls the position of Pramoedya's Orientalist archivist. Against the aesthetic judgment of the literary critic, Achebe and Naipaul each invoke an authoritative knowledge of languages and customs, turning from literary criticism back to the more traditional philological claim to be able to read the literary passage as a manifestation of a linguistic development of culture and history.

Achebe cites F. R. Leavis's famous criticism of Conrad's "adjectival insistence upon inexpressible and incomprehensible mystery"[23] as part of the development of his argument that Conrad bestows "human expression" on the European characters but withholds it from the African characters. What Achebe identifies here is not so much the psychological evidence of racism that is so memorable a part of the polemic of his critique. It is, rather, the literary mystification of language—and specifically, the fundamental absence of African languages—that Achebe locates in the passages he cites from Conrad's text. "Adjectival insistence," then, is a literary judgment whose linguistic-sounding precision is shown, from Achebe's postcolonial critical perspective, to turn on a question of traditional philology: the deliberate refusal, in Conrad's text, to take African languages seriously as the human expression of a historical and cultural development. One reason to call attention to this philological twist in Achebe's argument is to hold onto a part of the critical leverage that subsequent critics have sometimes overlooked, sometimes resisted, in calling attention to some of the narrative complexities in "Heart of Darkness" that Achebe ignores. The passages Achebe singles out for analysis of Conrad's "adjectival insistence" on "inscrutable," "incomprehensible," or "unspeakable" aspects of the African setting constitute a deliberate, but also complex and consequential reading of the way African languages, histories, and cultures are fundamentally dislocated by the literary modernism of Conrad's prose, which "eliminates the African as human factor"[24]— refusing the philological basis for considering Africa as a coherent object of linguistic, historical, or cultural study. One might indeed argue that the critical edge of Conrad's literary modernism is precisely evident in the way it turns against the racist presumptions of European efforts to make Africa over into an object of linguistic, historical, and cultural study. In order to demonstrate this, however, it would be necessary to respond in full to the challenge Achebe presents, in a variety of ways throughout his essay, to outline even more fully than he does how the absence of African languages is determined by a prior history of positive—and positivist—misrepresentation of African languages in European philology.[25]

V. S. Naipaul takes an almost diametrically opposed position to Achebe's. Citing a long passage from "Karain: A Memory," in which the narrator of the story describes the land that Karain has conquered on the coast of Mindanao, Naipaul at first seems to concede the point that Achebe makes about the "romantic" vagueness of Conrad's prose: "It is a passage that, earlier, I would have hurried through: the purple passage, the reflective caption." With Achebe's critique in mind, one might well recognize in Naipaul's cited passage the same effects of an "adjectival insistence" that deliberately mystifies the place and people being described—to cite only a part of Naipaul's passage: "It was still, complete, unknown, and full of a life that went on stealthily with a troubling effect of solitude; of a life that seemed unaccountably empty of anything that would stir the thought, touch the heart, give a hint of the ominous sequence of days."[26] Here, the adjectival (and adverbial) insistence seems a clear projection of the white narrator's incomprehension. Naipaul goes on, however, to find "a precision in its romanticism, and a great effect of thought and sympathy."[27]

For Naipaul, as with Achebe, a key part of the argument will turn on the psychology ("thought and sympathy") manifested by the passage. But there is also an anthropological side to Naipaul's reading that helps explain the striking difference between the two: whereas Achebe finds Conrad's depiction of Africans a distortion and disfigurement of the communities and peoples of which they are a part, Naipaul finds in Conrad's willful obscurity of description a truthful evocation of what he will later describe as "half-made societies"[28]—and he singles out as examples Karain himself, the figure of Wang "the self-exiled Chinese in *Victory*," and "the two Belgian empire builders" of "An Outpost of Progress."[29] Achebe and Naipaul, one might indeed conclude, are focused on two very different realities; the Conradian passage, for each, produces a different *mimesis*. Yet the way that mimetic reality is produced—denied, for Achebe; captured, for Naipaul—depends, for both, on the way the Conradian passage breaks the link between linguistic and literary expression on which nineteenth-century philology depends.

Both Achebe and Naipaul draw attention to the way Conrad turns from a description of the land to a description of the people. It is here that Naipaul finds a "precision" in Conrad's "romanticism": "the effort [of thought and sympathy] doesn't stop with the aspect of the land. It extends to all men in these dark or remote places who, for whatever reason, are denied a clear vision of the world."[30] Achebe, of course, traces a very different psychological and anthropological effort in Conrad's shift from describing the landscape of Africa to describing its people. What is already evident in the "adjectival insistence" of Conrad's landscape descriptions—the denial of language to Africans—becomes still more revealing when it comes to people, whose "place" is nowhere more fully defined as when their language is rendered incomprehensible (Achebe gives considerable satirical play to this point, echoing Naipaul's designation of "romanticism" by sarcastically saying that "As everybody knows, Conrad is a romantic on the side"[31]).

Achebe and Naipaul capture two sides of the movement Foucault outlines in the dissolution of comparative philology (and the human sciences generally)—into anthropology, on the one hand, and psychology, on the other.[32] The Conradian landscape description breaks the philological presumption of a connection between language and the people. This refusal to accord a language to the people depicted represents for Achebe an anthropology of racism, but for Naipaul a psychological insight. Both positions stem from a turn away from comparative philology. The power of the Conradian passage of literature—its exoticizing movement from a landscape to a people; in its contest of any enlightened perspective—derives from this crisis in the human sciences, whether taken as a refusal of philological presumption that language is the "human expression" of a people, or a recognition of the displaced relation of language to a people, and an individual's sense of racial identity. To the extent that these are two sides of the same coin, the classification "romantic" in each case might indicate what is shared—the romanticism of a philological "placing" of peoples according to language; the "precision" with which romantic philology displaces a person's racial and ethnographic identity. The way each writer considers the trope of Conrad's "darkness" (racial distortion, racial insight) reflects, indeed, their own postcolonial philological practice.

All three of these postcolonial literary examples (Achebe, Naipaul, and Pramoedya, whose citations from Conrad's "Karain: A Memory" we have already discussed in chapter 7) might be explained in terms of the aftereffects of the breakdown of the nineteenth-century "master science" of philology. The value in recognizing this lies in grasping how this eclipsed form of colonial knowledge and expertise (whether repudiated or nostalgically missed—and more likely some complex combination of the two)—determines the posture ascribed to the other figure, the literary critic, and the function of the isolated passage of literature. Informing both positions, albeit as opposed and inverted premises, is the premise of comparative philology: the law of internal historical change in language. The position of the literary critic, bound merely to an aesthetic appreciation of the literary passage, presumes this philological premise as a given of language, albeit in the very same gesture turning away from the linguistic principles (comparative linguistic study, the law of vowel and consonantal changes) on which the coherence of any given language is presumed to exist. The position of the more knowledgeable expert, on the other hand, is invested with a knowledge of languages and of the culture and customs of the users of the language, but without the objective scientific premise—the law of internal historical change that both connects and differentiates languages—on which nineteenth-century comparative philology was based. The foregrounding of the literary passage, in other words, holds in place the unresolved contradictions of linguistic knowledge and cultural authority once invested with scientific precision and objectivity in the master discipline of philology.

The philological (re)turn at the heart of French poststructuralist theories of the text, or *écriture*, does not, of course, precisely mirror (much less explain) the dynamic of contest and collaboration between the positions of literary criticism and linguistic expertise in the examples from Achebe and Naipaul. Nonetheless, they might be considered, along with the interplay between Orientalist philologist and critically trained police agent in Pramoedya's *House of Glass*, as variations of the same phenomenon—what Foucault calls the "contestation of philology" by literature. Each case, of course, involves an extremely complex set of interlocking linguistic and literary assumptions. To the extent that the example from *House of Glass* seems to stage a contest between two European philological traditions (Orientalist philology and French literary criticism), it appears to attribute the problem of philology to what Foucault characteristically invokes as "Western consciousness" (*"la conscience occidentale"*).[33] The philological imperatives at stake, however, can hardly be adequately grasped in such terms. If an abyss of interpretative priority is already opened up in the discrepancy between the European philological presumptions of the Dutch specialist of Javanese language and culture and the French-educated Menadonese police commissioner, how much more of a gap must there be between the overlapping secular, sacred, and political presumptions of Javanese and Malay philologies (*baca* and *karang*), ancient and modern, oral and written? A similar proliferation of differing traditions exists in the contrasting cases of Achebe and Naipaul, and these are multiplied all the more in the doubling and crossing over from scientific claims to linguistic knowledge to aesthetic claims to literary evaluation.

In the example from *House of Glass*, for example, to consider the formalist analysis of the passage chosen for our epigraph would need at the least to invoke all three of what Foucault outlines as those effects of the formation (and dissolution) of philology—positivist linguistic science (a proper translation of the passage); interpretive practice; and modernist self-referentiality. These stage both quintessentially European (or if you will "Western") philological problems; but parse them according to the displacement and estrangement of the coordinates presumed to bound those cultural categories. In the interplay between *linguistic* expertise and *literary* evaluation that characterizes the imperatives of postcolonial philology in this very general sense, the individual passage of literature foregrounds a *mise-en-abyme* of interpretative traditions. The example from *House of Glass* offers a striking, but in many respects quite characteristic displacement of exegetical traditions. Informing what we have characterized as the contest and collaboration between nineteenth-century Orientalist philological expertise and twentieth-century French literary criticism is, too, the crucial factor of Pangemanann's Christian faith. If this appears to play no role in the implied contest between Tuan L.'s faith in, and Pangemanann's lack of faith in, the reliability of documents, it becomes an increasingly important organizing factor in the documentary presentation of the novel as a whole, signaled by the novel's epigraph, a passage of Latin text—a citation from the Vulgate Magnificat—that will turn out, at the very end of the novel, to be the parting words with which Pangemanann delivers the confiscated notes of Minke to Nyai Ontosoroh. If the epigraph foregrounds a specifically Christian exegetical tradition, far from enclosing the documentary status of the novel within a Christian hermeneutic, the passage of Latin text stages a *mise-en-abyme* of philology.

Considering Foucault's threefold "compensations" for the founding and dissolution of nineteenth-century philology, the Latin text presents a positivist linguistic issue of translation for which the translation into *bahasa Indonesia* enacts a potential decolonization of the globalized form of print capitalism—what Derrida dubbed "globalatinization"[34]—opening the roman script to a constantly dialogized space of print literacy translating from Latin (the Vulgate) to French (the language of Pangemanann's education) to Dutch (Minke's notes) to *bahasa* (the medium of Pramoedya's novel). This constitutes, moreover, an active secularization that does not simply evacuate the exegetical moves of prior religious traditions of interpretation (the passage of religious text) but, rather, actively deploys those strategies of reading (literature contesting philology, in Foucault's terms); so that Pangemanann's conflicted Catholic conscience (itself split between Catholic and Protestant variants repeatedly invoked in the odd spelling of his name) is counterpointed against the awakening of a modernizing Islamic political consciousness—the narrative consciousness of Minke, the historical Tirto Adi Suryo. The question of how to interpret this deployment of Christian against Islamic interpretive traditions is lodged at the heart of the debate between Tuan L. and Pangemanann over the reliability of documents (the term *dipercaya* invokes the word for "faith" shared, and contested, by Christianity and Islam). If this split modernizing consciousness (Pangemanann's Christian versus Minke's Islamic narrative perspective) affects every passage of text, underwriting the very notion of a passage of text, it is not, however, to enclose the narrative as a whole within a tightly bound dialectic of opposition between Christianity and Islam. There is, it is true, an intimate proximity between these religious perspectives—and the philological practices associated with each (above all the appeal to a single God) are braided together to form what the Minke of *This Earth of Mankind* and the Pangemanann of *House of Glass* each call "modern" consciousness. But this "modern" consciousness (what Foucault calls *la conscience occidentale*) is, of course, that of the "native" first-person narrator whose most intimate sense of identity is premised on a difference from the colonizing "Western" other.

Pramoedya's Buru quartet enacts a reversal, in this regard, similar to other classic twentieth-century postcolonial novels—Achebe's *Things Fall Apart* and Naipaul's *A House for Mr. Biswas* are convenient examples: the colonized person (Minke and Pangemanann; Okonkwo; Mohun Biswas) occupies the position reserved for the colonizer. This characteristic postcolonial displacement of narrative priorities—what early postcolonial criticism dubbed "writing back to Empire"—is crucially accompanied, however, by a philological reversal in which the colonial language, now occupied by the "native" other, confronts the traditions and practices of the colonized not only as foreign (and variously primitive, ancient, barbaric, unenlightened, etc) but also as the special province of the colonizer's expertise. Thus, Pangemanann, at home in the modern romanized script of Latin, French, Dutch, and *bahasa Indonesia* finds himself dependent on the expertise of Tuan L. for a grasp of texts composed in traditional Javanese script. The suspicious hermeneutic that this engenders creates a far-reaching unsettling of the Orientalist imperatives of colonial philology, reversing in turn the priority of colonizing and colonized traditions and converting European languages into the literary and linguistic space of contestation over non-European traditions of reading, exegesis, and interpretation. Echoing Foucault's argument about the far-reaching effects of the discovery of comparative philology, but recognizing the necessarily "non-Western" fold that constitutes "Western consciousness" ("*la conscience occidentale*"), we might grasp how the colonial discipline of philology was, from its inception, shaped around an imperative to displace the centrality of European languages and literatures.

The Trope of Theory and the Passage of Postcolonial Philology

The theoretical problem of the trope is, in a nutshell, what I have been characterizing as the turn from literary to linguistic expertise in shaping the characteristic imperatives of postcolonial philology. If *trope* generally means any figurative use of language, the theoretical problem it poses is the question of how to distinguish between the literal, or standard meaning, and the figurative departure from that standard or literal sense. As elaborated most notably in the earlier work of Jacques Derrida, tropes—metaphor, for example, in Aristotle—are typically the place to look to see where the conceptual claims of philosophical texts come undone, or "deconstruct." Since literal, or proper meaning can only reveal itself through the figurative turn away from proper, or literal meaning, tropes exemplify the inherent instability of meaning, locating those moments of aporia that characterize Derrida's readings of philosophical texts.

Not only is this the problem posed by any individual passage of literature isolated for critical analysis; the term *trope* itself might be (and indeed classically has been) used to describe a passage of literature lifted out of context (either for critical analysis or for rhetorical display). John Guillory has argued that de Man's reliance on the term, in his call for a "return to philology," unwittingly smuggles this thematic definition back into what appears to be a more rigorous examination of the materiality of figurative language.[35] But this position, according to Marc Redfield, itself confuses the problematic ways in which tropes, for de Man, "always raise epistemological questions because they put into play the difference between literal and figurative meaning."[36] Redfield points out that Guillory mistakenly translates "trope into signifier" (when in fact "tropes are disruptive for de Man precisely because they twine together meaning [the "signified"] and the principle of the meaning's articulation [the "signifier"]"). But this mistake itself reveals an inherent theoretical instability in the reliance on tropes in twentieth-century literary criticism, one that reproduces the Saussurean turn from historical linguistics to structuralist, or semiotic approaches. Guillory's formulation for the way de Man stabilizes the literary around an investment in tropes remains useful: "literature = literary language = rhetoric = trope";[37] but this set of equivalences, far from guaranteeing the investment in literature, makes trope not only the privileged space of the literary but also—and in precisely the same movement—the space where the "literary" turns inside out to reveal its linguistic other side. This is so whether one attempts to analyze trope in a strictly linguistic sense or whether one attempts to isolate the "literariness" of the trope; the two are indeed braided together.

The theoretical interest in tropes, dominant throughout twentieth-century literary criticism, provides a counterpart to the focus on morphemes in nineteenth-century comparative philology. In its turn against the linguistic premise of comparative philology, literary criticism sought to draw on the rhetorical device of the trope to legitimize its analysis of literature. Whether we follow Guillory in viewing de Man's confusion of the linguistic properties of tropes as stabilizing a sense of the "literary," or whether we follow Redfield in viewing de Man focusing on the radically destabilizing nature of tropes, the theoretical preoccupation with rhetorical tropes epitomized by de Man (and itself turned into the trope of "theory"—whether as something to claim or something to resist) inevitably provokes an unsettling questioning of the disciplinary foundations of literary criticism. (De Man himself provided a succinct analysis of this phenomenon, figuring it as the "return to philology" in his 1982 essay of that title.) The controversies over de Man's early Nazi sympathies that erupted after his death served all the more to turn de Man-ian deconstruction into a symptomatic form of disciplinary crisis, although the controversies did nothing to resolve the theoretical problems his work posed, including the resistance to "theory"—as a trope, and as the theoretical problem of tropes.

Paul de Man's work, which in many respects would appear to stand at the furthest remove from what we are considering in terms of the imperatives of a postcolonial philology, nonetheless both analyzes and thematizes the contest between the literary and the linguistic, between literary criticism and philology, that I have argued provokes a suspicious return to philology from a postcolonial political perspective. The dialogue between Tuan L. and Pangemanann might be read as an allegory of de Man's "return to philology" not so much in the sense that it exposes the questionable motives of the profession of literary analysis, but rather in the sense that it enacts a questioning of the disciplinary basis—the textual, or documentary basis—of philology in the broadest sense. As readers of Pramoedya's Buru tetralogy we cannot escape the problem posed by the Javanese expert: the statement that documents are more reliable than the words of their authors provokes a dilemma, an *aporia,* particularly suited (both by temperament and training, as it were) to a deconstructive literary criticism. Deconstructive literary criticism, of course, would likely not consider this as a literary passage in the first place—and this is especially true of de Man, whose exclusive focus on a very narrow European set of canonical literary texts is conceded by proponents and critics alike. Far from disqualifying the relevance of such an approach in advance, this makes it all the more relevant in considering how our passage (and more particularly the way it deploys a trope of faith in the profession of philology) stages the vanishing object of philology. A de Manian reading of this passage, indeed, would call attention to the rigor with which de Man offers not so much literary readings of the texts he selects as a reading that shows the gaps on which such readings—and by extension the textual passages themselves—are premised.

In this sense, the general tenor of Guillory's critique of de Man— that his theory of trope is premised on an illusory sense of philological rigor—could be said to articulate precisely the point (and even the rigorously philological point) of de Man's readings. For postcolonial philology, the theory of the trope offers no sort of rigorous guarantee; it underscores, rather, a philological approach without guarantee. The trope is an index of what cannot be guaranteed, and therefore must be reread with considerable suspicion—with the suspicion, indeed, that the most important thing has been left out. In the dialogue between Tuan L. and Pangemanann this is thematized, as noted above, by the fact that the entire Buru quartet is premised on a loss of documents. But this is not simply a thematic. The distinction Tuan L. makes between "documents" and "the mouths of their own authors" submits, indeed, to a fairly straightforward deconstruction of the opposition between writing and speech, whereby the words of the archivist are turned against him by the text itself. This irony complicates, however, any stable sense of textual reference. Our faith in documentary evidence is solicited by the text, but only by making the "reliability" of words an infinitely questionable, disputable matter.

What happens, though, to the concept of the *literary*—of literary, as opposed to ordinary language; and of the specifically literary text, as opposed to the kinds of documents one would more ordinarily expect the official state archive to house—in this ironic contrast between "documents" and "the mouths of their own authors"? On the one hand, one might argue that Pramoedya's text is simply not concerned with this issue at all at this point; or, perhaps even more likely, that he is precisely *not* interested in the literary—that what is expressed, ironically, but through the mouth of the archivist, is a certain dismissal of the whole question of the literary, with literary language, and perhaps above all the question of style, rhetoric, and trope. To the extent that one may trace a resistance to the literary here, though, it is just here that the concept of the literary emerges; and specifically in the suspicious form of Pangemanann's (in this passage implied) skeptical response to Tuan L. In fact, the grammatical and rhetorical form of the passage in question is underwritten by a complicated set of debates over the literary value of documents.

The passage is a response to Pangemanann's question about Tuan L.'s reading of the "serimpi dance" as a chance for native rulers "to sleep with the dancers" (*"untuk memilih teman tidur sehabis wanita-wanita itu berserimpi memperagakan tubuh"*)—"You're making this up, Meneer, aren't you?...Do you know that for sure? After all, you have probably never left this building, Meneer" (*H*, 69) (*"Tuan mengada-ada...sudah sejauh itu pengetahuan Tuan? Padahal Tuan barangkali tidak pernah beranjak dari gedung ini?"* [*RK*, 69]). Perhaps in itself really a rhetorical question—about how he can know what he's saying about the Javanese documents he is reading and giving "lectures" about; these documents of "high" Javanese literature are credited by Tuan L. with both a literary and a documentary value that arouses Pangemanann's suspicion in part because he seems to doubt their aesthetic value and in part because he questions Tuan L.'s claim to cultural authority—both are implied in the resentment he shows toward the praise Tuan L. heaps on these Javanese texts. Tuan L.'s response, therefore, constitutes a complicated answer to all of the things insinuated into Pangemanann's questioning of his philological authority. Moreover, the rhetorical shape of Pangemanann's question anticipates the form of Tuan L.'s response in a way that anticipates the trope of the archive that underwrites—and undoes—the logic of Tuan L.'s profession of faith in documents: he has said, in effect, "how can you be sure of the truth if you've never been outside of the archives?" The logic of this inside/outside, in close proximity to the question of documents and textuality, informs the grammatical shape of the response "Because documents are more reliable"—that is, more reliable than what's taken to be "outside" documents. What is not visible in the passage

excerpted in the epigraph is the object of Tuan L.'s philology—
Javanese literature, about which he has been lecturing
Pangemanann (and will continue to do so). Yet in a complicated
way this is indeed the vanishing object of Pramoedya's own postcolonial philology. It is both what he writes *against* and, putting
under erasure in the deconstructive sense, what is shown to be at
the foundation of European philological faith. This Javanese
literary sensibility, the epitome of refinement and culture, has
simultaneously been passed over and remains as the very problem
of literary value, the hidden figure and thought (notably, in the
form of Minke), rehearsed by the passage.

In this way, the trope of documentary reliability in Pramoedya's
text deconstructs the reliance on tropes in the text of twentieth-
century theory. Reiterating both the need to solicit linguistic, or
philological, expertise and the suspicious lack of any such linguistic,
or philological, certainty, what we characterized earlier as the
imperative to archival truth in the Buru tetralogy surfaces here all
at once as the overriding concern of all the work of Pramoedya's
years of Buru incarceration (to provide a testimonial documentary
truth), as the literary conceit of the tetralogy (based on Minke's
notes), and as the merely contingent rhetorical posture. Each
linguistic element of the Dutch archivist's statement is much more
pointedly rhetorical in the original Indonesian text; just to consider
the first three words, "*Soalnya memang kertas-kertas,*" these might
alternatively be translated "This is the problem, for sure, mere
paper." One might take this still further, in a move that ought indeed
to be questioned both from a linguistic and from a literary-critical
perspective, but that cannot easily be discounted without at least
minimal expertise in each, to point out that the specific term for
"documents" here—*kertas-kertas*—is not only a rhetorically unstable
synonym for the other terms used for "documents" in the surrounding text (most notably *naskah*) but also underscores the sense of
oral play that, as discussed above, underwrites the literary sense of
writing, since *kertas* registers a specifically onomatopoeic sense,
meaning also "the sound of paper being crumpled."[38]

The notorious instability of the trope of poststructuralist theory
is very much connected to the problem of historical reference,
often characterized as a legacy of the formalist ahistoricism that
follows Saussure's theoretical shift from diachronic to structural
linguistics. As is clear from an attentive reading of Paul de Man
and Jacques Derrida, the deconstructive attention to tropes does
not involve a rejection of history. The problem of referentiality
posed by the *aporia* of any tropological system may not provide a
stable sense of historical reference; but the very instability of the
trope also poses, by the same token, an irreducible problem of historical reference.[39] This, indeed, is how the trope of the (un)reli-
ability of archival documents in Pramoedya's *House of Glass*

works—both in the general sense of activating readers' suspicion about the way the history of Indonesia has been documented in the twentieth century, and in the more particular sense of having precipitated my own attempt, here, to reread the way we read and write the history of literary modernism.

Inherent in the theory of the trope is a problem of history that inflects all of the imperatives of postcolonial philology. Derrida articulates this problem, in "White Mythology" (*"La mythologie blanche"*), as the problem of the history of metaphor. In one particularly useful moment, he pinpoints this problem of reference simultaneously as a history of philosophical approaches to metaphor and as "the proposition" of Hegel's "speculative and dialectical logic" (*"la proposition de sa propre logique spéculative et dialectique"*).[40] The commonplace distinction between "living and dead metaphors" is revealed—in a long passage cited from the *Aesthetics*—to outline "the movement of metaphorization" that "is nothing other than a movement of idealization": the "mass of metaphors" that originally ("in the first place") make up "every language" gradually lose their "metaphorical element" and become simply literal expressions, whose "first sensuous meaning" then needs to be reactivated in order for their "spiritual meaning" to become clear. The most fitting example of this movement—which, to repeat, Derrida points out is nothing other than the movement of dialectical thinking itself—turns out to be (as Derrida only later, toward the end of his essay, relates) the metaphor of the sun's movement from east to west, yielding the trope of "Western" consciousness, what Derrida typically characterizes as "Western" metaphysics: the sensuous sun's apparent rising in the east and setting in the west yields to the spiritual metaphor of enlightenment, but only through internalizing the complex tropological association of this extended metaphor—forgetting the initial sensuous perception that the sun rises in the east and recollecting in consciousness that, in fact, it is the earth that moves around the sun—can one come to understand fully the spiritual meaning of the metaphor, grasping (again) the whole movement of "Western" enlightenment.

The passage Derrida cites from Hegel's *Aesthetics* is particularly interesting in drawing attention to what might be called, from a philological perspective, the necessarily retroactive movement of metaphor; and tropes generally (metaphor itself sometimes serving as the master trope of tropes, sometimes being classified as one trope among others). Hegel seeks to distinguish between "living languages," in which "the difference between actual metaphors and words already reduced by usage to literal expressions is easily established," and "dead languages," in which "this is difficult because mere etymology cannot decide the matter in the last resort." Hegel goes on to explain the difficulty here—and it is in this seemingly quaint philological focus, itself a sort of *mise-en-abyme* of nineteenth-century comparative philology, for which "dead languages" present the key to understanding the laws of linguistic change (in etymology and a study of inflections) in "living languages," that Derrida locates the "proposition of [Hegel's] own speculation and dialectical logic":

> The question does not depend on the first origin of a word or on linguistic development generally; on the contrary, the question above all is whether a word which looks entirely pictorial, deceptive, and illustrative has not already, in the life of the language, lost this its first sensuous meaning, and the memory of it, in the course of its use in a spiritual sense and been *relevé* (*AUFGEHOBEN HATTE*) into a spiritual meaning.[41]
>
> *Dans les langues vivantes, cette différence entre les métaphores effectives* [wirkliche Metaphern] *et celles qui, à force d'usure* [durch die Abnutzung], *se sont abîmées et sont tombées au rang d'expressions propres* [eigentliche Ausdrücken] *est facile à établir; au contraire, cela est difficile dans les langues mortes, car ici la seule étymologie peut nous fournir l'ultime partage, dans la mesure où il s'agit non de revenir à l'origine première et au développement linguistique mais surtout de recherché si un mot qui paraît colorer et illustrer tout à fait à la manière d'une peinture, n'a pas perdu cette première sienne signification sensible et le souvenir de celle-ci dans la vie du langage et par son usage dans le sens spirituel, et s'il ne l'a pas ainsi RELEVÉ* [AUFGEHOBEN HATTE] *dans la signification spirituelle.*[42]

Philology, we might say, is compelled to confront this problem of metaphor in the text of "dead languages" as an undecideable problem of historical reference. But we might add two further points implicit in Derrida's argument. First, the problem of historical reference, itself the problem of priority between literal and figurative meaning that so preoccupies twentieth-century theory, attends the reading of any text where it is not obvious whether the metaphor is consciously or unconsciously deployed by the author (consider, for example—and it is not just one example among others—the use of the metaphor of "Western" consciousness). The second point is that, faced with this undecideable problem of historical reference in any text (and also any language, living or dead, considered in textual form or in any form of documentary evidence), philology must engage in a retroactive process of historical reconstruction. To the extent that Hegel figures the act of philology here in terms of the movement of dialectical philosophy, philology represents a reversal of the movement of consciousness coming to know itself, retroactively engaged in a process of recovering what has been remembered and what forgotten in the movement of history.

The theoretical problem of the trope not only helps illuminate the reversibility of the Hegelian dialectic; the specifically philological work inherent in the difficulty of unraveling the history of any one trope also underscores the extent to which the movement of consciousness described by the Hegelian dialectic is necessarily bound to a logic of retroactive knowledge (akin to Freud's concept of *Nachträglichkeit*). If we can identify this process in the theory of the trope, we might also say that its philological practice is made manifest in any passage of text, considering "passage" here all at once in the literal sense of any fragment of text, and in its fully metaphorical sense, including that sense that might translate the Hegelian process of *Aufhebung*—any passage of text that takes us through a thought process that went into the writing of the passage, reactivating the dead meaning of its content and coming to full consciousness of its higher spiritual sense.

The inherently retroactive philological response to the theoretical problem of the trope is central to the imperatives of any postcolonial philology. If in many ways this is implicit in a range of figures associated with postcolonial literature and theory (Said, Spivak, Bhabha), one of the more explicit of recent attempts to articulate this postcolonial imperative is Srinivas Aravamudan's reading of a "tropicopolitan" perspective in the eighteenth century. Drawing on an eighteenth-century dictionary definition of *trope* and appropriating the *O.E.D.*'s definition of *tropicopolitan* to describe a species dominant in tropical regions, he proposes the term as follows:

> I would like to propose the term tropicopolitan as a name for the colonized subject who exists both as a fictive construct of colonial tropology *and* actual resident of tropical space, object of representation *and* agent of resistance. In many historical instances, tropicopolitans—the residents of the tropics, the bearers of its marks, and the shadow images of more visible metropolitans—challenge the developing privilege of Enlightenment cosmopolitans.[43]

Adapting the term retrospectively to reconceive our historical understanding of the eighteenth century, what he calls "the critical stakes of tropicalization as retroactive change"[44] turn the theoretical problem of priority inherent in any tropology into a program for "postcolonial criticism that interrogates the ideological constraints of the national paradigm (and hence the very project of canonical literary history) but that also does justice to the accumulated archival richness of period specializations."[45] As Aravamudan's examples themselves richly show, the "retroactive change" enabled by such applications of what Derrida calls "tropic supplementarity" ("*la supplémentarité tropique*")[46] to literary history call attention to a contest of metropolitan colonial perspectives that has all along characterized the nature of colonial modernity. Many of Aravamudan's central examples confirm a historical point we have been following through the preceding studies—namely, that the hegemony of English national paradigms is itself deeply underwritten by prior Creole literary, historical, and cultural perspectives. Creole modernism has arguably always informed English modernism, constituting what Michael Dash characterizes as (reformulating Édouard Glissant) the "repeated detour in modernist thought."[47] As Dash's larger argument about "tropes and tropicality" emphasizes, however, this leaves open the question as to whether the historical priority of these Creole perspectives can displace the hegemony of English or must perpetually be reinscribed as exotic departures from the linguistic norm ("modernisms" in the O.E.D.'s first definition of that word).[48]

Decolonizing English and the O.E.D.

Postcolonial philological imperatives are at work in all these various theories of the trope. Both in a practical and a theoretical sense, these imperatives have shaped the preceding studies, their attempts to situate the linguistic-literary formations of English, Creole, and Indonesian modernisms, and their evaluation of the priority given to the individual passage of text held up for critical analysis. The sense of postcolonial philology to emerge is a philology without guarantees, but oriented toward as full as possible a retroactive accounting for the coordinates of transnational modernism. Drawing together a wide variety of studies that have long been premised on the theoretical critique and practical adaptation of comparative philology, such a postcolonial philology forms part of an unfinished, ongoing process of decolonizing English. Simultaneously encyclopedic in its historical, cultural, and comparative linguistic scope, and necessarily fragmentary and incomplete, this decolonizing of English follows the parallel precedent of the two philological projects that have defined the historical scope of this study: the formation of the O.E.D., on the one hand, and Pramoedya's attempt to document the formation of *bahasa Indonesia*, on the other.

These two philological projects, of course, stand in striking contrast, the one to the other. Whereas the O.E.D. represents the completion of a huge collective philological undertaking that, with the successive publication of different entries from the 1880s to the 1930s, constitutes an enduring archive documenting the linguistic and literary development of the English language, Pramoedya's work—and above all the work of Buru—is premised on the destruction of documents researching the history of the Indonesian language. Put this way, the contrast appears to confirm a political inequality that is all the more pronounced at the beginning of the twenty-first century: the hegemony of English as a language, as the language of globalization, continues to be supported by the authority of a huge colonial archive; while the destruction of Pramoedya's documents would appear to confirm a collective and globalizing loss of memory about the history of anti-colonial struggles. Yet these two projects interrelate in more important and more interesting ways than as emblems of domination and subordination. Pramoedya's efforts to recover the fragmentary documentation of the history of the Indonesian language during the turn of the century provide a model for how to read the *O.E.D.*'s archive of the English language.

In the gaps and biases of its colonial presuppositions, the *O.E.D.* documents the emergence of a set of modernist linguistic and literary questions, doubts, and suspicions. The principle of documentation by which each word is tracked according to a mini-anthology of quotations, passages of text that show the usage of words, makes the *O.E.D.* an archive of literary and linguistic fragments. This feature of what Hugh Kenner took to be an analogous sort of lapidary work to that of a Poundian or Joycean English modernism, turns each entry into a place where English words are constantly open to the destabilizing effects of a reading forced to consider the priorities of a word's history as it appears in this or that passage of text. The project of stabilizing and regulating "standard" English usage by placing each word in historical context has the effect of archiving the permanently destabilizing history of English; an archaeology, then, of the future decolonization of English.

In any *O.E.D* entry—as in any passage of literature grasped from a postcolonial philological perspective—we confront a range of different philologies and philological presumptions. Considering, by comparison, how the undocumented history of *bahasa Indonesia* shapes the imperatives of the dialogue between the colonial archivist and Pangemanann, we might sum up the range of things Pramoedya's decolonizing of tradition can apply to the work of decolonizing English implicit in the *O.E.D.* Between the dictionary definition of an English word and the citations used to illustrate that definition we can trace the same underlying set of questions opened up by the colonial archivist's contrast between the reliability of "documents" and the "mouths of their own authors." The most immediate object of philological study in this passage is, of course, Javanese—not Indonesian—but this is itself revealing for the way Pramoedya's passage stages the vanishing object of philology. Historically, the *O.E.D.* sets up an object of study analogous to the "Javanese" that is Tuan L.'s area of linguistic and literary expertise. What the *O.E.D.* in fact documents is the emergence of something closer to the *bahasa Indonesia* that shapes the dialogue in which Tuan L. articulates his reliance in documents. Attending to the distinction between the *literary* and *linguistic* emphases of the *O.E.D.*'s examples, one reads the literary examples as a "high" literary form of English that then is supplemented by those instances of ordinary usage given by newspapers or other nonliterary forms. The way these interact, however, enacts a far-reaching displacement of one's sense of "standard English"—somewhat analogous to the shift from Javanese to Indonesian. The relation between a definition and its citations consolidates the cultural capital of English as a stratification of different literary forms. Although it would be wrong to insist on a comparison between the high canonical assumptions of the *O.E.D.*'s citations and the stratified language of Javanese, while associating the everyday examples from newspapers or journals, by contrast, to Indonesian, what is revealing about the analogy is the recognition of an interplay between a presumed high literary competence (analogous to the archivist's expertise in Javanese) and an everyday discourse.

The analogy might be put this way: the *O.E.D.* seeks to build a total historical picture of the evolution of the English language, ambitiously grasping how the various strands of literary, extraliterary, and everyday language have contributed to producing a language similar to that of Javanese—a hierarchically organized language ("standard English") that engages speakers from different classes, using different forms of the language, but adhering to a common linguistic enterprise. This view of "standard English," however, confronts another language that occupies an overlapping and adjacent space—another level of stratification whose clearest cutting edge is the relation between English and non-English. Each *O.E.D.* dictionary entry, in this sense, rehearses a similar kind of confrontation as that between Tuan L. and Pangemanann over the question of Javanese documents: the confrontation between the expertise the dictionary offers and the way that expertise is put to use by readers.

The *O.E.D.*'s reliance on quotations provides the evidence for its claim to base the dictionary "on historical principles"; and indeed, the 1.8 million some quotations (as noted in the 1933 Preface) constitute a formidable archive of enormous literary and linguistic value. Yet between each example and its dictionary definition there exists a gap that opens up the question of the linguistic history of that word. The organizing historical principle of the *O.E.D.*'s deployment of quotations to illustrate the changing meaning of words and idioms relies on a positivist faith in being able to situate the individual passage of text within a single historical development. The need to evaluate the context from which the quotation has been taken, however, fundamentally shifts the certainty of the history being documented.

If the *O.E.D.* is dominated by the colonial biases of its main authors, this very bias foregrounds a "tropicopolitan" perspective (in Aravamudan's sense). One example (discussed in chapter 3) is the entry (in section B. 2) on *azure:* "Coloured like the unclouded sky; *orig.* of a deep intense blue, *now* usually of a soft clear bright blue, as is the sky of our more northern latitudes; sky-coloured, cerulean." It is not easy to separate the *historical* claims of this definition from cultural bias introduced by the phrase "our more northern latitudes."[49] This striking instance of what Aravamudan might describe as a metropolitan exclusion of a "tropicopolitan" perspective—by definition seeming to exclude those who live in more southern, tropical climates—raises the suspicion that *azure* might still be applied to the "deep intense blue" of more southern latitudes. Having once noticed the insinuation of such biases, however, the historical basis of each entry is open to a similar questioning of the historical priority accorded, on the evidence of the selected passages, to each word or idiom. The entry on *azure* (and its choice of characteristically poetic, metaphorical literary passages) itself is a highly complicated example of Derrida's "tropic supplementarity": the distinction between northern and southern perspectives turns on the metaphor that gives color (and different shades of color) to the word; and so, by extension, affects or afflicts every distinction the *O.E.D.* attempts to make between a meaning's "original" meaning and the meaning it has "now"—the movement of history figured as a movement of geography or, rather, literally and necessarily figuratively also as a movement of the sun. Having registered this contest between northern and southern perspectives, the dictionary entry opens up a historical question of priorities in cultural representation that is, in the strictly deconstructive sense, undecideable. It is impossible to decide whether the original definition claims a universal "we" that might equally be used in referring to "our southern latitudes" or whether it betrays a "northern" hemispheric collective identity. That doubt colors the entire range of historical and semantic distinctions informing the dictionary entry on *azure,* recalling what Ford Madox Ford claimed about Conrad's "indictment of the English language": "that no English word is a word; that all English words are instruments for exciting blurred emotions" (and recalling, too, of course, the special attention Ford and Conrad gave to the word *azure*).[50] The suspicion this provokes for a postcolonial philology is both theoretically and practically significant in marking the instability of the presumed order of historical priorities, turning the dictionary definition (and its anthology of quotations) into the evidence for a prior set of meanings than those given by the "standard" English meaning. The very insistence on calling attention to "our more northern latitudes"—like the biased perspective of Tuan L. in *House of Glass,* when he says that "documents" are far more reliable than the mouths of their authors—insinuates the excluded historical perspectives of those from more southern latitudes.

This problem of cultural-historical priority calls attention to the ways in which each entry of the *O.E.D.*, in its effort to locate the changing meaning of its word in reference to the quotations it selects, enacts a material displacement or dislocation of culture. This is not only a matter of the exclusion of cultural information that does not suit the dominant metropolitan norm of "standard English"—although, to be sure, all the entries of the *O.E.D.* need to be read with that suspicion. What makes the *O.E.D.* so valuable an archive for postcolonial philology is the way it documents the material dislocation of the "now" that appears to fix the colonial present-tense bias of the one who speaks of "our more northern latitudes" in the entry on *azure*. There is a material historical synchrony, as it were, in the relation of the word to the citations used to document the word's place in history. In the same movement that retroactively restores the "original" meaning of *azure* to give perspective to "our" present sense of the word, the dictionary entry invites a reading of the quotations as the material documentation of a contest of perspectives (a theoretical *différance*, in Derrida's formulation, but also what Lyotard calls the *differend:* the materiality of a disputed reading—e.g., over the color blue, its material properties in a scientific and also in a cultural sense). Any single passage of literature becomes a testing of the word's changing meaning against a literary authority, and also a testing of literary authority against other uses of the word. Literary authority—the cultural capital of a stratification of literary and linguistic values—is invoked in each citation. What the passage of literature registers is not merely a dispute over the meaning of words; refracted through the quoted passage is a material history of contest over cultural capital.

Pramoedya's use of the word *all-round* (discussed in chapter 1 and at the end of chapter 7) both overlaps with and departs from the English definition of the word in the *O.E.D.*, marking a striking gap in the *O.E.D.*'s philological record of the linguistic and cultural coordinates of the word: a gap between the colonial English associations of the *O.E.D.*'s definitions and the anti-colonial Indonesian sentiments attached to Pramoedya's mother's usage of this "foreign" word. The gap may in part be bridged through the example of C. L. R. James, whose *Beyond the Boundary* inflects the word with a West Indian ethos of cricket that resituates the colonial coordinates of the word within the long historical perspective of decolonization. C. L. R. James remains rooted, of course, in the same English-language experience as that of the *O.E.D.*—indeed, his contextualization of the word is in many respects far more convincing, more deeply rooted in an English-language experience, than the examples from the *O.E.D.* This recontextualization offers a paradigmatic instance of Creole modernism, reconstellating the English word with a set of cultural coordinates that gives it a depth of historical and political perspective seemingly absent from the transparent simplicity of its appearance in the *O.E.D.* In this sense, C. L. R. James points to a far-reaching contestation of a hegemonic colonial English perspective.[51] The Indonesian historical context suggested by Pramoedya's mother's use of the word opens this field of contestation wider still. The very distance between the English colonial coordinates of the *O.E.D.*, the West Indies coordinates of C. L. R. James's experience, and the Dutch East Indies coordinates of Pramoedya's mother's experience provides a window onto a contemporaneity of different, contested educational ideals. The gap in historical experience marked by what is left out of the *O.E.D.*'s definition signals a further contest of historical perspective, albeit one that remains fundamentally open and unresolved.

C. L. R. James's recontextualization of the word *all-round* stands in a similar kind of relation to the *O.E.D.* as does Raymond Williams's project, as realized in *Culture and Society* and *Keywords*. The "extraordinary advantage of the great Oxford *Dictionary*,"[52] as Williams puts it, provides a hugely important archival record, an extremely useful historical starting point for the sort of inquiry into "vocabulary" that Williams developed in those studies, and that laid the groundwork for contemporary cultural studies.[53] In a number of ways, what emerges from supplementing the *O.E.D.*'s definition of *all-round* with the perspective of C. L. R. James reinforces how cultural studies can capitalize on the three limitations Williams identifies in the *O.E.D.*: the historical period in which it emerged (1880s–1920s); its "primarily philological and etymological" principles; and its dependence on "the written language...as the real source of authority."[54] All three of these limitations are turned to an advantage in C.L.R. James's juxtaposition of the keyword *culture* with that cluster of associations whose historical (anti-colonial) significance eludes the *O.E.D.* definition of *all-round*. His use of the word reconstellates our understanding of the "structure of feeling" (in another of Williams's formulations) associated with both words (*culture* and *all-round*). The "extraordinary advantage" of the *O.E.D.* is not coincidentally linked to the limitations of its historical moment (the height of imperialism), of its philological and etymological biases (grounded in European comparative philology), and of the authority of the "written language." These limitations point to the ways in which the *O.E.D.* is a limiting archive—an archive in the sense developed by Brent Edwards (drawing on Foucault): "*archive*...not so much...a site or mode of preservation of a national, institutional, or individual past, but instead...a discursive system that governs the possibilities, forms, appearance, and regularity of particular statements, objects, and practices."[55] Yet the *O.E.D.*'s archive, in this sense, is also haunted by the kind of creolizing and diasporic cultural practices—including the phonographic and photographic traces of such structures of feeling—that haunt the work of Jean Rhys (as we discussed in chapter 4). The cultural capital of the *O.E.D.*'s linguistic and literary documentation of a hegemonic English is precisely what lays it open to the sort of contestation and reversal of historical perspective made available by the examples from C. L. R. James and Pramoedya.

Documents, in this sense, may be more reliable than the "mouths" of their authors because they provide data for the philologist that may have little do with the original "intentions" of the authors. If such a foreign—philological—reading of literature is what Tuan L. and the authors of the *O.E.D.* have in common, the manner in which each effects a fundamental estrangement of the literary and linguistic coordinates of their object of philology (Javanese and English, respectively) makes their philological expertise transformative in a way that turns the documents of their respective cultures into the documentation of a linguistic creolizing process, even—perhaps especially—where that creolizing process is contained or incorporated into efforts to shore up cultural value (the prestige of Javanese, "standard English"). In this sense, the citations in the *O.E.D.* also resemble the innumerable passages of text collected in Benjamin's *Arcades Project*. Their encyclopedic documentary reach is capable of effecting a rearrangement of perspectives or a reconstellation of "structures of feeling."

If each word in the *O.E.D.* has the potential to become a "dialectical image" in Benjamin's sense, a key feature of this potential is the way each English word not only enacts a historical displacement of standard English but also represents a force field of different interacting linguistic systems and "structures of feeling." *Azure* offers a visible instance of this in part because the Arabic and Persian sources of the word are displayed in the dictionary's description of its morphology, calling for the use of Persian script. In the original *O.E.D.*, the space of romanized print has not yet erased the multiplicity of scripts that underwrite the multilinguistic historical coordinates of the word.[56] *All-round*, by contrast, is a word that appears to embody the hegemony of a global English. The scope of that hegemony, however, only begins to emerge from the multilinguistic context within which *all-round* signifies a potentially revolutionary, anti-colonial word (a monolingualism or "globalatinization" of other, Creole or Indonesian experiences).

The cultural capital embedded in such words as *azure* and *all-round* is the result of a long and uneven history of overlapping, discontinuous, and contested cultural systems. This cultural capital can be measured by balancing the "extraordinary advantage" of the *O.E.D* against the striking disadvantages that faced Pramoedya in his efforts to document the historical formation of *bahasa*

Indonesia. The richness of archival historical perspective registered by the *O.E.D.* stands in dialectical relation to the necessarily limited documentary evidence available to Pramoedya. The very limitations of archival evidence confronting Pramoedya, however, produced a practice of reading that has important implications for reading the archival wealth of the *O.E.D.* Each entry of the *O.E.D.* is an effect of polyglossia that opens the word to a "heteroglossia" of present and future meaning. This creolizing effect also calls into question the written archive's depth of historical perspective—first, literally by reading as the prior "word of another" (Bakhtin's *raznorečie*) the written record of the word (the counter-historical move whereby the English meaning of the word *azure* or *all-round* is revealed in its Caribbean or West Indian context: producing, perhaps, a prior historical orientation other than that provided by the *O.E.D.*); and then by measuring the written record against gaps that signal a surrounding absence of other undocumented oral and written resources (as with Pramoedya's recollection of his mother's educational ideal, the word *all-round* functioning as a gap that potentially shows the links between discrepant, overlapping educational systems).

It is the imperative to read the *O.E.D.* both for the wealth of its linguistic and literary archive and for its gaps that recalls what Mignolo, discussing what gets obscured by the rise of alphabetic writing systems in the Renaissance, describes as "colonial semiosis." As noted earlier, Mignolo, following A. L. Becker, adapts Ortega y Gasset's two axioms for a "new philology": "(1) every word is exuberant, because it says more than intended; (2) every word is deficient, because it says less then expected."[57] The first axiom speaks to the rich "exuberant" field of English colonial and anti-colonial associations that may be found documented by the *O.E.D.* (taking advantage of that document together with the limitations and biases that call for a reading against its colonial grain—the word says more than its supposedly colonial articulation intended). The second axiom speaks to the lack—or rather loss—of referential context for understanding just what cluster of associations are evoked in the *O.E.D.*, or in any passage of literature. But these two axioms work to bring together dialectically the simultaneously exuberant and deficient semiotic fields of reference found, respectively, in the *O.E.D.*'s documentation of English and Pramoedya's documentation of Indonesian. Linking Mignolo's notion of "colonial semiosis" with what Raymond Williams does in taking off from the "extraordinary advantage" of the *O.E.D.*, while adjusting to its "limitations," we might conceive of the *O.E.D.* not only as a product of English modernism but also as its archival displacement, first by Creole modernism and then again by Indonesian modernism. In each entry's selection of illustrative passages of literature, one might recognize a "colonial semiosis" at work that reveals the overlapping imperatives in each of these three linguistic-literary formations. It is an archive that might be read, according to the three principles of a postcolonial philology outlined above, as: (1) identifying the semiotic drift of words between languages; (2) registering (more than intended) a dislocation of material culture; and (3) effecting a reversal of historical priorities (whereby the "colonial" field of reference is preceded by a logic of decolonization).

These three general postcolonial imperatives delineate together, then, a sequence of procedures for analyzing the individual passage of literature. In the first step, which our study has associated with the linguistic-literary formation of English modernism, the attempt to grasp a text's relation to the horizon of universal human history is confronted with the impasse of modernity: the form of the text's relation to history is only legible through the break from tradition that has shaped the text's fragmentary form, but literary modernism cannot define that break without recourse to some prior moment of modernity. This impasse already leads to the next step, which we have associated with Creole modernism: the passage of text is read as the product of a material contest over discrepant cultural perspectives. The final step, associated with Indonesian modernism, is to read the text as the site of a semiotic rift between overlapping, discrepant culture systems. The individual passage of literature remains a powerful touchstone for cultural capital precisely because it registers the gaps and breaks in cultural history. It is these gaps and breaks that link the alien genealogies of modernism and modernity we have been tracing through the linguistic-literary formations of English, Creole, and Indonesian modernisms. The theory and practice of postcolonial philology promises (but cannot guarantee) a way to read passages of literature as the gaps between and breaks in such overlapping and discrepant linguistic, literary, and cultural formations.

NOTES

Chapter 1

1. In his *Keywords: A Vocabulary of Culture and Society* (New York: Oxford University Press, 1985), Raymond Williams offers a useful distinction between the range of meanings associated with the word *modern* and the "more specialized" definition of *modernism:* "Modernism and modernist have become more specialized, to particular tendencies, notably to the experimental art and writing of c.1890–c.1940" (208).

2. A partial list of key critics whose work has helped consolidate Conrad's centrality to genealogies of English modernism includes: F. R. Leavis, Albert Guerard, Fredric Jameson, Edward Said, Geoffrey Galt Harpham. Consider also Michael Levenson, Marianne DeKoven, Michael North.

3. A partial list of critics who have placed Rhys at the heart of contested genealogies of Creole modernism includes: Wilson Harris, Peter Hulme, Kamau Brathwaite, Veronica Gregg, Sue Thomas, Judith Raiskin, Elaine Savory, Carolyn Vellenga Berman.

4. Benedict Anderson and James Siegel have been the two most important authorities writing in English on Pramoedya. Anderson's essays in his *Language and Power: Exploring Political Cultures in Indonesia* (Ithaca, N.Y.: Cornell University Press, 1990) and, implicitly, the argument of his *Imagined Communities: Reflections on the Origin and Spread of Nationalism* (London: Verso, 1991) have been the most influential; James Siegel's *Fetish, Recognition, Revolution* (Princeton, N.J.: Princeton University Press, 1997) emphasizes the significance of Pramoedya's nonfiction work for the history of Indonesian modernism. More recent English-language assessments of Pramoedya's significance for Indonesian modernism include Pheng Cheah's *Spectral Nationality: Passages of Freedom from Kant to Postcolonial Literatures of Liberation* (New York: Columbia University Press, 2003); and Razif Bahari, *Pramoedya Postcolonially: (Re-) Viewing History, Gender and Identity in the Buru Tetralogy* (Denpasar, Bali: Pustaka Larasan, 2007). See also Keith Foulcher, Henk Maier, Rudolf Mrázek. The first major book-length study of Pramoedya's life and work was A. Teeuw's Dutch-language *Pramoedya Ananta Toer: De verbeelding van Indonesië* (Breda: de Geus, 1993).

5. See, for example, Michael North, *The Dialect of Modernism: Race, Language, and Twentieth-Century Literature* (Oxford: Oxford University Press, 1994); Elleke Boehmer, *Empire, the National, and the Postcolonial, 1890–1920* (Oxford: Oxford University Press, 2002); and Brent Hayes Edwards, *The Practice of Diaspora: Literature, Translation, and the Rise of Black Internationalism* (Cambridge, Mass.: Harvard University Press, 2003).

6. See, for example, Richard Begam and Michael Valdez Moses, eds, *Modernism and Colonialism: British and Irish Literature 1899–1939* (Durham, N.C.: Duke University Press, 2007).

7. See, especially, Boehmer, *Empire, the National, and the Postcolonial;* and Edwards, *Practice of Diaspora*.

8. Susan Stanford Friedman, "Periodizing Modernism: Postcolonial Modernities and the Space/Time Borders of Modernist Studies," *Modernism/modernity* 13, no.3 (2006), 423–43, 426; 427.

9. Ibid, 428.

10. Françoise Lionnet, "Continents and Archipelagoes: From *E Pluribus Unum* to Creolized Solidarities," *PMLA* 123, no. 5 (October 2008), 1503–15; 1503.

11. Two rather different examples, both of which might be taken as successful efforts to create a paradigm shift in conceiving the coordinates of modernity, broadly conceived, are Mary Louise Pratt's *Imperial Eyes: Travel Writing and Transculturation* (London: Routledge, 1992); and Susan Buck-Morss's *Hegel, Haiti, and Universal History* (Pittsburgh: University of Pittsburgh Press, 2009).

12. It is notable, though, that Françoise Lionnet expands the scope of "creolization" to an archipelagic theoretical model that links the poetics of Caribbean writers with the politics of decolonization in the Philippines and Indonesia.

13. Roland Barthes's "The Death of the Author" (in *Image, Music, Text*, trans. Stephen Heath, 142–154 [New York: Hill and Wang, 1977]) provides one of the most celebrated statements of this predicament. Michel Foucault's "What Is an Author?" (in *Language, Counter-Memory, Practice: Selected Essays and Interviews*, trans., Donald F. Bouchard and Sherry Simon, 113–138 [Ithaca, N. Y.: Cornell University Press, 1977]) offers a reformulation, and critique, of Barthes, but reiterating the characteristically French modernist coordinates of Barthes's articulation (from Mallarmé to Proust). Edward Said's *Beginnings: Intention and Method* (New York: Columbia University Press, 1985) provides an especially useful and extended meditation on this problem, especially as it relates to what we consider here as the linguistic-literary formation of English modernism.

14. For ongoing debates about the validity of "world literature" as a category, its relation to new global paradigms of comparative study, and especially the legacy of Goethe's fragmentary comments on the category, see the essays in Christopher Prendergast's *Debating World Literature* (London: Verso, 2004); and Haun Saussy's *Comparative Literature in an Age of Globalization* (Baltimore: Johns Hopkins University Press, 2006).

15. Pramoedya Ananta Toer, *Tempo Doeloe: Antologi Sastra Pra-Indonesia* (Jakarta: Hasta Mitra, 1982), 9.

16. See Zdzisław Najder, *Joseph Conrad: A Life* (Rochester, N.Y.: Camden House, 2007), 72; North, *Dialect of Modernism*, 49–50.

17. Pratt, *Imperial Eyes*, 6.

18. I have discussed this at greater length in my *The Invention of the West: Joseph Conrad and the Double-Mapping of Europe and Empire*

(Stanford: Stanford University Press, 1995). See also Said, *Beginnings;* Geoffrey Galt Harpham, *One of Us: the Mastery of Joseph Conrad* (Chicago: University of Chicago Press, 1996); and J. H. Stape, "Narrating Identity in *A Personal Record*," in Jakob Lothe et. al., eds., *Joseph Conrad: Voice, Sequence, History, Genre* (Columbus, Ohio: Ohio University Press, 2008; 217–235).

19. Victor Hugo, *The Toilers of the Sea,* trans. Isabel F. Hapgood (New York: Signet, 2000), 35; *Les Travailleurs de la mer: Romans,* vol 3 (Paris: Editions du Seuil, 1963), 183.

20. Hugo, *Toilers of the Sea,* 93; Hugo, *Travailleurs,* 22.

21. Johann Wolfgang von Goethe, *Essays on Art and Literature,* ed. John Gearey, trans. Ellen von Nardroff and Ernest H. von Nardroff (Princeton: Princeton University Press, 1986), 228; Goethe, *Goethes Werke,* vol. 43 (Weimar: Hermann Böhlaus, 1908), 106.

22. Homi Bhabha, *The Location of Culture* (London: Routledge, 1994), 12.

23. Ibid.

24. See, in particular, Edward Kamau Brathwaite, *The Development of Creole Society in Jamaica* and *Contradictory Omens;* Édouard Glissant, *Le discours antillais* (1981) and *Poétique de la Relation* (1990), both of which are combined in the 1997 French text *Le discours antillais* (Paris: Gallimard, 1997) and its partial English translation as *Caribbean Discourse: Selected Essays,* trans. J. Michael Dash (Charlottesville: University Press of Virginia, 1989).

25. Glissant, *Caribbean Discourse,* 125; Glissant, *Discours antillais,* 408.

26. Glissant, *Caribbean Discourse,* 126; Glissant, *Discours antillais,* 410.

27. Anderson, *Imagined Communities,* 25.

28. Ibid., 47ff.

29. Carolyn Vellenga Berman's *Creole Crossings:Domestic Fiction and the Reform of Colonial Slavery* (Ithaca, N.Y.: Cornell University Press, 2006) explores at length the significance of this shift for domestic fiction throughout the nineteenth century and into the twentieth century. Situating Jean Rhys's work at the heart of her study—as we shall discuss further in part II—Berman also calls attention to Anderson's formulation of the "creole pioneers" of nationalism. Although she exaggerates the extent to which Anderson "defines these 'creole pioneers' as exclusively white settlers in the Americas" (5), the corrective draws attention to the complex contest over shifting alliances and antagonisms over racial identities and identifications that constitute the "creole pioneers" of early nationalism. Berman's critique—and adoption—of Anderson, is illuminated by Fawzia Mustafa's argument (in "Categories of Hybridity: Caribbean Proliferations" [talk delivered at the Association of Caribbean Studies 17th Annual Conference, Manaus, Brazil, 1995, TS, 8]) that "the originality" of Anderson's formulation is effective in large part because the inherent hybridity of the term "creole" makes it "a multiple signifier" whose "application, whether through race, sex, or culture is always political."

30. Glissant, *Caribbean Discourse,* 125; Glissant, *Discours antillais,* 408.

31. Ibid.

32. This has now become a key point of reference for the critical reception of Rhys's work. See, for example Gregg, Thomas, and Savory, as well

as the touchstone disagreement (discussed in Savory) between Brathwaite and Hulme over whether or not Rhys can be considered a West Indian writer.

33. The bracketed passage is not included in the English edition. Unless otherwise noted, all translations of passages omitted from the English translation of Pramoedya's prison notes, *The Mute's Soliloquy*, are my own.

34. Willem Samuels translates the key word "all-round" as "all around" and adds that the mother is using an "English" word. I have modified the translation to register the form of the "foreign phrase" (*kata asing*) as it appears in the original.

35. The word "all-round" appears as an English word in the *O.E.D.* and as an Indonesian word in John M. Echols and Hassan Shadily, *An Indonesian-English Dictionary* (3rd ed., Ithaca, N.Y.: Cornell University Press, 1989).

36. In "My Apologies, in the Name of Experience" Pramoedya lists *A Preliminary Study of the History of the Indonesian Language* and "the two volumes of *Pre-Indonesian Literature*" among a set of manuscripts destroyed. (See Alex G. Bardsley's translation [*Indonesia* 61 (April)], 11.)

37. A. Teeuw, *Modern Indonesian Literature*, vol. 1 (Dordrecht: Foris, 1986), 23.

38. Ibid., 22–23; Anderson, *Imagined Communities*, 133; Henk Maier, *We Are Playing Relatives: A Survey of Malay Writing* (Leiden: KITVL Press, 2004), 20–21; Adrian Vickers, *A History of Modern Indonesia* (Cambridge: Cambridge University Press, 2005), 80; Max Lane, *Unfinished Nation: Indonesia Before and After Suharto* (London: Verso, 2008), 272; and Tineke Hellwig and Eric Tagliacozzo, eds., *The Indonesia Reader: History, Culture, Politics* (Durham, N.C.: Duke University Press, 2009), 269–70.

39. Anderson, *Imagined Communities*, 133.

40. Cited in Anderson, *Imagined Communities*, 117.

41. Ibid., 118.

42. The historical 1913 article is referred to in the final volume of the tetralogy, but by this time Minke has been replaced by the first-person narrator of the police agent, Pangemanann.

43. James Siegel, *Fetish, Recognition, Revolution* (Princeton: Princeton University Press, 1997), 30–31.

44. Ibid., 28.

45. Anderson, *Imagined Communities*, 133.

46. Siegel, *Fetish, Recognition, Revolution*, 62.

47. Cited in Siegel, *Fetish, Recognition, Revolution*, 17.

48. Pramoedya, *Tempo Doeloe*, 1. This phrase—*semangat semasa*—might more literally be translated "feeling of the time"; but I borrow Raymond Williams's formulation here because Pramoedya's historical argument in the introduction to this anthology stands in revealing counterpoint to Williams's theoretical elaboration of "structures of feeling" (see, for example, *Marxism and Literature* [Oxford: Oxford University Press], 128–135).

49. So, for example, "The tales of 'modern' authors such as Hamka, Pramoedya Ananta Toer, and Shahnon Ahmad lend themselves very well to 'sweet' and 'melodious' recitation in the tradition of Hang Jebat's performance, keeping up the dialogue between sounds in the air and words on paper" (Maier, *We Are Playing Relatives*, 51).

50. Of the word for "reading," *baca*, Maier writes: "The translation we find in most dictionaries is 'to read,' but then 'to read' certainly does not cover everything that is evoked by *membaca*. *Baca* (and its variant *membaca*) refer to 'read' and 'recite' at once, to the movement of the eyes as well as to the movement of the vocal chords, to 'silence' as well as to 'sound,' but also to 'leaning on paper' and 'leaning on memory.' *Baca*, in other words, points in many directions, calling up a network of other words in its wake when we try to read it in its English mirror" (*We Are Playing*, 40). Maier goes on: "Closely related to *baca* and its connotations of memorable and, therefore, relevant knowledge is the term *karang*, which is usually translated as 'compose,' 'put in order,' 'formulate.' *Baca* and *karang* are best described as being two aspects of the same activity, one moving backward, the other moving forward: *baca* refers to the activity of repeating letters or sounds, *karang* refers to the activity of arranging letters or sounds into fragrant garlands—or bouquets—of words, sentences, fragments...everyone who is involved in the act of *baca* is also involved in the act of *karang*" (41–42).

51. Pramoedya, *Tempo Doeloe*, 1.

52. Michel Foucault, "What is an Author?" in *Language, Counter-Memory, Practice: Selected Essays and Interviews* (trans., Donald F. Bouchard and Sherry Simon, Ithaca, N. Y.: Cornell University Press, 1977); see esp. 123–124; and Michel Foucault, "Qu'est-ce qu'un auteur?" (*Bulletin de la Société française de Philosophie*, 63, No. 3 (1969), 73–104; esp. 83.

53. Ibid., 116; 78.

54. Toward the end of his life, reflecting back on the moment when he turned to write about his Polish background in *A Personal Record*, Conrad wrote to Charles Chassé, complaining about critics who "stuck" the "label" "Slavonism" on him because "they had discovered the existence of Russian authors": "I have asked myself more than once whether if I had preserved the secret of my origins under the neutral pseudonym of "Joseph Conrad" that temperamental similitude would have been put forward at all" (G. Jean-Aubry, *Joseph Conrad: Life and Letters*, vol. 2 [New York: Doubleday, 1927], 336).

55. Smith discusses Conrad's preoccupation with "the semiotics of his identity" not only on the evidence of the different signatures Conrad used corresponding roughly with the "three lives" of his Polish childhood (Konrad Korzeniowski), British merchant service (Joseph Conrad Korzeniowski), and literary career (Joseph Conrad), but also on the evidence of the "layering" of those signature identities (above all in the obsessive alternation between "K" and "C") in the marginal jottings of his manuscripts: "If he jotted these signs in books and used them to arrange his fantasy life, it is not surprising that he put them in those manuscripts that involve a deep sense of himself: *Lord Jim, Nostromo, Under Western Eyes*." See David R. Smith, "The Hidden Narrative: The *K* in Conrad," in Smith, ed., *Joseph Conrad's Under Western Eyes: Beginnings, Revisions, Final Forms* (Hamden, Conn.: Archon, 1991), 42–43.

56. See Joseph Conrad, *The Collected Letters of Joseph Conrad*, eds. Frederick Karl and Laurence Davies, vol. 1 (Cambridge: Cambridge University Press, 1983), 168.

57. I follow Rhys's biographer, Carole Angier (*Jean Rhys: Life and Work* [Boston: Little, Brown, 1990]), in spelling her first name "Gwendoline," although Rhys, in *Smile Please* (14), spells it "Gwendolen."

58. Peter Hulme, "The Locked Heart," 76.

59. For alternative accounts of the political context of this period of instability, see M. C. Ricklefs, *A History of Modern Indonesia Since c. 1300*, 2nd ed. (Stanford: Stanford University Press, 1993), esp. 253–56; Vickers, *History of Modern Indonesia*, esp. 140–41; and Lane, *Unfinished Nation*, esp. 26–41.

60. Jean Rhys, *The Letters of Jean Rhys*, eds. Francis Wyndham and Diana Melly (New York: Viking, 1984), 148.

61. If Pramoedya, rather than Toer, is the standard Indonesian way to refer to the author, it should be noted that the full name (along with such characteristic shortened references as "Pram") nonetheless also plays an important function in referring to the work of the author. For example, the legal historian, poet, and Conrad critic G. J. Resink, to whom Pramoedya dedicated the first two novels of the Buru tetralogy, preferred to call Pramoedya by his last name because of "its affinity with the Javanese word *toetoer*, for "storyteller" (see my "Pramoedya's Fiction and History: An Interview with Indonesian Novelist Pramoedya Ananta Toer," *Yale Journal of Criticism* 9, no. 1 (1996),163).

62. Pramoedya Ananta Toer, "Blora," trans. Harold Merrill, *Indonesia* 53 (April), 51.

63. The counterpoint between all three genealogies might be read according to the following three theoretical formulations: Edward Said's "affiliative theory" (see *The World, the Text, and the Critic* [Cambridge, Mass.: Harvard University Press, 1983]); Édouard Glissant's theory of "Relation" (for a succinct account, see Chris Bongie's *Islands and Exiles: The Creole Identities of Post-Colonial Literature* [Stanford: Stanford University Press, 1998], 59–60); and the idea of "playing relatives" that Henk Maier traces through Malay writing (*We Are Playing Relatives*).

64. C. L. R. James, *Beyond a Boundary* (New York: Pantheon, 1983), 20. Cf. Dash, *Other America*, 102–3.

Chapter 2

1. Conrad finished working on *The Rescue* in May 1919, while it was being published in serial form (from January to July 1919). It was published in book form in 1920.

2. Reporting to his aunt, Marguerite Paradowska, in May 1894 about his completion of the last chapter of *Almayer's Folly*, Conrad writes: "Il commence avec un *trio* Nina. Dain. Almayer. et il finit dans un long *solo* pour Almayer qui est presque aussi long que le Tristan-solo de Wagner" (*Collected Letters of Joseph Conrad*, eds. Frederick Karl and Laurence Davies, vol. 1 (Cambridge: Cambridge University Press, 1983), 155–56). Reporting to Edward Garnett in September 1895 about his completion of *An Outcast of the Islands*, Conrad writes: "It is my painful duty to inform you of the sad death of Mr. Peter Willems late of Rotterdam and Macassar who has been murdered on the 16th inst at 4 p.m. while the sun shone joyously and the barrel organ sang on the pavement the abominable Intermezzo of the ghastly Cavalleria" (Ibid., 245).

3. For extended recent discussions of the historical context of Conrad's Malay fiction, see Agnes S. K. Yeow, *Conrad's Eastern Vision: A Vain and Floating Vision* (New York: Palgrave Macmillan, 2009); and Robert Hampson, *Cross-Cultural Encounters in Joseph Conrad's Malay Fiction* (New York: Palgrave, 2000). For earlier discussions, see Lloyd Fernando, "Conrad's Eastern Expatriates: A New Version of His Outcasts" *PMLA*, 91,

no. 1 (January 1976), 78-90; Avrom Fleishman, *Conrad's Politics: Community and Anarchy in the Fiction of Joseph Conrad* (Baltimore: Johns Hopkins University Press, 1967); Eloise Knapp Hay, *The Political Novels of Joseph Conrad* (Chicago: University of Chicago Press, 1963); Heliéna Krenn, *Conrad's Lingard Trilogy: Empire, Race, and Women in the Malay Novels* (New York: Garland Publishing, 1990); John McClure, *Kipling and Conrad: the Colonial Fiction* (Cambridge, Mass.: Harvard University Press, 1981); Norman Sherry, *Conrad's Eastern World* (Cambridge: Cambridge University Press, 1966); and Ian Watt, *Conrad in the Nineteenth Century* (London: Chatto and Windus, 1980).

4. See especially Emily Apter, *The Translation Zone: A New Comparative Literature*. Princeton: Princeton University Press, 2006; and also the essays in Christopher Prendergast, ed., *Debating World Literature* (London: Verso, 2004).

5. Edward Said, *Culture and Imperialism* (New York: Vintage, 1994), 51.

6. On the circumstances of the composition and publication, see Max Lane's introductions to his English translations, and Joesoef Isak, "The Shaping of the Mute's Soliloquy" (Address delivered at Fordham University, April 24 1999. At http://home.earthlink.net/~agbardsley, accessed August, 2003). For a brief summary and interpretation of the entire tetralogy, see Benedict Anderson, *The Spectre of Comparisons: Nationalism, Southeast Asia and the World* (London: Verso, 1998), 292–93. For extended readings of the tetralogy, see Pheng Cheah, *Spectral Nationality: Passages of Freedom from Kant to Postcolonial Literatures of Liberation* (New York: Columbia University Press, 2003); Razif Bahari, *Pramoedya Postcolonially: (Re-) Viewing History, Gender and Identity in the Buru Tetralogy* (Denpasar, Bali: Pustaka Larasan, 2007); and Peter Hitchcock, *The Long Space: Transnationalism and Postcolonial Form* (Stanford: Stanford University Press, 2010).

7. Fernando Coronil, Introduction, in Fernando Ortiz, *Cuban Counterpoint: Tobacco and Sugar*, trans. Harriet de Onís (Durham, N.C. : Duke University Press, 1995), xl.

8. John Pemberton, *On the Subject of "Java,"* (Ithaca, N.Y.: Cornell University Press, 1994), 20.

9. For an extended discussion of this form of opera, see Manusama, *Komedie Stamboel of de Oost-Indische Opera* (Weltevreden: V. Electrische Drukkerij 'Favoriet," 1922); Tan Sooi Beng, *Bangsawan: A Social and Stylistic History of Popular Malay Opera* (Singapore: Oxford University Press, 1993); Adolf Maximilien Pino, *Komedie Stamboel: En Andere Verhalen Uit de Praktijk van het Binnenlands Bestuur op Java 1913–1946* (Leiden: Nautilus, 1998); Matthew Isaac Cohen, *The Komedie Stamboul: Popular Theater in Colonial Indonesia, 1891–1903* (Athens, Ohio: Ohio University Press, 2006). See also Rudolf Mrázek, *Engineers of Happy Land: Technology and Nationalism in a Colony* (Princeton: Princeton University Press, 2002), 147; and also Adrian Vickers's description of this "fascinating combination of local and trans-Asian arts, where Indonesian stories of the romantic prince Panji appeared alongside *The Merchant of Venice*, *Ali Baba*, and stories of the concubines of Batavia" (*A History of Modern Indonesia* [Cambridge: Cambridge University Press, 2005], 68).

10. Rob Nieuwenhuys, *Komen en Blijven: Tempo Doeloe—Een Verzonken Wereld* (Amsterdam: Querido, 1998), 163. For photographic reproductions of this and the other two photographs discussed, see my "Opera and the Passage of Literature," in Carola Kaplan, Peter Mallios, and Andrea White,

eds., *Conrad in the Twenty-First Century: Contemporary Approaches and Perspectives* (New York: Routledge, 2005), 103, 104, and 106.

11. Nieuwenhuys, *Komen en Blijven*, 164. In this photo we see the star singer, Marietje Oord, standing in the middle background. Although this is a "woman's orchestra" (*damesorkestje*), Nieuwenhuys notes that the figure seated in the middle foreground is a transvestite star called Theo Mac Lennan (165).

12. Ibid., 161. In this photo, it is not clear whether the man operating the hand organ is the servant supplying the entertainment, his somber face—by contrast to the smiles of the others—signaling that he is not himself amused; or whether he is an initiator of the masquerade, perhaps the one best able to conceal his smile.

13. Pramoedya Ananta Toer, *Tempo Doeloe: Antologi Sastra Pra-Indonesia* (Jakarta: Hasta Mitra, 1982), 1.

14. Cited in Mervyn Cooke, *Britten and the Far East: East Asian Influences on the Music of Benjamin Britten* (Woodbridge, Suffolk: Boydell and Brewer, 2001), 5.

15. Frantz Fanon, *The Wretched of the Earth*, trans. Constance Farrington (New York: Grove Press, 1961/1968), 210; Fanon, *Les damnés de la terre* (Paris: Maspero, 1970), 144.

16. Bernard Dupriez traces the naming of this literary device, *mise-en-abyme*, back to André Gide's use of the heraldic term *abyme* to explain the narrative effect of "disappearing repetition" (*A Dictionary of Literary Devices*, trans. Albert W. Halsall [Toronto: University of Toronto Press, 1991], 285). Jacques Derrida makes extensive use of the term (and the device), posing the question of Mallarmé, for example, "isn't it precisely such writing *en abyme* that thematic criticism—and no doubt criticism as such—can never, to the letter, account for?" See Jacques Derrida, *Dissemination*, trans. Barbara Johnson (Chicago: University of Chicago Press, 1981), 265; *"la pratique de l'écriture en abîme, n'est-ce pas ce dont la critique thématique—et sans doute la critique—en tant que telle—ne pourra jamais rendre à la lettre compte?"* (Derrida, *La dissemination* [Paris: Editions du Seuil, 1972], 297).

17. The phonograph music almost literally calls forth the characters from the first book: "Just as the phonograph was playing 'The Last Rose of Summer' and I had, by coincidence, opened my eyes, I saw a two-horse carriage pull up in front of the house. A young Eurasian girl alighted and then helped out a young boy. Then a Native woman descended who, in her turn, helped down a European. And the European man used a crutch" (*F*, 201); *"Waktu phonograf mengumandangkan* Bunga Ros Terakhir Musim Panas *dan kebetulan aku sedang membuka mata, kulihat sebuah kereta berkuda dua berhenti di depan rumah. Seorang gadis Peranakan Eropa turun, kemudian menolong turun seorang bocah lelaki. Kemudian seorang wanita Pribumi, yang pada gilirannya menolong turun seorang tuan Eropa. Dan tuan itu menggunakan tongkat ketiak"* (*J*, 194–95).

18. Benedict Anderson, *Language and Power: Exploring Political Cultures in Indonesia* (Ithaca, N.Y.: Cornell University Press, 1990), 243.

19. Just before the opera passage, the contemporary moment of *Almayer's Folly* is described as occuring "at the time when the hostilities between Dutch and Malays threatened to spread from Sumatra over the whole archipelago" (*AF*, 81). In 1995, Pramoedya succinctly described the plot of *Almayer's Folly* as "the story about a Balinese prince who is smuggling guns to organize resistance against Dutch colonial rule" (see my

"Pramoedya's Fiction and History: An Interview with Indonesian Novelist Pramoedya Ananta Toer," *Yale Journal of Criticism* 9, no. 1 (1996), 156).

20. Cedric Watts, *The Deceptive Text: An Introduction to Covert Plots* (Brighton: Harvester, 1984), 51.

21. He is described as "perfectly repulsive" with his "one eye and... pock-marked face, with nose and lips horribly disfigured by the small-pox" (*AF*, 38).

22. Said, *Culture and Imperialism*, 130.

23. Said reads the "monumentality" of *Aida*, built on "the authority of Europe's vision of Egypt," in historical relation to the geopolitical aims of the Khedive Ismail in the face of contending European interests. *Aida's* "Egyptian identity" reflects Cairo's "European façade, its simplicity and rigor inscribed on those imaginary walls dividing the colonial city's native from its imperial quarters" (*Culture and Imperialism*, 129).

24. Walter Benjamin, *Illuminations*, trans. Harry Zohn (New York: Schocken, 1969), 221; Benjamin, *Illuminationen: Ausgewählte Schriften* (Frankfurt: Suhrkamp, 1977), 141.

25. Theodor Adorno, "On the Fetish-Character in Music and the Regression of Listening," in his *Essays on Music* (Berkeley: University of California Press, 2002), 288–317.

26. "There was a phonograph on a low table with a small wheel on each of its four legs. The lower section of the phonograph table was used as a place to store music. The table itself was ornately carved. It must have been made to order" (*TE*, 28). The original Indonesian continues, making explicit the connection between the "beauty" (*indah*) of the furniture and the "beauty" (*terindah*) of Annelies: "*Semua indah. Dan yang terindah tetap Annelies*" (*BM*, 15) ["All beautiful. And then, constantly present throughout it all, the stunning beauty of Annelies" (my translation)].

27. "As music from *La Traviata* wafted around the room, so too laughter echoed inside me. The three of us were the worst play actors in the world. 'We're not here to admire that new phonograph,' I chided him. 'No doubt one of the many presents you have given Rientje'" (*H*, 34); "*Dengan membubungnya sebuah fragmen* La Traviata *membubung pula tawa bahak hatiku: kami bertiga sungguh pemain sandiwara terburuk di dunia. 'Kita bertemu bukan untuk mengagumi phonograf baru itu,' kataku menegur. 'Tentu itu hadiahmu yang kesekian untuk Rientje'*" (*RK*, 33).

28. Adorno, "On the Fetish-Character in Music," 298–99.

29. Julian Budden, *The Operas of Verdi*, vol. 2 (New York: Oxford University Press, 1979), 100.

30. "The Last Rose of Summer" appears in Flotow's *Martha*, first, in its original Irish melody form (though in German) sung by Lady Harriet, dressed up as a servant who has sold herself into debt-bondage. As the opera sorts out its convoluted plot of trans-class disguise, the Irish melody recurs four more times, in various modulations. The example provides a miniature signature motif for the way nineteenth-century opera effects an estrangement of literary tradition in the process of constituting another modular form alongside the forms of the novel and the newspaper that Benedict Anderson designates as modular vehicles for imagining the nation. The opera itself, then, rehearses a particularly interesting moment in European operatic tradition—the moment in which what Katie Trumpener calls "bardic nationalism," with its origins in late eighteenth-century English literary appropriations of Celtic forms (*Bardic Nationalism: the Romantic Novel and the British Empire* [Princeton: Princeton University

Press, 1997],)—gets reconstituted in a mid-nineteenth-century articulation of the dialectic between "national memory" and "imperial amnesia."

31. Ultimately, for Hegel, prose wins out over all the arts: poetry transcends music as art; and all the arts—necessarily grasped as "for us, a thing of the past"—are subsumed by philosophy in the dialectical movement of the universal spirit or mind toward Absolute Knowing. See *Aesthetics: Lectures on Fine Art*, trans. T. M. Knox (Oxford: Clarendon Press, 1998), 951; Hegel, *Ästhetik* (Berlin: Aufbau Verlag, 1955), 860–61.

32. See Georg Wilhelm Friedrich Hegel, *The Phenomenology of Spirit*, trans. A. V. Miller (Oxford: Oxford University Press, 1977), 441; Hegel, *Phänomenologie des Geistes* (Frankfurt: Ullstein, 1807/1980), 402.

33. After Conrad himself, Ford Madox Ford was the first to emphasize Conrad's debt to Flaubert, as discussed in the next chapter. For more recent assessments see Watt, *Conrad in the Nineteenth Century;* and Yves Hervouet, *The French Face of Joseph Conrad* (Cambridge: Cambridge University Press, 1990).

34. Gustave Flaubert, *Madame Bovary*, trans. Alan Russell (Harmondsworth: Penguin, 1950/1981), 78; Flaubert, *Madame Bovary* (Paris: Garnier-Flammarion, 1966), 98.

35. Michael North, *The Dialect of Modernism: Race, Language, and Twentieth-Century Literature* (Oxford: Oxford University Press, 1994), 49–50.

36. "How it came to pass that Babalatchi, fleeing for his life in a small canoe, managed to end his hazardous journey in a vessel full of a valuable commodity, is one of those secrets of the sea that baffle the most searching inquiry. In truth nobody inquired much. There were rumours of a missing trading prau belonging to Menado, but they were vague and mysterious" (*OI*, 55).

37. Hampson, *Cross-Cultural Encounters*, 100.

38. A story of two "flights"—the first from a rout by "white men," the second from their temporary asylum provided by the Sultan of Sulu—its narrative registers both in a single sentence: "On the cool mats in breezy verandahs of Rajahs' houses it is alluded to disdainfully by impassive statesmen, but amongst armed men that throng the courtyards it is a tale which stills the murmur of voices and the tinkle of anklets; arrests the passage of the siri vessel, and fixes the eyes in absorbed gaze" (*OI*, 54–55).

39. Hampson, *Cross-Cultural Encounters*, 109.

40. Jean-François Lyotard, *The Differend: Phrases in Dispute*, trans. Georges Van Den Abbele (Minneapolis: University of Minnesota Press, 1988), xi; *Le Différend* (Paris: Les Éditions de Minuit, 1983), 9.

41. Lyotard, *The Differend*, xi; *Le Différend*, 9.

42. Hampson and Stape disagree over whether this phrase—"that piratical and son-less Aeneas"—refers to Babalatchi or to Omar (see Hampson, *Cross-Cultural Encounters*, 215). The truncated form of the allusion surely contributes to this interesting dispute. When the phrase is read as an effect of the political "differend" over a shared, contested Malay-English piratical romance, I would suggest that both readings are possible and that their counterpoint generates a third—Stape's reading seems the most immediately probable, since Omar is presented as a father figure, while Babalatchi is not; but the ironic form of this anti-epic genealogy offers the possibility that the phrase might not only be extended to Babalatchi (who is, after all, by metonymy associated with the distorted

insurgent Islamic family romance of Omar and Aïssa) but also to Lingard, since it is the man he calls "son"—Willems, whose affair with Aïssa provides the plot for *An Outcast*—who comes closest to supplying what Omar (or Babalatchi) lack by way of a male heir. Omar, Babalatchi, and Lingard each offer different profiles of the father figure who fails to establish an imperial lineage.

43. See G. J. Resink, *Indonesia's History Between the Myths: Essays in Legal History and Historical Theory* (The Hague: W. van Hoeve, 1968), esp. "The Law of Nations in Early Macassar," 48ff, and "The Archipelago Under Joseph Conrad's Western Eyes," 315.

44. See Hans van Marle's note to the Oxford World's Classics editions of *An Outcast of the Islands*, 375 n. 46, and *Almayer's Folly*, 215.

45. This suggestion was made to me by G. J. Resink in Jakarta in 1995, in an interview Pramoedya himself helped arrange. The longstanding friendship between Pramoedya and Resink is indicated by the fact that Pramoedya dedicated *This Earth of Mankind* and *Child of All Nations* to Resink, or "Han," as he was nicknamed after the "Hanuman" character of *Ramayana wayang* plots (a nickname Resink himself discusses in his essay on the changing historical and political significance of *Mahabharata* and *Ramayana* plots in Javanese opera ["From the Old Mahabharata- to the New Ramayana-Order," *Bijdragen tot de Taal-, Land- en Volkenkunde* 131 (1975), no. 2/3, 214-235; 229]). Pramoedya often wrote of his gratitude toward Resink for saving his manuscripts when he was in Bukitduri prison in 1948–49. See *Nyanyi Sunyi Seorang Bisu* II, 179ff, and his comments in 1983 where he writes of "Resink's rescue work": "But for him, all these works would certainly have been destroyed, as happened to a number of my manuscripts from before 1947 and after 1965" (*"Perburuan* 1950 and *Keluarga Gerilya* 1950," 42).

46. Linked to the work of "covert plotting," and also to the narrative technique of what Ian Watt, before Watts, has called "delayed decoding," the "artistically defective" song deliberately disrupts narrative sequence to highlight the almost perverse insistence (what F. R. Leavis called "adjectival insistence" [*The Great Tradition: George Eliot, Henry James, Joseph Conrad* (London: Chatto, 1948), 177]) with which the narrative is arrested by long passages of impressionist tropical description. *An Outcast of the Islands* provides a host of examples, anticipating what Fredric Jameson has characterized as the "aestheticizing strategy" that produces "Conrad's sensorium" (*The Political Unconscious: Narrative as a Socially Symbolic Act* [Ithaca, N.Y.: Cornell University Press, 1981], 230). The narrative splits between the two "vagabonds" of the original title, the acoustic and visual registers of this "sensorium": the acoustic register belongs primarily to Babalatchi, while the visual register is associated with Willems. At the height of Lingard's lengthy moment of recognition, another sense intrudes—the sense of smell, which tends to exaggerate still more the offensive racism directed against Babalatchi, whose home it is that induces this sense: "[Lingard] could not command his memories that came crowding round him in that evil-smelling hut, while Babalatchi talked on in a flowing monotone" (*OI*, 223); and again, later, "The pungent taint of unclean things below and about the hut grew heavier, weighing down Lingard's resolution and his thoughts in an irresistible numbness of the brain" (*OI*, 229–30). The crisis of identity and consciousness induced in Lingard in the face of Willems's act of betrayal comes to a climax in an instance of literally abysmal taste: "discomposed...by its

unprovoked malevolence, by its ghastly injustice, that to his rough but unsophisticated palate tasted distinctly of sulphurous fumes from the deepest hell" (*OI*, 236).

47. One passage from Conrad to which Pramoedya twice returns is the moment in "Karain: A Memory" when Karain, on arriving in Java, finds "every man...a slave" (*TU*, 31). In his introduction to the nonfictional work of Tirto Adi Suryo, anthologized in the biography of the journalist on whom Minke is based, this allusion seems simply to illustrate the historical moment of extreme Dutch colonial subjection. Pramoedya does not explain that this is the perspective of a Bugis Malay character—a non-Javanese judgment on the state of Javanese society at the height of Dutch colonial rule. It is precisely this non-Javanese, outsider perspective, however, that seems most important for the other allusion, in a section from the Buru prison notes. Recalling the critique of "Javanism" developed through the tetralogy, Pramoedya, recording his response to a journalist's question about his opinion of the Indonesian "psyche," writes: "We should not be offended by what that Polish-born sailor-turned-writer wrote about the Javanese people: that everyone, from beggars to kings, is a slave"(my translation); *"Jangan sakit hati kalau seorang pengarang-pelaut kelahiran Polandia menamakan orang Jawa itu, dari pengemis sampai rajanya budak"* (*NS* I, 183).

48. GoGwilt, "Pramoedya's History and Fiction," 156.

49. W. E. B. DuBois, *The Souls of Black Folk* (New York: Signet, 1982), 45: "It is a peculiar sensation, this double-consciousness, this sense of always looking at one's self through the eyes of others, of measuring one's soul by the tape of a world that looks on in amused contempt and pity." What Paul Gilroy calls the "self-consciously polyphonic form" of *Souls* (*The Black Atlantic: Modernity and Double Consciousness* [Cambridge, Mass.: Harvard University Press, 1993], 115) articulates Du Bois's key formulation of "double consciousness" as an anticipation of that counterpoint between "the cultures of Europe, Africa, and America" that Fernando Coronil sees in a "contrapuntal reading of Said and Ortiz" ("Transculturation and the Politics of Theory: Countering the Center, Cuban Counterpoint," introduction to Ortiz, *Cuban Counterpoint*, xl).

50. According to Giorgio Agamben's examination of aesthetic taste, Minke fits the profile of that figure—the man of taste—who appears in Hegel's *Phenomenology of Spirit* as the very measure of "pure culture": the "absolute and universal perversion and alienation of the actual world and of thought...*pure culture*." Giorgio Agamben, *The Man Without Content*, trans. Georgia Albert (Stanford: Stanford University Press, 1999), 25.

51. Clifford Geertz, *The Religion of Java* (Glencoe, Ill.: Free Press, 1960), 231.

52. Nancy Florida, *Writing the Past, Inscribing the Future: History as Prophecy in Colonial Java* (Durham, N.C.: Duke University Press, 1995), 176.

53. Geertz, *The Religion of Java*, 238.

54. As Benedict Anderson points out, *bahasa Indonesia* "is a cultural fortress from which to cross swords with his heritage" (*Language and Power*, 219).

55. Minke's critique of "Javanism" calls attention to the pernicious practice of a sort of philological superstition influencing "every aspect of life": "Words, for example, had been made into mantras. They were considered to have their origins with powers above humankind and not with

social and economic life.... These words were looked upon as some kind of supernatural acronyms, freed from semantics, cut off from their etymology, severed even from the word's own meaning. This people of mine had become isolated from the development of science and modern knowledge, deliberately isolated by their European conquerors. They were the residents of colonialism's special nature reserve" (*F*, 374–75); "*Pada kekuatan kata, seperti dalam mantra-mantra. Dianggap kata berasal dari kekuatan-kekuatan di atas manusia, bukan dari kehidupan sosial-ekonomi...Kata dipandang sebagai akronom gaib, terlepas dari semantik, terpental dari etymologi, tercecer dari makna kata itu sendiri. Bangsaku, bangsa ini, telah terkucil dari perkembangan ilmu-pengetahuan, dikucilkan oleh para pemenang dari Eropa. Jadi semacam penduduk cagar alam kolonial*" (*J*, 372). The critique includes, too, "the literature [and way of life] of Java" ("*literatur dan kehidupan Jawa*"): "The *Mahabarata* and *Bharatayuddha* provided nothing to grab hold of for those who wanted to enter the modern era. These great epics had become obstacles to the people's advancement" (*F*, 373); "*Ramayana dan* Mahabharata *tak meninggalkan pegangan bagaimana memasuki dunia modern*" (*J*, 370).

56. Geertz, *The Religion of Java*, 280.

57. The English translation imposes a European musical sensibility—"harmony"—not suggested by the Indonesian words (literally: "a calm feeling that defies form"—and we might note in "perasaan" the presence of that all-important Javanese word *rasa*). "Harmony," indeed, seems in some respects precisely the wrong term to capture the particularly complex structure of gamelan music. According to Mantle Hood, "Unlike the primary tradition of the Western orchestra, founded on a large harmonic complex which moves in vertical structures, the gamelan moves in as many as twenty-five different horizontal strata" (Hood, "The Enduring Tradition: Music and Theater in Java and Bali" in *Indonesia*, ed. Ruth T. McVey, 452 [New Haven, Ct: Southeast Asia Studies, Yale University, 1963]), 452.

58. A. L. Becker, *Beyond Translation: Essays toward a Modern Philology* (Ann Arbor: University of Michigan Press, 1995), 232.

59. See Apter, *Translation Zone*, chapter 3.

60. Leo Spitzer, *Classical and Christian Ideas of World Harmony: Prolegomena to an Interpretation of the World "Stimmung"* (Baltimore: Johns Hopkins Press, 1963), 173.

61. Said, *Culture and Imperialism*, 318.

62. Spitzer, *Classical and Christian Ideas*, 46.

63. A revealing example of how this "abysmal taste" in opera stages a similar philological problem for historiography emerges in Ranajit Guha's critique of European models of historiography in *History at the Limit of World-History* (New York: Columbia University Press, 2002). Guha discusses the difficulty of translating the Sanskrit term *rasa* in order to highlight "the untranslatability of the Mahabharatic cycle in terms of the Western narrative paradigm." Having cited Sushil Kumar De to confirm the point Nancy Florida makes, in the Javanese context, about the "untranslatable" resonance of the word *rasa*, Guha writes: "For our purpose we shall use the simpler term *mood* or *attunement* (borrowing from the German *Stimmung*) interchangeably with *rasa*..." (63).

64. See note 48, chapter 1.

65. It is a picture we must read in at least these three different ways: an image of multi-cultural innovation; an image of violent colonial contest;

and an image of a new formation of political identity, ethnic affiliation, and national identification.

66. The significance of East Indies opera for Conrad and Pramoedya extends beyond this comparative reading of the Malay trilogy and Buru tetralogy. In Conrad's *Victory* the *mise-en-scène* for the romance of Heyst's rescue of Lena is inaugurated by a striking instance of "abysmal taste" in a specifically East Indies form of operatic music, Heyst's "unholy fascination" in the music of the Zangiacomo Ladies' Orchestra from which Heyst will rescue Lena: "nothing could have been more repulsive to his tastes, more painful to his senses, and, so to speak, more contrary to his genius than this rude exhibition of vigour" (*VI*, 68). The opening section of Pramoedya's prison memoirs contains a fascinating reflection on the "squealing *kroncong* songs" played over the loudspeakers as Pramoedya and his fellow prisoners were being shipped out to Buru. About this form of popular music evolved from the accompaniment to East Indies opera, Pramoedya writes: "*Kroncong* still had some power before independence, it still had some vitality—a vitality of a nation that was not yet free. As the Revolution erupted and passed, *kroncong* remained just a kind of narcissism, a posy of empty words, a culture of masturbation. Equal to the culture of great speeches and of puppet shadow theater" (cited and translated in Mrázek, *Engineers of Happy Land*, 196); "*Kroncong sebelum kemerdekaan masih punya gairah, masih mengandung vitalitas—vitalitas bangsa yang belum merdeka. Kroncong sehabis dan selama Revolusi justru tinggal jadi semacam narcisme, rangkaian kata kosong, masturbasiisme. Sejajar dengan pidatoisme dan wayangisme*" (*NS* I, 10).

67. For both, the *lingua franca* of Malay presents the problem of reading, which Henk Maier succinctly sums up in calling attention to the problem of translating the word *baca* into English: "The translation we find in most dictionaries is 'to read', but then 'to read' certainly does not cover everything that is evoked by *membaca*. *Baca* (and its variant *membaca*) refer to 'read' and 'recite' at once, to the movement of the eyes as well as to the movement of the vocal cords, to 'silence' as well as to 'sound,' but also to 'leaning on paper' and 'leaning on memory.' *Baca*, in other words, points in many directions, calling up a network of other words in its wake when we try to read it in its English mirror" (*We Are Playing Relatives: A Survey of Malay Writing* [Leiden: KITLV Press, 2004], 40).

68. "Counterpoint," for Said, is specifically "Western": "In the counterpoint of Western classical music, various themes play off one another, with only a provisional privilege being given to any particular one; yet, in the resulting polyphony there is concert and order, an organized interplay that derives from the themes, not from a rigorous melodic or formal principle outside the work" (*Culture and Imperialism*, 51).

Chapter 3

1. Pierre Bourdieu, *The Rules of Art: Genesis and Structure of the Literary Field*, trans. Susan Emanuel (Stanford: Stanford University Press, 1995), 121; Bourdieu, *Les règles de l'art: genèse et structure du champ littéraire* (Paris: Editions du Seuil, 1992), 104.

2. I follow the practice of spelling the *transatlantic review* with lower case initial letters as it first appeared in print. On the reasons for choosing the uncapitalized title, see Bernard Poli (*Ford Madox Ford and the Transatlantic Review* [Syracuse, N. Y.: Syracuse University Press], 43).

According to Poli, "Ford said he liked the effect of an uncapitalized name on the front of a shop in Paris and had found it an interesting coincidence that E. E. Cummings [sic] should not use capitals either." Following the inconsistency of the review itself, which sometimes capitalized its own title, scholars remain divided on how to cite the review. Poli uses capitals (as he does for e.e. cummings), but Hugh Kenner uses lower case, as do recent critics such as Max Saunders and Sara Haslam (*Ford Madox Ford and the City* [Amsterdam: Rodopi, 2005]).

3. Virginia Woolf, *The Common Reader: First Series* (New York: Harcourt Brace Jovanovich, 1925/1953), 231, 229.

4. Andreas Huyssen, *After the Great Divide: Modernism, Mass Culture, and Postmodernism* (Bloomington, Ind.:: Indiana University Press, 1986), vii–viii. Huyssen distinguishes between the anti-aestheticist moment of avant-garde practice and the retrospective assimilation of artistic experiment into an aesthetic modernist canon. Bourdieu's emphasis is somewhat different, claiming for French avant-garde literary modernism the production of an autonomous aesthetic field (and thus situating a "modernism" that precedes the moment of what Huyssen calls the "historical avant-garde"). Without exploring these characteristic confusions over the terminology and definition of "modernism," I think it is nonetheless useful to keep Huyssen's term alongside Bourdieu's if only because, although both offer ways to examine the close relationship between "low" and "high" cultural forms, neither is able to sustain clear distinctions that would succeed in extricating the classification of "modernism" from an ongoing difficulty in distinguishing between the two. So, Bourdieu's "consecrated avant-garde"—seemingly related to Huyssen's "modernism"—must itself be grounded in a dialectic of "low" and "high" culture. And Huyssen's "historical avant-garde" is itself part of the scene of consecrating itself as a "high" cultural field.

5. John Guillory, *Cultural Capital: The Problem of Literary Canon Formation* (Chicago: University of Chicago Press, 1993), esp. chap. 2.

6. Woolf, *Common Reader*, 229.

7. Ford Madox Ford, *Joseph Conrad: A Personal Remembrance* (New York: Ecco, 1924/1989), 90. (Hereafter abbreviated as *Remembrance*.)

8. Cf. Sue Thomas, *The Worlding of Jean Rhys* (Westport, Conn.: Greenwood, 1999), 85.

9. On Ford's change of names, see Max Saunders, *Ford Madox Ford: A Dual Life* (Oxford: Oxford University Press, 1996), vol. 1, 2ff.

10. See Samuel Hynes, "Conrad and Ford: Two Rye Revolutionists," in his *Edwardian Occasions: Essays on English Writing in the Early Twentieth Century* (London: Routledge, 1972); and Ezra Pound, "The revolution of the word began so far as it affected the men who were of my age in London in 1908, with the LONE whimper of Ford Madox Hueffer," cited in Saunders, *Ford Madox Ford*, vol. 1, 238.

11. Ford, in fact, fuses two separate letters—one from October 23, in which Conrad responds to Ford's announcement about starting a review "on exactly the same lines as the old *English Review*, except that it will be published in London & New York as well as here [Paris]" (J. H. Stape and Owen Knowles, eds., *A Portrait in Letters: Correspondence to and about Conrad* [Amsterdam: Rodopi, 1996], 216); and the other from November 10, in which Conrad responds to Ford's request to reprint "The Nature of a Crime" since, according to Ford, it "would have a certain literary and sentimental interest" (Stape and Knowles, *Portrait in Letters*, 223). This

complication of letters is complicated all the more by the fact that Ford cites from—and republishes in facsimile later—a letter Conrad reedited in response to an undated letter from Ford in which Ford requests, first, permission to "print the four or five lines from yr. letter wh. I have typed out," and, second, "could you possibly write for me about 3,000 words—of Personal Record?" (Stape and Knowles, *Portrait in Letters,* 221).

12. Ford Madox Ford, *It Was the Nightingale* (New York: Octagon, 1933/1975), 320.

13. For accounts of *The English Review* and *the transatlantic review,* see Mizener, *The Saddest Story: A Biography of Ford Madox Ford* (London: Bodley Head, 1971); Homberger, "Ford's *English Review*: Englishness and Its Discontents" (*Agenda* 27, no. 4 [Winter 1989]/28, no. 1 [Spring 1990]: 61-66); Bernard Poli, *Ford Madox Ford and the transatlantic review* (Syracuse: Syracuse University Press, 1967); and Nora Tomlinson, "The English Review: An Introduction." (http://www.modjourn.org/render.php?id=mjp.2005.00.104&view=mjp_object; accessed May 25, 2010).

14. Saunders, *Ford Madox Ford,* vol. 1, 156 and throughout. See also Todd K. Bender, *Literary Impressionism in Jean Rhys, Ford Madox Ford, Joseph Conrad, and Charlotte Brontë* (New York: Garland, 1997).

15. See the Conrad Supplement to *the transatlantic review,* vol. 2, no. 3, 337; and the Preface to Ford, *Remembrance.*

16. For a fuller account of these, see Elizabeth Foley O'Connor, "Perambulating the Metropolis: Women and Commodity Culture in James Joyce, Kate O'Brien, and Jean Rhys" (PhD diss. in progress, Fordham University).

17. For Jessie Conrad's letter to *The Times Literary Supplement,* see Frank MacShane, ed., *Ford Madox Ford: The Critical Heritage* (London: Routledge and K. Paul, 1972), 131–32.

18. See, in particular, Judith Butler, who turns to Freud's notion of repetition-compulsion to explain what Foucault misses about the Lacanian return to Freud: "repetition is not subjectivating in Lacan in the way that Foucault implies. In fact, repetition is not only the mark that subjectivation has in some sense *failed* to occur, but that it is itself a further instance of that failing" (*Bodies That Matter: on the Discursive Limits of "Sex"* [New York: Routledge, 1993], 249). See also Diana Fuss, *Identification Papers* (New York: Routledge, 1995).

19. Sigmund Freud, *Beyond the Pleasure Principle,* trans. James Strachey (New York: Norton, 1961), 6; Freud, *Gesammelte Werke* (Frankfurt: S. Fischer, 1941, vol.13, 9.

20. Ford's prodigious output defies easy classification; and so "reminiscences" might suitably apply to all of Ford's work, fiction and nonfiction alike. I have in mind, here, however, in order of my own priorities and interests, most especially Ford's *Reminiscence* (1924); *Return to Yesterday* (New York: Liveright, 1932/1972), which looks back on the founding and foundering of *The English Review;* and *It Was the Nightingale* (New York: Octagon, 1933/1975), which looks back on the founding and foundering of *the transatlantic review.*

21. Bourdieu, *Rules of Art,* 142; Bourdieu, *Règles de l'art,* 122.

22. Conrad and Ford, *The Nature of a Crime* (Garden City, N.Y.: Doubleday, Page, 1924), vi.

23. "Fragments From Work in Progress Or to Appear," *transatlantic review* 2, no. 1, 107; Conrad and Ford, *The Nature of a Crime,* ix.

24. Ibid., 108; xi. In the book form, "Collaborator" is spelled correctly.

25. Ibid., 107–8; ix.
26. Ford, *Remembrance*, 90.
27. "Fragments from Work," 108; Conrad and Ford, *Nature of a Crime*, x.
28. Ford, *Remembrance*, 25.
29. MacShane, *Ford Madox Ford*, 132.
30. Ibid., 133.
31. Ford, *Remembrance*, 31.
32. See Ford, *Remembrance*, 7, 186, 188. For an extended discussion of Conrad's borrowings from French writers, see Yves Hervouet, *The French Face of Joseph Conrad* (Cambridge: Cambridge University Press, 1990).
33. Ford, *Remembrance*, 6–7.
34. Ibid., 30.
35. Ibid., 31.
36. Ibid., 170.
37. Ibid., 170.
38. Ibid., 172.
39. Ibid., ii.
40. MacShane, *Ford Madox Ford*, 134.
41. Fredric Jameson, *The Political Unconscious: Narrative as a Socially Symbolic Act* (Ithaca, N.Y.: Cornell University Press, 1981), 208.
42. Edward Said, *The World, the Text, and the Critic* (Cambridge, Mass.: Harvard University Press, 1983), 99.
43. Jameson, *Political Unconscious*, 213.
44. Said, *World, Text, and Critic*, 100.
45. Jameson, *Political Unconscious*, 213.
46. Ibid., 231.
47. Ibid., 210.
48. Ford, *Remembrance*, 173.
49. Said, *World, Text, and Critic*, 109.
50. Ibid.
51. MacShane, *Ford Madox Ford*, 133.
52. Norman Sherry, *Conrad: The Critical Heritage* (London: Routledge and Kegan Paul, 1973), 110.
53. Albert Guerard, *Conrad the Novelist* (Cambridge, Mass.: Harvard University Press, 1958), 91.
54. See "The Charm of Empire," in Christopher GoGwilt, *The Invention of the West: Joseph Conrad and the Double-Mapping of Europe and Empire* (Stanford: Stanford University Press, 1995), chap. 2; and "Conrad's Alien Genealogies: Joseph Conrad's 'Karain: A Memory," Pramoedya Ananta Toer, and Postcolonial American Perspectives" (*Western Humanities Review*, LII, no. 2 (Summer 1998), 96–109.
55. Ford, *Remembrance*, 11.
56. Ford Madox Ford, "Joseph Conrad," *English Review* {{no volume number?}} (December 1911), 69.
57. Ibid., 70.
58. Ford, *Remembrance*, 20.
59. Ibid., 249.
60. Ibid., 230.
61. The *O.E.D.*, which traces the etymology of the English word back to the French, provides an example of the sense of the word's usage to indicate an adjustment of territorial boundaries, in a passage from W. E. H. Lecky, *England in the 18th Century*: "A few slight rectifications of territory were at the same time made."

62. I explore this at length in my *Invention of the West*; and see also "Joseph Conrad as Guide to Colonial History," in John G. Peters, *A Historical Guide to Joseph Conrad* (Oxford: Oxford University Press, 2010), 137–61. For contrasting discussions of Conrad's relation to Sir Hugh Clifford see, inter alia, John Marx, *The Modernist Novel and the Decline of Empire* (Cambridge: Cambridge University Press, 2005) and Agnes S. K. Yeow, *Conrad's Eastern Vision: A Vain and Floating Vision* (New York: Palgrave Macmillan, 2009).

63. See, as one point of reference on this critical reception, Thomas, *Worlding of Jean Rhys*, 49–51; and compare Elaine Savory, *Jean Rhys* (Cambridge: Cambridge University Press, 1998), and Veronica Marie Gregg, *Jean Rhys's Historical Imagination: Reading and Writing the Creole* (Chapel Hill: North Carolina University Press, 1995).

64. Ford, Preface to Jean Rhys, *The Left Bank and Other Stories*, cited in Sondra Stang, *The Ford Madox Ford Reader* (New York: Ecco Press, 1986), 244.

65. Ford, *It Was the Nightingale*, 280. To this variety of cultural backgrounds is later added the variety of artistic genres with which Paris "gyrated, seethed, clamoured, roared": "Painters, novelists, poets, composers, sculptors, batik-designers, decorators, even advanced photographers so crowded the boulevards that you could not see them for the tree-trunks" (282).

66. *transatlantic review* 2, no. 6, 683.

67. Ibid., 639.

68. See Carole Angier, *Jean Rhys: Life and Work* (Boston: Little, Brown, 1990), 134.

69. *transatlantic review* 2, no. 6, 641.

70. On this point, see Thomas, *Worlding of Jean Rhys*, 62; and Coral Ann Howells, *Jean Rhys* (New York: Harvester Wheatsheaf, 1991).

71. Rhys critics who explore aspects of this include Emery, Gregg, Thomas, O'Connor, Raiskin, and Savory.

72. Ford, *Remembrance*, 229.

73. Stang, *The Ford Madox Ford Reader*, 251.

74. Ibid., 289.

75. Ford, *Remembrance*, 170.

76. See Rhys's description of a particularly upsetting scene in the "elocution master's class" over the pronunciation of the word *froth* in the second, unauthorized part of the autobiographical *Smile Please* (83–84). And see Angier's discussion of the negative judgment passed on Rhys's "accent" as catalyst for her leaving the Academy of Dramatic Art (*Jean Rhys*, 49).

77. Hugh Kenner, *The Pound Era* (Berkeley: University of California Press, 1971), 101–2; Michael North, *The Dialect of Modernism: Race, Language, and Twentieth-Century Literature* (Oxford: Oxford University Press, 1994), chaps. 1 and 2.

78. Walter W. Skeat's *A Concise Etymological Dictionary of the English Language* (Oxford: Clarendon Press, 1911), distinguishing between *rum* meaning "liquor" and *rum* meaning "strange, queer," claims a Malay etymology for the first and a Gypsy etymology for the second. Yule and Burnell's Anglo-Indian glossary known as "Hobson-Jobson" (London: John Murray, 1903) confuses both meanings and claims for both a West Indian (Barbados) etymology as "the only probable history." The *Oxford English Dictionary* attempts a studied neutrality, noting only that the etymology is "obscure."

79. "It was Conrad who chose the title. He felt a certain sardonic pleasure in the choosing so national a name for a periodical that promised to be singularly international in tone, that was started mainly in his not very English interest and conducted by myself who was growing every day more and more alien to the normal English trend of thought at any rate in matters of literary technique" (Ford, *Return to Yesterday,* 365).

80. Stang, *Ford Madox Ford Reader*, 244–45.

81. Ibid., 245.

82. This problem, moreover, is constituted around the difficulty in remembering the precise color of the sea and sky at particular moments throughout the day—a problem of "local color" (or, in Ford's terms, "descriptive passage"), which, as Sue Thomas unearths, engages Rhys in a critical reading and rewriting of stereotypical descriptions of the West Indies. The keyword of such stereotyped tourist discourse is, it turns out, *azure*—the very same word over which Ford has Conrad agonize. (See Thomas, *Worlding of Jean Rhys,* 55–56.)

83. There is also a third version of "Vienne," as Elizabeth Foley O'Connor notes, that Rhys reworked for her 1968 collection *Tigers Are Better-Looking*. In an unpublished March 7, 1967, letter to Olywyn Hughes, Rhys describes the changes as "complicated" (see Savory, *Jean Rhys,* 152).

84. Ford, *Remembrance*, 11.

Chapter 4

1. Walter Benjamin, *Reflections: Essays, Aphorisms, Autobiographical Writings* (New York: Schocken, 1978), 157; Benjamin, *Illuminationen: Ausgewählte Schriften* (Frankfurt: Suhrkamp, 1977), 180.

2. Conrad's return to the scene of the "Malay seas" of his earlier work is generally credited to the visit he received from Captain Carlos M. Marris in September 1909, as recorded in a letter to his agent, Pinker: "I had a visit from a man out of the Malay Seas. It was like the raising of a lot of dead—dead to me, because most of them live out there and even read my books and wonder who [the] devil has been around taking notes" (*Collected Letters of Joseph Conrad,* eds. Frederick Karl and Laurence Davies, vol. 4, 1990, 277–78). See also Zdzisław Najder, *Joseph Conrad: A Chronicle* (Cambridge: Cambridge University Press, 1964), 352–53; and Frederick Karl, *Joseph Conrad: The Three Lives* (New York: Farrar, Straus and Giroux, 1979), 674–75. For revealing letters from Marris, see J. H. Stape and Owen Knowles, eds., *A Portrait in Letters: Correspondence to and about Conrad* (Amsterdam: Rodopi, 1996), 66–72.

3. Shari Benstock's landmark study argues that Rhys moved only at the periphery of avant-garde circles: "Like the women of her fiction, Rhys did not find a place for herself on the literary Left Bank; she was an outsider among outsiders, neither part of the café crowd nor an occasional visitor to Sylvia Beach's bookshop. Rhys lived outside the bounds of society, outside even the bounds of so loosely constructed and open a society as that of the Left Bank" (*Women of the Left Bank: Paris 1900–1940* [Austin, Tex.: University of Texas Press, 1986], 448). Deborah Parsons, however, noting that Jean Rhys "cannot be placed on Benstock's map" since the figures of her novels exist "on the borders of the expatriate social group of the salon," argues that this reveals a limitation in Benstock's map: "The map therefore serves actually to localize and confine the writers it places, ignoring those outside its boundaries, and neglecting representations of

the dynamic between, and movement within, city space. Benstock's "Left Bank," which evokes a sense of an insular female community, is thus curiously artificial. Her model and her map are essentially static and deny woman subject in modernism, and the woman writer of modernism, the freedom of the city" (*Streetwalking in the Metropolis: Women, the City, and Modernity* [Oxford: Oxford University Press, 2000], 149–50).

4. Fredric Jameson's *The Political Unconscious* provides a key point of reference, e.g.: "the sea is both a strategy of containment and a place of real business: it is a border and a decorative limit, but it is also a highway, out of the world and in it at once, the representation of work... as well as the absent work-place itself" (Ithaca: Cornell University Press, 1981, 210). See also Cesare Casarino, *Modernity at Sea: Melville, Marx, Conrad in Crisis* (Minneapolis: University of Minnesota Press, 2002); Robert Hampson, *Cross-Cultural Encounters in Joseph Conrad's Malay Fiction* (New York: Palgrave, 2000); my *The Invention of the West: Joseph Conrad and the Double-Mapping of Europe and Empire* (Stanford: Stanford University Press, 1995); and Jacques Darras, *Joseph Conrad and the West: Signs of Empire* (trans. Anne Luyat; London: Macmillan, 1982). For the particular significance of *The Shadow-Line*, see Jeremy Hawthorn's introduction to the Oxford World's Classics edition and two of the most authoritative biographies, Karl's *Joseph Conrad* (777ff) and Najder, *Joseph Conrad* (101ff).

5. Michel de Certeau, *The Practice of Everyday Life* (Berkeley: University of California Press, 1984), 134; De Certeau, *L'Invention du quotidien* (Paris: Union Générale d'Editions, 1980), 235.

6. Ibid., 135; 237.

7. Ibid, 150; 258.

8. Ibid., 135; 236.

9. Benjamin, *Reflections*, 157; Benjamin, *Illuminationen*, 179–80.

10. Marianne DeKoven examines at length the gendered logic of this scriptural economy of modernism using Irigiray's feminist deconstruction of the Platonic parable of the cave as a model for examining the gendered and sexualized "passage" in modernist texts—above all, the "vaginal passage" in Conrad's "Heart of Darkness." See *Rich and Strange: Gender, History, Modernism* (Princeton: Princeton University Press, 1991), especially 19–37, 85–138.

11. See, for example, Nancy Harrison, *Jean Rhys and the Novel as Women's Text* (Chapel Hill: University of North Carolina Press, 1988), 116–17; Sue Thomas, *The Worlding of Jean Rhys* (Westport, Conn.: Greenwood, 1999), 115–16; who follows Rachel Bowlby's extended discussion of the "impasse" in *Still Crazy After All These Years* (London: Routledge, 1992), 34–58; and Veronica Marie Gregg, *Jean Rhys's Historical Imagination: Reading and Writing the Creole* (Chapel Hill: University of North Carolina Press, 1995), 160. See also Parsons, *Streetwalking*, 144–45; and Victoria Rosner, *Modernism and the Architecture of Private Life* (New York: Columbia University Press, 2005), 1–2.

12. Many commentators argue that Rhys's female protagonists are not *flâneuses*, although the debate over whether they can or cannot be classified as such reproduces theoretical debates (Janet Wolff, Griselda Pollock, Rachel Bowlby, and Judith Walkowitz) over the category of *flâneur* and its combined gendered and class marking. See, in particular, Deborah Parsons's discussion of the status of the *flâneur* "as both historical figure and critical metaphor" (*Streetwalking,* 2) and her extended application of

the term throughout *Streetwalking*. See also Elizabeth Foley O'Connor's chapter on female *flânerie* in "Perambulating the Metropolis."

13. Walter Benjamin, *The Arcades Project* (Cambridge, Mass.: Belknap Press, 1999), 21; Benjamin, *Das Passagen-Werk* (2 Vols. Frankfurt: Suhrkamp, 1983) I, 70.

14. Benjamin, *Reflections*, 157; Benjamin, *Illuminationen*, 180.

15. Benjamin, *The Arcades Project*, 21.

16. Jacques Derrida, *Monolingualism of the Other: or The Prosthesis of Origin*, trans. Patrick Mensah (Stanford: Stanford University Press, 1998), 2; Derrida, *Le monolinguisme de l'autre: ou la prothèse d'origine* (Paris: Editions Galilée, 1996), 15.

17. Bowlby, *Still Crazy*, 57.

18. Ibid, 58.

19. Derrida, *Monolingualism*, 1; Derrida, *Le monolinguisme*, 13.

20. The literal meaning of the term and its figurative meanings (extending to the specific sense of a diplomatic stand-off) introduce a problem of topographical reference reproduced in the difficulty of tracing the word's French or English origins. The *O.E.D.* traces its etymology back to 1851, and cites Voltaire as the authority for the word's French origins. Voltaire, however, ascribes the French word to an *English* adoption of a lost French usage: "Nous avons renoncé à des expressions absolument nécessaires, dont les Anglais se sont heureusement enrichis. Une rue, un chemin sans issue, s'exprimait si bien par *non-passe, impasse* que les Anglais ont imité, et nous sommes réduits au mot bas et impertinent de *cul-de-sac* qui revient si souvent, et qui déshonore la langue française" (Voltaire, *Correspondance,* vol. 6 [Paris: Gallimard, 1980], 526). Here is a veritable "impasse" of modern national-linguistic etymology. The linguistic and cultural question of priority in relation between English and French delineates an Anglo-French modernism regulated according to a "monolingualism" of the other dominant language (French or English).

21. The precedent of Édouard Glissant's work is made explicit in Derrida, *Monolingualism*, 19; Derrida, *Le monolinguisme*, 36.

22. Entitled "From a 'dead-end' situation" ("*À partir d'une situation «bloquée»"*) the opening section of the Introduction poses the root problem of Martinique as "an inability to escape the present impasse" ("*une impuissance à sortir de l'impasse actuelle"*) (Édouard Glissant, *Caribbean Discourse: Selected Essays*, trans. J. Michael Dash [Charlottesville: University Press of Virginia, 1989], 1; Glissant, *Le discours antillais* [Paris: Gallimard, 1997], 13. In the first essay of the collection, the same figure is used to describe the situation of Martinique: "a people wedged in an impossible situation" (18) ("*peuple coincé dans un impossible*" [45]). Whether this is a specifically Martinican, or a more general Caribbean/Antillean formulation is, one might want to emphasize, one feature of the "impasse" of such a discourse. Chris Bongie argues that this "impasse" articulates Glissant's post-independence, postcolonial disenchantment with the project of decolonization (*Islands and Exiles: The Creole Identities of Post-Colonial Literature* [Stanford: Stanford University Press, 1998], 149–50).

23. Fernando Ortiz, *Cuban Counterpoint: Tobacco and Sugar*, trans. Harriet de Onís (Durham: Duke University Press, 1995), 102–3.

24. Glissant, *Caribbean Discourse*, 74, 75; Glissant, *Le discours*, 793, 794.

25. Paul Gilroy, *The Black Atlantic: Modernity and Double Consciousness* (Cambridge, Mass.: Harvard University Press, 1993), 75.

26. Brent Hayes Edwards, *The Practice of Diaspora: Literature, Translation, and the Rise of Black Internationalism* (Cambridge, Mass.: Harvard University Press, 2003).

27. Elaine Savory, *Jean Rhys* (Cambridge: Cambridge University Press, 1998), 117.

28. Gustave Flaubert, *Dictionary of Accepted Ideas*, trans. Jacques Barzun (Norfolk, Conn.: New Directions, 1954), 24; Flaubert, *Dictionnaire des idées recues* (Paris: A.G. Nizet, 1966), 120.

29. See, for example, Savory, *Jean Rhys*, 117–18; Thomas, *The Worlding of Jean Rhys*, 120; Gregg, *Jean Rhys's Historical Imagination*, 158; Delia Caparoso Konzett, *Ethnic Modernisms: Anzia Yezierska, Zora Neale Hurston, Jean Rhys, and the Aesthetics of Dislocation* (New York: Palgrave, 2002),165; and Christina Britzolakis, "'This way to the exhibition': Genealogies of Urban Spectacle in Jean Rhys's Interwar Fiction" (*Textual Practice* 21, no. 3 (2007), 457–482),463. Cf. also Erica Johnson, *Home, Maison, Casa: The Politics of Location in Works by Jean Rhys, Marguerite Duras, and Erminia Dell'Oro* (London: Associated University Presses, 2003), especially 48–49.

30. Thomas, 54–55.

31. Roland Barthes, *S/Z* (Paris: Éditions du Seuil, 1970), 10.

32. Cited in Benjamin, *Arcades Project*, 227. The original German for this passage reads: "[ich war], sowie alle anderen in diesem Hafen weilenden Seeleute ein blosser Gegenstand amtlicher Schreibereien und auszufüllender Formulare" (Benjamin, *Das Passagen-Werk*, 299).

33. Ibid.

34. Benjamin, *Reflections*, 155; Benjamin, *Illuminationen*, 178.

35. For more on the Paris Exhibition, see Britzolakis, "'This way to the exhibition.'"

36. Benjamin, *Reflections*, 155; Benjamin, *Illuminationen*, 178.

37. In the original German, the identities of Harbor Master and shipping master are confused in a parenthesis that identifies the latter with an earlier citation describing the former. This emphasizes all the more the problem of priority in mistaken racial identification. See Benjamin, *Das Passagen-Werk*, 299.

38. Benjamin, *Reflections*, 157; Benjamin, *Illuminationen*, 180.

Chapter 5

1. *The Letters of Jean Rhys*, eds. Francis Wyndham and Diana Melly (New York: Viking, 1984), 154.

2. Denise de Caires Narain, "Caribbean Creole: The Real Thing? Writing and Reading the Creole in a Selection of Caribbean Women's Texts," in *Essays and Studies 2000*, vol. 53 (Woodbridge, Suffolk: D. S. Brewer, 2000),105–6. Narain points to the 1950s as the period in which Caribbean writing began making use of "the rhythm and syntax of the demotic speech of the West Indies"—with such writers as Selvon, Salkey, Lamming, and Naipaul.

3. See Chris Bongie's application of the linguistic term "creole continuum" to this wider literary, cultural, and political formation (*Islands and Exiles: The Creole Identities of Post-Colonial Literature* [Stanford: Stanford University Press, 1998]), 23.

4. In her last chapter (entitled "The Helen of Our Wars: Cultural Politics and Jean Rhys Criticism"), Elaine Savory offers an excellent analysis of

how the debates between Hulme and Brathwaite reflect the wider contours of contest within critical responses to Rhys (*Jean Rhys* [Cambridge: Cambridge University Press, 1998], 196–225).

5. Mary Lou Emery, *Modernism, the Visual, and Caribbean Literature* (Cambridge: Cambridge University Press, 2007), 99.

6. Carolyn Vellenga Berman, *Creole Crossings: Domestic Fiction and the Reform of Colonial Slavery* (Ithaca: Cornell University Press, 2006), 171–72. It should be noted, however, that Berman explicitly points out that her purpose "is not to charge Rhys with white supremacy, but simply to dispute her monopoly on 'the real story' of Creole characterization."

7. Although I somewhat exaggerate the contrasting evaluations of Rhys in these two studies, the exaggeration usefully encapsulates the way Rhys's work itself has come to embody a potently contradictory political place within postcolonial studies. It might be noted that Emery's evaluation is premised almost entirely on a reading of the pre-World War II novels, while Berman's is premised almost entirely on a reading of *Wide Sargasso Sea*.

8. Berman, *Creole Crossings*, 38.

9. Ibid., 43.

10. The English translation underscores the literary fetish of this trope. Adding the parenthetical reference to Minke's notes (and excluding the additional phrase "and a smile on her lips that could demolish faith/confidence"), it connects this passage with its later repetition, and notably in the section that introduces the phrase "creole beauty," which I discuss in a moment.

11. Peter Hulme, "The locked heart: The Creole Family Romance of *Wide Sargasso Sea*" (in *Colonial Discourse, Postcolonial Theory*, eds. Francis Barker, Peter Hulme, and Margaret Iverson, 72–88 [Manchester, Eng.: Manchester University Press, 1994]). See, esp. 76: "*Wide Sargasso Sea*, as a writing out of [the] family history [of the Lockharts], a kind of extended autobiography or creole family romance, is offered as in some sense a 'compensation' for the ruin of that family at the time of Emancipation."

12. There are a number of passages from Jean Rhys's letters that support the kind of autobiographical reading that finds Rhys struggling with her own internalized racism. Berman cites one such letter, revealing the "racist" assumption that Christophine is "too articulate." Another letter that supports Berman's general claim for Rhys's effort to reserve the name of Creole for whites is equally revealing. In a letter to Selma Vaz Dias from April 27, 1953, explaining a well-established West Indian family, she offers the following parenthetical explanation: "All Creoles are not negroes. *On the contrary*" (*Collected Letters*, 108). This is a rather striking articulation of an impossible racist logic—a counterpart to the impasse of Creole consciousness in that its attempt to articulate the dominant place of white Creoles within West Indian society in fact reveals, in its duplicating negative forms, that "whiteness" can only take shape around a kind of pathological denial. This is, I argue, what gets articulated novelistically in Rochester's disavowal of Antoinette's Creole world and the construction of his own contradictory and pathological sense of white identity.

There are a number of passages from Pramoedya's prison memoirs that explicitly address his own sense of internalized racism, something for which he often uses the term "complex" (or "inferiority complex"). Most striking, in connection with the depiction of Annelies's "creole beauty," is his account of what he found beautiful in his first wife (this, in a letter to the daughter of that first wife): "she of the round face and large eyes. In the Dutch-language magazines of the time I'd often see pictures of American and European film stars, and their eyes were always so large, not at all like Indonesian eyes, not in the least like my mother's or father's eyes. Ever since I was a child, I'd thought large eyes to be more aesthetically pleasing; I wasn't attracted to the mongoloid features of my own race. And so it was your mother's eyes, with their hint of mixed blood, that enchanted me...." (*MS*, 193–94); "*Pada waktu kecil aku sering melihat-lihat gambar majalah-majalah Belanda. Bintang-bintang film Amerika dan Eropa itu selalu nampak bermata besar, bukan seperti mata sebangsaku yang kesipit-sipitan, tidak seperti mata ibuku, atau ayahku. Sudah sejak kecil mata besar itu menimbulkan perasaan estetik padaku, meninggalkan estetik mata* mongoloid. *Mata mamamu memang menarik aku, sekalipun di tengah-tengah masyarakat bermata kecil ia merasa malu sampai-sampai pernah menutupnya dengan kacamata netral*" (*NS* II, 174–75).

13. Frantz Fanon, *Black Skin, White Masks*, trans. Charles Lam Markmann (New York: Grove Press, 1952/1967), 9–10: "The white man is sealed in his whiteness. The black man in his blackness. We shall seek to ascertain the directions of this dual narcissism and the motivations that inspire it.... Concern with the elimination of a vicious circle has been the only guide-line for my efforts"; Fanon, *Peau noire, masques blancs* (Paris: Editions du Seuil, 1952), 7: "*Le Blanc est enfermé dans sa blancheur. Le Noir dans sa noirceur. Nous essaierons de determiner les tendances de ce double narcissisme et les motivations auxquelles il renvoie.... Le souci de mettre fin à un cercle vicieux a seul guidé nos efforts.*"

14. Clifford Geertz, "Java Jive," *New Republic* 214, no. 17 (April 22, 1996), 31–34.

15. Louis Couperus, *The Hidden Force*, trans. Alexander Teixeira de Mattos (Amherst: University of Massachusetts Press, 1985), 106; Couperus, *Mozaiek: een Keur uit zijn Werken* (Rotterdam: Nijgh and van Ditmar, 1949, 367.

16. Couperus, *Hidden Force*, 54; Couperus, *Mozaiek*, 329.

17. Couperus, *Hidden Force*, 54.

18. Couperus, *Mozaiek*, 329.

19. Couperus, *Hidden Force*, 55; Couperus, *Mozaiek*, 329.

20. Couperus, *Hidden Force*, 65; Couperus, *Mozaiek*, 338.

21. Couperus, *Hidden Force*, 106; Couperus, *Mozaiek*, 367.

22. Couperus, *Hidden Force*, 108; Couperus, *Mozaiek*, 369.

23. Couperus, *Hidden Force*, 197; Couperus, *Mozaiek*, 436.

24. Couperus, *Hidden Force*, 207–8.

25. Couperus, *Mozaiek*, 444.

26. Michel Foucault, *The History of Sexuality*, vol.1, trans. Robert Hurley (New York: Viking, 1980). But see also Ann Stoler's extended critique of Foucault in *Race and the Education of Desire* (Durham: Duke University Press, 1995).

27. Sigmund Freud, "Der Familienroman der Neurotiker," *Gesammelte Werke*, vol. 7 (Frankfurt: S. Fischer, 1941); Freud, "Family Romances," trans. James Strachey (New York: Avon, 1965); see also Françoise Verges, *Monsters and Revolutionaries: Colonial Family Romance and Metissage* (Durham: Duke University Press, 1999), 255.

28. See, for example, Sue Thomas, *The Worlding of Jean Rhys* (Westport, Conn.: Greenwood, 1999), 163; Nancy Harrison, *Jean Rhys and the Novel*

as Women's Text (Chapel Hill: North Carolina University Press, 1988), 232; and Savory, *Jean Rhys* (145–47).

29. Jean Rhys, *Wide Sargasso Sea*, 64.

30. See, esp., Gayatri Spivak, chapter 2 of *A Critique of Postcolonial Reason* (Cambridge, Mass.: Harvard University Press, 1999) and Benita Parry, chapter 1 of *Postcolonial Studies: A Materialist Critique* (London: Routledge, 2004). See also Judith L. Raiskin, *Snow on the Cane Fields: Women's Writing and Creole Subjectivity* (Minneapolis: University of Minnesota Press, 1996), 108; and Carine M. Mardorossian, "Shutting up the Subaltern: Silences, Stereotypes, and Double-Entendre in Jean Rhys's *Wide Sargasso Sea*" (*Callaloo* 22, no. 4 (1999), 1071–1090), 1071.

31. Homi Bhabha, *The Location of Culture* (London: Routledge, 1994), esp. chaps. 4 and 6.

32. The difficulty of disentangling the physical from the psychological weight of this image of Minke's "palakia tree" headache offers a suggestively "dialectical image," in Benjamin's sense, for the "impasse" of Minke's Creole consciousness, while underscoring, in counterpoint to our earlier discussion of the "impasse" of Rhys's Creole consciousness, the gendered, sexual logic of the "impasse" (in French, *sans issue*—i.e., without fruit) of modernity that Benjamin ascribes to Baudelaire.

33. See Kenneth Pomeranz and Steven Topik, *The World That Trade Created: Society, Culture, and the World Economy*, 2nd ed. (Armonk, N.Y.: M. E. Sharpe, 2006), 109 and 138ff.

34. Walter William Skeat, *Malay Magic: Being an Introduction to the Folklore and Popular Religion of the Malay Peninsula* (London: Macmillan, 1900), 333. A fuller account is given in the original article Skeat published on the subject ("Notes to Birth Customs," *Selangor Journal* 3, no. 17[May 3, 1895), 277: "Casting the child's horoscope: this may be done in several ways; i.e. either (a) by astrological calculations, (b) by the process called *Palakia* (Arab.) or *Palak* (Mal.) in which the Abjad (an alphabet whose letters have certain numerical values assigned to them) is used for casting up the letters of both parents' names."

Chapter 6

1. For a detailed historical investigation into this, see John Roosa, *Pretext for Mass Murder: The September 30th Movement and Suharto's Coup d'Etat in Indonesia* (Madison, WI: University of Wisconsin Press, 2006). See also Mary Zurbuchen, *Beginning to Remember: The Past in the Indonesian Present* (Singapore: Singapore University Press, 2005).

2. Chris GoGwilt, "Pramoedya's Fiction and History: An Interview with Indonesian Novelist Pramoedya Ananta Toer," *Yale Journal of Criticism* 9, no. 1 (1996), 156–57.

3. On Rinkes and *Balai Pustaka*, contrast A. Teeuw, *Modern Indonesian Literature*, vol 1 (Dordrecht: Foris, 1986), 13–15, with Henk Maier, *We Are Playing Relatives: A Survey of Malay Writing* (Leiden: KITLV Press, 2004), 163ff.

4. Ann Stoler, *Carnal Knowledge and Imperial Power: Race and the Intimate in Colonial Rule* (Berkeley: University of California Press, 2002), 48.

5. Jean Gelman Taylor, *The Social World of Batavia: European and Eurasian in Dutch Asia* (Madison, WI: University of Wisconsin Press, 1983), 147.

6. For definitions of the term *nyai*, see John M. Echols and Hassan Shadily, *An Indonesian-English Dictionary*, 3rd ed. (Ithaca, N.Y.: Cornell University Press, 1989), 392; Taylor, *Social World*, 30; Tineke Hellwig, *Adjustment and Discontent: Representations of Women in the Dutch East Indies* (Windsor, Ontario: Netherlandic Press, 1994), 31–32; Laurie Sears, "Introduction: Fragile Identities," in *Fantasizing the Feminine in Indonesia*, ed. Laurie Sears (Durham, N.C.: Duke University Press, 1996), 21; James Siegel, *Fetish, Recognition, Revolution* (Princeton, N.J.: Princeton University Press, 1997), 54.

7. Mikhail Bakhtin, *The Dialogic Imagination: Four Essays*, trans. Caryl Emerson and Michael Holquist (Austin, Tex.: University of Texas Press, 1981), see esp. 271–72.

8. Ann Laura Stoler, *Race and the Education of Desire* (Durham, N.C.: Duke University Press, 1995), esp. 95–136; and Stoler, *Carnal Knowledge*, esp.79–111.

9. Pramoedya Ananta Toer, *Sang Pemula* (Jakarta: Hasta Mitra, 1982), 296.

10. For a summary and discussion of Tirto's *Cerita Nyai Ratna*, see Adrian Vickers, *A History of Modern Indonesia* (Cambridge: Cambridge University Press, 2005), 62–65.

11. Pramoedya Ananta Toer, *Tempo Doeloe: Antologi Sastra Pra-Indonesia* (Jakarta: Hasta Mitra, 1982), 32; Siegel, *Fetish, Recognition, Revolution*, 54–93; Jean Taylor, "*Nyai Dasima*: Portrait of a Mistress in Literature and Film," in Laurie J. Sears, ed., *Fantasizing the Feminine*, 225–48.

12. See Tineke Hellwig, "Njai Dasima, een vrouw uit de literatuur," in *A Man of Indonesian Letters: Essays in Honour of A. Teeuw*, eds. C. M. S. Hellwig and S. O. Robson (Dordrecht: Foris, 1986), 48–66; Taylor, "*Nyai Dasima*"; Siegel, *Fetish, Recognition, Revolution*, 54–93.

13. Jean Taylor, "The World of Women in the Dutch Colonial Novel," *Kabar seberang sulating Maphilindo* 1 (1977), 26–41; 30.

14. Ibid.; Taylor, "*Nyai Dasima*," 248.

15. Pramoedya, *Tempo Doeloe*, 1.

16. Siegel, *Fetish, Recognition, Revolution*, 76.

17. Benedict Anderson, *Imagined Communities: Reflections on the Origin and Spread of Nationalism*, rev. ed. (London: Verso, 1991).

18. Gayatri Spivak, *A Critique of Postcolonial Reason: Toward a History of the Vanishing Present* (Cambridge, Mass.: Harvard University Press, 1999), 271.

19. Ranajit Guha and Gayatri Chakravorty Spivak, eds., *Selected Subaltern Studies* (Oxford: Oxford University Press, 1988), 44.

20. Sears, *Fantasizing the Feminine*, 23.

21. C. W. Watson, "Some Preliminary Remarks on the Antecedent of Modern Indonesian Literature," *Bijdragen tot de Taal-, Land- en Volkenkunde* 127, no. 4 (1971), 417–33; 423; Pramoedya, *Sang Pemula*, 294ff.

22. On Rinkes, see Pramoedya, *Sang Pemula*, esp. 151–71; and Doris Jedamski, "The Subjective Factor in Cultural Change," in *Pramoedya Ananta Toer: Essays to Honor Pramoedya Ananta Toer's 70th Year*, ed. Bob Hering (Stein: Yayasan Kabar Seberang, 1995), 190–210.

23. Pramoedya, *Sang Pemula*, 295; Wim Wertheim, "Pramoedya as Historian," in *Pramoedya Ananta Toer: Essays to Honor Pramoedya Ananta Toer's 70th Year*, ed. Bob Hering (Stein: Yayasan Kabar Seberang, 1995), 83.

24. Pramoedya Ananta Toer, *Realisme-Sosialis dan Sastra Indonesia* (Jakarta: Lentera Dipantara, 2003), 117, 114.

25. Pramoedya, *Sang Pemula*, 55.

26. An early attempt at reading Conrad's work in this way may be found in my "Conrad's Alien Genealogies: Joseph Conrad's 'Karain: A Memory,' Pramoedya Ananta Toer, and Postcolonial American Perspectives" (*Western Humanities Review*, LII, no. 2 [Summer 1998], 96–109).

27. Siegel, *Fetish, Recognition, Revolution,* 62.

28. Cited in Robert Hamner, *Joseph Conrad: Third World Perspectives* (Boulder: Three Continents Press, 1990), 31.

29. Hamner, *Joseph Conrad,* 33.

30. Cited in Hellwig, *Adjustment*, 33.

31. Cf. Joseph Conrad, *Almayer's Folly* (Garden City, N.Y.: Doubleday, Page, 1924), 112–13.

32. See Christopher GoGwilt, *The Invention of the West: Joseph Conrad and the Double-Mapping of Europe and Empire* (Stanford: Stanford University Press, 1995), 85.

33. GoGwilt, "Pramoedya's Fiction," 156.

34. It is also worth noting that Taminah's story ends up enacting some of the characteristic features of a *nyai* narrative, in what constitutes a curious translingual Malay-English coda to the novel as a whole. Babalatchi, recounting Almayer's story to Captain Ford, includes the tale of Taminah's death. In response to what the reader might suppose to be Ford's joking accusation that Babalatchi bought Taminah to be his own *nyai*, we read:

> "Nay, Tuan. Why do you speak bad words? I am old—that is true—but why should I not like the sight of a young face and the sound of a young voice in my house?" He paused, and then added with a little mournful laugh, "I am like a white man talking too much of what is not men's talk when they speak to one another." (*AF*, 207)

Foreclosing on a possible *nyai* narrative (and specifically, in terms of a transnational, English and Malay understanding of the domestic economy of *nyai* relations), this coda offers another instance of how Conrad reconstellates the problems of respectability and disrepute attached to the native *nyai* figure around the questionable figure (linguistic and literary) of the *tuan*.

35. Fredric Jameson, *The Political Unconscious: Narrative as a Socially Symbolic Act* (Ithaca, N.Y.: Cornell University Press, 1981).

36. Spivak, *Critique of Postcolonial Reason,* 4: "an unacknowledgeable moment that I will call 'the native informant' is crucially needed by the great texts; and it is foreclosed."

37. Stoler, *Carnal Knowledge*, 180.

Chapter 7

1. Pramoedya Ananta Toer, "My Apologies, in the Name of Experience," trans. Alex G. Bardsley, *Indonesia* 61 (April 1996), 4; "Ma'af: Atas Nama Pengalaman." *Kabar Seberang* 23 (1992), 1–9 (at http://home.earthlink.net/~agbardsley/prampage.html, accessed July 13, 2005), 3.

2. The epigraph to the first two volumes of the Buru tetralogy, echoing the metaphor of the "step by step" process of "writing to the roots," captures the sense in which Pramoedya's entire *oeuvre* may be conceived as an attempt to mark the gaps in historical record: "This narrow path has

been trod many a time already, it's only that this time the journey is one to mark the way" ("*Jalan setapak ini memang sudah sering ditempuh, hanya yang sekarang perjalan pematokan*"). In the original context, this forms a dedication to "Han" (G. J. Resink) that begins, "Han, certainly this is nothing new" ("*Han, memang bukan sesuatu yang baru*"), suggesting a parallel between the work of reconstructing lost historical work on Buru and the earlier "rescue work" Pramoedya attributes to Resink for saving his manuscripts from Bukitduri prison in 1948–49.

3. See Henk Maier, *We Are Playing Relatives: A Survey of Malay Writing* (Leiden: KITLV Press, 2004), 41–42.

4. Pramoedya, "My Apologies," 7; "Ma'af," 5.

5. In prefatory remarks for the English edition of *The Mute's Soliloquy*, Pramoedya wrote: "Most of my notes about the period before 1973 were destroyed: some I myself was forced to destroy in the interest of my own safety; others were destroyed by the authorities. I have no idea how many pages of notes I wrote in the end, but what we have here is some of what I managed to salvage" (*MS*, 5).

6. As I note in "The Voice of Pramoedya Ananta Toer: Passages, Interviews, and Reflections from *The Mute's Soliloquy* and Pramoedya's North American Tour" (*Cultural Critique* 55 [Fall 2003], 217–246, 243), there seems to be no corresponding formulation of "mute's soliloquy" in the published Indonesian and Dutch versions of *The Mute's Soliloquy*. However, as the translator and editor, Willem Samuels, points out in his concluding note, his translation is based not on those published versions but on the original, unedited transcript.

7. Pramoedya, "My Apologies," 6; "Ma'af," 5.

8. Ibid., 7; 6.

9. Ibid., 1; 1.

10. Maier, *We Are Playing Relatives*, 42.

11. Ibid., 41–42.

12. Goenawan Mohamad, "A Kind of Silence" (address given at the Asia Society, April 22, 1999; at http://home.earthlink.net/~agbardsley/goen.html; accessed August, 2003).

13. See A. Teeuw, *Pramoedya Ananta Toer: De verbeelding van Indonesië* (Breda: de Geus, 1993), 38; Max Lane, "Pramoedya, Racialism and Socialism," in *The Chinese in Indonesia* (Singapore: Select Books, 2007), 31; and Sumit Mandal, "'Strangers Who Are Not Foreign: Pramoedya's Disturbing Language on the Chinese of Indonesia," in *The Chinese in Indonesia*, trans. Max Lane (Singapore: Select Books, 2007), esp. 42–43.

14. Mandal, in *CI*, 35–54.

15. See Edward Said, *The World, the Text, and the Critic* (Cambridge, Mass.: Harvard University Press, 1983), who outlines his argument in the Introduction on "Secular Criticism" (1–30) and draws on it throughout the set of essays collected in this book.

16. Ibid., 19.

17. Benedict Anderson, *Language and Power: Exploring Political Cultures in Indonesia* (Ithaca, N.Y.: Cornell University Press, 1990), 219.

18. Ibid., 245.

19. Paul W. Van der Veur, ed., *Toward a Glorious Indonesia: Reminiscences and Observations of Dr. Soetomo*, trans. Suhami Soemarmo and Paul W. Van der Veur (Athens, Ohio: Ohio University Center for International Studies, 1987), 3–4.

20. Anderson, *Language and Power*, 262.

21. Michel Foucault, *Language, Counter-memory, Practice: Selected Essays and Interviews,* ed. Donald F. Bouchard (Ithaca, N.Y.: Cornell University Press, 1977), 139; Michel Foucault, "Nietzsche, la généalogie, l'histoire" (in *Hommage à Jean Hyppolite,* 145–172 [Paris: Presses Universitaires de France, 1971]), 145.

22. Anderson, *Language and Power,* 267.

23. Pramoedya, "My Apologies," 1; Pramoedya, "Ma'af," 1.

24. See Bardsley's note to the translation, Pramoedya, "My Apologies," 1.

25. John M. Echols and Hassan Shadily give the first definition for *lanjaran* in their *Indonesian-English Dictionary,* 3rd ed. (Ithaca, N.Y.: Cornell University Press, 1989); the second definition (along with a version of the first—specifically "supporting pole for climbing plant") is from Stuart Robson and Singgih Wibisono, *Javanese-English Dictionary* (Singapore: Periplus, 2002), 425.

26. The front cover of the third printing of the Indonesian edition describes the novel this way, although the novel itself is subtitled "a historical novel" ("*sebuah novel sejarah*").

27. Pramoedya Ananta Toer, *Arus Balik* (Jakarta: Hasta Mitra, 1995), 739. All translations are my own.

28. Pramoedya, "My Apologies," 3.

29. Pramoedya, "Ma'af," 5.

30. Maier, *We Are Playing Relatives,* 41–42.

31. Pramoedya, "My Apologies," 7; "Ma'af," 4.

32. Ibid., 7; 5.

33. Ibid., 6; 4.

34. See my "The Voice of Pramoedya Ananta Toer," 236; the original Indonesian is in the unpublished transcript of Pramoedya's typewritten responses, p. 2.

35. Pramoedya Ananta Toer, "*Perburuan* 1950 and *Keluarga Gerilya* 1950," *Indonesia* 36 (October 1983), 25–48; 25.

Conclusion

1. Seth Lerer, *Error and the Academic Self: The Scholarly Imagination, Medieval to Modern* (New York: Columbia University Press, 2002), 108.

2. Hugh Kenner, *The Pound Era* (Berkeley: University of California Press, 1971), 102. As Lerer notes, "the story of the *Oxford English Dictionary* has been written many times" (Lerer, *Error,* 108). See also Hans Aarsleff, *Study of Language in England, 1780–1860* (Princeton, N.J.: Princeton University Press, 1967); Tony Crowley, *Standard English and the Politics of Language,* 2nd ed. (New York: Palgrave Macmillan, 2003); Lynda Mugglestone, *Lexicography and the OED: Pioneers in the Untrodden Forest* (Oxford: Oxford University Press, 2000); and Simon Winchester, *The Professor and the Madman* and *The Meaning of Everything.*

3. Walter D. Mignolo, *The Darker Side of the Renaissance: Literacy, Territoriality, & Colonization* (Ann Arbor: University of Michigan Press, 2003), 9.

4. Ibid., 8. This "new philology" also provides a key model for Henk Maier's *We Are Playing Relatives: A Survey of Malay Writing* (Leiden: KITLV Press, 2004).

5. For illuminating discussions of the relationship between Pangemanann and the archivist see Laurie J. Sears, *Shadows of Empire: Colonial Discourse and Javanese Tales* (Durham, N.C.: Duke University

Press, 1996), 9ff; and Ann Laura Stoler, *Along the Archival Grain: Epistemic Anxieties and Colonial Common Sense* (Princeton: Princeton University Press, 2009), 17ff.

6. For especially illuminating discussions of this, see Bernard Cohn, "The Command of Language and the Language of Command," in his *Colonialism and Its Forms of Knowledge: the British in India* (Princeton, N.J.: Princeton University Press, 1996); and Vinay Dharwadker, "Orientalism and the Study of Indian Literatures," in *Orientalism and the Postcolonial Predicament*, eds. Carol and Peter van der Veer (Philadelphia: University of Pennsylvania Press, 1993).

7. Edward Said, *Beginnings: Intention and Method* (New York: Columbia University Press, 1985), 188.

8. For contrasting assessments of Edward Said, see, inter alia, Aijaz Ahmad, *In Theory: Classes, Nations, Literatures* (London: Verso, 1992), Emily Apter, *The Translation Zone: A New Comparative Literature* (Princeton: Princeton University Press, 2006), and Timothy Brennan, *Wars of Position: The Cultural Politics of Left and Right* (New York: Columbia University Press, 2006).

9. Cf. Jonathan Culler, *The Literary in Theory* (Stanford: Stanford University Press, 2007), 15.

10. Michel Foucault, *The Order of Things: An Archaeology of the Human Sciences* (New York: Vintage, 1973), 296; Foucault, *Les mots et les choses: une archéologie des sciences humaines* (Paris: Gallimard, 1966), 309.

11. Foucault, *The Order of Things*, 299–300.

12. Foucault, *Les mots et les choses*, 312–13.

13. Foucault, *The Order of Things*, 300; Foucault, *Les mots et les choses*, 313.

14. Chinua Achebe, *Things Fall Apart* (London: Heinemann, 1958), 176.

15. V. S. Naipaul, *Literary Occasions: Essays* (New York: Vintage, 2003), 45–46.

16. Ibid., 45.

17. V. S. Naipaul, *The Mimic Men* (New York: Vintage, 1967/2001), 38.

18. Ngũgĩ Wa Thiong'o, *Moving the Centre: the Struggle for Cultural Freedoms* (Oxford: James Currey, 1993), 3.

19. V. S. Naipaul, *The Return of Eva Perón* (New York: Vintage, 1981), 236.

20. Virginia Woolf, *The Common Reader: First Series* (New York: Harcourt Brace Jovanovich, 1925/1953), 229.

21. Chinua Achebe, *Hopes and Impediments: Selected Essays* (New York: Anchor, 1989), 12.

22. Naipaul, *The Return*, 231.

23. Achebe, *Hopes*, 5.

24. Ibid., 12.

25. Following Christopher Miller's study *Blank Darkness: Africanist Discourse in French* (Chicago: University of Chicago Press, 1985), one might see how Conrad's English is indeed premised on a prior French engagement with just this issue.

26. Cited in Naipaul, *The Return*, 231.

27. Ibid.

28. Ibid., 233.

29. Ibid.

30. Ibid.

31. Achebe, *Hopes*, 7.

32. Foucault, *The Order of Things*, 373ff; Foucault, *Les mots et les choses*, 385ff.

33. Foucault, *The Order of Things*, 282; Foucault, *Les mots et les choses*, 294.

34. See, for example, Jacques Derrida, *Acts of Religion* (New York: Routledge, 2002), 89.

35. John Guillory, *Cultural Capital: The Problem of Literary Canon Formation* (Chicago: University of Chicago Press, 1993), chap. 4.

36. Marc Redfield, "Professing Literature: John Guillory's Misreading of Paul de Man," in *Legacies of Paul de Man*, ed. Marc Redfield (New York: Fordham University Press, 2007), 118.

37. Guillory, *Cultural Capital*, 221.

38. See John M. Echols and Hassan Shadily, *An Indonesian-English Dictionary*, 3rd ed. (Ithaca, N.Y.: Cornell University Press, 1989), 289. Recall Henk Maier's point about the network of meanings suggested by the term *membaca* and its root, *baca*: "The translation we find in most dictionaries is 'to read,' but then 'to read' certainly does not cover everything that is evoked by *membaca*. *Baca* (and its variant *membaca*) refer to 'read' and 'recite' at once, to the movement of the eyes as well as to the movement of the vocal cords, to 'silence' as well as 'sound,' but also to 'leaning on paper' and 'leaning on memory.' *Baca*, in other words, points in many directions, calling up a network of other words in its wake when we try to read it in its English mirror" (*We Are Playing Relatives*, 40).

39. Two key examples of Paul de Man's treatment of this are "Semiology and Rhetoric" (in *Allegories of Reading: Figural Language in Rousseau, Nietzsche, Rilke, and Proust* [New Haven: Yale University Press, 1979]) and "The Rhetoric of Temporality" (in *Blindness and Insight: Essays in the Rhetoric of Contemporary Criticism* [2nd ed. Minneapolis: University of Minnesota Press, 1983]). Cf. also Harry Berger, Jr., *Situated Utterances: Texts, Bodies, and Cultural Representations* (New York: Fordham University Press, 2005), esp. Chap. 1.

40. Jacques Derrida, *Margins of Philosophy*, trans. Alan Bass (Chicago: University of Chicago Press, 1982), 225.

41. Cited in Derrida, *Margins of Philosophy*, 225.

42. Jacques Derrida, *Marges de la philosophie* (Paris: Editions de Minuit, 1972), 267.

43. Srinivas Aravamudan, *Tropicopolitans: Colonialism and Agency, 1688–1804* (Durham, N.C.: Duke University Press, 1999), 4.

44. Ibid, 10.

45. Ibid., 24.

46. Derrida, *Margins of Philosophy*, 220; Derrida, *Marges de la philosophie*, 261.

47. Michael J. Dash, *The Other America: Caribbean Literature in a New World Context* (Charlottesville: University Press of Virginia, 1998), 41.

48. The first citation for the *O.E.D.* definition of *modernism*:—"A usage, mode of expression, or peculiarity of style or workmanship, characteristic of modern times"—is from Jonathan Swift: "The corruption of English by those Scribblers, who send us over their trash in Prose and Verse, with abominable curtailings and quaint modernisms." By the time this *O.E.D.* definition was first published (March 1908), the more specialized definition of *modernism* (added to later editions of the *O.E.D.* and described by Raymond Williams [see chapter 1, note 1]) was already in circulation. As Matei Calinescu points out, moreover, this sense of the word comes from a

Latin American provenance: "The first to use the label of 'modernism' approvingly to designate a larger contemporary movement of aesthetic renovation was Rubén Darío, the acknowledged founder of *el modernismo* in the early 1890s" (*Five Faces of Modernity: Modernism, Avant-Garde, Decadence, Kitsch, Postmodernism* [Durham, NC: Duke University Press, 1987], 69). To this we might add the specifically Indonesian sense of the word *modernism* (*modernisme*) by which Pramoedya singled out the period of formative literature (*sastra gatra*), with the emergence of the first native press, associated with Tirto Adi Suryo (see Pramoedya Ananta Toer, *Realisme-Sosialis dan Sastra Indonesia* [Jakarta: Lentera Dipantara, 2003], 118)—echoed in Minke's fascination with the word *modern* in *TE*, 18 (*BM*, 4).

49. In *The Structure of Complex Words* (Ann Arbor: University of Michigan Press, 1967), William Empson addresses, and attempts to find a way to redress, the different types of "confusion" produced by the *O.E.D.*'s "struggle...to show the complete historical development of a word" (394).

50. Ford Madox Ford, *Joseph Conrad: A Personal Remembrance* (New York: Ecco, 1989), 229. See discussion in chap. 3.

51. As might be expected from the C. L. R. James who revised European genealogies of revolutionary history by giving priority to the example of the Haitian revolution in *The Black Jacobins* (New York: Vintage, 1989). On C. L. R. James, see, inter alia, Homi Bhabha, *The Location of Culture* (London: Routledge, 1994), 174; Chris Bongie, *Islands and Exiles: The Creole Identities of Post-Colonial Literature* (Stanford: Stanford University Press, 1998), 4; Dash, *The Other America*; and Aravamudan, *Tropicopolitans*, chap. 7.

52. Raymond Williams, *Keywords: A Vocabulary of Culture and Society* (New York: Oxford University Press, 1985), 18.

53. See, for example, Bruce Burgett and Glenn Hendler, eds., *Keywords for American Cultural Studies* (New York: New York University Press, 2007), 2–3.

54. Williams, *Keywords*, 18–19.

55. Brent Hayes Edwards, *The Practice of Diaspora: Literature, Translation, and the Rise of Black Internationalism* (Cambridge, Mass.: Harvard University Press, 2003), 7.

56. Underscoring the archival significance of the *O.E.D.*, it should be noted that this is also one of the most visible instances in which the online project of the *O.E.D.*, in its ambitious ongoing effort to update the dictionary, is also engaged in an effacement of its own archive; although it retains Greek, it drops Arabic and Persian script.

57. Mignolo, *The Darker Side of the Renaissance*, 8.

BIBLIOGRAPHY

Aarsleff, Hans. *The Study of Language in England, 1780–1860*. Princeton: Princeton University Press, 1967.
Achebe, Chinua. *Hopes and Impediments: Selected Essays*. New York: Anchor, 1989.
———. *Things Fall Apart*. London: Heinemann, 1958.
Adorno, Theodor. *Essays on Music*. Berkeley: University of California Press, 2002.
———. *Philosophie der neuen Musik*. Frankfurt: Suhrkamp, 1978.
———. *Philosophy of New Music*. Trans. Robert Hullot-Kentor. Minneapolis: University of Minnesota Press, 2006.
Agamben, Giorgio. *The Man Without Content*. Trans. Georgia Albert. Meridian Series. Stanford: Stanford University Press, 1999.
Ahmad, Aijaz. *In Theory: Classes, Nations, Literatures*. London: Verso, 1992.
Anderson, Benedict. *Imagined Communities: Reflections on the Origin and Spread of Nationalism*. Rev. ed. London: Verso, 1991.
———. *Language and Power: Exploring Political Cultures in Indonesia*. Ithaca, N.Y.: Cornell University Press, 1990.
———. *Mythology and the Tolerance of the Javanese*. 2nd ed. Ithaca, N.Y.: Southeast Asia Program, 1996.
———. *The Spectre of Comparisons: Nationalism, Southeast Asia and the World*. London: Verso, 1998.
Angier, Carole. *Jean Rhys: Life and Work*. Boston: Little, Brown, 1990.
Apter, Emily. *The Translation Zone: A New Comparative Literature*. Princeton: Princeton University Press, 2006.
Aravamudan, Srinivas. *Tropicopolitans: Colonialism and Agency, 1688–1804*. Durham, N.C.: Duke University Press, 1999.
Bahari, Razif. *Pramoedya Postcolonially: (Re-)Viewing History, Gender and Identity in the Buru Tetralogy*. Denpasar, Bali: Pustaka Larasan, 2007.
Bakhtin, Mikhail. *The Dialogic Imagination: Four Essays*. Trans. Caryl Emerson and Michael Holquist. Austin: University of Texas Press, 1981.
Barthes, Roland. *Le bruissement de la langue. Essais Critiques*. Vol. 4. Paris: Éditions du Seuil, 1984.

———. *Image, Music, Text*, trans. Stephen Heath. New York: Hill and Wang, 1977.
———. *S/Z*. Paris: Éditions du Seuil, 1970.
———. *S/Z: An Essay*. Trans. Richard Miller. New York: Hill and Wang, 1975.
Baucom, Ian. *Out of Place: Englishness, Empire, and the Locations of Identity*. Princeton: Princeton University Press, 1999.
Becker, A. L. *Beyond Translation: Essays toward a Modern Philology*. Ann Arbor: University of Michigan Press, 1995.
Begam, Richard, and Michael Valdez Moses, Eds. *Modernism and Colonialism: British and Irish Literature 1899–1939*. Durham, N.C.: Duke University Press, 2007.
Bender, Todd K. *Literary Impressionism in Jean Rhys, Ford Madox Ford, Joseph Conrad, and Charlotte Brontë*. New York: Garland, 1997.
Beng, Tan Sooi. *Bangsawan: A Social and Stylistic History of Popular Malay Opera*. Singapore: Oxford University Press, 1993.
Benítez-Rojo, Antonio. *The Repeating Island: The Caribbean and the Postmodern Perspective*. 2nd ed. Trans. James E. Maraniss Durham: Duke University Press, [1992] 1996.
Benjamin, Walter. *The Arcades Project*. Cambridge, Mass.: Belknap Press, 1999.
———. *Illuminationen: Ausgewählte Schriften*. Frankfurt: Suhrkamp, 1977.
———. *Illuminations*. Trans. Harry Zohn. New York: Schocken, 1969.
———. *Das Passagen-Werk*. 2 Vols. Frankfurt: Suhrkamp, 1983.
———. *Reflections: Essays, Aphorisms, Autobiographical Writings*. New York: Schocken, 1978.
Benstock, Shari. *Women of the Left Bank: Paris, 1900-1940*. Austin, Tex: University of Texas Press, 1986.
Berger, Harry. Jr. *Situated Utterances: Texts, Bodies, and Cultural Representations*. New York: Fordham University Press, 2005.
Berman, Carolyn Vellenga. *Creole Crossings: Domestic Fiction and the Reform of Colonial Slavery*. Ithaca: Cornell University Press, 2006.
Bernabé, Jean. *Éloge de la Créolité*. Paris: Gallimard, 1989.
Bernabé, Jean, Patrick Chamoiseau, and Raphaël Confiant. "In Praise of Creoleness." Trans. Mohamed B. Taleb Khyar. *Callaloo* 13 (1990): 886–909.
Bhabha, Homi. *The Location of Culture*. London: Routledge, 1994.
Boehmer, Elleke. *Empire, the National, and the Postcolonial, 1890–1920*. Oxford: Oxford University Press, 2002.
Bongie, Chris. *Islands and Exiles: The Creole Identities of Post-Colonial Literature*. Stanford: Stanford University Press, 1998.
Bourdieu, Pierre. *Les règles de l'art: genèse et structure du champ littéraire*. Paris: Éditions du Seuil, 1992.
———. *The Rules of Art: Genesis and Structure of the Literary Field*. Trans. Susan Emanuel. Stanford: Stanford University Press, 1995.
Bowlby, Rachel. *Still Crazy After All These Years: Women, Writing and Psychoanalysis*. London: Routledge, 1992.
Brathwaite, Edward Kamau. *Contradictory Omens: Cultural diversity and integration in the Caribbean*. Mona, Jamaica: Savacou Publications, 1974.
———. *History of the Voice: The Development of Nation Language in Anglophone Caribbean Poetry*. London: New Beacon Books, 1984.

———. *The Development of Creole Society in Jamaica, 1770–1820*. Oxford: Clarendon Press, 1971.
Breckenridge, Carol A., and Peter van der Veer. *Orientalism and the Postcolonial Predicament: Perspectives on South Asia*. Philadelphia: University of Pennsylvania Press, 1993.
Brennan, Timothy. *Wars of Position: The Cultural Politics of Left and Right*. New York: Columbia University Press, 2006.
Britzolakis, Christina. "'This way to the exhibition': Genealogies of Urban Spectacle in Jean Rhys's Interwar Fiction." *Textual Practice* 21, no. 3 (2007), 457–82.
Buck-Morss, Susan. *The Dialectics of Seeing: Walter Benjamin and the Arcades Project*. Cambridge, Mass: MIT Press, 1993.
———. *Hegel, Haiti, and Universal History*. Pittsburgh, Pa: University of Pittsburgh Press, 2009.
Budden, Julian. *The Operas of Verdi*. Vol. 2. New York: Oxford University Press, 1979.
Burgett, Bruce, and Glenn Hendler, Eds. *Keywords for American Cultural Studies*. New York: New York University Press, 2007.
Butler, Judith. *Bodies that Matter: on the Discursive Limits of "Sex."* New York: Routledge, 1993.
Calinescu, Matei. *Five Faces of Modernity: Modernism, Avant-Garde, Decadence, Kitsch, Postmodernism*. Durham, N.C.: Duke University Press, 1987.
Casarino, Cesare. *Modernity at Sea: Melville, Marx, Conrad in Crisis. Vol. 21: Theory out of Bounds*. Minneapolis: University of Minnesota Press, 2002.
Cheah, Pheng. *Spectral Nationality: Passages of Freedom from Kant to Postcolonial Literatures of Liberation*. New York: Columbia University Press, 2003.
Cohen, Matthew Isaac. *The Komedie Stamboul: Popular Theater in Colonial Indonesia, 1891-1903*. Athens, Ohio: Ohio University Press, 2006.
Cohn, Bernard S. *Colonialism and Its Forms of Knowledge: The British in India*. Princeton: Princeton University Press, 1996.
Conrad, Joseph. *Almayer's Folly: A Story of an Eastern River*. Ed. Jacques Berthoud. Oxford World's Classics. Oxford: Oxford University Press, 1992.
———. *An Outcast of the Islands*. Ed. J. H. Stape and Hans van Marle. Oxford World's Classics. Oxford: Oxford University Press, 1992.
———. *The Collected Letters of Joseph Conrad*. Eds. Frederick Karl and Laurence Davies. 9 vols. Cambridge: Cambridge University Press, 1983–2007.
———. *The Collected Works*. 26 vols. Garden City, N.Y.: Doubleday, Page, 1926.
———, and Ford Madox Ford. *The Nature of a Crime*. Garden City, N.Y.: Doubleday, Page, 1924.
Cooke, Mervyn. *Britten and the Far East: East Asian Influences on the Music of Benjamin Britten*. Woodbridge, Suffolk: Boydell & Brewer, 2001.
Coronil, Fernando. "Transculturation and the Politics of Theory: Countering the Center, Cuban Counterpoint." Introduction to Fernando Ortiz, *Cuban Counterpoint: Tobacco and Sugar,* trans. Harriet de Onís. Durham, N.C.: Duke University Press, 1995.
Couperus, Louis. *The Hidden Force*. Trans. Alexander Teixeira de Mattos. Rev. ed. Library of the Indies. Amherst: University of Massachusetts Press, [1900] 1985.

———. *Mozaiek: een Keur uit zijn Werken*. Rotterdam: Nijgh and van Ditmar, 1949.
Crowley, Tony. *Standard English and the Politics of Language*. 2nd ed. New York: Palgrave Macmillan, [1989] 2003.
Culler, Jonathan. *The Literary in Theory*. Stanford: Stanford University Press, 2007.
Darras, Jacques. *Joseph Conrad and the West: Signs of Empire*. Trans. Anne Luyat. London: Macmillan, 1982.
Dash, J. Michael. *The Other America: Caribbean Literature in a New World Context*. New World Studies. Charlottesville: University Press of Virginia, 1998.
de Certeau, Michel. *L'Invention du quotidien*. Paris: Union Générale d'Editions, 1980.
———. *The Practice of Everyday Life*. Berkeley: University of California Press, 1984.
de Man, Paul. *Allegories of Reading: Figural Language in Rousseau, Nietzsche, Rilke, and Proust*. New Haven: Yale University Press, 1979.
———. *Blindness and Insight: Essays in the Rhetoric of Contemporary Criticism*. 2nd ed. Minneapolis: University of Minnesota Press, 1983.
DeKoven, Marianne. *Rich and Strange: Gender, History, Modernism*. Princeton: Princeton University Press, 1991.
De Lange, Attie, Gail Fincham, and Wieslaw Krajka, Eds. *Conrad in Africa: New Essays on "Heart of Darkness."* Boulder, Colo.: Social Sciences Monographs, 2002.
Derrida, Jacques. *Acts of Religion*. New York: Routledge, 2002.
———. *Dissemination*. Trans. Barbara Johnson. Chicago: University of Chicago Press, 1981.
———. *La dissémination*. Paris: Éditions du Seuil, 1972.
———. *Marges de la philosophie*. Paris: Éditions de Minuit, 1972.
———. *Margins of Philosophy*. Trans. Alan Bass. Chicago: University of Chicago Press, 1982.
———. *Monolingualism of the Other: or The Prosthesis of Origin*. Trans. Patrick Mensah. Stanford: Stanford University Press, 1998.
———. *Le monolinguisme de l'autre: ou la prothèse d'origine*. Paris: Editions Galilée, 1996.
Dharwadker, Vinay. "Orientalism and the Study of Indian Literatures." In *Orientalism and the Postcolonial Predicament,* eds. Carol Breckenridge and Peter van der Veer. (pp. 158–83). Philadephia: University of Pennsylvania Press, 1993.
Dillon, Elizabeth Maddock. "The Secret History of the Early American Novel: Leonora Sansay and the Revolution in Saint Domingue." *Novel* 40, no. 1 (Spring 2006): 77–103.
Domínguez, Virginia R. *White by Definition: Social Classification in Creole Louisiana*. New Brunswick, N.J.: Rutgers University Press, 1986.
Du Bois, W. E. B. *The Souls of Black Folk*. New York: Signet, 1982.
du Perron, E. *Country of Origin*. Trans. Francis Bulhof and Elizabeth Daverman. Amherst: University of Massachusetts Press, 1984.
Dupriez, Bernard. *A Dictionary of Literary Devices*. Trans and adapted by Albert W. Halsall. Toronto: University of Toronto Press, 1991.
Echols, John M., and Hassan Shadily. *An Indonesian-English Dictionary*. 3rd. ed. Ithaca, N.Y.: Cornell University Press, 1989.
Edwards, Brent Hayes. *The Practice of Diaspora: Literature, Translation, and the Rise of Black Internationalism*. Cambridge, Mass: Harvard University Press, 2003.

Emery, Mary Lou. *Jean Rhys at "World's End": Novels of Colonial and Sexual Exile*. Austin: University of Texas Press, 1990.

———. *Modernism, the Visual, and Caribbean Literature*. Cambridge: Cambridge University Press, 2007.

Empson, William. *The Structure of Complex Words*. Ann Arbor: University of Michigan Press, 1967.

Fanon, Frantz. *Black Skin, White Masks*. Trans. Charles Lam Markmann. New York: Grove Press, [1952] 1967.

———. *Les damnés de la terre*. Paris: Maspero, 1970.

———. *Peau noire, masques blancs*. Paris: Éditions du Seuil, 1952.

———. *The Wretched of the Earth*. Trans. Constance Farrington. New York: Grove Press, [1961] 1968.

Fernando, Lloyd. "Conrad's Eastern Expatriates: A New Version of His Outcasts." *PMLA*, 91, no. 1 (January 1976), 78-90. Reprinted in Hamner, Robert, Ed. *Joseph Conrad: Third World Perspectives*. Boulder, Colo.: Three Continents Press, 1990.

Flaubert, Gustave. *Dictionary of Accepted Ideas*. Trans. Jacques Barzun. Norfolk, Conn.: New Directions, 1954.

———. *Dictionnaire des idées reçues*. Paris: A. G. Nizet, 1966.

———. *Madame Bovary*. Paris: Garnier-Flammarion, 1966.

———. *Madame Bovary*. Trans. Alan Russell. Harmondsworth: Penguin, [1950] 1981.

Fleishman, Avrom. *Conrad's Politics: Community and Anarchy in the Fiction of Joseph Conrad*. Baltimore: Johns Hopkins University Press, 1967.

Florida, Nancy. *Writing the Past, Inscribing the Future: History as Prophecy in Colonial Java*. Durham, N.C.: Duke University Press, 1995.

Ford, Ford Madox. *It Was the Nightingale*. New York: Octagon Books, [1933] 1975.

———. "Joseph Conrad." *The English Review*. 10, (December 1911): 68–83.

———. *Joseph Conrad: A Personal Remembrance*. New York: Ecco, [1924] 1989.

———. *Return to Yesterday*. New York: Liveright, [1932]1972.

———, Ed. *the transatlantic review, 1924*. 2 Vols. New York: Kraus Reprint, 1967.

Foucault, Michel. "Nietzsche, la généalogie, l'histoire." In *Hommage à Jean Hyppolite*. 145–72. Paris: Presses Universitaires de France, 1971.

———. *The History of Sexuality. Vol. 1: An Introduction*. Trans. Robert Hurley. New York: Vintage, 1980.

———. *Language, Counter-memory, Practice: Selected Essays and Interviews*. Ed. Donald F. Bouchard. Ithaca, N.Y.: Cornell University Press, 1977.

———. *Les mots et les choses: une archéologie des sciences humaines*. Paris: Gallimard, 1966.

———. *The Order of Things: An Archaeology of the Human Sciences*. New York: Vintage, 1973.

———. "Qu'est-ce qu'un auteur?" *Bulletin de la Société française de Philosophie* 63, no. 3 (1969), 73–104.

Foulcher, Keith. "The Early Fiction of Pramoedya Ananta Toer, 1946–1949." In *Text/Politics in Island Southeast Asia: Essays in Interpretation*, ed. D. M. Roskies (pp. 191–220). Athens: Ohio University Press, 1993.

Friedman, Susan Stanford. "Periodizing Modernism: Postcolonial Modernities and the Space/Time Borders of Modernist Studies," *Modernism/modernity* 13, no. 3 (2006), 423–43.

Freud, Sigmund. *Beyond the Pleasure Principle*. Trans. James Strachey. New York: Norton, 1961.

———. "Family Romances." Trans. James Strachey. Vol.9. London: Hogarth, 1909.

———. "Der Familienroman der Neurotiker." In *Gesammelte Werke*. (Vol. 7, pp. 227–31). Frankfurt: S. Fischer, 1941.

———. *Gesammelte Werke*. 18 vols. Frankfurt: S. Fischer, 1941.

———. *The Interpretation of Dreams*. Trans. James Strachey. New York: Avon, 1965.

Fuss, Diana. *Identification Papers*. New York: Routledge, 1995.

Geertz, Clifford. "Java Jive." *New Republic* 214, no. 17 (April 22, 1996): 31–34.

———. *The Religion of Java*. Glencoe, Ill.: Free Press, 1960.

Gilroy, Paul. *The Black Atlantic: Modernity and Double Consciousness*. Cambridge, Mass: Harvard University Press, 1993.

Glissant, Édouard. *Caribbean Discourse: Selected Essays*. Trans. J. Michael Dash. Caraf Books. Charlottesville: University Press of Virginia, 1989.

———. *Le discours antillais*. Paris: Gallimard, [1981/1990] 1997.

Goenawan Mohamad. "A Kind of Silence." Address given at the Asia Society, April 22, 1999. At http://home.earthlink.net/~agbardsley/goen.html, accessed August 2003

———. "Pasemon: On Allusion and Illusions." In *Menagerie 2* (pp. 119–35). Jakarta: Lontar, 1993.

———. *Sidelines: Thought Pieces from TEMPO Magazine*. Trans. Jennifer Lindsay. Jakarta: Lontar, 1994.

Goethe, Johann Wolfgang von. *Essays on Art and Literature*. Ed. John Gearey. Trans. Ellen von Nardroff and Ernest H. von Nardroff. Princeton: Princeton University Press, 1986.

———. *Goethes Werke. Vol. 43: Goethes Briefe*. Weimar: Hermann Böhlaus, 1908.

GoGwilt, Christopher. "Conrad's Alien Genealogies: Joseph Conrad's 'Karain: A Memory,' Pramoedya Ananta Toer, and Postcolonial American Perspectives." *Western Humanities Review*, LII, no. 2 (Summer 1998), 96–109.

———. *The Invention of the West: Joseph Conrad and the Double-Mapping of Europe and Empire*. Stanford: Stanford University Press, 1995.

———. "Pramoedya's Fiction and History: An Interview with Indonesian Novelist Pramoedya Ananta Toer." *Yale Journal of Criticism* 9, no. 1 (1996): 147–64.

———. "The Voice of Pramoedya Ananta Toer: Passages, Interviews, and Reflections from *The Mute's Soliloquy* and Pramoedya's North American Tour." *Cultural Critique* 55 (Fall 2003), 217–46.

Gordon, John Dozier. *Joseph Conrad: The Making of a Novelist*. Cambridge, Mass: Harvard University Press, 1940.

Gregg, Veronica M. *Jean Rhys's Historical Imagination: Reading and Writing the Creole*. Chapel Hill: North Carolina University Press, 1995.

Guerard, Albert. *Conrad the Novelist*. Cambridge, Mass: Harvard University Press, 1958.

Guha, Ranajit. *History at the Limit of World-History*. New York: Columbia University Press, 2002.

Guha, Ranajit, and Gayatri Chakravorty Spivak, Eds. *Selected Subaltern Studies*. Oxford: Oxford University Press, 1988.

Guillory, John. *Cultural Capital: The Problem of Literary Canon Formation*. Chicago: University of Chicago Press, 1993.

Hamner, Robert, Ed. *Joseph Conrad: Third World Perspectives*. Boulder, Colo.: Three Continents Press, 1990.
Hampson, Robert. *Cross-Cultural Encounters in Joseph Conrad's Malay Fiction*. New York: Palgrave, 2000.
Harpham, Geoffrey Galt. *One of Us: The Mastery of Joseph Conrad*. Chicago: University of Chicago Press, 1996.
Harris, Wilson. *Tradition, the Writer, and Society*. London: New Beacon, 1967.
———. *The Womb of Space: The Cross-Cultural Imagination*. Westport, Conn.: Greenwood, 1983.
Harrison, Nancy. *Jean Rhys and the Novel as Women's Text*. Chapel Hill: North Carolina University Press, 1988.
Haslam, Sara. Ed. *Ford Madox Ford and the City*. Amsterdam: Rodopi, 2005.
Hawthorn, Jeremy. *Joseph Conrad: Language and Fictional Self-Consciousness*. London: Edward Arnold, 1979.
———. *Joseph Conrad: Narrative Technique and Ideological Commitment*. London: Edward Arnold, 1990.
Hay, Eloise Knapp. *The Political Novels of Joseph Conrad*. Chicago: University of Chicago Press, 1963.
Hegel, Georg Wilhelm Friedrich. *Ästhetik*. Berlin: Aufbau Verlag, 1955.
———. *Aesthetics: Lectures on Fine Art*. vol.2. Trans. T. M. Knox. Oxford: Clarendon, 1998.
———. *Phänomenologie des Geistes*. Frankfurt: Ullstein, [1807] 1980.
———. *The Phenomenology of Spirit*. Trans. A. V. Miller. Oxford: Oxford University Press, 1977.
Hellwig, Tineke. *Adjustment and Discontent: Representations of Women in the Dutch East Indies*. Windsor, Ontario: Netherlandic, 1994.
———. "Njai Dasima, een vrouw uit de literatuur." In *A Man of Indonesian Letters: Essays in Honour of A. Teeuw*, eds. C. M. S. Hellwig and S. O. Robson (pp. 48–66). Dordrecht: Foris, 1986.
Hellwig, Tineke, and Eric Tagliacozzo, Eds. *The Indonesia Reader: History, Culture, Politics*. Durham, N.C.: Duke University Press, 2009.
Hering, Bob, Ed. *Pramoedya Ananta Toer 70 Tahun: Essays to Honour Pramoedya Ananta Toer's 70th Year*. Stein, Netherlands: Yayasan Kabar Seberang, III, nos. 24/5, 1995.
Hervouet, Yves. *The French Face of Joseph Conrad*. Cambridge: Cambridge University Press, 1990.
Hitchcock, Peter. *The Long Space: Transnationalism and Postcolonial Form*. Meridian Series. Stanford: Stanford University Press, 2010.
Homberger, Eric. "Ford's *English Review*: Englishness and Its Discontents." *Agenda* 27, no. 4 (Winter 1989)/28, no. 1 (Spring 1990): 61–66.
Hood, Mantle. "The Enduring Tradition: Music and Theater in Java and Bali." In *Indonesia*, ed. Ruth T. McVey. New Haven, Ct: Southeast Asia Studies, Yale University, 1963.
Howells, Coral Ann. *Jean Rhys*. New York: Harvester Wheatsheaf, 1991.
Hugo, Victor. *The Toilers of the Sea*. Trans. Isabel F. Hapgood. New York: Signet, 2000.
———. *Les travailleurs de la mer. Romans*, vol. 3. Paris: Éditions du Seuil, 1963.
Hulme, Peter. "The Locked Heart: The Creole Family Romance of *Wide Sargasso Sea*." In *Colonial Discourse, Postcolonial Theory*, eds. Francis

Barker, Peter Hulme, and Margaret Iverson. (pp. 72–88). Manchester, Eng.: Manchester University Press, 1994.

Huyssen, Andreas. *After the Great Divide: Modernism, Mass Culture, and Postmodernism*. Bloomington, Ind: Indiana University Press, 1986.

Hynes, Samuel. *Edwardian Occasions: Essays on English Writing in the Early Twentieth Century*. London: Routledge, 1972.

Isak, Joesoef. "The Shaping of the Mute's Soliloquy." Address delivered at Fordham University, April 24 1999. At http://home.earthlink.net/~agbardsley, accessed August, 2003.

James, C. L. R. *Beyond a Boundary*. New York: Pantheon, [1963] 1983.

———. *The Black Jacobins*. 2nd ed. New York: Vintage, [1938] 1989.

Jameson, Fredric. *The Political Unconscious: Narrative as a Socially Symbolic Act*. Ithaca, N.Y. Cornell University Press, 1981.

Jean-Aubry, G. *Joseph Conrad: Life and Letters*. 2 vols. New York: Doubleday, 1927.

Jedamski, Doris. "The Subjective Factor in Cultural Change." In *Pramoedya Ananta Toer 70 Tahun: Essays to Honour Pramoedya Ananta Toer's 70th Year*, ed. Bob Hering (pp. 190–210). Stein: Yayasan Kabar Seberang, 1995.

Johnson, Erica L. *Home, Maison, Casa: The Politics of Location in Works by Jean Rhys, Marguerite Duras, and Erminia Dell'Oro*. London: Associated University Presses, 2003.

Jones, Susan. *Conrad and Women*. Oxford: Oxford University Press, 1999.

Kaplan, Carola, Peter Mallios, and Andrea White, Eds. *Conrad in the Twenty-First Century: Contemporary Approaches and Perspectives*. New York: Routledge, 2005.

Karl, Frederick R. *Joseph Conrad: The Three Lives*. New York: Farrar, Straus and Giroux, 1979.

Kenner, Hugh. *The Pound Era*. Berkeley: University of California Press, 1971.

Kirschner, Paul. *Conrad: The Psychologist as Artist*. Edinburgh: Oliver, 1968.

Knowles, Owen, and Gene Moore, Eds. *The Oxford Reader's Companion to Conrad*. Oxford: Oxford University Press, 2000.

Konzett, Delia Caparoso. *Ethnic Modernisms: Anzia Yezierska, Zora Neale Hurston, Jean Rhys, and the Aesthetics of Dislocation*. New York: Palgrave, 2002.

Krenn, Heliéna. *Conrad's Lingard Trilogy: Empire, Race, and Women in the Malay Novels*. New York: Garland, 1990.

Krishnan, Sanjay. *Reading the Global: Troubling Perspectives on Britain's Empire in Asia*. New York: Columbia University Press, 2007.

Lane, Max. *Unfinished Nation: Indonesia Before and After Suharto*. London: Verso, 2008.

Leavis, F. R. *The Great Tradition: George Eliot, Henry James, Joseph Conrad*. London: Chatto, 1948.

Levenson, Michael H. *A Genealogy of Modernism: A Study of English Literary Doctrine, 1908-1922*. Cambridge, Eng.: Cambridge University Press, 1984.

Lerer, Seth. *Error and the Academic Self: The Scholarly Imagination, Medieval to Modern*. New York: Columbia University Press, 2002.

Lionnet, Françoise. "Continents and Archipelagoes: From *E Pluribus Unum* to Creolized Solidarities," *PMLA* 123, no. 5 (October 2008), 1503–15.

Loomba, Ania, Suvir Kaul, et al., Eds. *Postcolonial Studies and Beyond.* Durham, N.C. : Duke University Press, 2005.

Lothe, Jakob. *Conrad's Narrative Method.* Oxford: Oxford University Press, 1989.

Lothe, Jakob, Jeremy Hawthorn, and James Phelan. Eds. *Joseph Conrad: Voice, Sequence, History, Genre.* Columbus, Ohio: Ohio State University Press, 2008.

Lyotard, Jean-François. *The Differend: Phrases in Dispute.* Trans. Georges Van Den Abbele. Minneapolis: University of Minnesota Press, 1988.

———. *Le Différend.* Paris: Les Éditions de Minuit, 1983.

———. *The Postmodern Condition: A Report on Knowledge.* Trans. Geoff Bennington and Brian Massumi. Minneapolis: University of Minnesota Press, 1984.

MacShane, Frank, Ed. *Ford Madox Ford: The Critical Heritage.* London: Routledge and K. Paul, 1972.

Maier, Henk. "Boredom in Batavia: A Catalogue of Books in 1898." In *Text/Politics in Island Southeast Asia: Essays in Interpretation,* ed. D. M. Roskies (pp. 131–56). Athens: Ohio University Press, 1993.

———. "The Dream of Reality—The Writing of 'Blora.'" In *Pramoedya Ananta Toer 70 Tahun: Essays to Honour Pramoedya Ananta Toer's 70th Year,* ed. Bob Hering (pp. 62–72). Stein: Yayasan Kabar Seberang, 1995.

———. "From Heteroglossia to Polyglossia: The Creation of Malay and Dutch in the Indies." *Indonesia* 56 (October 1993): 37–65.

———. *We Are Playing Relatives: A Survey of Malay Writing.* Leiden: KITLV Press, 2004.

Manusama, A. Th. *Komedie Stamboel of de Oost-Indische Opera.* Weltevreden: V. Electrische Drukkerij 'Favoriet,' 1922.

Mardorossian, Carine M. "Shutting up the Subaltern: Silences, Stereotypes, and Double-Entendre in Jean Rhys's *Wide Sargasso Sea.*" *Callaloo* 22, no. 4 (1999), 1071–90.

Marx, John. *The Modernist Novel and the Decline of Empire.* Cambridge: Cambridge University Press, 2005.

McClure, John. *Kipling and Conrad: The Colonial Fiction.* Cambridge: Harvard University Press, 1981.

Meyer, Bernard C. *Joseph Conrad: A Psychoanalytic Biography.* Princeton: Princeton University Press, 1967.

Mignolo, Walter D. *The Darker Side of the Renaissance: Literacy, Territoriality, & Colonization.* Ann Arbor: University of Michigan Press, [1995] 2003.

Miller, Christopher. *Blank Darkness: Africanist Discourse in French.* Chicago: University of Chicago Press, 1985.

Miller, J. Hillis. *Fiction and Repetition: Seven English Novels.* Cambridge, Mass: Harvard University Press, 1982.

———. *Poets of Reality: Six Twentieth-Century Writers.* New York: Atheneum, 1974.

Mizener, Arthur. *The Saddest Story: A Biography of Ford Madox Ford.* London: Bodley Head, 1971.

Mohamad, Goenawan. See Goenawan Mohamad.

Moore, Gene, Ed. *Conrad's Cities: Essays for Hans van Marle.* Amsterdam: Rodopi, 1992.

Moran, Patricia. *Virginia Woolf, Jean Rhys, and the Aesthetics of Trauma.* New York: Palgrave Macmillan, 2007.

Morf, Gustav. *The Polish Shades and Ghosts of Joseph Conrad.* New York: Astra, 1976.

Moser, Thomas. *Joseph Conrad: Achievement and Decline*. Cambridge, Mass: Harvard University Press, 1957.

Mrázek, Rudolf. *Engineers of Happy Land: Technology and Nationalism in a Colony*. Princeton: Princeton University Press, 2002.

Mugglestone, Lynda. *Lexicography and the OED: Pioneers in the Untrodden Forest*. Oxford: Oxford University Press, 2000.

Murdoch, H. Adlai. "Rhys's Pieces: Unhomeliness as Arbiter of Caribbean Creolization." Callaloo 26, vol. 1 (2003): 252–72.

Murfin, Ross, Ed. *Conrad Revisited: Essays for the Eighties*. Tuscaloosa, Ala.: University of Alabama Press, 1985.

Murray, James A. H., et al. *A New English Dictionary on Historical Principles [O.E.D]*, 13 Vols. Oxford: Oxford University Press, [1884-1928, Supplement 1933], 1933.

Mustafa, Fawzia. "Categories of Hybridity: Caribbean Proliferations." Talk delivered at the Association of Caribbean Studies 17th Annual Conference, Manaus, Brazil. 1995. TS.

———. *V. S. Naipaul*. Cambridge Studies in African and Caribbean Literature. Cambridge: Cambridge University Press, 1995.

Nadelhaft, Ruth. *Joseph Conrad*. Atlantic Highlands, N.J.: Humanities Press, 1991.

Naipaul, V. S. *A House for Mr Biswas*. Harmondsworth: Penguin, [1961] 1969.

———. *Literary Occasions: Essays*. New York: Vintage, 2003.

———. *The Mimic Men*. New York: Vintage, [1967] 2001.

———. *The Return of Eva Perón*. New York: Vintage, 1981.

Najder, Zdzisław. *Joseph Conrad: A Chronicle*. Cambridge: Cambridge University Press, 1964.

———. *Joseph Conrad: A Life*. 2nd ed. [rev. ed. of above]. Rochester, N.Y.: Camden House, 2007.

Nakai, Asako. *The English Book and Its Marginalia*. Amsterdam: Rodopi, 2000.

Narain, Denise de Caires. "Caribbean Creole: The Real Thing? Writing and Reading the Creole in a Selection of Caribbean Women's Texts." In *Essays and Studies 2000*, vol. 53 (pp. 105–27). The English Association. Woodbridge, Suffolk: D. S. Brewer, 2000.

Ngũgũ wa Thiong'o. *Moving the Centre: The Struggle for Cultural Freedoms*. Oxford: James Currey, 1993.

Nieuwenhuys, Rob. *Komen en Blijven: Tempo Doeloe—Een Verzonken Wereld*. Amsterdam: Querido, 1998.

———. *Mirror of the Indies: A History of Dutch Colonial Literature*. Singapore: Periplus, 1999.

North, Michael. *The Dialect of Modernism: Race, Language, and Twentieth-Century Literature*. Oxford: Oxford University Press, 1994.

O.E.D. See James A. H. Murray et. al.

O'Connor, Elizabeth Foley. "The Thoroughly Modern Spectator: Women, the City, and the Marketplace." PhD dissertation, Fordham University, 2011.

Ortiz, Fernando. *Cuban Counterpoint: Tobacco and Sugar*. Trans. Harriet de Onís. Durham, N.C.: Duke University Press, 1995.

Parry, Benita. *Conrad and Imperialism: Ideological Boundaries and Visionary Frontiers*. London: Macmillan, 1893.

———. *Postcolonial Studies: A Materialist Critique*. London: Routledge, 2004.

Parsons, Deborah L. *Streetwalking in the Metropolis: Women, the City, and Modernity*. Oxford: Oxford University Press, 2000.
Pemberton, John. *On the Subject of "Java."* Ithaca, N.Y.: Cornell University Press, 1994.
Peters, John G. *Conrad and Impressionism*. Cambridge: Cambridge University Press, 2001.
———. Ed. *A Historical Guide to Joseph Conrad*. Oxford: Oxford University Press, 2010.
Pino, Adolf Maximilien. *Komedie Stamboel: En Andere Verhalen Uit de Praktijk van het Binnenlands Bestuur op Java 1913–1946*. Leiden: Nautilus, 1998.
Poli, Bernard. *Ford Madox Ford and the Transatlantic Review*. Syracuse, N.Y.: Syracuse University Press, 1967.
Pomeranz, Kenneth, and Steven Topik. *The World That Trade Created: Society, Culture, and the World Economy*. 2nd ed. Armonk, N.Y,: M. E. Sharpe, 2006.
Pramoedya Ananta Toer. 1980. *All That Is Gone*. Trans. Willem Samuels. New York: Hyperion, 2004.
———. *Anak Semua Bangsa*. Jakarta: Hasta Mitra, 1981.
———. *Arok Dedes*. Ed. Joesoef Isak. Jakarta: Hasta Mitra, 1999.
———. *Arok of Java*. Trans. Max Lane. Singapore: Horizon, 2007.
———. *Arus Balik*. Jakarta: Hasta Mitra, 1995.
———. "Blora." Trans. Harold Merrill. *Indonesia* 53 (April 1992), 51–64.
———. *Bumi Manusia*. Jakarta: Hasta Mitra, [1980] 1981.
———. *Cerita dari Blora*. Jakarta: Hasta Mitra, [1952] 1994.
———. *Child of All Nations*. New York: Penguin, 1996.
———. *The Chinese in Indonesia*. Trans. Max Lane. Singapore: Select Books, 2007.
———. *De pioneer: Biografie van Tirto Adhisoerjo*. Trans. Marjanne Termorshuizen. Amsterdam: Manus Amici, 1988.
———. *De stroom uit het noorden*. Trans. Henk Maier. Breda: de Geus, 1995.
———. *Exile: Pramoedya Ananta Toer in Conversation with André Vltchek and Rossie Indira*. Ed. Nagesh Rao. Chicago: Haymarket Books, 2006.
———. *Footsteps*. Trans. Max Lane. New York: Penguin, 1990.
———. *Gadis Pantai*. Jakarta: Lentera Dipantara, [1962] 2003.
———. *The Girl from the Coast*. Trans. Willem Samuels. New York: Hyperion, 2002.
———. *Guerillafamilie*. Trans. Cara Ella Bouwman. Breda: de Geus, 1990.
———. *Hoakiau di Indonesia*. Jakarta: Garba Budaya, 1998.
———. *House of Glass*. Trans. Max Lane. New York: Penguin, 1992.
———. *Jejak Langkah*. Jakarta: Hasta Mitra, 1985.
———. *Keluarga Gerilya*. Jakarta: Hasta Mitra, [1949] 1995.
———. *Lied van een stomme: Gevangene op Buru*. Trans. A. van der Halm. Amsterdam: Manus Amici, 1989.
———. *Lied van een stomme: Brieven van Buru*. Trans. Angela Rookmaaker en Alfred van der Helm. Amsterdam: Manus Amici, 1991.
———. "Ma'af, Atas Nama Pengalaman." *Kabar Seberang* 23 (1992), 1–9. At http://home.earthlink.net/~agbardsley/prampage.html, accessed July 13, 2005.
———. "My Apologies, in the Name of Experience." Trans. Alex G. Bardsley. *Indonesia* 61 (April 1996): 1–12.
———. *The Mute's Soliloquy: A Memoir*. Trans. Willem Samuels. New York: Hyperion, 1999.

———. *Nyanyi Sunyi Seorang Bisu: Catatan-catatan dari Buru.* Vol. 1 Jakarta: Lentera, 1995.
———. *Nyanyi Sunyi Seorang Bisu: Catatan-catatan dari Buru.* Vol. 2 Jakarta: Lentera, 1997.
———. "*Perburuan* 1950 and *Keluarga Gerilya* 1950." Trans. Benedict Anderson. *Indonesia* 36 (October 1983), 25–48.
———. *Realisme-Sosialis dan Sastra Indonesia.* Jakarta: Lentera Dipantara, 2003.
———. *Rumah Kaca.* Jakarta: Hasta Mitra, 1988.
———. *Sang Pemula.* Jakarta: Hasta Mitra, 1985.
———. *Tales from Djakarta: Caricatures of Circumstances and Their Human Beings.* Ithaca, N.Y.: Southeast Asia Program, 1999.
———. *Tempo Doeloe: Antologi Sastra Pra-Indonesia.* Jakarta: Hasta Mitra, 1982.
———. *This Earth of Mankind.* Trans. Max Lane. New York: Penguin, 1996.
Pratt, Mary Louise. *Imperial Eyes: Travel Writing and Transculturation.* London: Routledge, 1992.
Prendergast, Christopher, Ed. *Debating World Literature.* London: Verso, 2004.
Raiskin, Judith L. *Snow on the Cane Fields: Women's Writing and Creole Subjectivity.* Minneapolis: University of Minnesota Press, 1996.
Redfield, Marc, Ed. *Legacies of Paul de Man.* New York: Fordham University Press, 2007.
Resink, G. J. *Indonesia's History Between the Myths: Essays in Legal History and Historical Theory.* Selected Studies on Indonesia, vol. 7. The Hague: W. van Hoeve, 1968.
———. "From the Old Mahabharata- to the New Ramayan-Order." *Bijdragen tot de Taal-, Land- en Volkenkunde* 131 (1975), no. 2/3, 214–35.
Rhys, Jean. *After Leaving Mr. Mackenzie.* New York: Norton, [1930] 1985.
———. *The Collected Short Stories.* New York: Norton, 1987.
———. *Good Morning, Midnight.* New York: Norton, [1939] 1986.
———. *The Letters of Jean Rhys.* Selected and Edited by Francis Wyndham and Diana Melly. New York: Viking, 1984.
———. *Quartet.* New York: Norton, [1929] 1997.
———. *Smile Please.* New York: Harper & Row, 1979.
———. *Voyage in the Dark.* New York: Norton, [1934] 1982.
———. *Wide Sargasso Sea.* New York: Norton, [1966] 1985.
Ricklefs, M. C. *A History of Modern Indonesia since c. 1300.* 2nd ed. Stanford: Stanford University Press, 1993.
Roberts, Andrew. *Conrad and Masculinity.* London: Macmillan, 2000.
Robson, Stuart and Singgih Wibisono. *Javanese English Dictionary.* Singapore: Periplus, 2002.
Roosa, John. *Pretext for Mass Murder: The September 30th Movement and Suharto's Coup d'État in Indonesia.* Madison, Wisc.: University of Wisconsin Press, 2006.
Roskies, D. M. Ed. *Text/Politics in Island Southeast Asia: Essays in Interpretation.* Athens: Ohio University Press, 1993.
Rosner, Victoria. *Modernism and the Architecture of Private Life.* New York: Columbia University Press, 2005.
Ross, Stephen. *Conrad and Empire.* Columbia, Mo.: University of Missouri Press, 2004.

Said, Edward. *Beginnings: Intention and Method*. New York: Columbia University Press, 1985.
———. *Culture and Imperialism*. New York: Vintage, 1994.
———. *Orientalism*. New York: Vintage, 1979.
———. *Out of Place: A Memoir*. New York: Vintage, 1999.
———. *The World, the Text, and the Critic*. Cambridge, Mass.: Harvard University Press, 1983.
Saunders, Max. *Ford Madox Ford: A Dual Life*. 2 vols. Oxford: Oxford University Press, 1996.
Saussy, Haun, Ed. *Comparative Literature in an Age of Globalization*. Baltimore: Johns Hopkins University Press, 2006.
Savory, Elaine. *Jean Rhys*. Cambridge: Cambridge University Press, 1998.
Sears, Laurie, Ed. *Fantasizing the Feminine in Indonesia*. Durham, N.C.: Duke University Press, 1996.
———. *Shadows of Empire: Colonial Discourse and Javanese Tales*. Durham, N.C.: Duke University Press, 1996.
Sherry, Norman, Ed. *Conrad: The Critical Heritage*. London: Routledge & Kegan Paul, 1973.
———. *Conrad's Eastern World*. Cambridge: Cambridge University Press, 1966.
———. *Conrad's Western World*. Cambridge: Cambridge University Press, 1971.
Shiraishi, Takashi. *An Age in Motion: Popular Radicalism in Java, 1912–1926*. Ithaca, N.Y.: Cornell University Press, 1990.
Sieburth, Richard. "Benjamin the Scrivener." In Gary Smith, ed., *Benjamin: Philosophy, History, Aesthetics*. Chicago: University of Chicago Press, 1989. 13–37.
Siegel, James. *Fetish, Recognition, Revolution*. Princeton: Princeton University Press, 1997.
———. *Solo in the New Order: Language and Hierarchy in an Indonesian City*. Princeton: Princeton University Press, 1986.
Skeat, Walter W. *A Concise Etymological Dictionary of the English Language*. Oxford: Clarendon Press, 1911.
Skeat, Walter William. *Malay Magic: Being an Introduction to the Folklore and Popular Religion of the Malay Peninsula*. London: Macmillan, 1900.
———. "Notes to Birth Customs." *Selangor Journal* 3, no. 17 (May 3, 1895), 276–80.
Smith, David R., Ed. *Joseph Conrad's Under Western Eyes: Beginnings, Revisions, Final Forms*. Hamden, Conn.: Archon, 1991.
Spitzer, Leo. *Classical and Christian Ideas of World Harmony: Prolegomena to an Interpretation of the Word "Stimmung."* Baltimore: Johns Hopkins University Press, 1963.
Spivak, Gayatri. *A Critique of Postcolonial Reason: Toward a History of the Vanishing Present*. Cambridge, Mass.: Harvard University Press, 1999.
———. *Death of a Discipline*. New York: Columbia University Press, 2003.
Stang, Sondra. Ed. *The Ford Madox Ford Reader*. New York: Ecco Press, 1986.
Stape, J. H., and Owen Knowles, Eds. *A Portrait in Letters: Correspondence to and about Conrad*. Amsterdam: Rodopi, 1996.
Stoler, Ann Laura. *Along the Archival Grain: Epistemic Anxieties and Colonial Common Sense*. Princeton: Princeton University Press, 2009.

———. *Carnal Knowledge and Imperial Power: Race and the Intimate in Colonial Rule*. Berkeley: University of California Press, 2002.

———. *Race and the Education of Desire*. Durham, N.C.: Duke University Press, 1995.

Taylor, Jean Gelman. *The Social World of Batavia: European and Eurasian in Dutch Asia*. Madison, Wisc.: University of Wisconsin Press, 1983.

———. "The World of Women in the Dutch Colonial Novel." *Kabar seberang sulating Maphilindo* 1 (1977), 26–41.

Teeuw, A. *Modern Indonesian Literature*. Vol. 1. Dordrecht: Foris, 1986.

———. *Modern Indonesian Literature*. Vol. 2. The Hague: Martinus Nijhoff, 1979.

———. *Pramoedya Ananta Toer: De verbeelding van Indonesië*. Breda: de Geus, 1993.

Thomas, Sue. *The Worlding of Jean Rhys*. Westport, Conn.: Greenwood, 1999.

Trumpener, Katie. *Bardic Nationalism: The Romantic Novel and the British Empire*. Princeton: Princeton University Press, 1997.

Van der Veur, Paul W., Ed. *Toward a Glorious Indonesia: Reminiscences and Observations of Dr. Soetomo*. Trans. Suhami Soemarmo and Paul W. Van der Veur. Athens, Ohio: Ohio University Center for International Studies, 1987.

Van Marle, A. *De groep der Europeanen in Nederlands-Indië, iets over ontstaan en groei. Indonesië* 5 (1952): 77–121; 3 (1952): 314–41; 4 (1952): 481–507.

Verges, Françoise. *Monsters and Revolutionaries: Colonial Family Romance and Métissage*. Durham, N.C.: Duke University Press, 1999.

Vickers, Adrian. *A History of Modern Indonesia*. Cambridge: Cambridge University Press, 2005.

Voltaire, F. M. A. de. *Correspondance*. Vol. 6 Paris: Gallimard, 1980.

Watson, C. W. "Some Preliminary Remarks on the Antecedent of Modern Indonesian Literature." *Bijdragen tot de Taal-, Land- en Volkenkunde* 127, no. 4 (1971): 417–33.

Watt, Ian. *Conrad in the Nineteenth Century*. London: Chatto and Windus, 1980.

———. *Essays on Conrad*. Cambridge: Cambridge University Press, 2000.

Watts, Cedric. *The Deceptive Text: An Introduction to Covert Plots*. Brighton: Harvester, 1984.

White, Andrea. *Joseph Conrad and the Adventure Tradition*. Cambridge: Cambridge University Press, 1993.

Wiesenfarth, Joseph. *Ford Madox Ford and the Regiment of Women: Violet Hunt, Jean Rhys, Stella Bowen, Janice Biala*. Madison, Wisc.: University of Wisconsin Press, 2005.

Williams, Raymond. *Culture and Society: 1780–1950*. London: Chatto and Windus, 1958.

———. *Keywords: A Vocabulary of Culture and Society*. Rev. ed. New York: Oxford University Press, 1985.

———. *Marxism and Literature*. Oxford: Oxford University Press, 1977.

———. *The Politics of Modernism: Against the New Conformists*. London: Verso, 1989.

Winchester, Simon. *The Meaning of Everything: the Story of the Oxford English Dictionary*. Oxford: Oxford University Press, 2003.

———. *The Professor and the Madman: a Tale of Murder, Insanity, and the Making of the Oxford English Dictionary*. New York: Harper Collins, 1998.

Wolff, Janet. *Feminist Sentences: Essays on Women and Culture*. Berkeley: University of California Press, 1990.
Woolf, Virginia. *The Common Reader: First Series*. New York: Harcourt Brace Jovanovich, [1925] 1953.
Yeow, Agnes S. K. *Conrad's Eastern Vision: A Vain and Floating Vision*. New York: Palgrave Macmillan, 2009.
Yule, Henry and A. C. Burnell. *Hobson-Jobson: A Glossary of Colloquial Anglo-Indian Words and Phrases, and of Kindred Terms, Etymological, Historical, Geographical and Discursive*. London: John Murray, 1903.
Zurbuchen, Mary, Ed. *Beginning to Remember: The Past in the Indonesian Present*. Singapore: Singapore University Press, 2005.

INDEX

1965 coup (Indonesia). *See* events of 1965

Absolute Prose, 71–75, 80, 82, 89 (*see also* Conrad–Ford collaboration)
abysmal taste, 44–45, 48–51, 54–60
  and Conrad, 44–45, 48–51, 57–60
  defined, 44
  and differend, 51
  and Pramoedya, 44–45, 54–60
  See also aesthetic judgment, *mise-en-abyme*, taste
Achebe, Chinua, 227–234
  "An Image of Africa,"228
  Things Fall Apart, 227–228, 234
Adorno, Theodor, 47, 58
aesthetic judgment, 39–40, 43–51, 54–60, 135, 229–233
  and differend, 51
  and opera, 39–40, 43–44, 46–48, 51, 135, 183, 201
  and *mise-en-abyme*, 44, 183
  and literary and linguistic knowledge, 229–233
  See also taste
affair, 62, 66–67, 91
affiliation, 178, 186–188, 192, 195, 197, 201, 254 n.13
  and Pramoedya, 178, 186, 195, 197, 201
  and Said, 187–188, 192, 254 n.13
  See also filiation
Africa, 12, 41, 62, 79, 99–100, 227–228, 230–231
  Central Africa, 12, 62
  "Heart of Darkness," 99, 230–231

"An Image of Africa," 228
Things Fall Apart, 227–228, 234
afro-caribbean culture, 83, 105, 107
  music, 105, 107
  and black international modernism, 107
After Leaving Mr Mackenzie (Rhys), 64, 67, 90–92, 102, 104–105, 107, 110, 115, 169–170
  and affair with Ford, 67
  citation from *Almayer's Folly*, 64, 90–92, 105, 107–108, 110, 115, 169–170
  descriptive sea passage in, 92, 107
  Julia Martin, 64, 92, 102, 105, 107–108, 115, 169
  and memory, 91, 107, 170
  problem of reading, 92, 107, 115, 169
  subaltern reading effect in, 169
"Again the Antilles" (Rhys), 21–22, 92, 111, 113
  disputed passage of literature in, 22, 113
Agamben, Giorgio, 264 n.50
Aida (Verdi), 46, 261 n.23
Alexander the Great, 133, 134
alien genealogies, 34, 36, 183–197, 199, 202, 214, 251 (*see also* genealogy)
Almayer's Folly (Conrad), 12, 31, 39, 43–53, 57, 59, 64, 71, 76, 79–80, 87, 90–93, 105, 108, 110, 115, 166–167,

Almayer's Folly (continued)
  169–170, 173, 200–201, 203, 261
    n.21, 279 n.34
  Abdulla, 46
  Mrs. Almayer and *nyai* stereotype,
    166–167
  Babalatchi, 43, 45–47, 50–53, 59,
    203, 261 n.21, 262 n.36, 263–264
    n.46, 279 n.34
  cited by Rhys, 64–65, 90–93, 105,
    108, 110, 115, 169
  covert plot, 46
  Dain Maroola, 169–170
  and *Madame Bovary*, 48, 79, 80
  and *nyai* narrative form, 166–167,
    169–170
  Pramoedya's reading of, 53, 170,
    260 n.19
  Taminah, 169–170, 173, 279 n.34
  Verdi opera in, 43–47, 50, 57
all-round, 25–26, 35, 213–214,
    247–250, 256 n.34, n.35
  and C. L. R. James, 35, 247
  as English word, 26, 247, 256 n.35
  as Indonesian word, 26, 256 n.35
  and *O.E.D.*, 247, 256 n.35
  and Pramoedya, 25–26, 35,
    213–214, 247–250, 256 n.34
Amir Hamzah, 23, 24, 183, 184, 190
  Nyanyi Sunyi (Songs of Solitude),
    183, 184, 190
anagram, 23, 68, 115 (see also *Nature
  of a Crime, Voyage in the Dark*)
Anderson, Benedict, 8, 21–22, 27–29,
    36, 189–191, 194, 196, 214, 255
    n.29, 261 n.30
  cited by Pramoedya, 196
  "creole pioneers,"21–22, 255 n.29
  Imagined Communities, 8, 21–22,
    27, 29, 36, 161
  on Pramoedya's use of *bahasa
    Indonesia* and Javanese, 189,
    194, 264 n.54
  on Soetomo, 190–191
Angier, Carole, 257 n.57, 270 n.77
anglophonism, 5, 7, 9, 85, 88, 91,
    103–107, 110, 113–117, 140,
    142–145, 167–168, 211, 220
  and debates about Dutch East
    Indies, 167–168
  and historical models, 220
  Rhys's francophone English, 88,
    91, 103–107, 110, 113–117, 140,
    142–145, 211
  See also English, French,
    monolingualism

Anna Morgan. See under *Voyage in
  the Dark*
Annelies (Buru Quartet), 44–45, 47,
    130–134, 138–140, 145–148, 202,
    261 n.26, 275 n.10, 275–276 n.12
  enforced return to Europe, 138–139
  mental breakdown, 131, 133, 138,
    145
  and Minke, 134, 140, 145, 147–8
  and reading, 138
  See also creole beauty, creole
    family romance
anthropology, 224, 231–232
  and psychology, 231–232
anti-colonial nationalism, 4–8,
    27–28, 35, 40, 44–46, 53, 59, 131,
    139, 153–154, 160–162, 172,
    177–178, 192, 205, 217, 228, 244,
    247–248
  documenting, 4–5, 177–178,
    192–193, 217, 247–248
  and language, 6–8, 27–30, 35–36,
    35–36, 59, 160–162, 178, 205,
    217, 247–248
  and politics, 4–5, 40, 44–46, 53,
    131, 139, 153–154, 160–162, 178,
    217, 228, 244
  "National Awakening," 45, 191,
    193, 197
Antilles, 21, 82–83, 88, 105, 109,
    112–113
  on naming, 88, 113
  See also Caribbean, West Indies
anti-trope, 92 (*see also* trope)
aphorism. *See* proverbs, sayings
apology (*ma'af*), rhetoric of, 181, 201
  (*see also* offense)
aporia, 235, 237
Apter, Emily, 58
Arab (people), 16, 46, 78, 156, 166, 203
  harbor master in *Arus Balik*, 203
Arabic (language), 7, 29–30, 41, 57,
    87, 166, 170, 204–205, 207,
    211–212, 220, 249
  etymology of *azure*, 87, 249
  shift to romanized script, 205, 207,
    211
Aravamudan, Srinivas, 242–243, 246
Arcades Project (Benjamin), 97–98,
    118, 119, 123–126, 249, 274 n.32,
    n.37
  and Rhys, 97–98, 118
  "The Interior, the Trace," 119
  citation from Conrad's *The
    Shadow–Line*, 119, 123–126, 274
    n.32, n.37

archive, 9, 36, 40, 51, 53, 59, 107,
    200, 218, 220–222, 226, 233–234,
    237–244, 247–248, 250–251,
    279–280 n.2
  and Conrad, 51, 53
  Edwards on, 107, 248
  lost records of Indonesian history,
    26–27, 163–165, 177, 192–193,
    200, 218, 222, 279–280 n.2
  and *O.E.D.*, 9, 36, 218, 242–244,
    247–248, 250–251
  oppositional reading of, 51, 53, 226
  and postcolonial philology, 222, 239
  and Pramoedya, 53, 59 (*see also*
    archivist)
  and reevaluating modernism, 240,
    244, 250, 251
  reliability of. *See* archivist
  Said on, 40
  of transatlantic black modernism,
    107
  trope of, 238–239
archival gaps, 26, 163–164, 170,
    177–179, 184, 188, 191–193,
    195–197, 199–200, 207, 222,
    244, 247, 250–251
  and de Man, 237
  in documenting Indonesian
    history, 26–27, 163, 170, 177,
    184, 188, 192–193, 195–197,
    199–200, 222, 207, 279–280 n.2
  and *O.E.D.*, 244–245, 247, 250
  and passage of literature, 170, 184,
    196
  as resource for decolonizing
    tradition, 178, 184, 191, 195–196
archivist (*House of Glass*),
    220–222, 226, 229, 232, 234–235,
    237–239, 245, 249
  and reliability of documents,
    221–224
Aristotle, 235
  and metaphor, 235
Arok of Java (Pramoedya),
    177–178, 185, 207–211
  Dedes, 210
  and historical turning-point, 209, 211
  Javanese and Sanskrit scripts in,
    210–211
  narrative consciousness in, 209–210
  Oti, 210
  revolutionary and
    counter-revolutionary
    consciousness, 210
  and revolutionary family romance,
    209, 211

thirteenth-century setting, 177,
    178
  See also Arok
Arok (legendary Javanese figure),
    181, 185, 208–209, 211
  and trope of vicious circle, 185, 208
aria, 48, 49, 57 (*see also* opera, song)
Arus Balik (Pramoedya), 177–178,
    185, 202–205
  and Arabic influence, 203–204
  and Chinese in Indonesia, 185, 203
  as epic, 203
  and Europeans in Indonesia, 203
  harbor master in, 204
  and Islam, 204
  riddle of *malakama* fruit, 202–203
  sixteenth-century setting, 177–178,
    185, 202–203
atonality, 58
Auerbach, Erich, 58, 219
Austria, 12, 83
authorship, 10, 13, 15, 19, 22, 30–31,
    33–34, 49, 70, 213
  author's name, 30–31, 34, 49, 189
    (*see also* Conrad, Pramoedya,
    Rhys)
  Barthes on, 31
  and Conrad–Ford collaboration, 70
  Foucault on, 30–31
autobiography, 3, 9–10, 12, 14,
    18–20, 31, 33, 35, 67, 74, 81, 92,
    108, 122, 132, 139, 190, 197
  Conrad's autobiographical
    presence, 74–75, 81
  and creole family romance, 132, 139
  and model of Soetomo's
    Kenang–Kenangan, 190
  See also Mute's Soliloquy, A
    Personal Record, Smile Please
avant-garde, 35, 61–63, 65–66, 68, 75,
    98, 170, 225, 267 n.4
  consecrated, 61
  historical, 63
  rival national literary, 62
  Rhys and, 98
  See also Left Bank, modernism
Aymara (language), 220
azure, 72–73, 75, 85–87, 246–247,
    249–250, 271 n.82
  in Conrad's "Youth," 72, 75, 86
  Ford on, 72, 75, 86, 246
  O.E.D. entry on, 86–87, 246–247,
    249
  and European cultural memory,
    87, 246
  and tropicopolitan perspective, 246

Index 303

Babalatchi (*Almayer's Folly* and *An Outcast of the Islands*), 43, 45–47, 50–53, 59, 203, 261 n.21, 262 n.36, n.42, 263 n.46, 279 n.34
  as harbor master (*shahbandar*), 52
  name, 52, 53
  and narrative form of Malay trilogy, 50–51, 53, 59
  and *nyai* narrative form, 279 n.34
  and piracy, 51
  and racial stereotype, 43, 46–47, 52–53, 59
  and song, 50–51, 53
baca (reading), 29–30, 178–179, 183, 206, 209, 233, 257 n.50, 266 n.67, 283 n.38 (see also *karang*)
bahasa Indonesia. See Indonesian
Bakhtin, Mikhail, 11, 36, 77, 156, 250
  heteroglossia, 11, 77, 156, 250
Balai Pustaka, 23–24, 30, 154–155, 163, 165
  and D. A. Rinkes, 163, 154–155
  and *nyai* narrative form, 154, 163, 165
Balinese, 169, 170
Bardsley, Alex, 196
barrel organ, 47–49, 51, 57, 258 n.2 (*see also* hand organ)
Barthes, Roland, 31, 115, 254 n.13
  "The Death of the Author," 31, 254 n.13
Baudelaire, Charles, 100, 102, 277 n.32
Becker, A. L., 57, 220, 250
Benítez-Rojo, Antonio, 6, 83
Benjamin, Walter, 47, 97–98, 100, 102, 118–119, 121, 123–126, 219, 249, 274 n.37, 277 n.32, n.37
  Arcades Project, 97, 98, 118, 125, 219, 249
  citing Conrad, 119, 123–126, 274 n.32, n.37
  flâneur, 102
  "Paris, Capital of the Nineteenth Century," 102
  passage of literature, 126
  social space, 102, 125
  theory of the trace, 118–119, 121, 125
  race, 125–126
Benstock, Shari, 271–272 n.3
Berman, Carolyn Vellenga, 128, 255 n.29, 275 n.6, n.7, n.12
Beyond a Boundary (James), 35, 247
Bhabha, Homi, 7, 17, 22, 143, 242
  hybridity, 7, 143
  mimicry, 7, 22, 143
  "Sly Civility," 22
black transatlantic modernism, 83, 107
Black Jacobins (James), 7, 284 n.51
Black Skin, White Masks (Fanon), 132, 276 n.13
blank, 85–86, 98, 100, 104, 110, 119–120, 124–125
  and Conrad, 85, 99, 125
  and English modernism, 98, 104, 125
  and problem of white racial identity, 85, 98, 100, 104, 110, 124–125
  and Rhys, 85, 125
"Blora" (Pramoedya), 33
Boedi Oetomo, 45, 187, 189, 191–192, 198, 201
  founding of (1908), 45, 198
  and Javanese *priyayi* worldview, 201
  National Awakening, 45, 191, 193, 197
  and Pramoedya's father, 187, 192, 201
  Soetomo as founder, 189
Bongie, Chris, 273 n.22, 274 n.3
Borneo (Kalimantan), 45, 51, 76, 79, 170
Bourdieu, Pierre, 61–63, 68, 75, 91, 93, 267 n.4
  cultural capital, 61, 63, 75
  dialectic of distinction, 61, 63, 267 n.4
  literary field, 61–62, 75, 91
bovarysme, 49
Bowen, Stella, 67
Bowlby, Rachel, 103
Brathwaite, Kamau, 6, 7, 18, 128, 256 n.32, 274–275 n, 4
  creolization, 18, 128
  and Hulme, 128, 256 n.32
British Merchant Marine, 10, 74, 98, 124
  and racial hierarchies, 98, 124
Brontë, Charlotte, 20, 32, 110, 115, 148
  Jane Eyre, 20, 32, 115, 148
  Bertha Mason, 20, 32
  stereotype of creole, 110
Brooke, Rajah Sir James, 51, 53
  journals, 51, 53
  and piracy, 51
Bugis (people), 50, 52, 53, 264 n.47
  Wajo Kingdom, 50, 53

Bukitduri prison, 33, 184, 198, 214, 263 n.45, 279–280 n.2
Buru imprisonment (Pramoedya), 7, 23, 39–40, 139, 154, 177–178, 180, 183–184, 188, 192, 230
   conditions, 178, 180, 183–184, 188, 192, 259 n.6, 280 n.5
   dissident voice, 184
   and fellow prisoners, 177, 180, 222
   and trope of vicious circle, 180–181
Buru, work of (Pramoedya), 177, 179, 183–184, 192, 196–197, 199–200, 205, 243
   fragmentary form, 184, 196–197
   and historical documentation, 26–27, 200, 222, 243, 279–280 n.2
   principle of alien genealogy, 183–184, 196–197
   and passage of literature, 184, 196–197
   See also *Arok of Java*, *Arus Balik*, *Buru quartet*, *Mute's Soliloquy*
Buru quartet (Pramoedya), 7, 26–30, 39–47, 53, 57, 59–60, 131, 133–134, 139–140, 153–185, 191, 193, 198, 200–204, 212, 221–222, 226, 234, 237, 239, 256 n.42, 258 n.61, 259 n.6
   and creole family romance, 45–46, 131, 139–140, 198
   documentary basis of, 26–27, 45, 59, 157–158, 160–165, 177–178, 193, 222, 279–280 n.2
   epigraphs (*This Earth of Mankind*, *Child of All Nations*), 279–280, n.2
   fiction of documentation in, 153–154, 161–164, 171, 221–222, 226
   and history, 45, 59, 162–164, 177, 178, 185, 222
   and Javanism, 54–56, 147
   mise-en-abyme, 45–47, 140, 183
   Nyai Dasima in, 59, 158–162
   and *nyai* narrative form, 163–165, 170
   opera in, 44–45, 47, 53, 57, 60, 185
   and revolutionary family romance, 200, 201
   See also *Child of All Nations*, *Footsteps*, *House of Glass*, Minke, Pangemanann, *This Earth of Mankind*
Butler, Judith, 162, 268 n.18

Calinescu, Matei, 283–284 n.48
Capital. *See* cultural capital
Caribbean, 6–8, 21, 32–33, 63, 82–83, 85–88, 92, 109, 113–114, 110, 128–129, 133, 137, 149, 250
   creole continuum, 128, 132
   and Creole modernism, 128–129, 132–133, 149, 274 n.2
   on naming, 88, 113
   Rhys's childhood, 82–83, 85, 87–88, 92, 109, 119
carnival, 20, 118
Carpentier, Alejo, 7
Catholic. *See under* Christianity
Celebes (Sulawesi), 52, 53
Cerita Nyai Ratna (Tirto), 162
Césaire, Aimé, 7, 146
Chaucer, Geoffrey, 22, 113
Child of All Nations (Pramoedya, Buru quartet), 39, 45, 139, 163
   story of Surati and *Njai Paina*, 163
Chinese, 7, 29, 30, 41, 52, 59, 156–166, 185, 202, 212
   anti-Chinese measures in Indonesia, 185
   Babalatchi's name, 52
   The Chinese in Indonesia, 185–186
Chinese in Indonesia, The (Pramoedya), 185–186
   and alien genealogies, 185
   and trope of vicious circle, 185–186
Christianity, 57, 58, 159, 167, 171–172, 184–186, 204, 228, 233, 234, 235
   in *Arus Balik*, 204
   Catholic identity of Pangemanann, 171–172, 233–234
   Catholic–Protestant split, 234
   exegetical tradition, 234
   and Islam, 204, 234
   names, 172
   scripture, 58, 205, 233
   Things Fall Apart, 228
   trope of vicious circle, 184–186
   See also scripture
chromolithograph, 92–93, 105, 108
cinema, 108, 111, 154, 158
   and *nyai* narrative form, 154, 158
   Sasha Jansen's "film-mind" (*Good Morning, Midnight*), 108, 111
citation, 3, 4, 11, 15, 22, 35, 61–64, 68–73, 75, 78, 82, 86–88, 90, 105, 107, 110, 115, 118, 123, 125–126, 169–170, 173, 182, 196, 170, 173, 182, 196, 218, 227–235, 240–241, 244, 247, 249

citation (*continued*)
  Achebe citing Conrad, 228–232
  Achebe citing Yeats, 227–228
  Benjamin citing Conrad, 119, 123–126, 274 n.32, n.37
  Derrida citing Hegel, 240–241
  Ford citing Conrad, 68–73, 75, 78, 82
  Ford citing Rhys, 87–88
  modernist strategy of, 63–64
  and *O.E.D.*, 9, 15, 35–36, 218, 244–245, 247, 249
  Pramoedya citing Anderson, 196
  Pramoedya citing Conrad, 53, 170, 182–183, 196, 201, 264 n.47
  and problem of memory 71–72, 75, 82, 88
  Rhys citing Conrad, 64, 90–92, 105, 107–108, 110, 115, 169–170
  Rhys citing Dickinson, 110
  See also passage of literature, recitation
class, 47, 49, 55, 82, 92–93, 98, 102, 104, 108, 115, 121–124, 137, 143, 156–157, 161–162, 164, 169, 174, 194, 210, 245
  in *Arok of Java*, 210
  bourgeois private interior space, 98, 102, 121, 122
  creole landholding elite, 137
  and domestic relations, 114, 121–123, 156–157, 174
  and figure of *nyai*, 156, 161–163
  and genealogy, 194
  and prostitution, 115
  and "revolutionary Malay," 194
  and standard English, 245
  subaltern perspectives, 143, 161–162, 169, 174
  white middle-class identity, 92–93, 104, 108 *See also* distinction, cultural capital, *priyayi*
Classical and Christian Ideas of World Harmony (Spitzer), 58
Clifford, Sir Hugh, 81
collage, 65, 92
colonialism, 4–8, 11, 16, 20–21, 27–28, 30, 35–36, 40, 43, 45, 54, 57, 60, 76–77, 81, 113, 116–117, 120, 132, 135, 140, 153–156, 161, 169, 170, 180, 220–221, 242, 244, 246, 247, 250
  colonized, 27–28, 140, 153–154, 235, 242
  colonizer, 26–28, 140, 153, 154
  Dutch, 40, 46, 76, 81, 135, 154, 169, 170, 198, 220, 221

  and meaning of *creole*, 127, 135
  and meaning of *nyai*, 155–156
  territories, 6, 52, 76–77, 81, 269 n.62
  See also decolonization, Dutch East Indies, hegemony, Orientalism.
concubinage, 153–158 (see also *nyai*)
Conrad–Ford collaboration, 67–71, 79–80, 83, 85, 87, 267–268 n.11
  Conrad's break with Ford, 67, 80
  confusion of authorship, 70, 71
  Absolute Prose and search for the *mot juste*, 70–75, 80–82, 85, 89
  Romance, 70, 73, 80, 83
  See also Absolute Prose, Ford, *Nature of a Crime*, *Romance*
Conrad, Jessie, 67, 70
Conrad, Joseph, 3, 5, 7, 9–20, 23, 25–26, 30–35, 39–53, 57–82, 84–89, 98–99, 105, 119–124, 135, 153, 166–170, 173, 182–183, 196–197, 201–202, 212, 223, 228–229, 230–232, 246, 257 n.54, n.55, 258 n.2, 260–261 n.19, 261 n.21, 262 n.36, 262–263 n.42, 263–264 n.46, 264 n.47, 266 n.66, 267–268 n.11, 272 n.10, 274 n.32, n.37, 279 n.34
  autobiography, 10, 12–14, 16–19, 31, 48, 64, 71, 78, 80–81
  death, 62
  and *English Review*, 12–13, 16, 61, 64, 66–69, 71, 87, 271 n.80
  family romance, 16, 31–32, 34, 46, 52, 59, 76–77, 124, 166–167, 197, 200–202, 262–263 n.42
  father, 10, 13–14, 16–17
  and Ford Madox Ford. *See under* Ford, Ford–Conrad collaboration
  and Flaubert, 13, 48–49, 71–73, 80–81, 262 n.33
  Malay fiction, 39–41, 46, 52, 59, 63, 77–82, 85, 87, 166–170, 271 n.2
  Malay trilogy. See under *Almayer's Folly*, *An Outcast of the Islands*, *The Rescue*
  mother, 17
  and *nyai* narrative form, 166–169, 279 n.34
  and *O.E.D.*, 86, 87
  and opera, 39–44, 45–49, 50, 51, 57, 58, 60, 258 n.2, 266 n.66
  poetics of misnaming, 81, 170
  Polish background, 10–17, 31, 34, 119, 182

306   *Index*

pseudonyms, 31–32, 49, 68, 257 n.54, n.55
racism and critique in, 44–46, 52, 59, 201, 228
and *transatlantic review*, 61, 64, 69–70
See also *Almayer's Folly*, 73, 74 "The End of the Tether," "Heart of Darkness," "Karain: A Memory," *Lord Jim*, *The Mirror of the Sea*, *A Personal Record*, "The Secret Sharer," *The Shadow-Line*, "Typhoon," *Victory*, *An Outcast of the Islands*, *The Rescue*, *Victory*, "Youth."
Conradian passage, 19, 31, 62–65, 68–75, 78, 82, 87, 90–93, 98, 105, 108, 110, 115, 119, 123, 125, 202, 229–231, 263 n.46
and Achebe, 228–232
and Eliot, 63
and erasure of Malay settings, 65, 82
and Flaubert, 73
and Ford, 69–73, 75, 78, 82, 87
and F. R. Leavis, 229, 263 n.46
and problem of gender and race, 65, 91, 92, 93, 110, 125
and Mallarmé, 73, 74
and modernist style, 73–75, 82
and Naipaul, 229–231
and Pramoedya, 182–183, 196, 201, 264 n.47
and problem of memory, 71–73, 75, 82, 92–93, 125
and Rhys, 64, 65, 90–93, 105, 108, 110, 115
and Woolf, 62–65, 78
contact language, 11
contest, 3–4, 6–8, 21–23, 30, 34–36, 40, 52, 77, 81, 139–140, 159–161, 183, 201–202, 205, 212, 218, 224, 227, 233–251
legal, 52, 77, 81, 139–140, 159–161
literary-linguistic, 3–4, 6–8, 21–23, 201–202, 205, 218, 224, 227, 233–249
over passage of literature, 183, 201–202, 205, 218, 233–249
contrapuntal reading, 40–42, 46, 51, 53, 57–58, 200
and Coronil, 40–42, 264 n.49
and Said, 40–42, 46, 57–58, 60, 219, 264 n.49
contropare, 58
Coronil, Fernando, 40–42, 264 n.49

cosmopolitan, 13, 16, 34, 49, 83, 112, 133, 196, 242
vs. compatriotism, 112
creole as stereotype of, 133
and tropicopolitan, 242
counterpoint, 9, 40–43, 56–58, 60, 97, 109, 112–114, 131, 156, 212, 217, 219–220, 234, 258 n.63, 264 n.49
afro-caribbean forms of, 7, 41, 60, 107
and Biblical hermeneutics, 58
European forms of, 42, 57–58, 60, 266 n.68
Javanese and Indonesian forms of, 42–43, 57–58, 60
and philology, 57–58
and polyphony, 56–57, 60, 183
and Verdi, 57
See also contrapuntal reading, *contropare*, Cuban Counterpoint
Couperus, Louis, 135–137, 141–142, 146, 157
and creole heiress, 135–136, 141
and Dutch East Indies society, 137
The Hidden Force, 135–137, 142, 146
and witchcraft, 142
coup d'état of 1965. *See* events of 1965
covert plotting, 46–47, 50, 58, 263 n.46
creole (definitions), 21, 97, 109, 127–129
changing meaning, 97, 127–129, 142, 144, 148
creole continuum, 128, 132–133, 142, 274 n.3
demographic vs. linguistic definition, 128
English vs. Indonesian connotations, 129, 133–135
O.E.D. definition, 128–129, 142
stereotypes, 109–110, 112, 122, 128–131, 133, 136–137, 142–143
racialized definitions, 128–129, 131
creole (language), 6, 8, 11, 18–23, 26–28, 31, 34, 35, 85, 89, 104, 113, 128, 142–145, 148, 211–212, 243
Caribbean languages, 6, 8, 11, 85, 89, 128, 142–145, 243
and Conrad's English, 31
and Indonesian, 27–28, 148

Index 307

creole (language) (*continued*)
   patois, 89, 142–144
   and Rhys's francophone English, 104, 113, 211–212
creole beauty, 45, 47, 129, 130, 133, 139, 141, 202, 275 n.10
   in *This Earth of Mankind*, 45, 47, 129–130, 133, 139, 202, 275 n.10
   in *Wide Sargasso Sea*, 141, 143
creole consciousness, 88, 104, 108, 110–111, 113, 116–118, 126, 132–133, 277 n.32
   anteriority of, 123, 126
   "impasse" of 104, 110–111, 126, 148, 275 n.12
   and literariness, 110, 113
   and mass media, 113
   and Rhys, 88, 108, 113, 115, 117–118
   and racial identity, 111
creole family romance, 32–33, 45–46, 91, 111, 124, 131–133, 137–147, 197–198, 202, 275 n.11
   in *After Leaving Mr Mackenzie*, 91
   in Buru quartet, 45–46, 131–132, 137–140, 145, 147, 202
   and English modernism, 137
   Hulme's term, 131, 138, 275 n.11
   and Indonesian modernism, 137
   linguistic core, 145, 147
   and outsider perspective, 132–133, 140
   and racial identification, 132, 141, 202
   retrospective structure, 138–139
   in *The Shadow–Line*, 124
   in "Trio," 111
   in *Wide Sargasso Sea*, 131–132, 137–147, 275 n.11
creole heiress, 127, 129–132, 135–137, 140–141
   contradictory racial stereotype, 131, 136
   demonization of, 136
   and discursive shift in racial and sexual discourses, 136–137
   and Dutch East Indies society, 136–137
   in *The Hidden Force*, 135–137
   in *Jane Eyre*, 129–131
   and madness, 131, 136, 141
   nineteenth-century stereotype, 127, 129–131, 135–137
   and property rights, 140
   in *This Earth of Mankind*, 127, 129–132, 137, 140
   in *Wide Sargasso Sea*, 127, 129–132, 136–137, 140
Creole modernism, 3–9, 18–23, 27–35, 42, 60, 83, 127–133, 138, 143, 146, 149, 197, 200, 202, 218, 220, 243, 248, 250–251, 258 n.63
   and black transatlantic modernism, 83, 107
   and C. L. R. James, 248–249
   contrapuntal analysis, 42, 60, 200
   and English modernism, 6–7, 18, 22, 28, 30, 32, 35, 60, 83, 97, 127, 148, 197, 200, 202, 218, 243, 250–251
   and family romance, 31–32, 34, 133, 138, 197, 200
   and history of psychiatry, 146
   and Indonesian modernism, 7, 27–28, 30, 32, 35, 197, 200, 202, 218, 243, 250–251
   Rhys's response to, 128, 132–133, 138, 143, 200
   and stereotype of creole heiress, 130
créolité, 6, 128
creolization, 6–7, 14, 18, 20, 46, 97, 104, 107, 124, 128–129, 142, 146–148, 249–250, 254 n.12
   attempt to control in *Wide Sargasso Sea*, 145
   and *O.E.D.*, 249–250
   and *palakia* tree headache, 147
   in *The Shadow–Line*, 124
   theories of, 128, 143, 148
   See also creole (language)
Crowley, Tony, 86
Cuban Counterpoint (Ortiz), 7, 40–42, 60, 107
cultural capital, 3–4, 8–9, 34, 36, 40, 42, 45–46, 59, 61, 63–64, 75, 77, 81–87, 89, 202, 219–220, 245, 247, 249, 251
   and citation of passages, 3–4, 63–64, 247, 249, 251
   and distinction, 42, 75
   European, 40, 45–46, 84, 89
   linguistic and literary, 3–4, 63–64, 77, 81–87, 245, 247, 249, 251
   of modernist memory, 84, 251
   and opera, 59
   See also passage of literature, symbolic economy
cultural studies, 4, 40, 219, 248
culture, 107, 181, 185, 195, 201, 207, 209–210, 218–219, 227, 247–248, 251
culture systems, 219, 249, 251

kampung culture, 181, 185, 195, 201, 207, 209–210
  keyword, 248
  material dislocation of, 107, 218–219, 227, 247, 251
  See also aesthetic judgment, *rasa*, taste, transculturation
cummings, e. e., 66, 266–267 n.2

Dain Maroola (*Almayer's Folly*), 46, 80
  betrayal of, 46, 80
  Ford confuses with Dain Waris, 80
Dain Waris (*Lord Jim*), 80
dalang (*wayang* puppet master), 55, 56
dam, 84–86, 105
  O.E.D. entry on, 86
Darío, Rubén, 283–284 n.48
Dash, Michael, 243
Daum, P. A., 157
Debussy, Claude, 42
Narain, Denise de Caires, 128, 274 n.2
de Certeau, Michel, 100, 125
de Man, Paul, 235–237, 239
  and problem of historical reference, 239
  and imperatives of postcolonial philology, 236
  return to philology, 235–237
  trope of theory and theory of trope, 236–237
decolonization, 4–8, 28, 33, 35, 40, 128, 132, 135, 146, 177–179, 212, 217, 243–251, 254 n.12
  and colonialism, 5, 135, 244, 247
  and English, 243, 243–251
  history of, 4–8, 146, 179, 244, 247
  and Pramoedya's experience, 40, 177, 179
  and psychoanalysis and psychiatry, 146
  and Rhys, 128, 132
  and tradition, 177–179, 211–212, 217
  See also anti-colonial nationalism, Fanon, postcolonial philology
deconstruction, 36, 101, 115, 235, 237, 239 (see also de Man, Derrida)
Dedes, Queen (*Arok of Java*), 208, 210–211
  and Pramoedya's mother, 208, 210
  and narrative consciousness in

Arok of Java, 210–211
DeKoven, Marianne, 272 n.10
department stores, 102–103, 120
Derrida, Jacques, 103–104, 115, 234–235, 239–242, 246–247, 260 n.16
  citing Hegel, 240–241
  différance, 247
  and Glissant, 104
  globalatinization, 234, 249
  mise-en-abyme, 260 n.16
  Monolingualism of the Other, 103–104
  "White Mythology," 240–241
dialect, 9, 11, 14, 15, 23, 28, 34, 49, 57
dialectic, 48, 57, 59–61, 92–93, 98, 101–102, 111, 118, 121–123, 126, 172, 249, 277 n.32
  arrested dialectic of Minke's anti-colonial consciousness, 172
  of abysmal taste in opera, 57, 59–60
  deadlocked dialectic of Creole memory, 111
  dialectical image (Benjamin), 60, 118, 249, 277 n.32
  of distinction (Bourdieu), 61, 267 n.4
  Hegelian dialectic, 48, 92–93, 240–241
  spatial dialectic, 101–102, 121–123
  standstill of dialectics (Benjamin), 98, 126
diaspora, 107, 249
  practice of diaspora (Edwards), 107
  black transatlantic modernism, 249
  See also afro-caribbean culture
Dickens, Charles, 12, 15–17, 138
  Nicholas Nickleby, 15
  Our Mutual Friend, 138
Dickinson, Emily, 105, 110–111
differend, 51, 52, 77, 81–82, 142–143, 247, 262 n.42
  and Conrad's genealogy of Malay–English history, 52, 77, 81–82, 167, 262 n.42
  defined, 51
  as legal dispute, 52, 142
  and narrative form, 51–52
  and *obeah* in *Wide Sargasso Sea*, 142–143

Index 309

distinction, 42, 47, 61, 74
  dialectic of, 61, 267 n.4
  See also Bourdieu, class, cultural capital
domesticity, 119–123, 128, 141, 143, 153, 155–157, 165–167, 169–171, 174
  in Conrad's Malay fiction, 166–169
  da, 143
  domestic fiction, 128, 255 n.29
  domestic partner rights, 165
  domestic servants, 141, 143, 153, 155, 157, 173, 174
  economy of, and reading, 170, 171, 174
  huishoudster (housekeeper), 155–156
  and international law, 153, 165, 167, 169
  See also interiority, *nyai*, Taminah, Tuminah
Dominica, 10, 87, 89, 92, 108–109, 112–113, 116
Dominica Herald and Leeward Islands Gazette, 21–22, 113
Donizetti, Gaetano, 48
  Lucia di Lammermoor, 48
"double consciousness" (Du Bois), 53–54, 148, 264 n.49
drama, 154, 158, 160, 182 (*see also* East Indies opera, melodrama, opera)
Du Bois, W. E. B., 53, 264 n.49
Dutch (language), 7, 23–28, 34, 53, 135, 139, 154–155, 157, 159–160, 167, 170, 175, 181, 193, 196, 205, 207, 212, 233–235
  and Minke's notes, 234
  and *nyai* narrative form, 154, 159–160, 167, 170, 175
Dutch (literature), 23–26, 135, 154, 157
  modernism, 154
  trope of creole in, 135
  women writers, 157
Dutch East Indies, 27, 39, 44, 46, 51, 53, 55, 75–77, 81, 135–137, 154–157, 161, 166–167, 174
  abolition of slavery in 1860, 155
  and British controlled Malay territories, 76–77, 81, 167
  British interregnum, 166
  and lifting of immigration restrictions on women, 157
  and *nyai-tuan* cohabitation, 154–156, 161, 167
  sociological significance of creole trope for, 135–137
  See also Indonesia, Malay archipelago

East Indies opera, 30, 41–42, 59–60, 124, 158, 160–161, 266 n.66
  and *nyai* narrative form, 30, 158, 160–161
  and *The Shadow–Line*, 124
  See also opera
Eckermann, Johann Peter, 16
écriture, 31, 224 (*see also* writing)
Edwards, Brent Hayes, 107, 248
Eliot, T. S., 35, 63, 84, 218
Emery, Mary Lou, 128, 275 n.7
Empson, William, 284 n.49
"End of the Tether, The" (Conrad), 99
England, 6, 78, 89, 116
English (language), 6–23, 26–28, 31, 35, 49, 60–64, 71–72, 74, 83–87, 103–105, 143, 167, 184, 196, 212, 219–220, 243–251
  American English in *wayang*, 57
  and Anglo–Saxondom, 84
  and creole, 20, 143
  decolonization of, 243–251
  "Englishness" of English words, 86, 87
  and French, 71, 72, 74, 81, 83, 85, 103, 104
  grammar, 16, 17
  and *lingua franca*, 10, 17, 18, 49
  linguistic and literary capital, 86, 87, 245, 249
  and Malay, 50, 60, 63, 76, 77, 80, 81, 167
  monolingualism, 103, 114, 116, 249
  and *O.E.D.*, 8, 35, 86, 87, 244–247, 250
  and Pramoedya, 184
  Rhys's accent, 84–86
  standard English, 11, 86, 212, 245, 247, 249
  See also Conrad, Conradian passage, Rhys
English modernism, 3–18, 30–36, 39, 42, 49, 60–68, 73–75, 78, 80–83, 86, 88–89, 91, 93, 97–100, 104, 107–110, 127, 135, 148, 153, 166, 169–171, 174, 197, 200, 202, 218, 220, 228, 243, 250–251, 254 n.13, 258 n.63
  and black transatlantic modernism, 107
  and blankness of memory, 98, 104
  and Conradian passage, 65, 73, 80, 82, 91, 93, 99, 100, 169, 170

and contrapuntal analysis, 42, 60, 200
and Creole modernism, 6–7, 18, 28, 30, 32, 35–36, 60, 97, 127, 135, 148, 153, 170, 197, 200, 202, 218, 243, 250–251
and *English Review*, 12, 13, 61, 63, 66–68
and family romance, 31–32, 34, 197
and French modernism, 73–75, 81–82, 91, 110
and Indonesian modernism, 7–8, 28, 30, 32, 35–36, 60, 135, 153, 166, 170–171, 174, 197, 200, 202, 218, 243, 250–251
and *nyai* narrative form, 166, 169, 171, 174
and passage of literature, 34, 57, 61, 64–65, 82, 89, 91, 93, 108, 251
repetitive formation of, 5, 61, 67, 74, 78, 89, 93, 98, 110, 127, 148
and *transatlantic review*, 61–63, 66, 68–69
English Review, 12, 13, 16, 61, 63, 65–71, 78, 87, 89, 271 n.79
founding of, 61
name, 87, 89, 271 n.79
enlightenment, 100, 125, 181, 194, 240, 242
European models, 181, 194
Pramoedya on, 181, 194
scriptural economy, 125
and trope of "Western" consciousness, 240
tropicopolitan challenge to, 242
epic, 51, 52, 203, 262 n.42
in Conrad, 51, 52, 203, 262 n.42
in Pramoedya, 203
estrangement, 48, 57, 59–60, 181–186, 192, 195, 201–202, 204, 228, 233, 249, 261 n.30
of literature, 48, 57, 59–60, 261 n.30
from within Javanese tradition, 181–186, 192, 195, 201–202
of Islam and Christianity, 204
of Igbo and English, 228
and postcolonial philology, 233, 249
See also alien genealogies, tradition
ethnic identity, 10, 29–30, 36, 41, 52, 60, 166 (*see also* race)
etymology, 86–87, 189, 193, 240–241, 248

Javanese etymology, 189, 193, 264–265 n.55
Eurocentrism, 57, 88, 219, 223
Europe, 4, 12–13, 15–18, 23, 26–27, 29–30, 34, 41, 42, 45–50, 53–55, 59, 62–63, 68, 71–72, 79, 83, 84–85, 89, 100, 104, 110, 128, 133–134, 138–139, 141, 148, 153–154, 156, 158, 166, 168, 171–173, 187, 203–204, 212, 219, 221–222, 229–232, 264 n.50
avant-garde, 63
and counterpoint, 42, 57
crisis of consciousness, 48, 53, 84, 115
definition of European, 168
enforced return of creole heiress to, 133, 138, 139
and enlightenment, 100, 181, 194
grand narrative tradition, 48, 100
grand opera, 42, 44–48, 53, 57, 60
and human sciences, 187, 224, 231, 232
and music, 50, 53
naming systems, 148, 149, 173
novel form, 11, 158, 198
prewar Central Europe, 84
romanticism, 49, 71–72, 230, 232
suspicion of, 222
taste, 54, 55, 264 n.50
See also metropolitan, Orientalism, philology
events of 1965 (*peristiwa 1965*), 26, 139, 154, 177–180, 185–186, 197, 200, 202, 209, 222
and trope of vicious circle (*lingkaran setan*), 179, 180, 186, 197
and loss of Indonesian historical documents, 200, 222
and *Wide Sargasso Sea*, 202
exegesis (*see under* textual study)
expatriate communities, 62, 82–83, 107, 112, 270 n.65, 271 n.3
explication de texte, 172, 222–223 (*see also* textual study)

fairy tales, 20, 50
family romance, 10, 16, 31–33, 46, 52, 59, 76–77, 124, 131, 137, 140, 166–167, 179, 197–202, 207
in Conrad, 16, 31–32, 34, 46, 52, 59, 76–77, 124, 166–167, 197, 200–202, 262–263 n.42
and Freud, 137–138, 140, 198
and genealogies of modernism, 31, 137, 197, 200, 202

Index 311

family romance (*continued*)
  and narrative form, 138, 140, 202
  in Pramoedya, 33–34, 45–46 131, 137, 139–140, 179, 197–202, 205–209, 211–212
  and racial heritage, 137–140, 202
  and reading, 10, 31, 138, 197–198, 200, 202, 207, 213
  in Rhys, 32–33, 91, 111, 131, 137–147, 197–198, 200, 202, 275 n.11
  See also creole family romance, genealogy
Fanon, Frantz, 43, 50, 132, 140, 146, 276 n.13
  Black Skin, White Masks, 132, 276 n.13
  vicious circle of black-white relations, 132, 276 n.13
  Wretched of the Earth, 43, 50
feminism, 67, 162, 164, 165, 268 n.18, 272–273 n.12
  Tirto Adi Suryo and, 164, 165
fetishism, 47, 105, 120, 148, 202, 261 n.26
  commodity, 47
  and literature, 105, 148
  and music, 47
  racial, 47, 148, 202
feudalism. *See under* Javanese culture
figurative use of language. *See* trope
filiation, 178, 186–188, 191–192, 195, 197, 201
  "link in the chain" (*mata rantai*), 188, 191, 195
  "natural filiation" (Said), 187–188, 192
  and Pramoedya, 178, 186–187, 195, 197, 201
  and Said, 187–188, 192, 254 n.13
  See also affiliation
film. *See* cinema
flâneur, 102, 272 n.12
  and Baudelaire, 102
  and Benjamin, 102
flâneuse, 102, 114, 120, 272–273 n.12
  and Rhys, 102, 114, 120, 272 n.12
Flaubert, Gustave, 18, 48–49, 61, 71–73, 79–81, 87, 109, 222
  bovarysme, 48
  Un Coeur Simple, 222
  and Conrad's style, 73, 80, 81
  creole stereotype, 109
  Madame Bovary, 48–49, 71, 79
  and opera, 48–49
  and Pangemanann, 222

Florida, Nancy, 54, 265 n.63
Flotow, Friedrich von, 47, 261 n.30
  Martha, 47, 261 n.30
  "The Last Rose of Summer," 47, 261 n.30
Footsteps (Pramoedya, Buru quartet), 39, 44, 47, 54–56, 146–147, 163, 181, 200, 260 n.17
  and Javanism, 54–56, 147
  opera passage, 44, 47
Ford, Ford Madox (Hueffer), 12, 13, 32, 61–75, 77–84, 87–90, 268 n.20, 270 n.66
  affair with Rhys, 62, 66–67, 82
  and Conrad, 61–78, 80–84, 87–88
  and English modernism, 61–69, 77, 81–83, 90
  and *English Review*, 12, 13, 61, 63–65, 69–71, 78
  and memory, 62–63, 65, 68–78, 80–83, 87–88
  misspelling Marlow, 72, 75, 77–78
  name, 65, 68
  and pastiche, 71, 78
  Preface to *The Left Bank*, 82, 87–88
  and shell shock, 68, 69
  and *transatlantic review*, 32, 61–70, 78, 82–84, 87, 89, 266–267 n.2
  unreliability of, 63, 69, 70–71
  See also Conrad–Ford collaboration, *English Review*, *Joseph Conrad: A Remembrance*, *transatlantic review*
foreclosure, 162, 165–168, 170–174, 279 n.36
forgetting, 65, 67–69, 75, 77, 87, 91, 207
  and history of print culture, 207
  and wartime trauma, 67–69
  See also memory
Foucault, Michel, 30–31, 136–137, 192, 223–225, 231–235, 248, 254 n.13, 268 n.18
  on shift in discourses on race and sexuality, 136–137
  on dissolution of human sciences, 231
  on genealogy, 192
  on linguistic turn, 224–225
  and Said, 223
  "Western consciousness," 233–235
  "What is an Author,"30–31, 254 n.13
France, 12, 64, 71, 72, 174
Francis, G., 29, 158, 165, 166
  (see also *Nyai Dasima*)

French (language), 6–7, 13–14, 32, 61–62, 64, 71–75, 77, 80–82, 84–85, 103, 109–110, 115, 117, 140, 142–145, 172, 220, 222, 225, 232–235
  and Conradian passage, 73–75, 82
  and English, 71–74, 81, 103
  and Malay, 81
  monolingualism, 103
  and Pangemanann's education, 172, 222, 233–235
  patois, 89, 142–144
  and Rhys's francophone English, 88, 91, 103–107, 110, 113–117, 140, 142–145, 211
French modernism, 13, 31, 61–62, 71, 73–75, 77, 80–82, 91, 109–110, 225
  and English modernism, 73–75, 81–82, 91, 110
Freud, Sigmund, 34, 67, 74, 137–138, 198–199, 242
  on compulsion to repeat (*Wiederholungszwang*), 67, 74, 268 n.18
  on family romance, 34, 137–138, 198
  Nachträglichkeit (retroactivity), 242
  Oedipal complex, 198–199
Friedman, Susan Stanford, 5–7
The Fugitive (Pramoedya), 198–199

Gadis Pantai. See *The Girl from the Coast*
gamelan, 24, 42, 44, 50, 54–57, 60, 183, 201, 204, 265 n.57 (*see also* counterpoint, music, opera, polyphony, *wayang*)
Girl from the Coast (Pramoedya), 27, 178, 193, 197
  and lost trilogy, 27, 178, 193, 197
Gandhi, Mahatma, 25
Gaps. See archival gaps, history, memory
Garnett, Edward, 12, 70, 73, 75
Geertz, Clifford, 54, 56, 134
gender, 32, 41, 46, 65, 100, 124, 140, 161, 169, 174, 272 n.10, 277 n.32
genealogy, 3–6, 8, 10, 30, 34–36, 52, 60, 64, 78, 98, 110, 118, 129, 153, 164, 166–167, 174–175, 178–179, 183–197, 199–200, 202–205, 207, 209, 211, 217, 226
  and *The Chinese in Indonesia*, 185, 186

  contest over, in romanized script, 205
  and creole heiress, 129
  and critique, 183–197, 203–207, 211, 214
  and family romance, 34, 52, 197, 199–200, 202, 207, 213, 262 n.42
  family tree (*silsilah*), 191
  and Foucault, 192
  and genetic laws, 187–188, 191, 193–195
  Javanese genealogy, 188–195, 202–203, 207, 209, 213
  of Malay–English history, 77, 81, 82, 167, 262 n.42
  of modernity in Benjamin and Rhys, 98, 118
  and Nietzsche, 192
  and *nyai* narrative form, 164, 207
  and passage of literature, 179, 194–197, 200, 214
  principle of in Pramoedya, 178, 184, 188–197
  See also alien genealogies
genetic laws, 187–188, 191, 193, 194–195
  and aphorisms, proverbs, sayings, 193
  hukum warisan, 187, 193
  and Mendel, 193
  and Pramoedya's principle of genealogy, 191, 193
Generation of 1945, 7
German (language), 62, 63, 83, 84, 181, 194, 196, 220
  Austrian German, 83
German modernism, 62
German philology, 58, 221
Germany, 12
Gide, André, 61–62, 68, 260 n.16
Gilroy, Paul, 83, 107, 264 n.49
Glissant, Édouard, 6, 7, 18–19, 21–22, 83, 104, 107, 128, 243, 273 n.22
  creolization, 6, 18, 104, 107, 128
  opacity, 6
  poetics of relation, 6, 104
  precedent for Derrida, 104
globalization, 244, 249 (*see also* English, *lingua franca*)
globalatinization, 234, 239
Gloomy Sunday (*Sombre dimanche*), 106
Goenawan Mohamad, 183
Goethe, Johann Wolfgang von, 11, 16, 17, 28

Index   313

Good Morning, Midnight (Rhys),
  97–112, 116, 118–120, 122, 125,
  132
  and black transatlantic
    modernism, 107
  creole narrative consciousness,
    104, 106, 108–111, 125
  creole hammock stereotype, 112, 118
  and English identity, 99, 119, 122
  impasse, 101–106, 108–110
  interior, relation to exterior space,
    in 101–103, 109, 119–120, 122
  interior monologue, 103–104, 119,
    122, 125
  and London, 102, 109, 120, 122
  and memory, 106, 109, 111
  music and song, 105–109
  Paris setting, 97, 102–104, 107, 120
  Sasha Jansen, 101–103, 105–106,
    108–111, 119, 132
  department stores, 102–103, 120
  title and Emily Dickinson, 105,
    110–111
  See also monolingualism
gong, 55, 56 (*see also* gamelan)
Greek (ancient), 58, 64, 199, 205, 221
Guerard, Albert, 77
Guerilla Family (Pramoedya),
  198–199
Guha, Ranajit, 162, 265 n.63
Guillory, John, 63, 235–237
  and de Man on tropes, 235–237
Gulf of Siam, 99, 124

Hadji Moekti, 158, 163
  Hikayat Siti Mariah, 163
Hampson, Robert, 51, 262 n.42
Hamzah, Amir. *See* Amir Hamzah
hand organ, 41, 43, 47–48, 59, 260
  n.12 (*see also* barrel organ)
harbor master (*shahbandar*), 52, 119,
  203, 274 n.37
  and *Arus Balik*, 203
  Babalatchi as, 52
  and international law, 52
  and *The Shadow-Line*, 119, 274
    n.37
harmony, 56–58, 265 n.57
  and atonality, 58
  and disharmony, 56, 58
  European and Javanese harmonic
    systems, 57–58, 265 n.57
  tonality, 58
Harris, Wilson, 7
"Heart of Darkness" (Conrad), 79,
  85, 100, 124, 229, 230
  absence of African languages in,
    230
  "blank spaces" in, 85, 100
  cited by Achebe, 229–230
  cited by Eliot, 63
  French Belgian context of, 85
Hegel, Georg Wilhelm Friedrich, 48,
  51, 92–93, 240–242, 262 n.31
  Aesthetics, 48, 240–241, 262 n.31
  Derrida and, 240–241
  dialectic, 48, 92–93, 240–242, 262
    n.31
  and grand narrative tradition, 48
  master-slave dialectic, 92–93
  Phenomenology of Spirit, 48
  reversal of dialectic, 241–242
  trope of enlightenment, 240–241
hegemony, 7–8, 28, 35, 99, 182, 205,
  207, 212, 243–244, 249
  British hegemony over sea trade,
    99
  Javanese hegemony over
    Indonesia, 182, 205
  linguistic hegemony, 7, 8, 35, 207,
    212, 243–244, 249
  of standardized English, 212,
    243–244, 249
Helen (of Troy), 64, 78, 128
heliotrope, 110, 112
Hemingway, Ernest, 66, 85
hermeneutics, 58, 172, 221–222, 226,
  235
  Biblical, 58
  and Pangemanann, 172
  suspicious, 221–222, 235
heteroglossia, 11, 77, 156, 207, 250
Hidden Force, The (Couperus),
  135–137, 142, 146
  and creole stereotype, 135–136
Hikayat Siti Mariah (Hadji Moekti),
  163
Hinduism, 56, 203, 209–211
  and scripture, 56, 209–211
  goddess Pradnya Paramita,
    207–208
  shift from Javanese Hinduism to
    Hindu Javanism, 209–211
Hindu Javanism. *See under*
  Hinduism
history, 39, 41, 45–46, 51–53, 59,
  162–163, 165, 177–181, 188, 191,
  197, 200, 202, 207, 209, 220, 222,
  239–241
  ambiguity and, 52, 53
  and *Arok of Java*, 177, 209
  and *Arus Balik*, 177

314   *Index*

and Conrad's fiction, 39, 46, 51–53, 59, 77
Hegelian dialectic of, 240–241
of Indonesia. *See under* Indonesia
and lost documentation of Indonesia, 26–27, 163–165, 177, 192, 193, 200, 202, 218, 222, 267, 258 n.61, 279–280 n.2
material traces, 118, 165
of print culture, 207
shift from Javanese Hinduism to Hindu Javanism, 209–211
See also archive, archival gaps, Buru quartet, Buru work, decolonization
Homer, 9, 11, 15, 23
Hood, Mantle, 265 n.57
House for Mr Biswas, A (Naipaul), 227
House of Glass (Pramoedya, Buru quartet), 39, 45, 59, 172–173, 220–222, 226–227, 232–234, 239–240, 246, 256 n.42
citation from Vulgate Magnificat, 233–234
housemaid, Tuminah, 173
theft of Minke's documents, 172–173, 221–222, 226, 234
title metaphor, 172–173
trope of documentary reliability, 239–240
See also archive, archivist, Buru quartet, Pangemanann
huishoudster (housekeeper), 155–156 (see also *nyai*)
Hugo, Victor, 13–14
Toilers of the Sea, 13–14
hukum warisan, 187, 193 (*see also* genetic laws)
Hulme, Peter, 32, 128, 131, 138, 255–256 n.32, 274–275 n.4, 275 n.11
and creole family romance, 32, 131, 138, 275 n.11
debate with Brathwaite, 128, 256 n.32, 274–275 n.4
Huyssen, Andreas, 63, 267 n.4
hybridity, 7, 31, 41, 60, 113, 128–129, 143–144, 172, 255 n.29
fear of, 113
and opera, 41, 60
and Pangemanann, 172
theories of, 128–129, 144

Igbo, 228
language and culture in *Things Fall Apart*, 228

imagined communities. *See under* Anderson
impasse, 18, 22–23, 98, 101–106, 108–111, 113, 122, 125, 148, 202, 273 n.20
as blocked-off street, 101–102
of creole consciousness, 110–111, 118, 123, 148
as figurative predicament, 101
in *Good Morning, Midnight*, 101–102, 108–110, 122, 125
and interior monologue 103–104, 122, 125
as London or Parisian street architecture, 102, 122
and monolingualism, 106, 116, 122
as rhetorical predicament, 103, 122
imperialism, 7, 40, 46, 248 (*see also* colonialism)
impressionism, 63, 70, 72–73, 77, 79, 84, 88–89
and Conrad, 73
and Ford, 63, 70, 72–73, 77, 79, 88–89
and Rhys, 84
India, 25, 54, 162
Indo, 24, 26, 55, 59
Indonesia, 6, 24, 33, 40, 43–45, 52, 76, 139, 166, 155, 177–180, 184–185, 197–200, 202–203, 240, 249, 254 n.12
anti–Chinese measures (1960), 185
arrival of Europeans, 203
arrival of Islam, 203
events of 1965, 26, 139, 154, 177–180, 185, 186, 197, 200, 202, 209, 222
independence struggle (1945–7), 198, 199, 200
inter-island relations, 52
Majapahit Empire, 202
naming of (1922), 198
Oath of Youth (1928), 8, 27, 198
political crisis of 1957–1965, 33
thirteenth-century setting of *Arok of Java*, 177, 178
sixteenth-century setting of *Arus Balik*, 177, 178, 202
See also archival gaps, Buru quartet, Buru work, Dutch East Indies
Indonesian (*bahasa Indonesia*; language), 6, 8–10, 16, 23–30, 33, 35–36, 54, 57, 60, 134, 146–147, 161–162, 178, 184, 189, 194, 201, 205–206, 217–218, 234–235, 243–245, 247, 249

Index   315

Indonesian (*continued*)
  and national consciousness, 8, 27–30, 36, 42, 161–162
  and Javanese, 24–26, 33, 54, 245
  and *lingua franca* Malay, 10, 16, 24, 26–30, 161–162, 205
  Minke's choice of, 201
  and *nyai* narrative form, 161–162
  and *O.E.D.*, 8–9, 35, 36, 217, 243–245, 247–248
  Pramoedya's use of against Javanese, 54, 189, 194, 206, 264 n.54
  pre–Indonesian, 10, 23, 27, 29–30, 161, 178
  and revolutionary Malay, 104, 206
  and romanized print, 8, 29–30, 205–206
  in *wayang*, 57
  and world literature, 24, 28, 30
Indonesian archipelago. *See* Malay archipelago
Indonesian modernism, 3–9, 28–32, 35–36, 39, 42, 60, 133, 135, 153–155, 158, 162, 164–166, 171, 174, 177–178, 181, 190–191, 197, 200, 211–212, 214, 217–218, 220, 226, 243, 250–251, 258 n.63
  and Amir Hamzah, 23–24, 183–184, 190
  and Balai Pustaka, 154, 165
  and Creole modernism, 7, 28, 30, 32, 35–36, 133, 135, 153, 197, 200, 218, 243, 250–251
  and displacement of European models, 181, 250
  and English modernism, 7, 28, 30, 32, 35–36, 135, 153, 166, 174, 197, 200, 218, 243, 250–251
  and family romance, 31–34, 45–46, 131, 137, 139–140, 179, 197–202, 205–209, 211–212
  and *nyai* narrative form, 158, 162, 164–166, 171, 174, 191
  and *O.E.D.*, 35–36, 250
  and passage of literature, 35–6, 57, 170–172, 184, 196–197, 201, 214, 218, 251
  socialist-realist, 164
  and Soetomo's *Kenang-Kenangan*, 190
  See also genealogy, pre–Indonesian, Pramoedya
interior monologue, 103–104, 119–120, 122, 123, 125 (*see also* narrative first person)

interiority, 97–98, 101–103, 109, 115, 118–126
  Benjamin on, 118, 121
  creole anteriority, 122
  private interior space, 98, 101–103, 121, 124
  social and psychological space, 90, 101–103, 125
  and spatial dialectic, 101–102, 121–123
  See also domesticity, narrative first person, space
international law, 52, 153, 165, 167, 169
interpretation. *See* literary criticism
irony, 43–44, 46–47, 51, 57, 59, 77, 86, 201, 221, 227, 237–238
  in Conrad, 43–44, 46–47, 51, 57, 77, 201
  etymological, 86
  and faith in documents, 221, 237–238
Isak, Joesoef, 259 n.6
Islam, 52, 139, 146, 147, 159, 184–186, 203–204, 234, 263 n.42
  and *Arus Balik*, 203–204
  and Christianity, 204, 234
  marriage, 139
  militancy, 59
  modernizing consciousness, 234
  stereotyping of in *Nyai Dasima*, 159
  and trope of vicious circle, 184–186
It Was the Nightingale (Ford), 66, 270 n.65

James, C. L. R., 7, 35, 247, 249, 284 n.51
  and word *all-round*, 35, 247
  Beyond a Boundary, 35, 247
  Black Jacobins, 7
  and decolonization, 247
James, Henry, 12, 13, 65
Jameson, Fredric, 73–75, 170, 263 n.46, 272 n.4
Jane Eyre (Brontë), 20, 32, 110, 115, 123, 129–131, 133, 148
  and creole heiress, 130–131
  Bertha Mason, 20, 32, 115, 129, 130–131, 133, 148
  and marriage plot, 130–131
  stereotype of creole in, 110, 130–131
Japanese, 82, 83, 146, 198
jargon, 10–11
Java, 55, 57, 135, 183, 202–204, 222 (*see also* Indonesia, Javanese)

Javanese (language), 23–27, 33, 34, 42, 53–57, 134, 146–148, 156–157, 159, 165, 170, 172, 174, 177–214, 220–221, 226, 233, 238, 245, 249
  lanjaran, 197
  Pramoedya's use of, and Indonesian, 54, 189, 197, 206, 212
  script, 26, 204–205, 207, 209–211, 220, 235
  See also *baca*, *karang*, Javanese culture
Javanese culture, 24–26, 34, 42–45, 53–57, 60, 134, 165, 170, 172, 181–182, 185, 188–195, 198, 201–203, 206–207, 209–210, 213, 226, 239–239
  family structure, 165, 198, 201, 213
  and feudal hierarchies, 34, 188–189, 200–201, 212
  genealogy, 188–195, 202, 203, 207, 209, 213
  kampung civilization and, 181, 185, 195, 201, 207, 209–210
  legend of Arok, 181
  literature, 24–26, 53, 56–57, 134, 182, 198, 226, 233, 238–239
  music, 42–45, 54–57, 60
  names, 148–149, 170, 172, 190, 192
  priyayi sensibility, 45, 53–56, 189, 201, 206, 239
  superstitions, 146–147
  See also Javanism
Javanese people, 55–56, 182, 201, 221, 226
Javanism, 54–56, 147, 180–181, 188, 201, 297, 210, 226, 265 n.47, 264–265 n.55
  and *Arok of Java*, 210
  and Minke, 54–56, 147, 181
  and Orientalism, 54
  and rhetoric of apology and offense, 201, 207
  and trope of vicious circle, 180–181, 201
Javocentrism, 226 (*see also* Javanese culture, Javanism, *rasa*)
Jones, Sir William, 221
Joseph Conrad: A Personal Remembrance (Ford), 61, 63–74, 77, 79–85
  Absolute Prose and search for the *mot juste*, 70–75, 80–82, 85, 89
  confusion of narrative voice in, 70

confusion over Conrad's Malay characters, 80
  See also Conrad–Ford collaboration, Ford
Judaism, 109, 185, 186
Joyce, James, 35, 66, 84, 85, 218, 244
judgment, 172, 173 (*see also* aesthetic judgment)
Julia Martin. See under *After Leaving Mr Mackenzie*

Kamudi (Conrad's proposed pseudonym), 31–32, 49
Kant, Immanuel, 51
"Karain: A Memory" (Conrad), 76, 77, 80, 182–183, 201, 230, 264 n.47
  Naipaul cites from, 230
  Pramoedya cites from, 182–183, 201, 264 n.47
karang (composition), 29, 178–179, 183, 206, 209, 213, 233, 257 n.50 (*see also baca*, "Flowers for Mother")
Kartini, 165
Kartodikromo, Marco, 59
Keluarga Gerilya (Pramoedya), 198–199
Kenang-Kenangan (Soetomo), 190, 192–193, 213
Kenner, Hugh, 86, 218, 244
krontjong, 41, 266 n.66 (*see also* East Indies opera, music)
Komedi Bangsawan. See East Indies opera
Komedi Stamboul. See East Indies opera
Kommer, H., 158, 163
  Tjerita Njai Paina, 163

labor, 102–103, 119, 165
Lacan, Jacques, 67, 268 n.18
Lakamba (*Almayer's Folly*), 43–47, 50
Lane, Max, 259 n.6
language, 3–36,
  grammar, 16, 17, 224
  linguistic coordinates of modernism, 3–36
  and media, 107
  monolingualism, 6, 103–104, 106, 114, 116, 122, 125, 249, 273 n.20
  multilingualism, 77, 206, 219–220, 249, 250
  relation of written to spoken, 10, 15, 18–21, 25–26, 29, 36, 73, 145, 161, 182, 206

Index   317

language (*continued*)
  vernacular, 15, 72, 87
  See also linguistics, philology, scripts, writing; *and see under* individual languages
"The Last Rose of Summer" (Flotow), 47, 261 n.30
Latin, 58, 64, 205, 221, 233–235
law, 52, 58, 139–140, 142, 153–154, 157, 159, 163, 165, 167–168, 172
  colonial courts, 139, 154, 157, 159
  dispossession of native rights, 140
  and domestic relations, 153, 157, 165, 167–168, 172
  international, 52, 153, 165, 167, 169
  Islamic law, 139
  legal analysis, 58
  legal dispute, 52, 142
  Mixed Marriage Act of 1898, 157, 168
  legal rights of women, 163, 165, 172
  racial legislation, 139, 157, 168
Lawrence, D. H., 12, 66
Leavis, F. R., 229, 263 n.46
Left Bank and Other Stories (Rhys), 82, 87, 89, 92, 97, 105, 111
  Ford's Preface to, 82, 87
  trio of Antillean/Caribbean stories in, 92, 105, 111–113
Lenglet, Jean (Rhys's first husband), 32, 67, 83
Lerer, Seth, 218, 281 n.2
Lewis, Wyndham, 12, 66
Lingard, Tom (Malay trilogy), 34, 39, 46–47, 49–53, 76–77, 79–80, 166–167, 201, 263 n.42
  and family romance, 52, 76–77, 166–167, 201, 263 n.42
  and opera, 47, 49, 50
  and piracy, 51–52, 77
lingkaran setan (vicious circle), 179–188, 193–198, 201–205, 208–209, 212
  and Arok legend, 185, 208
  breaking from, 180, 188, 194–196
  and enlightenment, 181, 193, 194–195
  and fragmentary form of Buru work, 180, 198
  and gamelan, 183, 201
  and Javanese *kampung* civilization, 201, 208
  and passage of literature, 195–196, 198, 205
  religious connotations, 184–186, 205
  See also vicious circle

lingua franca, 9–28, 35, 49, 60, 157, 161, 174, 266 n.67
  English, 10, 17, 18, 49
  Malay, 10, 16, 24–28, 32, 60, 157, 161, 174
  Lowell's "spiritual *lingua franca*," 9, 11, 14–16, 23–25, 28
  See also pre–Indonesian
linguistic turn, 223–226, 229, 231–232, 235–236
  in Achebe and Naipaul's reading of Conrad, 232
  Foucault on, 224–225
  and Saussure, 223–224
  and non–Western fold of "Western consciousness,"235
  See also linguistics, literary criticism, philology
linguistics, 218, 225, 233–234, 239
  and dissolution of philology, 218, 223–224, 233
  historical (diachronic), 218, 223–224, 236, 239
  and literature, 218, 223–224, 229
  and Saussure, 223–224, 236, 239
  synchronic, 218, 224, 236, 239
link, 187–188, 192–193, 195, 200, 214, 226–227
  and break, 192–193, 195, 200, 214, 226–227
  genetic and cultural links, 187, 195
  mata rantai, 188, 195
  See also "Mata Rantai," tradition
Lionnet, Françoise, 6, 254 n.12
literal meaning. *See* trope
literacy, 10, 18–21, 26, 30, 113, 137, 174
  print literacy, 20–21, 30, 113
  See also baca, karang, orality, reading
literary criticism, 4, 6, 40, 43–44, 57–58, 171–173, 218–219, 221–227, 233, 235–237, 241, 260 n.16
  and Biblical hermeneutics, 58
  close reading of texts, 172, 222–223
  and cultural studies, 219
  exegetical abyss, 57, 233
  formalist principles, 218, 225, 233
  Foucault on, 224–225
  and linguistic turn, 223–226
  modernist theories of textuality, 223–226
  musical harmony, 58
  and Orientalism, 221–227, 233
  and philology, 218–219, 221–224, 226–227, 233

practice, 4, 57, 171–173, 222–223, 225–226, 233 (*see also* citation, close reading, exegesis, *explication de texte*, interpretation, tropes)
suspicious hermeneutics, 221–222, 235
theory, 4, 6, 219, 223–226, 233, 236, 241 (*see also* linguistic turn, philology, tropes)
vicious circle of racism and critique in Conrad, 43–44
See also contrapuntal reading
literary field, *see* Bourdieu
literary form, 48, 53, 56–60, 64, 71–73, 75, 160, 182–184, 198, 203, 217–218, 226, 238
alien genealogies of, 182–183, 194–7
and Conrad, 72–73, 75
crisis in, 53
and estrangement in opera, 48, 56–60
Malay and Indonesian, 23–24, 50, 183–184, 190
and linguistic form, 218, 226, 245
and ordinary language, 238, 245
See also aesthetic judgment, *baca*, epic, *karang*, narrative form, *nyai* narrative form, philology
London, 16, 76, 83, 87, 97, 109, 110, 117, 120–122
Lord Jim (Conrad), 77, 80, 99, 167–170
and *nyai* narrative form, 167–169
title and translation of *tuan*, 77, 167, 168, 169
Lowell, James Russell, 9, 11, 14, 15, 21, 23–24, 28, 35
Lucia di Lammermoor (Donizetti), 48
Lyotard, Jean–François, 51–52, 142 (*see also* differend)

ma'af. See apology, offense
Macassar, 46
Madame Bovary (Flaubert), 48–49, 71, 79
bovarysme, 49
and opera, 48–49
madness, 131, 133, 136, 138–141, 143, 148
and creole heiress stereotype, 131, 136, 141
Mahabharata, 173, 182–183, 195–196, 208, 210, 214, 265 n.55
in *Arok of Java*, 210

Javanese version, 210
passages from, 182, 195, 210, 214
Maier, Henk, 29–30, 178–179, 183, 185, 206, 209, 256 n.49, 266 n.67, 283 n.38
Malacca, 168
malakama fruit, 202–204
Malay (language), 7–10, 16, 23–24, 26–32, 49–50, 60, 63, 80–81, 134, 154–161, 163, 165–168, 170, 174, 178, 184, 194, 196, 199, 205, 207, 212, 233
and Conrad, 49–50, 60, 77, 80–81, 167–168
lingua franca Malay, 10, 16, 24, 26, 28–29, 32, 60, 157, 161
linguistic and literary capital, 81
and *nyai* narrative form, 154–161, 163, 166–168, 170
and "revolutionary Malay," 194
and script, 205, 207
See also Indonesian, *lingua franca*, pre–Indonesian
Malay archipelago, 7, 10, 39, 46, 51–52, 63, 65, 71, 76–79, 81, 85, 87, 168–170, 202
British vs. Dutch controlled territories, 76–77, 81, 87
erasure of setting in Conrad, 65, 76–77, 79, 81, 168–170
inter-island relations, 52
piracy and, 51–52, 77
and "Karain: A Memory," 76–77
and "Youth," 76–77, 87
See also Borneo, Malay peninsula, Malaysia, Indonesia, Java, Sumatra
Malay peninsula, 76, 78, 203
Malay trilogy (*Almayer's Folly, An Outcast of the Islands, The Rescue*), 16, 32, 34, 39–60, 63, 76–77, 79–80, 166–167, 200–201, 203
compared to Pramoedya's Buru quartet, 39–60
Dutch vs. British and, 76–77, 166–167
and family romance, 52, 59, 63, 76–77, 166–167, 201, 262 n.42
fragmentary narrative logic, 53, 203
narrative consciousness in, 49, 59–60
and opera, 43–48, 53, 59–60
See also *Almayer's Folly*, Babalatchi, Lingard, *An Outcast of the Islands*, *The Rescue*

Index 319

Malaysia, 76, 81
Mallarmé, Stéphane, 31, 73, 74, 260 n.16
  l'oeuvre pur, 31, 73, 74
Mandal, Sumit, 186
Mann, Thomas, 58, 62, 68
Mannoni, Octavio, 146
Manusami, 158, 166
Marlow, 19, 72–73, 75–78, 81, 87, 89, 99, 100, 167–168
  and Malay settings, 77, 81, 87, 168
  and *nyai* narrative form, 168
  spelling of, 72–73, 75, 77–78
Marlowe, Christopher, 77–78, 89
  and Marlow, 77–78, 89
  Doctor Faustus, 78
marriage, 130–131, 136–137, 139, 141, 153, 157, 161, 165–168, 172–173
  arranged, 131
  European vs. *nyai-tuan* cohabitation, 157, 161, 167
  and Conrad's Malay fiction, 166–168
  and Islamic law, 139, 161
  Mixed Marriage Act of 1898, 157, 168
  mixed marriage, 167, 168
  and naming, 172, 173
  and racial politics, 136–137
  and women's rights, 165
  See also creole heiress, *nyai*
Martha (Flotow), 47, 261 n.30
Martinique, 21, 22, 104, 105, 107–111, 122, 123, 140
  and *Good Morning, Midnight*, 104–105, 107–111, 122, 123
  and impasse, 104, 273 n.22
  and music, 105, 107, 108
  characters in "Trio" (*Left Bank*), 111
  in *Wide Sargasso Sea*, 140
Marya Zelli. See under *Quartet*
Mas (Javanese form of address), 34, 189, 192, 212, 214
  and Pramoedya's father's name, 189, 192, 212, 214
"Mata Rantai" ("One Link in the Chain"), 187–189, 191, 193, 195
  ambiguity of meaning, 191, 195
  and breaks in chain of tradition, 187–188
  genetic vs. traditional links, 187–188
  and vicious circle trope, 195
Maupassant, Guy de, 87

McKay, Claude, 128
mechanical reproduction. See media
Medan Prijaji, 162–165
media, 20, 41, 43, 47–49, 51, 53, 55, 57, 59–60, 92–93, 105–109, 111, 113–114, 118, 122, 124, 154, 165, 182, 249, 258 n.2, 259 n.10, 260 n.11, n.12, n.17, 261 n.26, n.27
  barrel organ, 47–49, 51, 57, 258 n.2
  chromolithograph, 92–93, 105, 108
  cinema, 108, 111, 154, 158
  and creole consciousness, 105–109, 113, 114
  hand organ, 41, 43, 47–48, 59, 260 n.12
  mass media, 47, 105–109, 111, 113, 114, 118
  and mechanical reproduction, 47, 48, 59, 92, 93, 108 (*see also* print)
  and *nyai* narrative form, 154, 165
  phonograph, 47, 53, 55, 59–60, 105–108, 111, 249, 260 n.17, 261 n.26, n.27
  photography, 20, 41, 59, 122, 124, 249, 259 n.10, 260 n.11, n.12
  translation across, 57, 108, 111
  See also literary form, newspaper, novel, opera, print
melodrama, 60, 159, 170, 204
  in *Arus Balik*, 204
  Nyai Dasima as melodrama of stereotype, 159, 170
memoir. *See* autobiography
memory, 61–93, 97, 104–112, 118, 122, 127, 177, 179–180, 183, 177–214, 207, 222
  anti-trope of, 92, 93, 105, 108
  as cultural problem, 62, 72, 75–79, 84–85, 87–89, 91–92, 97, 127
  Conrad and Malay culture, 65, 71–72, 76–79, 81–82, 85, 87, 93
  Ford and, 62, 72, 75–79, 84–85, 87–89, 91–92, 97, 127
  Freud and, 67–68
  and mass media, 47, 105–109, 111, 113, 118
  and memory loss, 67, 68, 69, 85, 93, 111
  modernist, 68–82, 91, 92, 93, 97, 104
  Rhys and Caribbean culture, 85, 88–91, 97, 104–113, 116, 118, 127
  Pramoedya and historical memory, 26–27, 163–165, 177–214, 222, 239–240
  and shell shock, 67–69

320 *Index*

and "Youth,"75–77, 81, 87
  See also archive, archival gaps, history
Menadonese, 171–172, 221, 233
Mendel, Gregor, 193, 195
metaphor, see trope
metropolitan, 4, 40, 97, 104, 109–110, 112, 116–117, 120–122, 131, 219, 242, 246–247
  capital cities in Rhys, 97, 104, 109–110, 117, 120, 122
  and tropicopolitan, 242, 246
  See also Europe
Mignolo, Walter, 220, 250
Mimic Men, The (Naipaul), 228
mimicry, 7, 22, 143
Mindanao, 230
Ming, Hanneke, 167
Minke (Buru quartet), 27, 28, 44–48, 53–56, 130, 133–134, 138–140, 145–148, 153–154, 156–158, 161, 163–164, 171–174, 181–183, 200–202, 221–222, 226, 234, 239, 256 n.42
  and Annelies, 130, 133–134, 138–139, 145–146, 148
  biological infertility, 146, 200, 277 n.32
  and choice of languages, 201
  creole family romance, 45–46, 131, 133, 138–140, 145, 202
  education, 45, 53–54, 56, 172
  mother, 55, 154, 173, 201
  musical taste, 45, 47, 53–56, 183, 201, 260 n.17
  name, 53, 147–148
  narrative consciousness, 45, 53–55, 171–173, 201, 221–222, 226, 234, 239
  Nyai Ontosoroh, 154, 156, 158, 161, 200–202
  and *palakia* tree headache, 146, 147, 277 n.32
  and Pangemanann, 47, 153, 155, 163, 171–174, 221–222, 226, 234, 256 n.42
  priyayi sensibility, 53–56
  and psychiatry, 133–134
  split racial and cultural identity, 45, 53, 146–147, 201–202
  and word "modern," 47, 283–284 n.48
  See also Buru quartet, Pangemanann, Tirto Adi Suryo
Mirror of the Sea, The (Conrad), 70
mise-en-abyme, 44–45, 51–52, 57–59, 140, 183, 233–234, 241, 260 n.16
  defined as narrative mirroring, 44, 260 n.16
  of interpretative traditions, 233
  and passage of literature, 233
  of philology, 58–59, 234, 241
misrecognition, 62, 65, 82, 88–89, 93, 114, 119, 146
  and cultural backgrounds, 88
  and Ford and Rhys, 119
  creole (mis)recognition, 132, 133, 134
  workplace misrecognition, 119
Mixed Marriage Act of 1898, 157, 168
"Mixing Cocktails" (Rhys), 87–88, 92, 111, 113, 117–118
  naming of Antilles/West Indies in, 88
  Ford cites from, 87–88
  title as code for racial intermixture, 113
Modern Language Association of America, 11
modernism, 3–9, 13, 17, 30–36, 42, 49, 61–63, 65, 73–75, 83–84, 86, 88, 91, 97, 100, 110, 153, 164, 170–171, 173, 175, 197, 200, 217–218, 224–225, 230, 233, 240, 243–244, 251
  black transatlantic, 83, 107
  canonical American and European, 4–7, 13, 31, 35, 61–63, 65–66, 71, 73–75, 80, 82–84, 86, 88, 91, 171
  creole trope and, 109–110
  contrapuntal reading of, 42, 200
  and dialect, 49
  definitions of, 4–7, 243, 253 n.1, 267 n.4, 283 n.48
  French, 13, 31, 61–62, 71, 73–75, 80, 82, 91
  genealogies of, 3–6, 8, 30, 32, 34–36, 158, 197, 200
  German, 62
  and linguistic turn, 224–225
  and *O.E.D.* entry on, 243, 283–284 n.48
  and passage of literature, 34–36, 57, 61, 64–65, 82, 89, 91, 93, 126, 170–172, 184, 196–197, 201, 214, 217–218, 223, 225–226, 243, 251, 272 n.10
  periodizing, 5, 6, 7
  philology and, 224, 225
  primitivist, 88
  transnational, 3–5, 8, 30, 32, 36, 83, 107, 153, 170, 175, 178, 197, 243

Index   321

modernism (*continued*)
　See also Creole modernism,
　　English modernism, Indonesian
　　modernism
modernity, 5–8, 36, 44, 47, 59, 60, 97,
　　115, 157
　colonial, 157, 243
　and creolization, 97
　impasse of, 251
　metropolitan, 97
　racialized, 110
　See also Creole modernism,
　　English modernism, Indonesian
　　modernism, modernism
Moerman, Maryvonne, 33
Mohamad, Goenawan. *See*
　　Goenawan Mohamad
monolingualism, 6, 103–104, 106,
　　112, 116, 122, 125, 249, 273 n.20
　and Derrida, 103–104, 249, 273
　　n.20
　and Rhys, 103–104, 106, 114, 116,
　　122, 125
　See also multilingualism
Monolingualism of the Other
　　(Derrida), 103–104, 249, 273
　　n.20
mood, 56, 265 n.63 (*see also* taste,
　　rasa)
Moore, Thomas, 48
Moslem. *See* Islam
mot juste, 70, 72, 73, 82, 85 (*see also*
　　Absolute Prose, Conrad–Ford
　　collaboration)
mourning, 91, 138
Mrázek, Rudolf, 184
music, 40–45, 56–58, 60, 105, 107,
　　113, 182–183, 265 n.57
　Caribbean, 41–42, 105, 107
　European, 40–41, 44, 56–57, 60
　Indonesian, 42–43, 55–56, 60, 183,
　　265 n.57
　See also counterpoint, harmony,
　　media, opera, polyphony, song,
　　tonality
Mustafa, Fawzia, 255 n.29
Mute's Soliloquy (Pramoedya), 10,
　　23–27, 33, 56, 177–180, 182–189,
　　191, 193–197, 199, 205–209,
　　212–214, 222, 264 n.47, 280 n.5
　and *baca* and *karang*, 179–180, 206
　different editions and translations
　　of, 177, 187, 190, 193–194, 213,
　　280 n.6
　English and Indonesian titles of,
　　180, 183–184, 280 n.6

"Farewell to Wayang," 56, 179,
　　182–183, 185, 209–210
"Final Release," 182
"Flowers for Mother," 23–26,
　　29–30, 179, 188, 194, 197, 199,
　　205–206, 212–214
fragmentary form of, 178, 180,
　　184, 196, 222, 280 n.5
"One Link in a Chain," 27, 179,
　　187, 188–189, 191–199,
　　213–214
principle of genealogy in, 178,
　　183–184, 187–188, 191–197,
　　199
vicious circle (*lingkaran setan*),
　　180, 183–185, 194–195, 197
See also Buru prison internment,
　　Buru work
"My Apologies, in the Name of
　　Experience" (Pramoedya), 177,
　　180, 182, 185, 193–195, 203,
　　208–210
　and Arok legend, 181, 185,
　　208–209
　on arrival of Islam in Indonesia,
　　203
　trope of vicious circle, 180–181,
　　185, 195, 209
mysticism, 147, 181, 189, 193, 199,
　　210
　Javanese mysticism, 181, 189, 193,
　　210

Nahautl (language), 210
Naipaul, V. S., 7, 17, 227–234
　citing "Karain," 230–232
　compared to Achebe, 230–232
　"Conrad's Darkness," 229–231
　on Conrad's romanticism, 232
　A House for Mr Biswas, 227
　The Mimic Men, 228
names, 30–34, 115, 140, 145, 170,
　　172, 189–192, 212–214, 257 n.54,
　　n.55, n.57, 258 n.61
　Conrad, 31–32, 49, 68, 257 n.54,
　　n.55
　European order of naming, 172, 173
　Javanese naming, 190, 192
　Pramoedya, 33–34, 189, 191–192,
　　214, 258 n.61
　Rhys, 32, 82–83, 116, 238, 257 n.57
　women's names, 173
Nana (Zola), 32, 115–117
Napoleon, 133, 134, 166
narrative consciousness, 28, 32–33,
　　45, 49, 53, 55, 103–107, 111, 113,

115–116, 153–154, 164, 169, 172, 198, 201, 203–205, 234
and ambiguous priority of cultural memory, 105–106
in *Arus Balik*, 203–204
and black transatlantic modernism in Rhys, 107, 111
and creole consciousness in Rhys, 88, 104–106, 111, 113, 116
in Conrad's Malay trilogy, 45, 49, 53, 201
and Hegel, 48, 92
and irony, 43–44
and *mise-en-abime*, 44–45, 53
in Pramoedya's Buru quartet, 45, 49, 53, 55, 153–154, 164, 172, 201, 234
and Rhys's narrative voice, 83–85, 88, 92, 103–107, 111, 113, 115, 143, 169
and romanized script, 205
and subaltern reading effect, 160
See also narrative first person, narrative form
narrative first person, 98–99, 102–105, 111–113, 115–116, 119–120, 122–123, 126, 132, 140, 153, 163, 172, 221, 234
in Conrad's later Malay tales, 98–99, 120
disruption in Pramoedya's Buru quartet, 153, 163, 172–173, 221–222, 234, 256 n.42
dismantling of in Rhys's "Trio," 112–113
in Rhys, 98, 99, 102–108, 111–113, 115, 116, 120, 122, 132, 140
recursive structure in Conrad and Rhys, 99, 122
See also interior monologue, narrative consciousness, narrative form
narrative form, 45, 51–53, 57, 60, 75, 80, 100, 105–106, 138, 153–154, 159, 161–163, 183
of Conrad's Malay trilogy, 45, 49, 53, 60, 80
and Conrad's "Youth," 75
and differend, 51–52
and family romance, 138, 140, 202
grand narrative, 48, 51, 100
and history, 45, 53, 60
and memory, 85, 105, 106
and *mise-en-abyme*, 45, 51–53, 57, 183
modernist rupture of, 100

and Rhys, 105, 106
See also literary form, narrative consciousness, narrative first person, *nyai* narrative form
National Awakening. *See under* Boedi Oetomo
national identity, 8, 10, 21, 34, 111, 123, 131, 169, 170 (*see also* anti-colonial nationalism)
nationalism. *See* anti-colonial nationalism
native (*pribumi*), 156, 166, 171–173
foreclosure of, and passage of literature, 171
native informants, 173, 279 n.36
transition from native to European, 172–173
Nature of a Crime (Ford and Conrad), 66, 68–70, 83, 267–268 n.11
Ford's repetitive citing from, 69–70, 267–268 n.11
pseudonym Baron Ignatz von Aschendrof, 66, 68
negro spiritual, 184, 214
newspaper, 21–23, 27, 35, 113, 159–160, 165–167, 227, 244
Dutch language, 159–160
proto-nationalist press, 27, 165–166
See also *Dominica Herald and Leeward Islands Gazette*, *Medan Prijaji*, *Poetri Hindia*, *Straits Times*
Ngũgĩ wa Thiong'o, 228
Nietzsche, Friedrich, 192
Nieuwenhuys, Rob, 41, 59–60, 259, n.10, 260 n.11, n.12
Tempo Doeloe, 41, 59–60
North, Michael, 49, 86
novel, 21, 48, 49, 138, 158, 227
European novel form, 138, 158, 227
and family romance, 138
See also literary form, narrative form
nurse, 10, 19–20, 26, 118, 114, 118
nyai, 153–163, 165–170, 172–174, 200–201
contradictory social form of, 156–157, 161–162, 174, 201
and debates about mixed marriage, 167
and domestic partner rights, 165
Dutch stereotype, 155–156, 158–159, 166
erasure of in Conrad, 169–170

Index   323

nyai (*continued*)
   Javanese meaning of, 156
   and subaltern perspectives, 161–163, 173
   and *tuan*, 154, 157–158, 160, 163, 165–167, 279 n.34
   and Taminah (*Almayer's Folly*), 279 n.34
   and Tuminah (*House of Glass*), 174
Nyai Dasima (Francis), 29, 59, 158–163, 165–166, 168, 170
   different versions, 158, 166
   English *tuan* in, 166
   as index of *nyai* narrative form, 158, 160, 162
   historical text of, 162–163
   and *lingua franca* Malay, 161
   plot of, 158, 159
   and problem of reading, 160–162
   subaltern figure of, 161–162
Nyai Mina (Tirto), 162
nyai narrative form, 30, 153–155, 157–172, 174–175, 178, 184, 200, 202, 204, 207, 279 n.34
   and Conrad's Malay fiction, 166–169
   and Creole modernism, 170, 200, 202
   and disappearance of, 153–155, 162, 165, 174–175, 202
   and East Indies opera, 30, 158, 160–161
   as foundational for Indonesian modernism, 162, 171, 174, 178, 200, 202, 207
   and historical documentation, 162–165, 175, 178, 202
   and Pramoedya's revolutionary family romance, 207
   and problem of reading, 160–165, 170–171, 175, 178, 200
   and subaltern reading effect, 162–164, 171
   and title of *Lord Jim*, 169
   See also, *Cerita Nyai Ratna*, *Hikayat Siti Mariah*, *Nyai Dasima*, *Nyai Mina*, *Nyai Permana*, *Tjerita Njai Paina*
Nyai Ontosoroh (Buru quartet), 139, 154–166, 170, 171, 172, 200, 201, 234
   name Sanikem, 156, 157, 171, 172
   and *nyai* narrative form, 166, 170
   and Pangemanann, 172, 234
   and Pramoedya's mother, 201
   as prefiguring Indonesian anti-colonial nationalism, 154, 165, 200, 201
   and revolutionary family romance, 200, 201
Nyai Permana (Tirto), 162, 164, 165, 170
   as index of vanishing form of *nyai* narrative, 165

Oath of Youth, 8, 27
obeah, 142, 144–147
O.E.D. See *Oxford English Dictionary*
Oedipus complex, 198–199, 202, 204–206
Oedipus Rex, 199
offense, 194–195, 201
   and genealogy, 194–195
   rhetoric of apology and, 181, 201
   vicious circle, 201
Old Javanese, 57
opacity, 6, 10, 14, 35, 116
opera, 30, 39–60, 135, 158, 160–161, 201, 258 n.2, 261 n.27, n.30
   abysmal taste, 58, 60
   aesthetic form, 40, 47–48, 53, 57, 60
   aesthetic judgment, 39–40, 43–46, 48, 50, 53, 55, 57–58, 60, 135, 201
   aria, 48–49, 57
   European, 40–42, 44, 46, 56–58, 60
   distortion through recording, 47–48
   estrangement of literary text, 48, 57, 60, 135, 261 n.30
   Javanese, 42, 53–58, 60, 201, 263 n.45
   and literary criticism, 58, 60
   and *nyai* narrative form, 158, 160–161
   and philology, 58
   and political consciousness, 54–55
   See also East Indies opera, passage of literature
orality, 18–21, 29, 36, 73–74, 145, 179–180, 182, 206, 233, 239, 250
   and creole language, 18–19
   and form of Nyai Ontosoroh's narrative, 161
   and form of Pramoedya's Buru work, 179–180, 239
   and literacy, 18–21, 29, 145, 233, 239 See also *baca*, creolization, *karang*, language, writing
Orientalism (Said), 54, 219, 221, 223, 226

Orientalism, 52, 54, 87, 219–223, 233, 235
　definitions, 221
　and Javanism, 54
　and philology, 221, 223, 235
Ortega y Gasset, 220, 250
Ortiz, Fernando, 7, 40–42, 60, 107, 264 n.49
　Cuban Counterpoint, 7, 40–41, 60, 107
　on transculturation, 107
Otago (ship), 99
Outcast of the Islands, An (Conrad), 39, 46–47, 50–52, 76, 166, 262 n.42
　Aïssa, 46, 50
　Babalatchi, 46, 50–52
　Lingard, 166
　and *nyai* narrative form, 166
　Omar el–Badavi, 46, 51–52
Oxford English Dictionary, 8–11, 15, 35–36, 86–87, 217–218, 242–251, 256 n.35, 284 n.49, n.56
　and colonial semiosis, 250–251
　and decolonization of English, 244, 247–248
　entry on *all-round*, 247, 256 n.35
　entry on *azure*, 86–87
　entry on *creole*, 128–129
　entry on *dam*, 86
　entry on *impasse*, 273 n.20
　entry on *lingua franca*, 9, 11, 15, 23, 35
　entry on *modernism*, 243, 283–284 n.48
　entry on *philology*, 218
　entry on *rectification*, 269 n.61
　entry on *tropicopolitan*, 242
　gaps and biases in, 244, 246–248, 250
　historical principles of, 86, 218, 245
　Hugh Kenner on, 86, 218, 244
　and Indonesian, 8–9, 35–36, 217, 243–245, 247–248
　linguistic and literary capital, 245, 247, 249–250
　and modernism, 35–36, 86, 218, 243–244, 248, 250–251, 283 n.48
　and the passage of literature, 9, 15, 35–36, 218, 244–47, 249–251
　and Persian script, 249
　and Raymond Williams, 219, 248, 250
　and Victorian habits, 218
　See also archive, English, hegemony, standard English

page, 13–14, 18–20, 22–23, 32, 72–73, 100, 115, 227
　printed page vs. oral recitation, 72–73, 227
　and textuality, 100
palakia tree seed, 146–147, 277 n.32
　headache image in *This Earth of Mankind*, 146–147
　as problem of classification, 147
　and creolization, 147
Palembang (Sumatra), 78–79
　spelled Parabang, 78–79
Palestine (ship), 75
Pangemanann (*House of Glass*), 45, 47, 49, 153, 155, 163–164, 171–174, 205, 221–222, 226, 229, 232–239, 244–246, 256 n.42
　Catholic conscience, 171–172, 233–234
　dialogue with archivist, Tuan L., 220–222, 226, 229, 232–239, 244–246
　as distinct from the historical F. D. J. Pangemanann, 163
　formulaic modernism of, 173–174
　and literary criticism, 172, 222
　policing of Minke, 47, 155, 163, 172, 221, 226
　shift from Minke's narrative consciousness, 153, 163, 172–173, 221–222, 234, 256 n.42
　theft of Minke's manuscripts, 172–173, 221–222, 226, 234
　and D. A. Rinkes, 163
　split narrative consciousness, 171–173
Pangemanann, F. D. J., 163
　Tjerita Rossina, 163
　Tjerita Si Tjonat, 163
pantun, 50
Paris, 42, 62, 82, 84, 87, 90–91, 97–98, 100–101, 105, 107, 109, 112, 120, 123, 219
　1889 Exposition, 42
　1937 Exposition, 120
　Benjamin on, 98, 100, 219
　and expatriate communities, 62, 82–83, 107, 112, 270 n.66, 271 n.3
　"impasse" as feature of street architecture, 101
　See also Baudelaire, black transatlantic modernism, *transatlantic review*
Parsons, Deborah, 271–272 n.3, 272–273 n.12

Index　325

passage of literature, 3–4, 8–9, 15,
    19, 22, 31, 34–36, 51, 57, 62–65,
    68–73, 82, 88–90, 92–93, 101,
    105, 108–109, 113, 115, 118, 125,
    169, 170, 182–184, 195–196, 207,
    212, 214, 217–219, 223–224,
    217–219, 223–227, 229, 232, 235,
    237, 242–244, 246–247, 249–251
  and Benjamin's arcades, 126, 249
  and Bible, 57, 58, 205
  and Conradian passage, 19, 31,
    62–65, 68–73, 82, 90, 92, 93, 105,
    108, 169, 170, 182, 183
  and contest over romanized script,
    205
  and Creole modernism, 34, 35, 36,
    217, 218, 251
  and cultural capital, 4, 9, 36
  and decolonizing tradition, 173,
    183–184, 195–196, 207, 212, 214
  and differend, 51
  dispute over Chaucer passage, 22,
    113
  and English modernism, 34–36, 57,
    61, 64–65, 82, 89, 91, 93, 218, 251
  fetishized, 105, 108
  and foreclosure of native, 171
  and genealogy, 195–196
  and Indonesian modernism,
    35–36, 57, 170–172, 184,
    196–197, 201, 214, 218, 251
  from *Mahabharata*, 182, 195, 210,
    214
  and law, 52, 58
  and linguistic turn, 225–226, 232,
    235
  as *locus classicus*, 227
  modernist emphasis on, 218, 223,
    225–226, 243
  and *O.E.D.*, 9, 15, 35–36, 218,
    244–47, 249–251
  and opera, 47–48, 51, 57–60
  and passage into literacy, 15, 18–19
  and *pesangon*, 184, 214
  and Pramoedya's revolutionary
    family romance, 207
  as problem of narrative
    consciousness, 92, 93, 109, 113,
    171
  purple passage, 229–230
  and scripture, 56–58, 204–205,
    209–211, 233–234
  and sea passage, 75, 101
  See also aphorism, Conradian
    passage, citation, pastiche,
    proverb, saying, song, text, trope

pastiche, 71, 74, 78, 79
patois, 14, 89, 117, 142–145
percussion, 42, 56
periodizing, 5–7
Persian (language), 249, 284 n.56
Personal Record, A (Conrad), 10,
    12–14, 16–19, 31, 48, 64, 71, 78,
    80–81
  as model for Ford's *Joseph Conrad*,
    64, 78, 80–81
pesangon, 184, 214
philogyny, 145
philology, 4, 9, 11, 15, 35, 56–59, 129,
    134–135, 146, 192–193, 218–237,
    240–241, 248–250
  and Achebe's critique of Conrad, 230
  and African languages, 230
  and Biblical hermeneutics, 58
  and counterpoint, 57–58
  and critical genealogy, 192
  and de Man, 235–237
  dissolution of, 218, 223–226, 231,
    233–234
  European comparative philology,
    4, 11, 218–219, 221–226, 231,
    235, 248
  Foucault on, 192, 224, 233–234
  German tradition of, 58, 221
  and Hegel, 241
  and Indonesian studies, 134, 233
  laws of linguistic change in, 221,
    224–226, 232, 235, 241
  linguistic knowledge, 219, 221,
    225–227, 229, 231–232
  and literary criticism, 218–219,
    223–226, 233–234, 237
  and literary form, 56–57, 224,
    225–226
  as "master science," 218, 221–225,
    232
  Mignolo's "new philology," 220, 250
  mise-en-abyme of, 234
  and Nietzsche, 192
  O.E.D. entry on, 218
  and Orientalism, 220–223,
    226–227, 233
  and postcolonial philology, 4, 9,
    218–219
  Pramoedya and, 192–193, 219
  return to, 218–219, 223–226,
    233–234, 237
  and romanticism, 232
phonograph, 44, 47, 53, 55, 59, 60,
    105, 108, 111, 249, 260 n.26, 261
    n.27
  gramophone, 105, 108, 111

326   *Index*

photography, 20, 41, 59, 92–93, 105, 122, 124, 249, 250 n.10, 260, n.11, n.12
  chromolithograph, 92–93, 105
  in Nieuwenhuys, 41, 59, 259 n.10, 260, n.11, n.12
  and photomontage, 65
  as riddle of representation, 41, 59
  in *The Shadow-Line*, 122, 124
  See also cinema, media, print
pidgins, 11
piracy, 51, 52, 77
plagiarism, 71
playing relatives, 29, 185, 197
  (*see also* Maier)
Poetri Hindia, 165
poison, 142–143, 158
Poland, 12, 17
Poli, Bernard, 266–267 n.2
policing, 45, 47, 155, 163
Polish, 10, 12, 14–15, 17, 31, 34, 98, 119, 182
political organizations, 45, 154, 163, 187
  Sarekat Prijaji, 54
  Sarekat Islam, 163
  Boedi Oetomo, 45, 187
political unconscious, 170–171
polyphony, 29–30, 56–57, 60, 183
Portuguese, 203, 205, 220
postcolonial philology, 4, 9, 218–220, 222–223, 227–228, 232–233, 236–237, 239–240, 242–243, 246–247, 251
  in Achebe and Naipaul, 232
  imperatives of, 218–220, 227, 233, 236, 240, 242–243, 251
  and Mignolo's "new philology," 220
  and *mise-en-abyme* of interpretative traditions, 233
  and *O.E.D.*, 247, 251
  and passage of literature, 227, 232–233, 251
  Pramoedya's, 239
  and return to philology, 237
  and Said's *Orientalism*, 223
  and theories of trope, 243
  See also philology
postcolonial studies, 4, 7, 18, 20, 33, 76, 83, 127–129, 162, 166, 219, 227, 234–235, 242
  and Creole modernism, 18, 127–129
  theories of hybridity and race, 129
  and term "subaltern," 162

Wide Sargasso Sea as touchstone for, 83, 127
"writing back" to Empire, 7, 235
See also Bhabha, postcolonial philology, Said, Spivak
poststructuralism, 31, 239
Pound, Ezra, 12, 35, 63, 66, 84, 218, 244, 267 n.10
"revolution of the word," 66, 267 n.10
Pradnya Paramita (Hindu goddess), 207, 208, 210
Pramoedya Ananta Toer, 3–5, 7–11, 23–35, 39–48, 50, 53, 55–60, 127, 130–131, 133–135, 138–139, 153–166, 170–175, 177–214, 217–218, 220–222, 226, 229, 232, 237, 239, 243–244, 247–251
  autobiography, 10, 23–30, 35
  Bukitduri prison, 33, 184, 263 n.45, 279–280 n.2
  Buru exile, 23, 39–40, 139, 154, 177–178, 180–181, 183–184, 188, 192, 239
  destruction of documents, 26–27, 164, 178, 180, 184, 192–193, 197, 200, 222, 279–280 n.2
  father, 23–27, 33–34, 179, 187–189, 191–194, 197–198, 200–201, 207, 212–214
  historical research, 26–27, 164, 177–178, 192–193, 217
  mother, 10, 23–30, 35, 179, 194, 197–198, 201, 207–208, 210, 212–214, 247
  name, 33–34, 189, 191–192, 212, 214, 258 n.61
  on race, 132–133
  reading of Conrad, 53, 170, 182–183, 196, 201, 260 n.19, 264 n.47
  and Resink, 258 n.61, 263 n.45, 279–280 n.2
  revolutionary family romance, 33, 34, 179, 197–202, 205–209, 211, 212
  See also *Arok of Java*, *Arus Balik*, "Blora," Buru quartet, *Child of All Nations*, *Footsteps*, *Fugitive*, *Gadis Pantai*, *Hoakiau di Indonesia*, *House of Glass*, *Keluarga Gerilya*, *Mute's Soliloquy*, *Sang Pemula*, *Tempo Doeloe*, *This Earth of Mankind*, *Realisme–Sosialis*

Index   327

Pratt, Mary Louise, 11
prayer, 56
pre–Indonesian (language and literature), 7, 23, 27, 29–30, 32, 36, 42, 59, 153, 158, 160–161, 163–164, 170, 178, 200, 205, 207
  and archival gaps, 200
  and East Indies opera, 42, 59
  and question of readership, 29–30, 42, 59, 158, 160, 163, 178
  and *nyai* narratives, 158, 160, 164, 170, 178
  and shift to print culture, 205, 207
print, 20–23, 27, 29–30, 34, 36, 113, 154, 160–161, 166, 207, 227, 234
  and globalatinization, 234
  print capitalism, 21–23, 113, 234
  print literacy, 20–21, 30, 113
  print medium, 154, 161, 166, 227
  and romanized script, 29, 207
  See also *baca*, *karang*, media, newspaper, orality
priority, 60, 70–71, 75, 82–84, 86–88, 91–93, 97, 104–105, 110, 116, 125, 127, 170, 202, 233–235, 241, 243–244, 246–247, 251
  of cultural memory, 83–84, 86–87, 91, 93, 97, 104, 116, 125, 127, 170
  and Creole, English, and Indonesian modernisms, 60, 92, 110, 170, 202, 211, 243, 251
  between citation and recitation, 70–71, 75, 82, 88
  of English words, 86–87, 104–105, 244, 246
  of French modernism, 71, 110
  between mimesis and self-referentiality, 75
  of history, 251
  of interpretation, 233, 241, 247
  postcolonial reversal of, 234–235, 251
priyayi (Javanese aristocracy), 53–56, 201
  crisis of political consciousness, 54
  and gamelan and *wayang*, 53–56
  and *rasa*, 54
  worldview, 54, 56, 201
  See also Javanese culture, Javanism, Minke, *Sarekat Priyayi*
proverbs, 193–197 (*see also* passage of literature, sayings)
prostitution, 47, 102, 108, 115, 116, 118, 146
  and Baudelaire, 102

"market value" of women, 108
  and *Voyage in the Dark*, 115, 116
pseudonym, 31, 32, 49, 82, 83, 115, 116, 257 n.54, n.55
  Baron Ignatz von Aschendrof, 66, 68
  Kamudi (Conrad), 31, 32, 257, n.55
  "neutral pseudonym" Joseph Conrad, 31, 32, 257 n.54
  and Rhys, 82, 83, 115, 116
psychiatry, 133, 145, 148, 224
  history of and *This Earth of Mankind*, 145
  and human sciences, 224
  See also Fanon, Freud, madness, psychoanalysis
psychoanalysis, 67, 133, 145 (*see also* Fanon, Freud, madness, psychiatry)

Quartet (Rhys), 67, 89, 101, 104, 111, 113
  and affair with Ford, 67
  cubist portrait of Ford as Heidler, 89
  Marya Zelli, 101, 113, 132
Quechua (language), 220

race, 7, 11, 21, 23, 29–31, 41, 47, 110, 128–129, 132, 137, 143–144, 148, 161, 166, 169, 174, 232
  fetish of, 47, 132, 148
  as trope, 11, 110, 232 (*see also* philology)
  reading, 21, 23, 29–30, 41, 132, 137, 161, 166, 169, 174, 232
  theories of, 7, 31, 128–129, 143, 144
racial identity, 16, 20, 32, 36, 45–47, 52–54, 59, 65, 92–93, 110–111, 118, 124–125, 131–132, 136, 141, 148, 166, 169–170, 174, 264 n.49
  ambiguity of, 52, 110 (*see also* creole)
  and Conradian passage, 65, 92–93, 110, 169, 170, 174
  fetishized, 47, 132, 148
  mixed, 16, 45, 110, 125, 131, 132, 136, 166, 169
  and narrative form, 43, 46, 52, 59, 98, 111, 118
  split, 20, 32, 36, 45, 53–4, 148, 264 n.49 (*see also* "double consciousness")
  stereotyped, 43, 46, 52, 54, 59, 124, 135, 141

328 *Index*

racism, 22, 43–4, 46, 52–54, 110, 132, 136–137, 145, 201, 202, 228–230, 232, 275 n.12
   in Conrad, 43–44, 46, 52–53, 201, 228–230, 232
   in Pramoedya, 53–54, 132, 201–202, 275–276 n.12
   in Rhys, 22, 110, 132, 202, 275 n.12
Raffles, Sir Stamford, 166
Raiskin, Judith, 142
Ramayana, 173, 182, 265 n.55
rasa (taste), 54, 265 n.63
   and Javanese *priyayi*, 54
reading, 10, 12–20, 24–26, 29–31, 35, 42, 45, 65, 70, 75, 78, 90–91, 115, 132, 134, 137–138, 160–162, 165–167, 169–170, 172, 174–175, 179, 183, 197–202, 204, 207, 209, 235, 247
   baca, 29–30, 178–179, 183, 206, 209, 233, 257 n.50, 266 n.67, 283 n.38
   Conradian irony, 44, 52
   Conradian passage, 65, 78, 90–91, 169, 170, 174
   Conradian readership, 75, 167
   contrapuntal reading, 40–42, 46, 51, 53, 57–58, 200
   and family romance, 10, 31, 137–138, 197–213
   and economy of domestic labor, 170, 174
   hierarchy of reading effects in Rhys, 93, 115
   and race, 132, 137, 166, 169, 174
   learning to read, 10, 12–15, 18, 19, 20, 23, 26, 30
   reading aloud, 13–16, 18, 25, 26, 70
   Rhys, and problem of reading modernism, 90 91, 115, 169
   subaltern reading effect, 162–163, 169, 171, 174
   See also *nyai* narrative form, pre–Indonesian
realism, 74, 75, 90, 100, 101, 164
   breakdown of, 100
   socialist realism, 164
Realisme–Sosialis dan Sastra Indonesia (Pramoedya), 164
recitation, 56, 57, 70–71, 74–75, 196
   in *wayang*, 56, 57
   Ford on Conrad, 70–71, 74–75
   and Pramoedya's Buru work, 196
   See also *baca*, citation
rectification, 81, 269 n.62

Redfield, Marc, 236
Rees Williams, Ella Gwendoline. See Rhys, Jean.
religion, 161, 174, 184, 185, 186, 203, 227, 234
   and vicious circle (*lingkaran setan*), 184–186
   See also Christianity, Islam, Judaism, passage of literature
repetition, 5, 57, 61, 67–69, 72–75, 77, 89, 163, 180, 196, 206, 212, 223
   and citation, 61, 69, 206
   and *baca* and *karang*, 206
   composition of *Mute's Soliloquy*, 180, 196
   and English modernism, 5, 61, 68–69, 73–74, 77, 89
   filiation and affiliation, 192
   Freudian compulsion to repeat, 67–68
   and linguistic turn, 223
Rescue, The (Conrad), 32, 39, 47, 49–51, 80, 82, 258 n.1
   Edith Travers, 49–50
   Hassim, 80
   and opera, 47, 49–50
   See also Lingard, Malay trilogy, piracy
Resink, G. J., 52, 258 n.61, 263 n.45, 279–280 n.2
Revolution. See anti-colonial nationalism, decolonization, revolutionary family romance
revolutionary family romance, 24, 179, 197–202, 205–209, 211, 212
rhetoric, 103, 235, 236, 238
Rhys, Jean, 3, 5, 7, 9–11, 18–23, 26, 30, 32–35, 61–67, 71, 82–93, 97–117, 119, 127–149, 153, 169–170, 197–198, 200, 202, 211–212, 249, 255 n.29
   autobiography, 10, 18–20, 23, 26, 32, 92, 117, 270 n.77
   Caribbean background, 82–83, 85, 88–89, 92, 105–106, 108–109, 111–113, 116–117, 119
   and black transatlantic modernism, 107
   citing Conrad, 64–65, 71, 89–90, 92, 105, 115, 169–170
   and creole consciousness, 21–23, 88, 98, 108, 113–114, 116, 132, 277 n.32
   creole family romance, 32–33, 91, 111, 131–133, 137–147, 197–198, 275 n.11

Index   329

Rhys, Jean (*continued*)
   and English accent, 84–86, 112, 270 n.77
   first appearance in print, 61, 82
   first husband Jean Lenglet, 32, 67, 83
   and *flâneuse*, 102, 114, 120, 272–273 n.12
   and Ford, 61–62, 64–67, 82, 84, 87, 89–90
   francophone English, 88, 91, 103–107, 110, 113–117, 140, 142–145, 211–212
   interiority, 101–104
   and memory, 63, 65, 85, 88–93, 97, 104–114, 116–117, 127, 132
   mother, 20
   name, 32, 82–83, 116, 138, 257 n.57
   narrative voice, 83–84, 86, 103–107, 112–113, 115–116
   and nurse Meta, 10, 19–20, 26
   and Indonesian political crisis, 1957–1965, 33
   and racial identity, 132, 257 n.57, 275 n.12
   studies in reading modernism, 90–93, 108, 110, 115, 169, 170
   as West Indian writer, 128, 256 n.32
   See also "Again the Antilles," *After Leaving Mr Mackenzie*, *Good Morning Midnight*, *Left Bank*, "Mixing Cocktails," *Quartet*, *Smile Please*, "Trio," "Vienne," *Voyage in the Dark*, *Wide Sargasso Sea*
rights, 140, 164, 165, 172, 184
   native rights, 140
   women's rights, 164, 165
Rigoletto (Verdi), 44, 46, 47
Rinkes, D. A., 154–155, 163–164
   and Pangemanann, 163
   and Tirto, 155
Robinson Crusoe, 23–24, 100
Romans, 79
romanized script, 8, 23, 26, 29–30, 205, 212, 220, 234–235, 249
   contest over, 205
   and *O.E.D.*, 249
   shift from Arabic to, 205
   See also globalatinization, print, script, writing
romance, 46, 51, 76, 198;
   see also family romance
romanticism, 49, 71–72, 230, 232;
   see also philology

rooms, 99, 101–102, 105, 108, 122–123, 125
   hotel, 101–102, 105, 122–123, 125
   interior space, 101–102
   and streets, 101–102, 105, 108
Royal Academy of Dramatic Art, 86, 270 n.76
rum, 84–86, 105, 270 n.78
Rushdie, Salman, 17
Russia, 17

Said, Edward, 40–42, 46, 54, 57–58, 60, 73–75, 187–188, 192, 219, 221, 223, 226, 242, 254 n.13, 264 n.49, 266 n.68
   Beginnings, 223, 254 n.13
   contrapuntal reading, 40–42, 46, 57, 60, 219
   on Conrad, 73–75, 223
   Culture and Imperialism, 40, 46, 58
   filiation and affiliation, 187–188, 192, 280 n.15
   Orientalism, 54, 219, 221, 223, 226
   secular criticism, 192, 223, 226
   The World, the Text, and the Critic, 223
   on Verdi's *Aida*, 46, 261 n.23
Sambir (Malay trilogy), 43, 45–46, 50, 53
Sandiman (Buru quartet), 44, 54–55, 59
Sang Pemula (Pramoedya), 158, 162–165, 182, 264 n.47
Sanikem (Buru quartet), 156–157, 161, 171–172 (*see also* Nyai Ontosoroh)
Sanskrit (language), 57, 209–211, 220–221, 265 n.63
   script, 209–211, 220
   shared roots of with Greek and Latin, 221
Sarekat Islam, 163 (*see also* political organizations, Tirto Adi Suryo)
Sarekat Priyayi, 54 (*see also* political organizations, Tirto Adi Suryo)
Sasha Jansen. See under *Good Morning, Midnight*
Saunders, Max, 66
Saussure, Ferdinand de, 223–224, 236, 239
Savory, Elaine, 108, 274–275 n.4
sayings, 20, 26, 190, 193–197, 199, 202, 205, 214
   and alien genealogies, 196–197
   and Pramoedya's critical genealogy, 194–197, 199, 205

See also passage of literature, *pesangon*, proverbs
Scott, Sir Walter, 12, 17, 118
script, 8, 23, 26, 29–30, 205–206, 212, 220, 234–235, 249–250
  alphabetic writing systems, 250
  Arabic, 205, 220
  Javanese, 26, 204–205, 209–211, 220
  Malay, 205, 207
  Persian, 249, 284 n.56
  romanized, 8, 23, 26, 29–30, 205, 212, 220, 234–235, 249
  Sanskrit, 209–211, 220
  See also print
scripture, 56–58, 204–205, 209–211, 233–234 (*see also* Christianity, Hinduism, Islam, Javanese, Judaism)
Sears, Laurie, 162
"Secret Sharer, The" (Conrad), 99
Semarang (Java), 41
semiotic drift, 219, 251
sexuality, 46, 67, 101–102, 123–124, 136–137, 169, 174, 277 n.32
  colonial politics, 136–137, 169
  discursive shift, 136–137
  and race, 136–7, 169
  See also domesticity, gender, marriage
Shadow-Line, The (Conrad), 98–99, 119–126, 274 n.32, n.37
  cited by Benjamin, 119, 123–126, 274 n.32, 274 n.37
  and creole family romance, 124
  and creole stereotype, 122, 124
  domestic relations, 122–124
  interior monologue and interior space, 120–122, 125
  and racial identity, 99, 122–124
  spatial dialectic and narrative form, 120–125
  title, 99
  trope of sea passage, 98–99
  See also Benjamin, Conrad, Rhys
shadow puppet theater. *See* gamelan, opera, *wayang*
Shakespeare, William, 13–14, 16, 17, 22
  Two Gentlemen of Verona, 13, 16, 17
shops. *See* department stores
Siam (Thailand), 99, 124, 169–170, 200
  Gulf of, 99, 124
  national identity of Taminah, 169–170, 200

Siegel, James, 28–29, 158, 161, 166, 202, 207
  Fetish, Recognition, Revolution, 29, 202
  on *Nyai Dasima*, 158, 161, 166
silsilah (Javanese family tree), 191
Singapore, 76
Soetan Sjahrir, 184
Skeat, Walter W., 270 n.79
Skeat, Walter William, 147, 277 n.34
slavery, 36, 90, 92–93, 155–156, 161, 169–170, 182, 200, 210–211
  abolition of in Dutch East Indies, 155
  in *Almayer's Folly*, 65, 90, 92–93, 169–170, 200
  in *After Leaving Mr Mackenzie*, 65, 90, 92–93, 169–170, 200
  in *Arok of Java*, 210, 211
  and Hegelian dialectic, 92–93
  and Javanese people, 182
  and narrative consciousness, 92–93, 169
  See also domesticity, *nyai*
"Sly Civility" (Bhabha), 22
Smile Please (Rhys), 10, 18–20, 23, 26, 32, 92, 117, 270 n.77
Smith, David R., 31, 257 n.55
Soetomo, 190–193, 196, 213
  on Javanese genealogy, 190, 193
  Kenang-Kenangan, 190, 192, 193, 213
song, 20, 48–50, 55–57, 105–109, 111, 114, 117, 144, 145, 182–184, 214
  aria, 48–49, 57
  in Conrad, 48–50, 57
  in Pramoedya, 55–57, 145, 180, 182–184, 214
  in Rhys, 105–109, 111, 114, 117, 144–145
  Babalatchi's, 50, 53
  suluk, 56–57
  text of, 48, 56–57, 105, 184
  and title of *Mute's Soliloquy*, 180, 183–184
space, 98, 101–103, 105, 119, 120–125, 242
  dialectic of private and public space, 101–102, 105, 108, 122–123
  as impasse, 101–102
  metropolitan, 98, 219
  private interior space, 98, 101–103, 121, 124
  public space, 98, 101–102, 119, 120
  sea, 98, 101

tropical, 242
See also domesticity, impasse, interiority, rooms, streets
Spanish (language), 7, 205, 220
Spitzer, Leo, 58, 219
  Classical and Christian Ideas of World Harmony, 58
Spivak, Gayatri, 161–162, 172, 174, 242, 279 n.36
standard English. *See* English
Stape, J. H., 262 n.42
Stein, Gertrude, 66
stereotype, 21, 43, 47, 109–110, 112–113, 122, 124, 127–130, 133–134, 136–137, 141–142, 144, 157–160, 166, 202
  of creole heiress, 127–130, 136–137, 141
  of *nyai*, 157–160, 166
  racial, 43, 46, 52, 54, 59, 124, 135, 141
Stoler, Ann Laura, 155, 157, 174–175
Straits Settlements, 76
Straits Times, 166–167
Strassler, Karen, 174–175
streets, 97–101, 108, 114–116, 118, 120, 122, 125
  in *Good Morning, Midnight*, 98–101, 108, 120, 122
  and impasse, 101
  and Paris arcades, 98
  and passage of literature, 101
  relation of rooms to, 101–102, 105, 108
  See also Benjamin, space
street piano. *See* barrel organ, hand organ
structure of feeling, 29, 59, 248–249, 256 n.48
  translation of *semangat semasa* 29, 59, 256 n.48
  Williams on, 248, 256 n.48
subaltern, 161–163, 166, 169, 170–171, 173–174
  and Christophine (*Wide Sargasso Sea*), 145
  Guha's definition, 162
  and *nyai* narrative form, 161–162, 166, 169–170, 173–174,
  reading effect, 162–163, 169, 171, 174
Suharto, 154
Sukarno, 154
Sulawesi (formerly Celebes), 52, 53
Sulu, 52, 167

suluk, 56, 57 (*see also* song)
Sumatra, 78, 79
Sundanese (language), 158, 162, 174, 205
superstition, 56, 146, 173 (*see also* witchcraft)
Surabaya (Java), 44
Surati (*Child of All Nations*), 163
Suwardi Surjaningrat, 27–29, 59, 256 n.42
symbolic economy, 32, 64, 67–68, 82–83, 90 (*see also* cultural capital)

Tales of Unrest (Conrad), 76
Taminah (*Almayer's Folly*), 169–170, 173–174, 200, 279 n.34
  as *nyai* figure, 170, 279 n.34
  and Tuminah (*House of Glass*), 170, 173–174
taste, 40, 43, 47, 54, 59, 135, 201, 263 n.46, 264 n.50 (*see also* abysmal taste, aesthetic judgment, *rasa*)
Taylor, Jean Gelman, 155–158
television, 20
tempo doeloe, 41–42, 45, 51, 59
Tempo Doeloe (Pramoedya), 29–30, 42, 59, 158, 160, 163, 256 n.48
Tempo Doeloe (Nieuwenhuys), 41, 59
"Temps Perdi" (Rhys), 89
testimony, 139, 154, 161, 166, 177, 221–222, 239
  and archival truth, 222, 239
  textual, 221
text, 48, 56–58, 75, 105, 205, 218–219, 221, 223–227, 232, 234
  as fragment, 218, 251
  modernist autonomy of, 75, 224–225
  modernist theories of, 223–226, 232
  passage of scripture, 57–58, 205, 234
  of song, 48, 56, 57, 105, 184
  relation to culture, 219, 221, 226–227
  See also literary criticism, passage of literature, philology, textuality
textuality, 10, 31, 75, 100, 223–225, 232
  and *écriture*, 31, 224–225, 232
  and modernist practices, 63–64, 75, 100, 223–226, 232
  See also literary criticism, passage of literature, philology, text
textual study, 4, 57–58, 218–219, 222–223, 227

and culture, 218–219, 221, 227
exegesis, 57
explication de texte, 172, 222–223
and Oriental scholarship, 223
and literary modernism, 218
See also literary criticism, passage of literature, philology, text, textuality
Thackeray, William Makepeace, 13
Theocritus, 9, 11, 15, 23
Things Fall Apart (Achebe), 227–228, 234
Third World, 4, 161–162
This Earth of Mankind (Pramoedya, Buru quartet), 39, 45, 47, 127, 129–135, 137–140, 146, 150, 156, 158–160, 171
  Annelies's deportation to Europe, 133, 138–139
  Annelies's mental breakdown, 131, 133, 138
  creole beauty, 45, 47, 129–130, 133–135, 146, 261 n.26
  creole family romance, 137–138
  creole heiress, 127, 129–130, 135, 140
  and European novel form, 138, 158
  palakia tree headache image, 146
  Pangemanann's reading of in *House of Glass*, 171
  psychoanalysis and psychiatry, 133, 145–146, 159
Thomas, Sue, 113, 271 n.82
Tirto Adi Suryo, 27–29, 44–45, 54, 153–155, 157–158, 162–165, 182, 200, 234, 264 n.47, 283–284 n.48
  Cerita Nyai Ratna, 162
  closure of newspapers, 165
  erasure from historical record, 45, 163–165
  feminist agenda, 164–165
  Medan Prijaji, 162–165
  Nyai Mina, 162
  nyai narratives of, 157–158, 163–165
  Nyai Permana, 162, 164–165, 170
  modernizing Islamic political consciousness, 234
  Poetri Hindia, 165
  political organizations, 54, 163
  Pramoedya's biography of, *Sang Pemula*, 158, 162–165, 182, 264 n.47
  Sarekat Islam, 163
  Sarekat Priyayi, 54
  See also Minke

Tjerita Njai Paina (Kommer), 163
Tjiang, O. S., 158, 166
Toer, Pramoedya Ananta. See Pramoedya Ananta Toer
Toilers of the Sea (Hugo), 13–14
tonality, 58, 60 (*see also* atonality, harmony, music)
trace, 119, 121, 124
tradition, 29–30, 111, 113, 117, 177–214, 217, 220, 225–226, 233, 235, 244, 251, 266 n.67
  breaks in, 187–188, 191–195, 214, 225, 251
  decolonizing, 117, 177–214, 217, 220, 226, 235, 244
  estrangement of, from within, 181–184, 192, 195, 214
  genetic vs. traditional links, 187–188, 193, 195
  hukum warisan (laws of tradition/ genetic laws), 187, 193
  Javanese and Indonesian problem of, 190–192
  loss of literary, 111, 113
  of Malay reading/composition, 29–30, 178–179, 183, 206, 209, 233, 257 n.50, 266 n.67, 283 n.38
  passage of literature and, 183–184, 195, 212–214
  warisan (legacy), 182–183, 193, 214
  See also affiliation, filiation, genealogy
transatlantic review, 32, 61–70, 78, 82–84, 87, 89, 266–267 n.2
transculturation, 6, 11, 97, 107
translation, 3, 9–10, 13–16, 25, 27–31, 35, 57, 62, 71–73, 83–85, 88, 103–108, 111, 116–117, 134, 144, 156, 167–168, 174–175, 194, 205, 212–213, 233–234
  across media, 57, 105, 107–108, 111
  and Conrad–Ford method of composition, 71–73, 84, 85
  and decolonization, 234
  of *nyai*, 156, 167–168, 175
  and Rhys's francophone English, 88, 91, 103–104, 106–107, 111, 116–117, 144
  and transculturation, 107
  untranslatability, 103, 144, 175
  See also language, monolingualism, multilingualism, *lingua franca*
transnational modernism. See black transnational modernism,

Index   333

transnational modernism (*continued*)
  Creole modernism, English modernism, Indonesian modernism, modernism trauma, 67–69, 139, 153–155, 172, 174–175, 200
  and events of 1965, 139, 154, 200
  Ford's wartime shell shock, 68–69
  linguistic, 172, 174
  and *nyai* narrative form, 153, 155, 172, 174–175
  and psychoanalysis, 67
Traviata (Verdi), 47, 261 n.27
"Trio" (Rhys, *Left Bank*), 92, 111–112
Trollope, Anthony, 12
trope, 75, 92–93, 98–99, 108–110, 113, 116, 134–136, 143, 218, 235–243
  anti-trope, 92, 108
  Aravamudan on, 242–243
  of archive, 238–239
  of creole, 109, 134–136
  defined, 235
  de Man on, 235–237
  Dash on, 243
  of enlightenment, 240
  Guillory on, 235–236
  heliotrope, 110, 112, 240, 246
  and problem of history, 240–241
  linguistic and literary properties of, 235–236, 238, 240–241
  of literature and race, 11, 110, 232
  metaphor and, 235, 240, 241
  as passage of literature, 235
  Redfield on, 236
  relation of figurative to literal, 235–236, 241
  retroactive movement of, 240
  of sea passage, 75, 98
  of theory, 236–237
  and unreliability, 237, 239
  of vicious circle, 179–181, 183–185
  of voyage, 116, 118
  See also linguistic turn, literary criticism
tropicopolitan, 242, 246
tropics, 92, 105, 108, 121, 242
Trovatore (Verdi), 43, 46, 48, 51, 57
Trumpener, Katie, 261 n.30
tuan, 77, 154, 157, 159–160, 163, 167–168
  and *nyai*, 154, 157, 159–160, 163, 167–168
  and *Lord Jim*, 77, 167–168
Tuan L. (*House of Glass*). *See* archivist

Tuminah (*House of Glass*), 173–174
  and Taminah (*Almayer's Folly*), 173–174
  and *nyai* narrative form, 174
Two Gentlemen of Verona (Shakespeare), 13, 16–17
"Typhoon" (Conrad), 62
Tzara, Tristan, 66

Verdi, Giuseppe, 40, 43–49, 53, 56, 261 n.23
  Aida, 46, 261 n.23
  Rigoletto, 44, 46, 47
  Traviata, 47, 261 n.27
  Trovatore, 43, 46, 48, 51
  See also barrel organ, hand organ, phonograph
Vergès, Françoise, 137
vernacular, 15, 72, 87
vicious circle, 43, 52, 132, 149, 179–188, 193–198, 201–205, 208–209, 212
  Conrad, racial stereotype and critique, 43, 52, 201
  Fanon, black-white relations, 132
  Pramoedya, *lingkaran setan*, 179–188, 193–198, 201–205, 208, 209, 212
  See also lingkaran setan, racism
Vickers, Adrian, 259 n.9
Victory (Conrad), 79, 266 n.66
Vienna (Austria), 83–84, 87, 89, 105
"Vienne" (Rhys), 66, 83–86, 88–89, 104, 271 n.84
Virgil, 51, 58
Voltaire, 273 n.20
Voyage in the Dark (Rhys), 32, 101–102, 111, 115–118
  Anna Morgan, 101, 115, 118
  anagram of Zola's *Nana*, 115
  Francine, 118
  francophone English effect of title, 116

Wajo (Sulawesi), 50, 53 (*see also* Bugis)
Walcott, Derek, 7
warisan (legacy), 214 (*see also* genetic laws, *hukum warisan*, tradition)
Watt, Ian, 263 n.46
Watts, Cedric, 46, 50, 263 n.46
  covert plotting, 46, 50
Watson, C. W., 162
wayang (shadow puppet theater), 24, 42, 54–57, 59–60, 185, 198, 201,

204, 207, 209 (*see also* gamelan, Javanese culture, opera, *priyayi*)
We Are Playing Relatives (Maier). *See* Maier
Welsh (language), 32
West Indies, 20–21, 33, 85, 88, 109, 113, 128, 140, 247, 249–250
  on naming, 88, 113
  See also Antilles, Caribbean
"Western" consciousness, 240–241
whiteness, 21, 32, 85, 92–93, 98, 104, 108, 110, 117–118, 121–126, 128, 131–132, 135–136, 139, 143, 168
  béké, 143
  and word "blank," 85, 98, 100, 104, 110, 124, 125
  contradictory racial stereotype of creole, 131, 136
  creole white, 32, 104, 110, 122, 124–125, 131–132, 135–136, 143
  as impossibility of identity, 93, 98, 104, 108, 123–126
  narrator of "Karain," 231
  and supremacist redefinition of creole, 128
  vicious circle of black-white relations, 132
  See also race, racial identity, racism
Wide Sargasso Sea, 7, 18, 19, 21, 32–33, 83, 85, 97, 104, 115–116, 118, 123, 127–133, 135–145, 147–148, 198, 200, 202
  Antoinette, 20, 32, 115, 129–131, 133, 136, 138, 140–141, 143–144
  Christophine, 19, 118, 141–145
  creole family romance, 131–132, 137–145, 147
  creole heiress, 127, 129–131, 135, 137, 140
  creole linguistic register, 104, 143–145, 147
  obeah, 142, 143–144, 146–147
  title, 127
  as touchstone text for postcolonial studies, 83, 127
Wiederholungszwang (compulsion to repeat), 67–69, 74, 268 n.18
  (*see also* Freud, repetition)
Wiggers, F., 158, 163
  Dari Boedak Sampe Djadi Radja, 163
Williams, Raymond, 219, 248, 250, 253 n.1, 256 n.48, 283–284 n.48
  Culture and Society, 248
  Keywords, 219, 248

on *O.E.D.*, 219, 248, 250
  See also cultural studies
Windward Islands, 10
witchcraft, 142, 146, 158, 159
  (see also *obeah*)
women, 47, 101–102, 104–106, 108, 110, 113, 115–116, 118, 124, 128, 132, 146, 154–155, 157, 161–162, 164–165, 169, 172–174
  characters in Rhys, 101–102, 104–106, 108, 113, 132 (see also under *After Leaving Mr Mackenzie*, *Good Morning Midnight*, *Quartet*, *Voyage in the Dark*, *Wide Sargasso Sea*)
  and Dutch East Indies, 154, 157
  and legal rights, 164–165, 172
  and prostitution, 47, 102, 108, 115–116, 118, 146
  and race, 124, 128
  and slavery, 155
  and subaltern voices, 161–162, 169, 173–174
  writers, 110, 154, 157, 165
  See also domesticity, feminism, gender, law, *nyai*, *nyai* narrative form
Woolf, Virginia, 62–65, 71, 78, 229
Wordsworth, William, 228
workplace, 102–103, 119–120, 121
  Benjamin on, 119
  vs. domestic space, 119–121
worlding, 10, 17–18
world literature, 10–11, 15–18, 20–21, 23–24, 26, 28, 206, 212
  Goethe's *Weltliteratur*, 11, 16, 17, 28
Wretched of the Earth (Fanon), 43, 50
writing, 10, 12–19, 23, 25, 26, 29–31, 100, 178–179, 183–184, 195–196, 201, 204–207, 209, 212–213, 233, 248, 257 n.50, 266 n.67, 283 n.38
  Malay forms (*baca* and *karang*), 29–30, 178–179, 183, 206, 209, 213, 233, 257 n.50, 266 n.67, 283 n.38
  O.E.D.'s dependence on, 248
  and orality, 10, 14–15, 18–19, 21, 23, 29, 36, 72, 145, 161, 184, 195, 206, 224
  and script, 205–207
  scriptural economy, 100
  See also archive, archival gaps, *baca*, *écriture*, *karang*, print, script, text, textuality
Wyndham, Francis, 127

Yeats, W. B., 228
"Youth: A Narrative" (Conrad), 72–77, 80–81, 86–87, 99, 100
  azure, word, in, 72, 75, 86–87
  elision of Malay setting, 76–77, 81
  and Ford citing, 72–73
  and memory, 75–77, 87
  and Orientalism, 87
  The Shadow–Line revisits, 99
  splitting of names in, 75–76

Zola, Émile, 32, 115–117
  Nana, 32, 115–117

www.ingramcontent.com/pod-product-compliance
Ingram Content Group UK Ltd.
Pitfield, Milton Keynes, MK11 3LW, UK
UKHW042005230426
12048UKWH00009B/571